EMPIRE OF PURITY

POLITICS AND SOCIETY
IN MODERN AMERICA

*Gary Gerstle, Elizabeth Hinton, Margaret O'Mara,
and Julian E. Zelizer, Series Editors*

For a full list of titles in the series, go to https://press.princeton.edu/series
/politics-and-society-in-modern-america

Empire of Purity

THE HISTORY OF AMERICANS'
GLOBAL WAR ON PROSTITUTION

EVA PAYNE

PRINCETON UNIVERSITY PRESS

PRINCETON & OXFORD

Published by Princeton University Press
41 William Street, Princeton, New Jersey 08540
99 Banbury Road, Oxford OX2 6JX

press.princeton.edu

All Rights Reserved

Library of Congress Cataloging-in-Publication Data

Names: Payne, Eva, 1982– author.
Title: Empire of purity: the history of Americans' global war on prostitution / Eva Payne.
Description: Princeton: Princeton University Press, 2024 | Series: Politics and society in modern America | Includes bibliographical references and index.
Identifiers: LCCN 2024002554 (print) | LCCN 2024002555 (ebook) | ISBN 9780691256979 (hardback) | ISBN 9780691257068 (ebook)
Subjects: LCSH: Prostitution—United States. | Sex work—Government policy—United States. | Social problems—United States. | Human trafficking—Law and legislation. | BISAC: SOCIAL SCIENCE / Prostitution & Sex Trade | HISTORY / United States / 19th Century
Classification: LCC HQ144 .P39 2024 (print) | LCC HQ144 (ebook) | DDC 306.740973—dc23/eng/20240220
LC record available at https://lccn.loc.gov/2024002554
LC ebook record available at https://lccn.loc.gov/2024002555

British Library Cataloging-in-Publication Data is available

Editorial: Bridget Flannery-McCoy and Alena Chekanov
Production Editorial: Theresa Liu
Jacket / Cover Design: Jessica Massabrook
Production: Erin Suydam
Publicity: Kate Hensley and Kathryn Stevens
Copyeditor: Karen Verde

Jacket images: Photographs from *First Enquiry on Traffic in Women and Children - Cuba, 1924–1926*. Courtesy of the United Nations Library & Archives Geneva.

This book has been composed in Arno

Printed in the United States of America

10 9 8 7 6 5 4 3 2 1

CONTENTS

EMPIRE OF PURITY

Introduction

TWO ROADS TO RIO

MARIE FRANÇOISE Yvonne Biaggioni felt a wave of relief as she stepped onboard the SS *Valdivia* on the evening of April 30, 1924. As the spire of Marseille's Notre-Dame de la Garde Basilica faded into the darkening sky, she reflected on her escape. A ballet dancer, she earned only a limited and insecure income which she sometimes supplemented by selling sex, both in her home of Marseille as well as elsewhere in France. But her boyfriend "abused her and took her money," and so, like many young French women in the aftermath of the First World War, she left home.[1]

Biaggioni was not the only member of her family to do so. Her younger sister had departed France at age 15 to seek employment in Russia, Egypt, Italy, Spain, and Germany, working as an "Oriental dancer" and sleeping with men "to make extra money." After the war, economic devastation pressed many people to migrate and earn money however they could.[2] In Biaggioni's family, at least three and likely all four sisters exchanged erotic and sexual labor for money, security, and survival.

Crossing the Atlantic, Biaggioni knew she would miss her family, especially the 2-year-old girl she called her "adopted daughter"—a term unmarried women often used to avoid the stigma that fell on children conceived out of wedlock. But she knew the money she could earn abroad could change their lives. While she had initially planned to go to Buenos Aires, Argentina, she learned that immigration officials there would not admit women who had previously sold sex. So Biaggioni settled on Rio de Janeiro, Brazil, where there were "less difficulties placed in a woman's way."

As the ship crossed the Atlantic, Biaggioni subsidized her voyage through sexual exchange. She had sex with several men on the ship, including the purser, who changed her cabin at no cost. A slim, 5'4" woman with "reddish hair," Biaggioni looked younger than her 36 years (though we cannot be sure she gave officials on the ship her real age). Upon arriving in Rio on May 16, 1924, Biaggioni immediately set about making money at a pención, or brothel, in the Lapa neighborhood, a bohemian entertainment district where the authorities tolerated commercial sex.

White French women like Biaggioni commanded higher prices and were subjected to less police surveillance and harassment than Afro-Brazilian and Eastern European Jewish women. French women were particularly in demand for practicing "perversion," slang for oral sex.[3] Biaggioni spent most evenings going out to casinos, where she ate, drank, watched the entertainment, and picked up clients. She frequently entertained "high officials, such as members of the Staff of the Ministry of Foreign Affairs, the Police Delegate of this District, and others of high rank," some of whom kept regular appointments with her.

While Biaggioni paid 70 mil reis (approximately 7 US dollars) a day to the madam for room and board, she earned around 200 mil reis (approximately 20 US dollars) a day, leaving her plenty of money to open a "nice savings account" at the Italo-French Bank of Brazil. She regularly sent money back to France to support her family and "adopted" daughter. But she also harbored more ambitious plans. Using the ship's purser on the SS *Valdivia* to pass messages, Biaggioni sent for her sisters Charlotte, age 25, and Pauline, age 20, and included money for their passage. She planned to "open a pención herself," where she and her sisters could keep all their earnings. After several years, they would all return to France "with a great deal of money saved up."

On July 12, 1924, an American visited the brothel not to purchase sex, but to spy on its dwellers and to learn all he could about the inner working of the vice economy. Tall, with a medium build, brown hair, and brown eyes, he looked to be in his early thirties.[4] We do not know what name he gave, but it was certainly not his real one, Paul Michael Kinsie. He examined the physiognomy of the women and listened to the languages they spoke. In New York–accented English, or perhaps a few words of broken French, he may have chatted with a few of the women and the brothel owner. As he could only speak English and Yiddish, he often had to rely on his observations and instincts—or, perhaps, biases—rather than conversations.

When Kinsie and Biaggioni met, she did not give her real first name, presenting herself as Yvonne Françoise, her middle names. Kinsie soon took his leave and moved on to another brothel—or maybe he stayed longer with one of the women; the record is silent. When he got back to his hotel, he wrote a report on his findings, signed only with the number 70, to assure that his identity remained concealed.

Did Biaggioni believe the story Kinsie told her? Perhaps he posed as a prospective client or said he wanted to place one of his "girls" at the brothel, or promised to take her to Buenos Aires, where she could make more money. Yet Biaggioni may have found Kinsie suspicious. Indeed, she may have already caught wind of the League of Nations study on the "traffic in women," and suspected Kinsie, as well as another man she spoke with on the SS *Valdivia*, of working as undercover investigators.

To League investigators, Biaggioni appeared doubly suspicious. She traveled from her home country to another to sell sex, making her a potential trafficking victim. But because she planned to send for her sisters—one of whom was under 21 years old, and thus, according to League officials, unable to consent to prostitution—Biaggioni was also a potential trafficker.[5]

Kinsie's journey to Rio took a very different route than Biaggioni's. Born in New York City in 1893, Kinsie grew up in a Jewish family in the Chelsea neighborhood. The 1915 Census listed him as a hat salesman who worked for the family business.[6] But as early as 1913, at just 20 years old, Kinsie also worked as an undercover investigator attempting to root out prostitution in American cities.[7]

In the early twentieth century, reform-minded private citizens and public officials in many American cities worried about the pervasiveness and visibility of prostitution, particularly the red-light districts where police informally tolerated commercial sex, often located in African American and immigrant neighborhoods or just outside the city limits. The American Social Hygiene Association (ASHA), an organization headquartered in Kinsie's hometown of New York City, took the lead in this work. With funding from billionaire businessman and philanthropist John D. Rockefeller, Jr., the ASHA sent its agents around the country to investigate vice districts and stamp them out. Kinsie soon became one of the organization's most valuable employees.

Kinsie possessed a remarkable ability to dissemble. He could pose as a client or pimp to get the measure of a red-light district. He could easily strike up conversations with young women, flirt with them, and get them to reveal information about the commercial sex industry and their place within it. He also misled officials. During one 1913 investigation in Lancaster, Pennsylvania, Kinsie lied in a sworn affidavit while describing his findings in the city and gave his age as 24, perhaps to increase his credibility.[8] Although he claimed to have a college degree from the University of Kentucky, there is no record of him graduating.[9]

When the United States entered the First World War, Kinsie's investigative career took off. He joined the US Army and worked for a special division run by ASHA personnel, which rewrote US military prostitution policy, criminalized prostitution in most states, and helped arrest tens of thousands of women. After crossing the country to eradicate prostitution near military training camps, Kinsie traveled to France to conduct investigations in the aftermath of the armistice, which led to the harassment and arrest of women there. While the war may have been devastating for French women like Biaggioni, making it both more difficult to marry and to eke out a living on their own, it offered an opportunity for the ASHA and its star investigator to spread the antiprostitution gospel.

In 1923, the League of Nations—the international governing body formed at the war's end—resolved to investigate the international dimensions of the traffic in women. Even though the United States declined to join the League, the League's trafficking committee selected Americans from the ASHA, the self-proclaimed world experts on prostitution, to take the lead. For the ASHA, an international investigation of trafficking provided the perfect pretext to spread American-style policy around the globe, particularly criminalizing commercial sex and curbing the migration of people deemed sexually immoral. As the most trusted and prolific investigator for the ASHA, Kinsie spent three years traversing the Atlantic, roaming Europe, crisscrossing the Americas, and searching for trafficked women in North Africa. In most places he posed as a trafficker to infiltrate the international trafficking rings the League believed were operating. He recorded his conversations and observations from sixty cities across four continents and shared this data with his ASHA colleagues, who compiled it into a final report to present to the League's Committee on Traffic in Women and Children.

Kinsie and his colleagues furnished the League with crucial data for conceptualizing and defining trafficking. "There is a constant stream of foreign women proceeding to certain countries," the final report declared. This "stream" itself provided evidence that "a traffic of considerable dimensions is being carried on."[10]

Their investigation imprinted a particularly American vision of trafficking on the League of Nations' anti-trafficking work, one that understood all women's migration for sexual labor as trafficking. And the final report, full of the supposed hard data extracted through the undercover investigative process, supported the American viewpoint. These definitions and data formed the basis of international agreements in the 1930s, which defined all prostitution as forced trafficking. The solution to the problem of trafficking, then, involved criminalizing commercial sex and limiting migration, policies framed as a means of protecting women.

How should we understand these two roads to Rio? According to the League's trafficking investigators, prostitution endangered not only Biaggioni, but the moral and physical health of the world. But in the eyes of women like Biaggioni, violent partners, economic precarity, police harassment, and difficulty migrating often posed more pressing dangers than the act of sexual exchange itself. In fact, while Kinsie surely saw himself as part of a prestigious scientific and policymaking community that rescued women around the world, Biaggioni had reason to see his work as nefarious. After all, Kinsie and his ASHA colleagues laid the foundation for policies that entrapped women, deprived them of customers, surveilled them, prevented them from traveling, and made it hard for them to earn a living, even in locales with legal commercial sex industries.

In the end, as this book will show, Kinsie's view won out—we still live with it today. But it is crucial to learn as much as we can from women like Biaggioni. Their archival traces reveal the structural constraints, the everyday dilemmas, and the strategies of mutual aid and creative resistance that shaped women's migration, labor, and lives.[11] From Kinsie's vantage, such factors remained largely irrelevant or invisible.

American Sexual Exceptionalism

In the 1870s, a group of British anti-slavery and women's rights activists began to attack what was a fairly ubiquitous mode of prostitution control in many European countries and their colonies in the nineteenth century. Under this policy regime, termed *réglementation* by the French officials who developed it, and "regulationism" or "regulation" in English, governments tolerated and oversaw the commercial sex industry by licensing brothels and registering prostitutes, whom physicians regularly examined for venereal disease.[12] These British activists, soon joined by their brethren on the Continent and in the United States, termed their movement "abolition" and themselves "new abolitionists," to signal their desire to abolish state-regulated prostitution, just as governments had abolished chattel slavery. Reformers also adopted the phrase "social purity" to describe their goal of purifying society from sexual ills.[13]

At first, this transatlantic abolitionism had a distinctly feminist bent. Its adherents argued that state-regulated prostitution both caused and resulted from women's political, social, and economic inequality, which any real solution to the problem of prostitution would have to address.[14] The feminist abolitionist position rejected licensed prostitution because it infringed on women's civil liberties and constituted state overreach.[15] The state-regulated brothel, they argued, was the primary driver of sex trafficking, the forced transport of women for forced prostitution. But by the late nineteenth century, another group who opposed regulated prostitution increasingly gained power in the United States and Europe. These "paternalist abolitionists," to use Jessica Pliley's term, hoped to abolish regulation not because it harmed women, but because it encouraged prostitution and immorality. They also argued, as feminists did, that regulation caused sex trafficking. Impelled by concerns over disease and crime, however, they worked to replace state-regulated prostitution with "laws that targeted 'bad' women while also treating women as children."[16] Unlike their feminist predecessors, they stressed carceral, rather than economic and political solutions to the "problem" of prostitution.

In the early twentieth century, a group of American reformers took the logic of paternalist abolitionism even further. While Americans initially had worked as junior partners to the British, as the United States gained power on the world stage they also gained power to shape the international fight against prostitution and trafficking. Under the banner of "social hygiene," they continued to reject state-licensed prostitution, but as a part of a larger platform to eradicate prostitution and the prostitute herself.[17] Much like Americans who advocated for the federal prohibition of alcohol and opium in the early twentieth century, these prostitution prohibitionists saw the federal government, particularly the US military, as their most powerful ally.[18] They pushed for laws that criminalized and prohibited commercial sex, as well as immigration restrictions that made supposedly sexually suspicious migrants subject to exclusion and deportation. And they succeeded, passing laws prohibiting prostitution in the 1910s that remain on the books and continue to be enforced. Indeed, the United States has been a global outlier in its insistence on prohibition as a policy approach and its tolerance for creating criminals through criminalizing acts, identities, and substances it deems immoral.[19]

As they attacked commercial sex, Americans developed a strong sense of what I term sexual exceptionalism, that is, the belief that American national character was rooted in—and visible through—the superior sexual morality of the people and their government. The term links the ideology of American exceptionalism to the concept of "sex exceptionalism," that is, that American culture, as well as law, have treated sex as essentially and categorically distinct from other aspects of human life. Its proponents articulated American sexual exceptionalism through multiple idioms, including the racial language of Anglo-Saxon bloodlines, medical discourses about low rates of venereal disease, religious claims about Protestant Christian sexual reserve, and political arguments about the sexual self-control necessary for democratic self-governance. Debates over prostitution and trafficking buttressed broader national narratives about American exceptionalism. As David Bell notes, "political narratives about America's exceptional character served to justify various projects of national aggression against both Native and foreign peoples, but they also highlighted what Americans saw as their best qualities and their moral duties, giving them a standard to live up to."[20] Reforming prostitution policy at home and abroad were thus two sides of the same coin.

Recent scholarship has shown the value of bringing together the histories of sexuality and statecraft, illuminating how delineating and policing normative sexual arrangements has expanded the reach of local and state governments, as well as the US federal government.[21] *Empire of Purity* examines how the state came to recognize, define, and act on the "problem" of commercial sex. It traces how the US government increasingly circumscribed normative heterosexual intercourse in the decades before—and concurrently with—the period when it also constructed a homosexual-heterosexual binary in federal policy.[22] As scholars have shown, policing prostitution and trafficking created new federal bureaucracies such as the FBI, restructured urban geographies, reinforced gendered and racial hierarchies, and strengthened colonial rule.[23]

Yet the wide-reaching goals and effects of US anti-prostitution and trafficking efforts, I argue, are only visible by following actors and policies as they crossed borders.[24] I trace the exercise of US power across multiple kinds of jurisdictions, from the US mainland, to US territories, occupations, and even other sovereign states. In doing so, a new picture emerges, one that illuminates both the workings of US power and the ideological construction of normative heterosexuality. By focusing on sexuality while attending to gender and race, the book pursues a different kind of "Atlantic crossings" of progressive reform, one in which Americans did not simply adopt European policies, but actively tried to shape them.[25]

This expansion of US power occurred not only through the spread of American ideology, as scholars have suggested of America's "moral empire," but also through direct attempts to shape and enforce policy in other places—both colonies and sovereign states. At times, US prostitution policy followed the model of the "colonial boomerang," as US officials first tested policies in colonies and then applied them on the mainland.[26] Yet at other times, US officials first implemented mainland policies in one colonial test case and then elsewhere outside of the mainland. While other scholars have revealed the US government's interest in regulating sexual contacts between US soldiers and local women, *Empire of Purity* demonstrates the expansive and interconnected nature of American reformers' efforts, which were not limited to one imperial site but reflected their global ambitions.[27]

Moreover, US prostitution policy was forged through entanglements with other imperial powers. These transimperial encounters reflected the fact that just as countries interact, so do imperial formations, which include both state and non-state actors.[28] Americans had long looked to the British Empire to make sense of their own imperial ambitions and anxieties.[29] In the late nineteenth century, a trans-Atlantic cadre of abolitionists attempted to close British imperial regulated brothels in India, while also calling on US cities not to adopt regulation. After 1898, US officials embraced Spanish imperial forms of regulated prostitution in the Philippines, while an American and European reform network criticized them. France and the United States, both imperial powers during WWI, battled over which country had the more scientific and civilized prostitution policy. And in the post–WWI moment, debates over prostitution policy at the League of Nations were also about how empires should properly govern.

Empire of Purity brings together the insight that public-private partnerships have fueled the expansion of state power, with an interest in zooming the lens out beyond the nation-state.[30] It demonstrates that partnerships between the state and private philanthropic organizations dedicated to eradicating prostitution and trafficking extended the US government's role in the sexual lives of its citizens as well as those who found themselves under its governance around the globe. In fact, such public-private partnerships could advance US policy interests in international governance even in the absence of explicit US state involvement. ASHA members, for example, promoted an American-style prohibitionist prostitution policy at the League of Nations, even as they did not officially represent the United States.

Americans' ambition to spread sexual morality abroad intertwined with their avowed commitment to expanding liberty: proper sexual governance paved the way for the success of democratic political forms. Although by WWI Americans often made the connections between sex and democracy explicit, prior to it they more often used the language of civilization. Leaders of private reform organizations, and, by the turn of the century, the US state, promoted sexual self-control for men and women as the cornerstone of civilization.

Civilizational ideology integrated anxieties about race, gender, sexuality, national identity, religion, and class into a unified, hierarchical continuum that allowed for the ranking of individuals and peoples.[31]

While nineteenth-century Americans employed the language of civilization to claim a status equal to European nations, by the twentieth century they used it to justify American global power.[32] Unsurprisingly, Americans with social, political, and economic clout positioned those like themselves—white, male, American, Protestant, and middle-class—at the top. Reform-minded white women forged their own claims to power by arguing for women's inherently civilized natures—more civilized even than white men—because of women's lack of and ability to control sexual impulses.[33]

Yet, these activists believed, civilizational hierarchies were not completely fixed. Individuals and peoples could move between the stages. With the proper tutelage uncivilized peoples could move forward; but if corrupted by vices, and particularly sexual vices, civilized peoples could move backward. A government that regulated or tolerated prostitution encouraged physical and mental degeneration among its citizenry, a sure path to national decline. Moreover, anti-prostitution activists argued, the problem of prostitution could extend beyond national borders: through trafficking, sexual vice in any part of the world could infect the United States. The efforts of American private reform organizations and US state officials to shape prostitution and trafficking policy abroad could also thus protect the United States itself.

US officials and private reform organizations drew on the growing moral authority of humanitarianism in their quest to disseminate American sexual laws and mores abroad. Many scholars have noted the imperial roots of humanitarianism and humanitarian interventions, often based on upholding the supposedly universal moral values that governed civilized societies.[34] Here again, US officials and private-citizen reformers argued for American sexual exceptionalism. For much of the nineteenth century the US government stood wary of humanitarian intervention into the affairs of sovereign states, concerned that European empires would use it as a pretext to intervene in the United States.[35] But when the United States declared war on Spain in 1898, it soon became a proponent of humanitarian intervention by military force. As Kristin Hoganson has shown, both US officials and the popular press positioned the United States as the masculine savior of feminized Cuba from the rapacious clutches of Spain.[36] Unlike European empires who jostled for supremacy through war, US officials argued, the United States only used force to spread civilization, rather than pursue its own self-interest.[37]

The post–WWI moment marked a new stage of humanitarian activity. The League of Nations claimed oversight over a range of issues, including the traffic in women, further marking the issue as one of universal humanitarian concern rather than national interests. Such framing, however, allowed the US government, as well as other governments, to pursue policies that allowed states to more tightly control the labor and mobility of populations in the name of humanitarian anti-trafficking work.[38]

Ideas about religion played a crucial, though not always visible, role in conceptions of American sexual exceptionalism. Within the United States, native-born white Protestants often framed Jewish and Catholic immigrants as sexually deviant and unassimilable. Drawing on long-standing anti-Semitic tropes of Jews as "prone to lust" based on their practices of circumcision and polygamy, critics claimed that Jews produced the majority of "filthy publications."[39] Catholic clerical celibacy confounded the gendered and familial norms of American Protestantism. Popular exposés of convent life related torrid tales of young nuns—sometimes Protestant-born girls tricked into conversion by conniving nuns and priests—and held captive for the sexual pleasure of lecherous clergymen.[40]

Countries that Americans associated with Catholicism also bore the taint of sexual immorality. The close ties between the Spanish government and Catholic Church rendered the nation sexually suspicious in the American cultural imagination.[41] American popular culture portrayed France, where Catholicism predominated despite the country's avowedly secular political culture, as a place of sexual excess and rampant prostitution.[42] In the early twentieth century, sensationalist white slavery literature decried the "French traders," "Jew traders," and "Polish Jewesses" who entrapped native-born white Protestant girls.[43] Such narratives positioned Protestantism as inherently sexually moral—and fundamentally American—in contrast to the foreign faiths of Judaism and Catholicism. Thus, on a global scale, American Protestants understood religion, sexual morality, and national identity as closely intertwined.

By the twentieth century, American social hygiene reformers had pledged to study sexual problems "in the spirit and with the methods of modern science, education, and enlightened morality," rather than from the supposedly religious and sentimental perspective that had animated the social purity reformers who came before them.[44] Yet the purportedly secular vision of sexual morality they espoused rested on Protestant conceptions of sexual self-control in service of the family and nation.[45] By recasting Protestant sexual morality in the allegedly secular terms of science, as well as civilization, they argued for its universality, and thus applicability, around the world.

Of course, in many ways, Americans imagined their sexual exceptionalism. Many other countries understood their own sexual mores and policies as the most modern, scientific, and moral. And Americans weren't unique in their concerns over prostitution and trafficking. As many scholars have shown, British, French, Latin American, and Eastern European reformers also attacked prostitution and trafficking with zeal.[46]

But the US government's relationship to prostitution did follow a different path than that of Britain, France, and other European states. First, the United States remained primarily a rural society in the nineteenth century; governments generally implemented licensed prostitution in urban centers. And the US federal government, comparatively weak, left it entirely to local governments to solve questions of prostitution control. Unlike many European powers, the United States did not maintain a strong standing military, the arm of the state that often pushed for licensed prostitution near garrisons. Indeed, the Civil War marked the US military's first small-scale attempt at licensing, when Union commanders oversaw brothels at camps in Memphis and Nashville, Tennessee, but abandoned such projects of prostitution regulation after the war's end.[47]

Moreover, the United States was primarily a settler colonial society until the turn of the century. As imperial powers with administrative colonies, Britain and Spain, for example, had to manage sex between local women of color and white metropolitan troops, administrators, and workers. In contrast, as US federal control expanded westward after the American Civil War, it largely displaced Native American populations and attempted to replace them with white families. Although data on women who sold sex in the West are scarce, white women formed the majority, working in saloons, brothels, and even mobile wagons in the mining towns, construction sites, and military garrisons where single men gathered.[48] Not until the United States gained its own administrative colonies after the War of 1898 did the federal government begin to seriously address the question of regulated prostitution. It quickly followed the colonial model set by the British, Spanish, and Dutch Empires, and regulated prostitution in the Philippines, Cuba, and Puerto Rico.[49]

Yet, much as the United States tried to "hide" its empire more broadly, US officials carefully swept these experiments with regulation under the rug.[50] A stated policy of prostitution prohibition (or at least, prohibiting US officials to license it) sent a clear message to the American people, and indeed, the world, that the US empire differed from the British or French model. It did not matter that US military and administrative presence expanded the commercial sex markets in Manila and San Juan after the War of 1898. It did not matter that prohibition as a policy left no room to mitigate the harms of sex for pay between soldiers and locals, which, of course, continued to occur. What mattered was that the sex was less visible to mainland Americans.[51]

This sacrifice of women and local communities to maintain the image of exceptional American sexual purity was, as Mary Louise Roberts has termed it, "the price of discretion."[52] As the United States gained power on the global stage in the twentieth century, particularly after WWI, officials and non-state reformers further enforced an American vision of right sexuality abroad, which only served to increase their sense of exceptionalism. Using the fight against prostitution and trafficking, powerful Americans attempted to remake other countries in their own image and enhance US global standing in an imperial age.

Seeing Sexual Labor and Migration

In this book, I approach sex trafficking as a "historically contingent concept," as Philippa Heatherington and Julia Laite call it, rather than a discrete problem.[53] Trafficking has long been a flexible and contested category.[54] Often, state officials as well as non-state reformers have used that flexibility to target some people and leave others be. They mobilized discourses of trafficking at particular moments to obtain their desired political aims, often while occluding those very goals.

Indeed, the flexibility of the terms "white slavery," "trafficking," and "prostitution" was the point. US officials and non-state reformers "institutionalized ambiguity," to use Katrina Quisumbing King's term, by constructing definitions and policies that accommodated seemingly contradictory ideas.[55] Prostitution, as a legal term, was slippery. Police could arrest so-called sexually suspicious women for anything from soliciting to loitering to vagrancy, as well as committing a sex act for money. White slavery and trafficking proved similarly flexible. Both state officials and private reform organizations at times treated prostitutes as victims and at other times as criminals, and debated whether they deserved punishment or protection. These unresolved ambiguities allowed officials to use their discretion, to choose, case by case, from a wide range of options.

How reformers and state officials understood the problem of prostitution mattered too. Some saw it as an issue of women's rights; others, of disease and public health; some believed it to be a problem of morality; still others considered it one of crime and social order; many insisted it originated from the sexually debased foreigners arriving in the United States; and most understood it as some combination of these factors. The way people defined prostitution had ramifications for who should have the authority to enforce laws and policies. Questions of jurisdiction played out over both governmental and geographic territory.

As US officials and non-state reformers institutionalized ambiguity into the structures of prostitution and trafficking policies, such policies gained teeth through discretionary policing. As Anne Grey Fischer has shown, the power of law enforcement officials to target some women as of concern to the state, signaled largely by virtue of their class, race, and ethnic backgrounds, is a cornerstone of police power. Discretion, states Fischer, is the "power to determine whether a woman is hailing a taxi or soliciting motorists for sex."[56] Even when women arrested for prostitution used the courts to advocate for themselves, they rarely prevailed.[57] Migrating women faced similar discretionary power at borders, as immigration officials evaluated their physiognomy, clothes, and comportment for signs of latent immorality.[58]

Yet women who sold sex, like Biaggioni, often articulated other ways of conceptualizing commercial sex and migration. Then and now, people use the word "prostitute" to signify an identity, a means of dividing women into categories of "good" and "bad" according to their sexual behavior. Most women, however, engaged in commercial sex less as a vocation than a gig, something they interspersed with other work, moving in and out of the commercial sex economy. While I use the term "prostitute" to capture the worldview of my actors, I use terms such as "woman who sold sex" and "sex worker" to reflect my analytical voice. Although "sex work" is anachronistic, coined by the sex worker activist Carol Leigh in 1978, it captures many women's insistence that they sold sex to make money, bringing issues of labor and economics to the fore. Moreover, it positions them as workers: as Heather Berg argues, sex work is not exploitative because it is sexual, but because it is labor under capitalism.[59]

Following several decades of feminist scholarship, I situate prostitution as a form of labor.[60] Like these scholars, I contend that state policing of prostitution often harmed women, and that even feminist efforts to "rescue" prostitutes or purported trafficking victims frequently made their lives more precarious.[61] This is not to say that women who sold sex did not suffer from violence and coercion. Many did. But such abuses threatened all working women—and especially migrant working women—across industries and locations.

To see the exploitation of women as a problem limited to the sex industry conceals the structural "push and pull" factors that led women to migrate and sell sex.[62] To set sexual labor and migration apart from all other forms of labor and migration makes the full lives of women in the commercial sex industry harder to see. It sets up a false dichotomy, as Elisa Camiscioli has shown, between "coercion and choice" that erases the structural factors that constrained women's lives.[63] It obscures the growth of global capitalism and its attendant inequalities of gender, race, and class. It ignores the increased flow and new routes of migration, particularly in the twentieth century.[64] It makes women's sexual, reproductive, and care work invisible.

The story of Americans' global sexual reform projects can only be told by bringing disparate sources together from collections within and outside of the United States. The papers of reform organizations in Europe and the United States, alongside US government documents, disclose reformers' motivations and strategies for attacking sexual vice. French military archives and those of US colonial and military administrations detail how local elites used US anti-prostitution efforts to advance their own goals, while petitions of complaint show working-class people protesting such policies as despotic. League of Nations reports on trafficking and the raw data collected by the League's American undercover agents show the perspectives of women migrants who moved between various forms of labor, including sexual labor, to support themselves and their families. But they also reveal how Americans inserted their own definitions of trafficking into international conventions, definitions that directly contravened what most women told them.

These sources overwhelmingly privilege the voices of those who sought to inflict an idealized vision of sexual order onto the bodies of women. *Empire of Purity* is not a story about the local conditions under which women performed sexual labor and their experiences, though it draws on many excellent works that do just that.[65] When we do see women's accounts, they are usually mediated: taken from interviews at prisons or recorded as investigative reports—much like the story of Marie Biaggioni, whose life we can only glimpse through the notes of two investigators who spoke with her and her family.

But inscribed in state archives are also forceful claims of people and communities who demanded their rights. People like Rubersinda Herrdia, a Dominican woman who lodged a complaint with the US military government denouncing the injustice of her twenty-five-day prison sentence for prostitution. Or Rosita Hall, on whose behalf the West Indian Labour Union wrote to US officials in the Panama Canal Zone to protest Hall's arrest for prostitution.

Or Aline Legros, a French woman whose family decried her arrest and forcible vaginal inspection for venereal disease at the hands of US military doctors.[66]

We need to understand how US power inheres in international prostitution and trafficking policies to reckon with the harm that many of these policies have done and continue to do to people who sell sex; specifically, how carceral and violent state intervention into women's lives came to be framed as protection. In following US officials and members of private organizations around the world, I risk simply reinscribing my actors' blind spots, as well as their own sense of self-importance. Yet I still believe that it is important to track the workings of US power, at once more limited than my actors believed it to be but also more expansive and harmful than they could imagine.

1

The "New Abolitionists"

THE POLITICS OF PROSTITUTION
IN THE LATE NINETEENTH CENTURY

THE VOICE OF EMINENT American abolitionist William Lloyd Garrison rang out to the women and men of his London audience as he urged them to stand up against the "great immorality"—indeed, an immense "impiety against God"—that had corrupted the soul of the British Empire. An American "on foreign soil," he was an "intermeddler, an agitator," yet he affirmed his right to confront "iniquity" and "immorality" wherever he found it, claiming "the earth is the Lord's."[1]

The evil of which Garrison spoke was not chattel slavery: the year was 1877 and an alarming new form of "pollution" was spreading. At a time when Southern states had begun to dismantle the gains of Reconstruction, Garrison no longer saw the plight of African Americans as his primary calling.[2] Instead, he exhorted his audience to take action on what he and other veteran reformers saw as the current global scourge: the sexual slavery of white women in state-regulated prostitution. Although not an entirely novel phenomenon, in the late nineteenth century government efforts to regulate the business of prostitution faced unprecedented criticism for entrenching rather than alleviating the plight of women who sold sex. Drawing upon their experiences in transatlantic anti-slavery agitation, Garrison and many others identified "state regulated vice" as the central moral and political injustice of the day.

But Garrison's was not the only vision of transatlantic reform circulating in late nineteenth-century public discourse. With the growing movement of people and ideas, debates about commercial sex spanned Europe and the United States and followed the path of imperial expansion into Asia, Africa, and Oceania. One group of activists, comprising male medical doctors and colonial officials, deemed prostitution a social reality and a public health risk: the state should regulate it through a system of licensing and medical inspections. Another group, drawn from the anti-slavery, women's rights, and temperance movements, fought against any legislation that licensed prostitution. Instead, through lobbying, public campaigns, and moral and religious education, they targeted what they saw as the root cause of prostitution: the double standard of morality that tacitly condoned extramarital sex for men, while punishing women for any appearance of sexual impropriety. This double standard, they contended, both caused and resulted from the widespread social and economic problems that drove many women to prostitution.

This set of reformers called themselves "new abolitionists," drawing on the moral authority and political success of the movement to abolish chattel slavery.[3] Yet there was an irony to this appellation. As Americans expressed horror that the regulation system could treat white women as chattel, they turned away from the violence, including sexual violence, that African American women had faced under slavery and continued to experience after emancipation. Their movement built on Anglo-American networks, emphasizing the sexual morality and political liberalism of white, Anglo-Saxon, Protestant countries, both in contrast to purportedly decadent European countries and supposedly savage Asian, African, and Oceanic peoples.[4]

Yet regulated prostitution called the morality and the civilizing mission of the British Empire into question. Indeed, at times even British reformers characterized the United States as an exceptional country because it had not embraced regulation on a large scale.[5] Comparisons between the two countries allowed Americans to construct a new narrative about their exceptionalism, based on the United States' supposedly superior laws and mores regarding sex. In the wake of the Civil War, Americans used the fight against state-regulated prostitution to position themselves as sexually exceptional and restore their moral superiority, damaged by the stain of slavery.

Prostitution in Europe

For much of Western European history, governments implicitly tolerated prostitution, and prostitutes occupied widely recognized, if perilous, positions within the social hierarchy.[6] At the opening of the nineteenth century, European scientists and administrators began to construe prostitutes as threats to public hygiene and sanitation rather than as social outcasts.[7] Popular conceptions of disease held that prostitutes emitted putrid miasmas that could spread syphilis and other illnesses to those around them.[8]

In 1802, Paris mandated the medical examination of prostitutes for venereal disease, marking the first systematic attempt to regulate prostitution as a matter of disease control. By 1810, new regulations required Parisian prostitutes to register with the morals police and submit to surveillance, compulsory medical inspection, and quarantine in the prison hospital if found to carry an infection. Women, as well as brothel madams, paid a fee for registration and inspection, which financed the system and, as some angry citizens charged, padded the pockets of the police and physicians who carried it out.[9] Given the onerous requirements of registration, compliance always posed a problem. Thus, the morals police soon began to register women whom they suspected of selling sex, turning sexual policing into a means of controlling all "irregular" women.[10]

The "Parisian system" quickly spread through France and to other European cities, as well as throughout European empires.[11] Termed *réglementation* in French, commentators writing in English used the term "regulation," or "regulationism," to describe it. With imperial expansion, controlling women's sexual labor and the purported health risk it posed took on new importance, though its contours varied in different colonial settings.[12] Maintaining an empire required masses of soldiers, administrators, and laborers. Medical and popular wisdom at the time held that these men needed sexual release for the sake of their health. At times tacitly, but often overtly, colonial officials encouraged them to seek local women for sex.[13]

By the early nineteenth century, the British Empire was the largest and most powerful of European empires. But military officials and politicians worried that high rates of venereal disease threatened its dominance. Syphilis and gonorrhea caused the majority of hospital admissions among British soldiers in India through most of the nineteenth century.[14] Moreover, doctors had little success in treating it. Popular methods included applying vinegar to the genitals and administering mercury through pills or topical applications, which often resulted in mercury poisoning.[15] In India, British officials attributed the spread of venereal disease to Indian women, whom they saw as morally and racially inferior vectors of contagion. As early as the late eighteenth century, concerns about venereal disease led British officials in India to open "lock hospitals," prison hospitals where prostitutes deemed diseased received treatment. British officials in India also implemented the "bazaar system" in many places, providing each regiment with prostitutes who traveled with them and underwent regular inspections for disease.[16]

Although British officials in the colonies developed multiple means of controlling prostitution, the British metropole came late to regulated prostitution in comparison to European countries such as France and Germany. While metropolitan British cities had opened their own lock hospitals for the treatment of poor prostitutes in the eighteenth and nineteenth centuries, they had not implemented forms of licensing. But by the 1850s, concerns over venereal disease and moral order led British physicians and social critics to look more favorably on the Parisian system. Between 1864 and 1869, British Parliament passed a series of Contagious Diseases Acts, which allowed for the medical inspection of suspected prostitutes in garrison towns and ports in southern England and Ireland. The first act, small in scope, attempted to limit the spread of venereal disease in the military, but subsequent acts broadened the state's power, using the police to surveil and control poor women.[17]

Following the passage of a third Contagious Diseases Act in 1869, a group of clergymen and physicians banded together to form the National Association for the Repeal of the Contagious Diseases Acts. They excluded women at the first meeting because of the supposedly obscene subject matter. While they eventually opened membership to women, a group of reform-minded women decided to found their own parallel but autonomous organization, the Ladies' National Association for the Repeal of the Contagious Diseases Acts. Josephine Butler, already a well-known anti-slavery activist and advocate for women's education and suffrage, led the organization.[18]

Butler and the Ladies' National Association believed that the Contagious Diseases Acts violated women's civil liberties and sacrificed women from the lower classes to satisfy upper- class men's lust. Instead of portraying women who sold sex as greedy, sexually deviant, and diseased, she argued that the narrow range of occupations open to women and the low wages they received forced them to turn to prostitution. As she wrote, in the city of Liverpool "there are 9,000 women who follow this profession, because there is *none other* open to them."[19] She argued against the criminalization of prostitution and punishment of prostitutes, particularly when men who purchased sex escaped without consequence.

Butler believed in the "moral reclaimability" of the prostitute, since selling sex did not change a woman's essential nature. Like any other woman, Butler stressed, the prostitute deserved respect for her civil liberties, including the right not to have her body forcibly examined.[20] Under regulation, any woman branded a "common prostitute" by an officer of the morals police was subject to forced inspection for venereal disease. Medical officials examined women's internal genitals with a speculum, defined by an anti-regulationist physician as a "large expanding steel instrument" for "forcing open . . . the very centres of feeling," causing not only pain and humiliation for all women, but potentially violating innocent virgins falsely identified as prostitutes.[21] Indeed, American women reformers would later refer to such inspections as "surgical rape."[22]

Abolitionists challenged not only the moral authority of regulationist physicians, but their scientific authority as well. While military physicians and officials emphasized that these examinations protected soldiers and the public from venereal disease, abolitionists charged that they actually spread it by way of the speculum, which went "hot from the body of one woman into the next" while tainted with "subtle organic poison."[23] The authority of the state to forcibly examine dangerous women's bodies versus women's right to bodily integrity formed a key axis of the conflict over regulation in the decades that followed.

Prostitution in the United States

The history of prostitution in the United States took a somewhat different course than in Britain and continental Europe, though not as different as American reformers often supposed. As in Europe, prostitution had been part of the landscape of American cities since the colonial period, while religious authorities, moral reform groups, and city officials periodically attempted to suppress it. Unlike many European cities in the nineteenth century, however, American municipalities tended not to police prostitution through the inspection and detention of diseased prostitutes, instead using ordinances about public order.[24]

In the United States, much like in Europe, domestic and imperial anxieties over race and class shaped debates over prostitution. But the American experiences of chattel slavery, immigration, and settler colonialism inflected them in particular ways, producing a distinctly American narrative about prostitution and race. At the same time, regional differences shaped the way reform-minded citizens identified the "problem" of prostitution, as well as its possible solutions.

The early nineteenth century saw waves of attack against what Clare A. Lyons terms the more "expansive sexual culture" of the early republic's coastal cities.[25] In the 1820s and 1830s, Boston, New York, and Philadelphia conducted raids on the known vice districts and brothels where a growing portion of commercial sex took place.[26] The confluence of the Second Great Awakening's religious revivals with the increasing visibility of commercial sex in rapidly developing urban centers stimulated the formation of new reform organizations targeting sexual sin. Moreover, in the same period, the issue of child prostitution rose to the fore, joining anxieties over juvenile delinquency with concerns over sexual morality. Middle- and upper-class evangelicals founded a range of organizations devoted to rescuing and reforming prostitutes, including those focused particularly on young girls.[27]

Indeed, young girls increasingly sold sex by the 1830s, compelled by many of the same factors that led women into sexual commerce, including low wages, as well as abandonment by or death of wage-earning parents or family members. Largely poor, white, and native-born women comprised the majority of prostitutes in Northeastern cities, many of whom had migrated to burgeoning metropolises from nearby rural areas. In 1836, employers paid women an average of 37.5 cents per day, while the estimated cost of living stood at between 21.4 cents and 25 cents per day. Women and girls who sold sex on the streets and in brothels could earn four to six dollars a night sleeping with two to three men.[28] Historian Timothy J. Gilfoyle estimates that 5–10 percent of all women in New York between the ages of 15 and 30 sold sex, with the number rising during frequent economic depressions.[29]

While some reformers did blame low wages, many devoted their energies to attacking the double standard of sexual morality, which permitted licentious men to visit prostitutes without sacrificing their respectability while condemning those same women as outcasts. Women-led organizations, such as the New York Female Moral Reform Society, decried the dangers that male lust posed to the innate purity of white women and girls. Prostitution offended the middle- and upper-class white gender ideology of the day, which held that white women maintained the purity of the home, while men ventured into the public and commercial spheres. By seducing and exploiting innocent women, devious men shirked their role as protectors and commercialized what should happen only within the bounds of marriage, tainting both the public and private spheres. The republic's health and survival, reformers argued, depended on the citizenry's sexual behavior.[30]

In both the North and South before the Civil War, chattel slavery stood as paradigmatic for American conceptions of labor, gender, and racial hierarchy. Americans had long used the language of slavery to critique coercive labor practices beyond chattel slavery. As early as the 1790s, indentured servants trafficked from Europe to North America were termed white slaves. During the nineteenth century, British and American workers decried the "white slavery" of child labor and the "wage slavery" of poor white workers.[31] More-over, activists also used the term to indicate the powerlessness of certain groups under the existing social order. In the years before the Civil War, white women arguing for suffrage compared their subordination to patriarchy with the status of enslaved African Americans.[32]

In the 1830s, Northern white abolitionists began to place sexuality at the center of their conception of the slave South.[33] As Ronald Walters has shown, abolitionists expressed concern that "the South was a society in which man's sexual nature had no checks put upon it."[34] Much like prostitution, the institution of slavery endangered white slave owners and their wives and children, as well as the enslaved women under their control. As an anonymous article published in 1840 in the *Liberator* railed,

> The system of slavery, In this country, Is a system of Incest, pollution and adultery—legalized by law, and sanctified in the name of Christianity. There is nothing like it beneath the sun for all manner of uncleanness, for habitual debauchery, for beastly prostitution. . . . It is not denied by any one, that twenty-five hundred thousand human beings, of both sexes, are herded together in the South, like cattle; that the marriage institution is to them null and void; that they have no protection for their virtue; that slaves are as regularly bred for the market as sheep and swine. Slaveholders are, almost without exception, whoremongers and adulterers. Having unlimited dominion over their female captives, the temptation to commit lewdness is, in ninety-nine cases out of a hundred, irresistible.[35]

In this view, slavery was a system of prostitution, even bestiality, sanctioned and made legal by the government. It violated all the tenets of civilized sexual morality, destroying marriage, motherhood, the family, and the sexual purity of white as well as Black women. These reformers painted slavery and prostitution as analogous, arrangements unsanctioned by contracts.[36] Yet while reformers figured white women as victims of the sexual system of slavery—the suffering wives of "adulterers"—they often imagined Black women as so degraded by enslavement that they had become inherently licentious and pre-disposed to prostitution.[37]

After Emancipation, the trope of slavery remained crucial to debates over prostitution. In the South, anxieties about the ability of Black people to work under a regime of free labor, rather than slavery, led cities such as Baltimore to use vagrancy laws to target Black people, including women in commercial sex, and particularly those who worked on the streets. Efforts to make prostitution

less visible pushed it from commercial districts and "respectable" neighborhoods, isolating it into poorer neighborhoods increasingly populated by
African Americans, who were denied good wages and housing stock. Such
segregation further fueled stereotypes of Black women as immoral and sexually available.[38] In former slave states, and increasingly in Northern cities
where freedwomen migrated, Black women sold sex to Black men, as well as
to white men who hoped to recreate their sexual fantasy of slavery through sex
with light-skinned Black women.[39]

In the North, too, prostitution became more visible in the years surrounding the Civil War, as the sex trade grew increasingly brothel-based and integrated into cities' commercial and leisure spaces. The intertwined phenomena
of industrialization, urbanization, and immigration meant that more people
from more places—immigrants from Europe and to a lesser extent East Asia;
African Americans from the South and native-born white rural Americans—
flooded cities to work in low-wage jobs, swelling the ranks of sex workers and
their customers.

By the mid-1850s to mid-1860s, greater numbers of immigrant women
began to sell sex in Atlantic coastal cities, particularly Irish women, though in
most of the country native-born white women still outnumbered foreign sex
workers.[40] Native-born white women who sold sex were often the daughters
of artisans and farmers, while immigrant women's fathers generally worked as
unskilled laborers. Most women who turned to commercial sex had previously
been employed in domestic service or the garment industry, marked by long
hours, difficult physical labor, low pay, and little control over their own time.[41]
As local governments vacillated between tacitly allowing and harshly repressing prostitution, police frequently and repeatedly arrested women and imprisoned them for sentences of three to six months.[42]

In the industrializing North reform-minded citizens indicted cities, which,
they argued, were teeming with immigrants and controlled by corrupt governments, as the wellsprings of prostitution. Reformers, journalists, ministers,
and police officials all believed that urban prostitution posed a problem but
gave wildly different estimates of its impact. In 1867, one newspaper reported
that 25,000 prostitutes stalked the streets of New York City, or approximately
20 percent of young women, while a reform organization put the number at
21,000, or 13 percent of the population. In contrast to these likely inflated figures, the police department issued a report putting the number at 2,562, or
2 percent, probably minimizing the extent of commercial sex happening on its
watch.[43]

On the West Coast, white laborers, reformers, and politicians focused on East Asian immigrants. They charged Chinese men in cities such as San Francisco with fueling brothel- and crib-based prostitution, in which women lived and worked in small shacks. Impelled by poor economic circumstances in China, male Chinese laborers had come to California in large numbers, lured by the gold rush of 1848–50, and continued to arrive in the western United States to construct the growing railroad network and drain swamps to develop farmland. The 1870 census counted 63,000 Chinese men living in the United States; by 1880, that number rose to 105,000. Many Chinese men came to the United States as indentured workers. White American workingmen felt threatened by this influx of low-paid foreign labor. At a time of deep concern over the distinction between free and coerced labor, white workers portrayed Chinese men as similar to enslaved African Americans.[44]

White Americans extended this analogy to Chinese women in gender-specific ways, leading concerned citizens and politicians to decry the "yellow slave traffic" in Chinese prostitutes. Male laborers generally came alone, with men representing 90 percent of all Chinese immigrants. Often, the same brokers who facilitated this transit, and subsequently trapped these men in conditions of indentured labor, also sold and indentured to brothels the small numbers of Chinese women who did travel to the United States.[45] A vocal nativist campaign against the flow of Chinese contract labor, whether in commercial sex, construction, or agriculture, prompted the US Congress to pass the first federal immigration restriction, the 1875 Page Act. The act specifically excluded criminals, prostitutes, and "Oriental" contract laborers, marking the first federal law against prostitution.[46]

Many white reformers believed that Chinese prostitutes were redeemable, even though immigration officials viewed them as inherently sexually immoral.[47] In 1874 in San Francisco, Presbyterian women missionaries opened the Chinese Mission Home as a place of refuge for Chinese prostitutes. In such homes, Chinese women could live under the watchful eyes of white Protestant matrons, who would convert them to Christianity, train them for domestic service, industrial work, and Christian marriage, and thus make them into respectable, if not fully assimilable, immigrant workers and wives.[48]

As the United States expanded westward through wars and seizures of Native American land, women sought out frontier encampments of predominantly male soldiers and laborers, trading their sexual and domestic services for money and goods. Available data from Wyoming and Colorado suggest that white women—both native-born and European immigrant—comprised the majority of sex workers, though smaller numbers of Black, Chinese, Mexican, and Native American women also sold sex.[49] Women in commercial sex, and particularly brothel madams who owned their own buildings, occasionally built substantial wealth in the sex industry.[50] Yet most women in the American West eked out only meager livings through selling sex, much as they did in the other professions available to them.[51]

Although frontier towns and military garrisons relied on these women's sexual labor, local and military officials made no systematic attempts to register women or inspect them for disease. This is not to say they were indifferent. In towns like Cheyenne, Wyoming, much as in the urban Northeast, local officials levied fines against brothels that functioned as a form of taxation, allowing the brothels to continue operating despite local ordinances against them. The military also relied on informal toleration in and near garrisons across regions, from Wyoming and Dakota Territory to Texas and New Mexico. While officials often denied that they permitted prostitution, in practice they encouraged it.[52]

Even though white, native-born women predominated in commercial sex, US territorial officials often pointed to Native American women as particularly dangerous vectors of disease and disorder, using this alleged fact to justify the expansion of state power over them. As one official in New Mexico noted, "Prostitution prevails to a great extent among the Navajos, the Maricopas, and the Yuma Indians, and its attendant disease . . . have more or less tainted the blood of the adults" as well as the children. He proposed, as a solution, the exercise of tighter military control over Native American populations.[53] Such a solution reflected post–Civil War US government policy, which further restricted the mobility of Native Americans, and indeed, as Ned Blackhawk puts it, the "the most intimate forms of Indian life."[54] In fact, the presence of US soldiers, and the attendant poverty and loss of land, led increasing numbers of Native American women to sell sex in military encampments, as well as trade it for food and clothing. Moreover, US officials' enforcement of the reservation system devastated Native American economies and populations, likely pushing more women into sexual exchange as a means of survival.[55]

In the post–Civil War period, then, prostitution was not a new phenomenon; it became visible in new configurations and at a scale that disconcerted native-born white Americans. Burgeoning brothels, segregated commercial sex districts, and rowdy saloons became sites of battle, even as many men actively participated in the sexually charged "sporting culture" of the time.[56] Sexual transactions between different races and ethnicities provoked anxieties about miscegenation, as well as new concerns about the spread of disease. As native-born white Americans attempted to categorize the racial and ethnic "others" within what they regarded as "their" country, they could assert their supremacy by discerning deviant sexual behavior. In this way, fights over the causes of prostitution in the United States were also fights about who could be an American.

"Social Evil" Ordinances

Even as American debates over prostitution took on distinctive forms, Americans still looked to Europe for solutions to the problem. Throughout the nineteenth century, small groups of American medical doctors, influenced by their European counterparts, called for French-style regulated prostitution to stem the spread of venereal disease. As in Europe, large urban centers and military garrisons in the United States served as important sites of experimentation with systems of regulation.

In 1857, William Sanger, the physician at New York City's detention center for women on Blackwell's Island, conducted the first comprehensive qualitative and quantitative American study of prostitution and venereal disease. In a thick volume that examined historical and contemporary laws and customs regarding sexuality and prostitution throughout the world, Sanger suggested that 7,860 women engaged in some form of prostitution in New York City alone. With most between 15 and 29 years old, these women represented approximately 6 percent of white women in their age bracket.[57] He concluded that prohibitory measures had done nothing to reduce these numbers. Sanger expressed strong support of regulation. For public health reasons, he argued, America should follow the "Parisian system."[58]

During the Civil War, the Union army did just that. Union troops seized Nashville, Tennessee, in March 1862, and by winter of that year military officials worried that prostitutes were spreading venereal disease to soldiers and civilians. At first, the military attempted to solve the problem by rounding up 1,500 of the offending white women and placing them on a train to Louisville, under guard. Yet according to the Nashville press, Black women flocked to the city to replace them, and soon the deported white women returned. After his prohibitionist strategy failed, the provost marshal resorted to a regulationist one. Under his orders, the military issued each prostitute a license. A woman then paid a fee of 50 cents per week and submitted to a weekly genital examination for venereal disease. If infected, doctors confined women in a special hospital; if they defied regulations, Union officials incarcerated them in the workhouse.[59]

While Union officials had implemented regulation as a last resort, military physicians argued that it had been an "undoubted success," although an "imperfect" one, particularly in comparison to the robust Parisian system. As the physician in charge of Nashville's hospital for women lamented, "we have here no Parisian 'Bureau des Moeurs,' with its vigilant police, its careful scrutiny of the mode of conduct of houses of prostitution, and its general care of the public welfare, both morally and in its sanitary consideration." Still, he argued, the Nashville system made venereal disease "traceable" to the women who supposedly spread it, who then could be swiftly "arrested and examined."[60] After the war's end, however, the military discontinued the regulation system it had implemented in Nashville, as well as a similar system in Memphis, Tennessee.

In addition to providing an opportunity to experiment with methods of prostitution control, the Civil War also allowed the government to produce broad statistics on venereal disease in the army and to investigate its transmission. The numbers proved shocking: at its 1867 height, 21.7 percent of men were infected with venereal disease.[61] Moreover, in the post–Civil War period the American scientific community and popular press began to publicize new European models of disease transmission, including germ theory.[62] Alarmed physicians and politicians amplified their calls for American cities to adopt the European model of regulation as a means of controlling disease and maintaining social order.[63]

One of the most high-profile attempts at regulation occurred in St. Louis, Missouri. In 1870, the city council passed the "Social Evil Ordinance," which appointed six physicians, under the auspices of the City Board of Health, to inspect registered prostitutes in the six districts of the city. Police incarcerated women diagnosed with venereal disease in a "Social Evil Hospital" for treatment. Monthly fees paid by prostitutes and madams financed the system. "The tax has accumulated quite a fund," noted one newspaper.[64] In adopting the euphemism "social evil," the city council framed prostitution as a danger to society as a whole, thus justifying its regulation.[65] While the St. Louis Medical Society claimed that this system would give "the salutary and beneficial results which have for a long time obtained in Europe," official statistics suggested otherwise.[66] Perhaps it slightly lowered rates of syphilis, but it failed to reduce the number of women selling sex or to make them fully subservient to police control.[67]

Building on the supposed success of regulation in St. Louis, commercial and industrial centers such as Detroit, Minneapolis, Buffalo, Philadelphia, Cincinnati, San Francisco, Cleveland, Louisville, Savannah, Indianapolis, Davenport, Omaha, and Baltimore, conducted their own experiments with regulation, seeing it as a viable means of managing venereal disease, controlling prostitution, and generating revenue through fees and fines.[68] Marion Sims, often termed the "father of modern gynecology" for his medical experiments on enslaved women, supported "sanitary inspection and control." His involvement illustrates how controlling the bodies of enslaved women formed part of the genealogy of regulated prostitution in the United States. After his 1876 presidential address to the American Medical Association on the issue, the Association distributed 10,000 copies of his speech in an attempt to sway public opinion.[69]

As municipalities attempted to license prostitution they found themselves confronted by an organized and vocal cadre of women's rights activists and former anti-slavery campaigners. These women, including Susan B. Anthony, Elizabeth Cady Stanton, and Julia Ward Howe, saw thwarting regulation as crucial to the fight for women's social and political equality. At a time when respectable women did not discuss the social evil at all, let alone in public, they began to speak out about regulated prostitution on the lecture circuit.[70] In 1874, reformers set their sights on ending regulation in St. Louis. After collecting 100,000 signatures on a petition, they rolled it to the state legislature in "a wheelbarrow decorated with white ribbons and accompanied by a group of innocent young girls attired in white."[71] The bill to repeal the Social Evil Ordinance easily passed.[72]

Social Purity and White Women's Rights

At the same time as Anthony, Stanton, and Howe fought regulation in American cities, Josephine Butler was looking outside of Britain for allies. In 1875, she formed the British, Continental, and General Federation for the Abolition of Government Regulated Prostitution, which later changed its name to the International Abolitionist Federation. Having learned of the fight against regulation in St. Louis, Butler sought to extend the Abolitionist Federation to the United States. This transatlantic alliance would shape the direction of prostitution reform in both countries.

For British and American reformers, Anglo-American cooperation signaled the blessings of God on the continuation of the movement to abolish slavery.[73]

As Butler remarked, "the skeptical might laugh" at her crusade to end regulated prostitution, "but it was not very long ago since it was said to be impossible to do away with slavery in America."[74] Just as many white abolitionists highlighted their own efforts to end slavery rather than the struggles of enslaved people to free themselves and shape their own futures, Butler and her allies often stressed their own role in emancipating prostitutes. While they railed against regulated prostitution, as well as the economic straits that forced many working women into part-time or occasional prostitution, they also gained new political power for themselves and white women like them.[75]

The joining of the British and American new abolitionist movements rested on a sense of shared racial and religious heritage. Reformers of both nationalities subscribed to a belief in a mythical Anglo-Saxonism that sustained their liberal political systems and civilized culture and thus made them natural allies. Their affinity rested on a shared Protestant faith, in opposition to the Catholicism of regulationist countries, particularly France.

On her 1875 continental tour, Butler recounted how Europeans had extolled her, "We are ready, we only waited for you, Anglo-Saxons, to take the lead." Several years later, Butler congratulated women in St. Louis for warding off regulation, but emphasized that they had to remain vigilant. "Powerful women" and "pure, self-governed men, of the real old Anglo-Saxon type" had to take up the fight against regulation everywhere.[76] Dr. Elizabeth Blackwell, the British-born reformer and first woman to receive a medical degree in the United States, proclaimed that regulation would "uproot our whole national life, and destroy the characteristics of the Anglo-Saxon race" by allowing forced bodily examinations. Garrison, too, argued that regulation was "sapping the foundation of society on both sides of the Atlantic," stressing the danger it posed to Anglo-American civilization.[77]

At Butler's suggestion, the Abolitionist Federation sent two prominent spokesmen, Henry J. Wilson and Congregationalist Reverend J. P. Gledstone, on a tour of the northeastern United States. Traveling from New York to Washington, DC, Baltimore, Philadelphia, and Boston, they held meetings with clergymen, veteran abolitionists, politicians, YMCA members, moral reformers, and physicians, including small but growing numbers of women doctors. In every city, Wilson and Gledstone helped to organize "Vigilance Committees" that would act as American arms of the Abolitionist Federation, once again building on the moral capital of the local Vigilance Committees that had helped those attempting to escape enslavement before the Civil War.[78]

Anti-slavery and women's rights luminaries including Garrison, Lucy Stone, Mary Livermore, and Susan B. Anthony rallied behind Wilson and Gledstone, thereby attracting large crowds. Their visit catalyzed the founding of the New York Committee for the Prevention of State Regulation of Vice (New York Committee). Led by Aaron Macy Powell, the former editor of the *National Anti-Slavery Standard,* and Abby Hopper Gibbons, a well-known abolitionist and social welfare reformer, the New York Committee lay the groundwork for the increasingly powerful organizations that superseded it. As the promise of Reconstruction faded, the old abolitionists threw their full weight behind new abolitionism.[79]

Working through existing networks of reformers, the Abolitionist Federation spread its message across the United States.[80] At the annual International Temperance Convention in Philadelphia, members distributed tracts for temperance workers to take home. In turn, American activists, including Julia Ward Howe, attended the 1877 International Congress for the Abolition of Government Regulation of Prostitution in Geneva, Switzerland. More than five hundred men and women from twelve European countries as well as the United States attended, strengthening transatlantic ties.[81] They formed committees to fight regulation in cities across the country, and in 1881 began publication of the first American anti-regulationist journal *The American Bulletin,* renamed *The Philanthropist* in 1886.

At a time of broad debate over the place of sexuality in American culture, however, new abolitionist activists stood out of step with both mainstream sexual culture as well as other strains of reform. In the 1870s, federal postal agent Anthony Comstock wanted to force all public conversations about sex back into a tightly locked box (even as he had to exhaustively catalog sexual behaviors, images, texts, and items to achieve this goal). At the other extreme, "free love" advocate Victoria Woodhull argued for sexual unions with multiple partners, without interference from the state. American social purity reformers shared Comstock's conservative views on sex—that it should remain private, marital, heterosexual, and procreative—yet like Woodhull, wanted open conversations about sexuality and an end to the cultural and legal double standard that condoned extramarital sex for men but condemned women who sold sex as a means of survival.[82]

Yet despite these roadblocks, the movement continued to gain steam as the Woman's Christian Temperance Union (WCTU) took up the new abolitionist cause. Its leaders and members quickly realized that their concern about the evils of alcohol overlapped in significant ways with the problem of prostitution. Soon after its founding in 1874, the WCTU began rescue work for prostitutes. In 1883, it organized work against social evil, focused on holding men accountable for visiting prostitutes, and in 1885 formed the "Department of Social Purity."[83]

Modifying the common term "social evil," "social purity" announced activists' aim to go beyond simply decrying or suppressing prostitution. Instead, they sought to purify society as a whole through ending sexual vice and the double standard, attacking the root of the problem rather than its symptoms.[84] The WCTU's Department of Social Purity soon eclipsed temperance work and emerged as a powerful ally for the abolitionist cause, with active branches spread throughout the United States and the British Empire and a well-developed organizational structure for attacking sexual vice through legal, preventative, and reformative means.[85]

Through new abolitionists' savvy use of print culture, newspapers on both sides of the Atlantic published stories about the downfall of innocent girls at the hands of libertine men, most notably famed investigative reporter William T. Stead's 1885 exposé of child prostitution in London. They campaigned to raise the age of consent to sex, an issue that united broad concerns over sexuality, prostitution, and the protection of women and children. Many Americans were horrified to learn that the age of consent stood between 10 and 12 in most states, and just 7 in Delaware: a man who had sex with a young girl committed a crime only if proven that he had used force and she had struggled. Through petitioning, publicity campaigns, and targeting state and later, federal legislation, social purity reformers raised the age of consent in most states.[86]

By the mid-1880s, the US social purity movement conducted a national campaign with transatlantic dimensions. Moreover, they learned how to run an effective movement. At the Abolitionist Federation's regular international congresses, activists on both sides of the Atlantic shared a growing repertoire of legal, educational, religious, and journalistic strategies to aid their fight against sexual vice.[87]

Feminism, Medicine, Eugenics

From its inception, new abolitionism had a feminist orientation.[88] British and American feminist abolitionists linked the fight against regulated prostitution directly to women's social, economic, and political rights, with many advocating women's suffrage as a central piece of their platform. In a lecture on "Social

Purity," Susan B. Anthony identified the cause of all prostitution as "woman's dependence" on men, arguing that "the first and only efficient work must be to emancipate woman from her enslavement." Not only should women vote, but they needed equal access to employment. As Anthony put it, "whoever controls work and wages, controls morals."[89] Class, too, as well as gender, made some women particularly vulnerable. Aaron Macy Powell believed that "the regulation system imperils the liberty and security of all women, especially poor women and working girls."[90]

In fact, feminists argued, regulation undermined not only women's rights but the entire liberal political system, predicated on individual rights. In Britain, Josephine Butler pointed out that all women might face registration as prostitutes, genital examinations, and imprisonment with very little proof. Since a justice of the peace alone determined whether to register a woman, the process violated the right to a jury trial and habeas corpus. Butler posed a simple question: "Shall we have liberty in lust, or shall we have political freedom? We cannot retain both."[91]

Feminist abolitionists remained wary of solutions to the problem of prostitution based on state intervention, which often involved the use of force. Dr. Elizabeth Blackwell advised reformers not to "stir up the police to a violent clearance of loose women off the streets" or attempt to close brothels "until you can offer honest work to the inmates."[92] Blackwell's sister, physician Emily Blackwell, warned that the movement against regulation might turn into a movement to replace regulation with a "repressive system" that arrested women, a pattern she had seen taking hold in Europe.[93] With women denied the right to vote on both sides of the Atlantic, feminist abolitionists knew that men alone created and enforced laws, making them unfriendly toward women. As Emily Blackwell remarked, forming "associations for the active dissemination of information, and propagation of juster views" would remedy the problem of prostitution.[94] Moral suasion, rather than legal force, could transform society.

While feminist abolitionists emphasized the moral might of their position, they also made scientific arguments. Women's medical education in the United States expanded dramatically in the late nineteenth century, when nineteen new women's medical schools opened. The number of female physicians in the country rose from under 200 in 1860 to 2,432 in 1880 and to more than 7,387 by 1900. In contrast, in 1881, only twenty-five women doctors practiced in England and Wales. While some American women physicians sought advanced training in European surgical techniques and laboratory medicine, women from around the world often traveled to the United States to attend medical school.[95]

Many members of the first generation of women to attend medical school put their weight behind social purity reform, arguing that they had come to their anti-regulation stance through their medical training, not in spite of it. Elizabeth Blackwell emphasized that her opposition to regulation rested on her experience as "a physician acquainted with the physiological and pathological laws of the human frame . . . with a positive and practical knowledge rarely possessed by women."[96] Similarly, American Dr. Rebecca C. Hollowell used her training as a physician to reject the regulationist argument that "prostitution springs from the *inexorable law of necessity*," a "legitimate craving that must be gratified for the maintenance of health." Citing Blackwell's medical research, Hollowell contended that men did not need sexual release because the body, male or female, governed itself by a "law of self-adjustment" which allowed for a "*healthy* discharge" of the reproductive organs through menstruation and spontaneous seminal emission.[97] In addition to its fundamental immorality, prostitution violated the laws of health for both men and women.

American women physicians also incorporated eugenics into their arguments against regulated prostitution. Despite the fact that British scientists pioneered eugenics, Josephine Butler complained that the American new abolitionist and physician Caroline Forbes Winslow and "her set" held views that tended "too much into making people into orderly breeding machines," ignoring the possibility that "miracles of grace" could transform even the most downtrodden people.[98] Many white American women fretted that violations of the rules of health and morality could lead to the "degeneration" of individuals and society as a whole. For a time in the 1880s, the WCTU published the *Journal of Heredity*, reflecting its concern that heredity influenced alcohol consumption and prostitution and that these vices in turn harmed future generations.[99]

Purity activists generally employed a Lamarckian conception of evolution, which held that acquired characteristics were heritable. As WCTU missionary and physician Nancy Monelle-Mansell argued, "there is in human nature a tendency for propensities to crystalize and to become fixed elements of character and physique, and to pass on from one generation to the next."[100] Not only could the prostitute and customer pass on venereal disease to innocent wives and children, but they could also pass on the very tendency to sexual excess. As one reformer argued, "Social Vice and National Decay stand to each other as parent to child, cause to consequence. . . . The prevalence and increase of the Social Evil among a people is a sure sign and symptom of national de-generacy."[101] This idea made it even more important for white middle-class women to exercise their power as a civilizing force against regulated prostitu-tion and any form of sexual vice.

While British and Continental physicians largely favored regulation, the social purity movement in the United States successfully convinced many in the male-dominated medical profession of their arguments. Powell placed ar-ticles articulating the scientific and moral position against regulation in lead-ing American medical and public health journals.[102] By the 1880s, many male medical doctors rejected regulation using arguments very much like those of social purity reformers. Emphasizing masculine self-control in language simi-lar to that of Blackwell and Hallowell, New York physician Charles Kitchell argued, "if the passions of men were dominated by reason, noble thinking and a true appreciation of the dignity and purpose of the sexual relation, prostitu-tion would be unknown."[103] By the mid-1890s, the New York Academy of Medicine, as well as organizations of physicians in other cities, issued public statements against regulation and in favor of male chastity.[104]

Licensed Women

Even as the abolitionist position gained strength in the United States in the late twentieth century, regulationists and abolitionists continued to clash over how to address prostitution. Yet reformers on both sides largely ignored how women who sold sex experienced and discussed different regimes of prostitu-tion control. Mobility marked these women's lives: movement from other countries to the United States, from rural areas to cities, from one city to an-other during police crackdowns, and between sexual labor and other forms of employment.[105] While state regulation allowed women to sell sex, it also placed significant constraints on their freedom of movement and their finances.

Some of the clearest evidence of women's experience of regulation comes from St. Louis. In March 1871, eight months after the city implemented a sys-tem of licensing, the health department reported that "the bawds were not reconciled to its restraint. They regarded it simply as a new device for persecu-tion, and scores left the city, rather than submit to its provisions."[106] Yet many women remained to sell sex in the rapidly industrializing city. Between July 1870 and March 1873, officials registered 2,685 prostitutes, including 1,904 native-born white women and 326 "colored" women, followed by smaller numbers of German, Irish, and other European immigrants, with 402 European women registered in total.[107]

Although the Social Evil Ordinance recognized prostitution as a legal profession, it subjected women to increased surveillance and arrest, similar to their experiences in cities that actively enforced anti-prostitution ordinances. Under regulation, remarked Health Officer Dr. William L. Barrett, police arrested women in greater numbers because they were "made amenable to law and kept constantly under its eye." Moreover, women often faced re-arrest; Barrett noted that one woman had been arrested forty-five times in one year. While the number of brothels increased after the ordinance (from 119 to 133), the number of women working out of private apartments decreased from 205 to seven. To authorities, such numbers demonstrated the success of their efforts in "concentrating prostitutes . . . to inspect and police them more thoroughly."[108]

The entanglement of policing with public health produced carceral outcomes. If a woman received a venereal disease diagnosis, the police promptly detained her in the Social Evil Hospital. As one journalist observed, "Many of the girls are taken from their 'homes' and carried to the hospital without any previous notice or warning," preventing them from leaving the city or seeking private treatment. The hospital, around four miles from downtown St. Louis, housed Black and white women in separate buildings. While white women lived in a large brick house, Black women lived on the second floor of a gatehouse, in likely more uncomfortable conditions. While the white women's building boasted indoor plumbing, the journalist reported that "just now the pipes are frozen and the institution suffers from a lack of water." A staff of two policemen, one male physician, and a husband-and-wife team who served as matron and steward guarded, treated, and provided for the women's basic needs.[109]

Although available accounts of women's perspectives are mediated through a journalist's pen, white women incarcerated in the Social Evil Hospital presented themselves as savvy women who demanded their rights as workers. Most women portrayed themselves neither as downtrodden, as abolitionists depicted them, nor as disease vectors, as pro-regulation officials rendered them. They expressed ambivalence about the licensing system, recognizing it as "an outrage upon their liberties," while also conceding that it gave them access to health care and "some protections."[110]

These women understood the St. Louis Social Evil Hospital as "their property." After all, the fees the city charged them—ten dollars per month for madams and six for prostitutes—funded the hospital. They complained about the quality of the food because, as one pointed out, "our money purchases these things; we are beholden to no one and have nothing to be grateful for." While officials attempted to reform their "appetites," women demanded stewed chicken, oysters, and butter with every meal; one woman called for "such food as we have been accustomed to," suggesting that some women could afford a high standard of living through sexual labor.[111]

The hospital required women to remain in their wards, which housed between three and eighteen prisoners, and allowed visitors only once a week. Women's treatment plans often kept them in the hospital for six months to over a year. Women repeatedly attempted to escape the hospital: on Christmas Day, 1872, six women ran away but were caught.[112] Eventually officials took away women's shoes to impede their flight.[113] Women protested that they "feel something like criminals" in the hospital. They repeatedly demanded access to tobacco, snuff, and a social room in which to enjoy themselves. Because "the city grants them a license," women argued, "they have a perfect right to dispose of their time and persons as they please."[114]

Yet women preferred the Social Evil Hospital to the other institutions, such as the "Female Guardian Home," which sought to place women in "respectable" employment, most likely as domestics.[115] The hospital, women emphasized, was "not a reformatory," nor should it be. It did not require women to perform domestic or other work. Instead, in good weather women walked the grounds and played croquet. When in their wards, women played cards, told fortunes, chatted, knitted, and napped. "Very few are fond of work," a journalist observed, "and their past life furnishes no incentive to ply the needle," a low-wage job in which women might work fifteen to eighteen hours a day to earn a subsistence wage.[116] Unsurprisingly, despite regulationists' claims that the hospital could incentivize women to leave the sex industry, few women did so. As a journalist noted, women stated that other types of work "would be about as bad as the woes of the present, without any of the present's enjoyments."[117]

Registered women in St. Louis offered their own critique of regulated prostitution, illuminating the limitations of both the regulationist and the abolitionist positions. Regulation could benefit women, they suggested, because it acknowledged that prostitution was a job. In fact, it paid better than any other job available to women. At the same time, the regulation system punished women, imposing difficult constraints even on those who managed to remain outside of the hospital. The women confined at St. Louis's Social Evil Hospital pointed out the hypocrisy of the system, but in ways that differed from social purity arguments. The problem was not solely that regulation instantiated a gendered double standard. Instead, they contended, if prostitution was legal and the city reaped financial benefits from it, then women had the right to set their own living and working conditions.

Race, Slavery, and Social Purity

Arguments about labor—forced or free—abounded in social purity rhetoric, even as reformers did not understand prostitution as a form of work. When the old abolitionists took up the new abolitionist cause, they not only equated regulated prostitution with slavery, but they also began to argue that white prostitutes endured worse conditions than Black women had under slavery. To do so, as Jessica Pliley has argued, they created a new "mythology" about African American slavery. In their formulation, chattel slavery had only deprived Black people of the profits of their labor, while the prostitution of white women stole their virtue—an even worse fate. This framing elided both the racial hierarchy central to American chattel slavery and the sexual exploitation of Black women under it, an issue that had previously been at the forefront of white American abolitionist critiques of slavery.[118] Moreover, it ignored that ongoing sexual violence against Black women, lynching, and the sharecropping system represented the most obvious continuity with chattel slavery, increasingly sanctioned by Jim Crow laws.

As social purity reformers equated prostitution with slavery, they placed commercial sex at the center of pressing battles over the nature of American political and economic life. Concerns over "white slavery" did not reach their apogee until the early twentieth century (see chapter 3). But the bloodshed of sectional conflict was still recent, giving the concept of slavery new political currency, as debates swirled around the meanings of labor, liberty, and race. The post–Civil War free labor ideal put the contract, agreed to by two fully consenting parties, at the center of social relations. Significantly, both the labor contract and the marriage contract were civil agreements between eligible consenting adults. The idea that all forms of prostitution amounted to slavery rested on the belief that a woman would not and could not consent to sex outside of the marital contract.[119]

In the 1870s, European anti-regulationists increasingly began to label white women in regulated prostitution as slaves, almost always in conjunction with a comparison to the enslavement of African Americans in the United States.

As French novelist Victor Hugo wrote of the "traite des blanches," or traffic in white women, "the slavery of black women is abolished in America, but the slavery of white women continues in Europe; and laws are still made by men in order to tyrannise over women."[120] American new abolitionists adopted this rhetoric and, by the mid-1870s, their anti-prostitution arguments commonly employed the language of slavery.[121] Speaking of the plight of Parisian prostitutes incarcerated in the prison hospital St. Lazare, American Purity Alliance president Aaron Macy Powell noted that they had "a more 'forlorn hope,' indeed, than that of the former American slave. . . . God forbid that there shall be established in this and other American cities, a yet more damnable slavery in the form of 'localized' and 'legalized' prostitution."[122]

As abolitionists shifted from decrying the sexual mistreatment of Black women under slavery to the supposedly worse conditions of white prostitutes, they transferred their critique of the sexual conditions created by the slave system onto the formerly enslaved.[123] Powell and his colleagues remained concerned about the sexual morality of African Americans. Yet they expressed ambivalence about the causes of Black immorality and whether it was inborn—and thus impossible to change—or the result of Black culture, shaped by the legacy of slavery, and thus reformable.

Some white reformers placed the blame squarely on the innate hypersexuality of Black women. *The Philanthropist*, the American Purity Alliance's official organ, printed a letter from a white Presbyterian minister who wrote to call attention to a new "field for operations . . . among the colored people." In his view, "the greatest impediment to the civilization and christianization of the colored people is lewdness and prostitution." Such qualities had a biological basis, as well as a cultural basis, he explained. "Their animal passions are very strong, and they have had but little in the past to curb them and nothing to teach them how to control them." In one small town, he found that "25 negro women went to that town every night to place their bodies on a commercial basis with men, white men."[124] In his framing, lascivious Black women stood at fault for such sex across the color line.

Yet other white social purity reformers did not accept racially deterministic explanations for the promiscuity of Black women, instead pointing to the legacy of slavery. As *The Philanthropist* noted, "sexual immorality and intemperance" were "the chief hindrance to progress on the part of the colored people at the present time." These problems resulted from slavery, which "destroyed the home" and left "inevitably a deplorable legacy of immorality."[125] Such cultural explanations, however, elided the structural factors, such as the sharecropping system, sexual violence by white men against Black women, and the rise of Jim Crow, which maintained white supremacy and impeded African American social, political, and economic equality.

Middle-class Black reformers also took up social purity, at times collaborating with the white social purity movement but, in the face of white racism, often working through their own channels. While white social purity reformers focused on the spread of regulated and tolerated prostitution, Black reformers decried the sexual mistreatment and violence Black women faced in the Jim Crow South.[126] *The Philanthropist* kept the majority-white social purity movement abreast of developments in Black social purity circles through printing the writings and speeches of its leaders.

Like their white counterparts, middle-class Black reformers often pointed to slavery as the root cause of sexual immorality. They also trained their focus on Black women. Fisk University Professor Eugene Harris adopted a cultural explanation and blamed slavery for the "moral laxity" of Black women. At a time when African Americans faced the onslaught of white violence, lynching, and disenfranchisement, Harris believed that Black women had a special duty to uplift the Black community. As he explained, "if the *pure* women among us affiliate with the *impure*, and treat their offenses with leniency, it will be hard for the public to discriminate with certainty between them." Thus, respectable Black women must vocally condemn Black prostitutes and other sexually "impure" women, so that white people would not paint the entire race with the same brush.[127]

Prominent Black women, including Mary Church Terrell, a suffragist and advocate for African American rights, also joined the social purity movement. Yet in contrast to the cultural explanations that Harris and white reformers used to explain the prevalence of Black women in commercial sex, Terrell argued that slavery had created social and political structures that encouraged sexual violence against Black women by white men. Terrell indicted the racism embedded in the legal system, noting "the courts of our country do not protect the colored women from the white men who ruin them." Indeed, the criminalization of marriage across the color line facilitated the sexual exploitation of Black women. As Terrell explained, "the courts are handing down decisions exonerating the men for the ruination of colored women on the theory that the traffic is better than inter-marriage."[128]

Moreover, Terrell and others charged white women purity reformers with purposefully ignoring the plight of Black women. "As a class the women of the south have not lifted a finger to save the colored women from vice," Terrell protested.[129] Suffragist, anti-slavery activist, and writer Frances E. W. Harper reported that Philadelphia's midnight Mission, an organization that provided refuge for prostitutes and unmarried pregnant women, had denied Black women entry. As Harper put it, "Black and white could sin together, but they could not be rescued in that home together."[130] These critiques made visible the role that white women played in the subjugation of Black women, refusing to help, and even blaming them, while turning a blind eye to the behavior of white men.

Like white purity reformers, Terrell looked abroad to make comparisons between sexual morality in the United States and other countries. Yet she did so to argue for the exceptional sexual morality of Black women in the face of slavery, Jim Crow, and white violence. "In spite of the fateful heritage of slavery," Terrell asserted, "in spite of the fact that the white men may despoil the colored girls in the South without fearing the penalty of the law," Black women were not promiscuous. In fact, she claimed, "statistics compiled by men who would not falsify in favor of my race, show that immorality among colored women is not so great as among women whose environment is similar to theirs in Italy, Germany, Sweden and France."[131] The problem white purity reformers needed to solve, then, was not Black women's immorality, but their sexual exploitation by white men who went unpunished. While white social purity reformers turned their attention overseas to critique regulated prostitution in Europe and its colonies, Terrell used international comparison to redirect the attention of white reformers back toward their Black countrywomen.

Conclusion

A critique of state-regulated prostitution initially animated the social purity movement. Just as the US government had wrongfully allowed and then righteously abolished slavery, so too could it stop regulation from taking hold on its shores and extirpate it in Europe. After American activists joined the British-led fight against state-regulated prostitution, they broadened their scope to include all prostitution, and indeed, sexual vice of any type, particularly when it involved young, white victims. By the 1890s, the once-fringe social purity movement had become mainstream, making the single standard of morality and male sexual restraint the American middle-class ideal. This ideal ignored the ongoing prevalence of prostitution, still a visible part of urban life and a source of income for tens of thousands of women.[132]

Through their efforts, however, the new abolitionists brought sexual matters into public conversations in unprecedented ways. While their publications, lobbying, and lectures popularized their cause and won broad support, their discourse had unintended consequences. The social purity movement loosened the strictures that had kept sexual matters out of polite society and the public arena, unleashing a proliferation of new conversations and debates about sex.[133]

Through their debates, abolitionists and regulationists made sex the subject of public policy. They also raised questions about the particular nature of American sexual morality. Should the United States follow the supposedly scientifically advanced European model of regulated prostitution? Or should the United States, as an exceptionally moral nation, chart its own path away from old-world vice? New abolitionists landed staunchly on the side of American exceptionalism, positing regulated prostitution as fundamentally foreign to the United States. Powell deemed it "a gigantic, iniquitous, old-world system of sensua[l] slavery for women and degradation for men," enforced by "despotic old-world governments" that threatened American womanhood and "public morality."[134]

The ideal of American gender relations formed a crucial part of reformers' belief in the special role that the United States and white American men and women could play in the global fight against sexual vice. As WCTU president Frances Willard argued, regulation and the sexual double standard had been defeated in the United States because "the manhood of America is the noblest and most masterful on earth, because it has most mastery of itself."[135] British reformers echoed this conclusion. Americans had repeatedly foiled the plans of regulationists, Abolitionist Federation representative J. P. Gledstone noted, because no one could "establish an odious tyranny in the midst of a free people, and [degrade] women in the land where she is most honored."[136] For social purity reformers, the sexual self-control of white men and the sexual purity of white women defined American national character.

In a world increasingly interconnected through immigration and empire, however, American reformers could not be complacent. British reformers contended that Americans could play a crucial role in the fight against European state-regulated prostitution. At the same time, they argued, joining the abolitionist campaign benefited the United States' self-interest. As they warned, "Europe is constantly sending hosts of men and women to people the new world, all of whom carry with them the habits, the principles, the prejudices, the prepossessions, something of the moral atmosphere of the countries in which they were born and bred. The purification of Europe from any moral pollution is the purification of one of the fountains of American life."[137] New immigrants arriving on US shores could endanger American sexual exceptionalism.

But Americans were also curious about how, as self-described sexually exceptional people, they might help those mired in the evils of both native "savage" sexuality and imperial state-regulated prostitution. British reformers observed that reports from India and China particularly affected Americans. Such stories "pricked their hearts to the quick, and opened their eyes to see that they might sometime find their country as deeply implicated in immorality as ours."[138] Indeed, the United States' acquisition of a new overseas empire in 1898 would arouse the attention of state and military officials—as well as social purity reformers—to the issue of prostitution in new ways. Over the following decades, Americans' fight to purify their own country became inseparable from their quest to reform the laws and mores of other countries.

2

Purifying Empire

INDIA, THE PHILIPPINES, AND THE WAR OF 1898

IN 1907, Dr. Katharine Bushnell and Elizabeth Wheeler Andrew, two American missionaries and social purity reformers, reflected on their decades-long fight against state-regulated prostitution in the United States and throughout the British Empire. All women, they argued, should feel outrage that colonial officials registered and licensed prostitutes in India and China and examined their bodies for venereal disease. "There is a solidarity of womanhood that men and women must reckon with," they argued. "We cannot, without sin against humanity, ask the scoffer's question, 'Am I my sister's keeper?'—not even concerning the poorest and meanest foreign woman," Bushnell and Andrew declared, "for the reason that *she is our sister*."[1]

Bushnell and Andrew remained committed to freeing their "sisters" in the "Orient" from the "slavery" of prostitution. British imperial rule as well as the immorality of American and European merchants, they argued, bore the blame. At the same time, however, their sense of "solidarity" with foreign prostitutes also reflected their growing concern that these women's exploitation posed "a great peril to American womanhood." While in the United States, "women have self-reliance and self-respect in a Christian country," Asian immigration and US imperialism in the Pacific introduced the "Oriental slave-prostitute" to American shores, and American as well as Chinese men exploited her. "Christian womanhood will fall," they predicted, if American women did not fight regulated prostitution everywhere they found it: in American cities, in US territories in the Caribbean and Pacific, or in the British Empire.[2]

Bushnell's and Andrew's writings illuminate a series of debates that emerged in the late nineteenth century between Anglo-American social purity activists, military officials, and civil governments. At their core, these debates raised questions about the nature of empire. How did the fates of metropolitan and colonial women intertwine? Was state-regulated prostitution in colonies such as India an unfortunate yet necessary aspect of the imperial project, which protected white women and families in the metropole? Or did it erode the health, morals, and civilization of both colony and metropole? Once a government licensed and regulated prostitution in its colonies, would it import regulation back to the metropole, as the British government had done? Or did state-regulated prostitution, which seemed to inevitably travel with the soldiers of empire, prove the fatal flaw of imperialism itself? For Americans, such debates were also crucially about the nature of American exceptionalism.

Americans first addressed these pressing questions in British India. In the 1880s, after the successful repeal of the metropolitan Contagious Diseases Acts, Josephine Butler turned her attention to the Acts regulating prostitution still in effect in India and enforced in far more punitive ways toward women than they had been in the metropole.[3] Butler's American associates joined her, with the Woman's Christian Temperance Union (WCTU) playing a key role.

But Americans had a particular relationship to India. Even as they stressed a shared Anglo-Saxon racial, political, and religious heritage, they positioned themselves as outsiders as they critiqued the British government's failure to protect Indian women from Indian men as well as from white soldiers. While "the British Government must deal with 'a condition and not a theory,'" WCTU President Frances Willard remarked, "we in America have practically no standing army; we have no 'oriental difficulties.'"[4] As a purportedly non-imperial state, the United States thus maintained its exceptional status as a country that did not regulate prostitution.

The War of 1898 made the United States an empire along the European model, forcing American social purity reformers to reevaluate the promises and dangers of imperialism. The US government framed the war as a means of helping the Philippines, Cuba, Puerto Rico, and Guam throw off the cruel yoke of Spanish rule. At the same time, many Americans argued, the peoples of those countries were unfit to fully govern themselves. Even as the United States saw the British Empire as a staunch ally in the global civilizing mission, the United States positioned itself as a fundamentally different kind of imperial power through its program of "benevolent assimilation," one motivated by a purported desire to uplift others rather than extract resources from them.[5]

Yet in the Philippines, the US government, like British in India, faced the reality of administering an overseas territorial empire. While this administrative colonialism built on the US government's experience of settler colonialism in the American West, it also came with new challenges, including different means of managing interracial interactions, especially sex. Indeed, as Tessa Winkelmann argues, "interracial intercourse was not a peripheral outcome of the occupation of the islands; rather it was a cornerstone."[6]

At first, American social purity activists had high hopes for the US government to act as a civilizing force in its new territories. After all, they themselves had already been working to civilize India, in the absence of any formal US government presence. With the backing of the government, Americans believed they might effect even more profound transformations. Filipinas—their bodies, their beauty, their ugliness—became a fixation for Americans.[7] Would the United States fall prey to the same sexual problems that plagued the British Empire and threatened its self-image as a civilizing power? Or could it chart a new, benevolent path and uplift benighted people toward sexual civilization while also keeping the metropole's health and morality intact?

Social Purity in India

For American purity activists, India served as an important testing ground for defining themselves, both against supposedly savage racial others and against their Anglo-Saxon peers. The context of the British Empire reframed ideas about racial difference in terms of civilization, a discourse through which white women positioned themselves as experts. By claiming the roles of saviors and sisters of Indian women, while ignoring the widespread sexual violence against African American women at home, white American women could continue to claim that the United States stood at the pinnacle of civilization.

Much American overseas activity in the nineteenth century centered on the "Indian subcontinent." Indeed, American merchants saw India as a lucrative field for trade, while philosophers and proponents of liberal religion took an Orientalist interest in Indian religious texts and practices. Moreover, India was the site of the first American overseas mission in 1812.[8] In the decades after the Civil War, as missionary organizations expanded, India remained an important field for American missionaries. In this period, too, women increasingly served missions, representing 60 percent of Protestant missionaries by the 1890s.[9] Building on the infrastructure created by the British Empire, American women missionaries believed that they were participating in a shared, Anglo-American project to Christianize and civilize Indians.

The explosive growth of transnational women's voluntary reform organizations in the late nineteenth century also fueled Anglo-American social purity efforts in India. The WCTU emerged as one of the most prominent. Women involved in foreign mission work and WCTU members significantly overlapped. While not an explicitly missionary organization, Protestant Christianity fundamentally shaped the WCTU's agenda, as did a missionary impulse to convert the world to its set of values, including temperance, sexual restraint, and women's emancipation. From its inception, as Ian Tyrrell has shown, the WCTU had an expansive vision of not just the United States but the globe as its field of work.[10]

While WCTU president Frances Willard stood staunchly behind social purity reform, she also shrewdly understood that she could bring more British women to the WCTU by joining the fight against regulated prostitution.[11] In 1883, the WCTU formed what became the Department of Social Purity, which addressed sexual vice under the rubrics of prevention, reformation, and legislation. The same year, Willard proposed the establishment of a World's WCTU to formalize the international ties the WCTU had already fostered. By the mid-1890s, the American WCTU alone printed a total of 118 million pages of literature and published regular columns in 883 newspapers. With a membership of 150,000 dues-paying women by 1891, rising to almost 200,000 by 1900, and branches in every state as well as Europe and Asia, the WCTU stood poised to reach a large audience and advance the social purity cause.[12]

To understand the position of women of color in "foreign" lands, American women missionaries and WCTU workers drew on religious and anthropological understandings of society as evolving from savagery through barbarism and finally to civilization, with white, Anglo-American Protestants at the pinnacle. Sexual arrangements also defined these stages, with monogamy as characteristic of civilization. Women's missionary publications decried Indians' practice of polygamy, child marriage, and temple prostitution; their sexually explicit religious texts; and the subservience of Indian women to their husbands. White feminists argued that civilized societies encouraged women's advancement, while women's inequality signaled decline and degeneration. At the same time, they advanced a gendered view of civilizational progress, holding that women from barbarous places took up civilization and Christianity far more readily than men.[13]

As American women participated in Anglo-American reform and missionary networks, they framed Americans as more civilized than both "heathen" Indians and their supposedly civilized, supposedly Christian, British imperial "rulers."[14] White American women worried that contact with "eastern" cultures and peoples had already harmed Britain. WCTU round-the-world missionary Mary Clement Leavitt was "convinced" that child prostitution in England resulted from "English intercourse with Asia, and the transplanting of eastern customs to the west." Yet American women also indicted British imperial governance and the immorality of British settlers in India for failing to civilize India. American medical missionary Emily Brainerd Ryder argued that when "the Hindu" looked at "the daily lives of the Europeans that have invaded his country" and read all about their "domestic discord or infidelity," he understandably chose to adhere to "the teachings of his ancestors." "The civilization of the enlightened world demands protection" for Indian women from Indian men, Ryder wrote.[15] If the British government would not protect them, then American women would have to rise to the occasion.

In 1891 Dr. Katharine Bushnell and Elisabeth Wheeler Andrew got the chance to do just that. An 1888 exposé of the regulation system in India—including the publication of British military circulars calling for the provision of "attractive" women for soldiers—had led the British government to suspend the Indian Contagious Diseases Act. Yet reports continued to reach Butler that British military officials regulated prostitution in India to satisfy the sexual needs of white British troops, contravening the law. An investigation conducted by two British men failed to uncover conclusive evidence of regulation. So Butler chose Bushnell and Andrew, both American WCTU women with long experience fighting prostitution and "white slavery." Butler believed that Bushnell's expertise as a trained physician and former missionary to China, as well as the two women's lack of ties to the British authorities, would enable them to collect information that officials might deny to Brits.[16]

During their first months in India, Bushnell and Andrew reported, British officials categorically denied the existence of government licensed brothels, forced inspections, and lock hospitals for the treatment of venereal disease. So they decided to use local interpreters and make their way into cantonments—permanent British military stations—under the pretense of purely missionary work in order to conduct, in essence, an undercover investigation. Through the interpreters, they spoke to more than three hundred women held in brothels in the cantonments. These included Indian women, the children of Indian mothers and white British fathers, and former mistresses of British soldiers who had cast them aside.

As Bushnell and Andrew recounted, women, some as young as ten, told them of being violently beaten, raped, and set on fire by British soldiers, and made to undergo repeated forced inspections for venereal disease, which Bushnell and Andrew termed "surgical rape." While British officials contended that Indians recognized prostitution as a profession and women there felt no shame in selling sex, Bushnell and Andrew recounted women's tearful stories of being forced to work in the brothels and held against their will. Andrew described the paradoxical position of the Indian prostitute: she is "declared to be 'a necessity'—yet she is denounced and pursued as relentlessly as if she was the deliberate enemy of all social and domestic order and peace."[17]

In 1893, Bushnell and Andrew returned to Britain and revealed their findings, creating precisely the scandal Butler had hoped would advance the abolitionist cause. In government hearings in London, they gave testimony and produced their journals, interview notes, a detailed table of the scheduled venereal disease examinations at each cantonment, and an examination ticket they obtained from an Indian woman. Their exposé received attention in popular newspapers and reform publications across the United States and Britain. After the British commander of the military forces in India accused the women of lying, other officials verified their findings. Under pressure, the commander issued a public apology, putting in clear relief the righteousness of Bushnell's and Andrew's work and the perfidy of British military officials in India. In response, Parliament passed the 1895 Cantonment Amendment Act, which explicitly forbid the military from keeping regimental brothels, giving the trans-Atlantic new abolitionists another victory.[18]

Yet Bushnell and Andrew's investigation precipitated what the famed suffragist Reverend Anna Garlin Spencer described as "a great rift in the leading womanhood of our generation in respect to a great moral question." At stake, as Bushnell and Andrew put it, was the question of which "innocent wives and children" should Anglo-American women work to protect: "the British or the Indian"? Political changes in Britain, and military leaders' insistence on regulating prostitution to manage venereal disease, led the British government to once again reinstate licensed prostitution in India in 1897. American social purity advocates expressed surprised when some white British women vocally supported this move, including Lady Henry Somerset, vice president of the World's WCTU and a seeming ally of the social purity cause. Somerset and more than one hundred other elite white women argued that regulated prostitution in the colony provided crucial protections for white British soldiers and their "future wives" and "unborn offspring" at home.[19]

After widespread outcry and fierce pressure from British and American WCTU members, Somerset eventually recanted. But the episode undercut the World's WCTU power, including its ability to apply pressure on national governments.[20] Despite the transatlantic publicity against regulation generated by Bushnell and Andrew, the British government, and particularly the military, held fast to the axiom of regulated prostitution as a colonial necessity.

Even though American social purity advocates did not, as they had hoped, abolish regulated prostitution in India, their efforts gave them new language for conceptualizing American sexual exceptionalism. Bushnell and Andrew repeatedly tied regulated prostitution to the subordination of all women—British, American, and Indian. After all, governments denied all women key political and economic rights, resulting in their gendered and often sexual subjugation. Yet the two women framed regulated prostitution as a particularly British imperial practice, which, like venereal disease, spread as a contagion. Supporters of regulation in India, Bushnell and Andrew charged, attempted "to contaminate public sentiment" such that the British government might reintroduce regulation and carry it over to the United States.[21]

Moreover, Bushnell and Andrew worried, such regulationist agitation was working. In five American states, regulationists had introduced legislation for compulsory examination of women deemed prostitutes. Aaron Macey Powell argued that it was "most important for America" to agitate against regulation in England and India, because regulation there would "greatly encourage and strengthen regulation propagandists in this country." For Bushnell and Andrew, regulated prostitution represented a fundamental threat not only to the British civilizing project in India, but to the very existence of civilized, liberal democracies like Britain and the United States. "When a Government begins to drag down the moral character of its subjects," they warned, "it has begun to dig out its own foundations."[22]

Bushnell and Andrew drew analogies to chattel slavery to advance their criticism of the British government in India. Such rhetoric proved particularly provoking to Britain, which at the time positioned itself as the anti-slavery empire. The climate did not sap white Britons of their morality in India, Bushnell and Andrew argued, but rather the extractive labor practices they enacted, both sexual and industrial, which the two compared to those "in the Southern States of American before the Civil War." The fate of the British Empire stood in the balance: "England virtually owns a whole nation of slaves in her control of India, and the effect of this fact upon the morals of that country will depend wholly upon whether she rules to redeem her subjects or to enrich herself."[23] The United States had taken the path away from slavery toward civilization;

now Britain could follow suit by ending regulated prostitution. Only then could it act as a benevolent civilizer.

As Bushnell and Andrew's writings suggest, African Americans played an important ideological role in Americans' arguments against state-sanctioned sexual vice in India. Yet in turning to India as the site of the next battle over the "slavery" of prostitution, white American social purity advocates also turned away from the violence, including sexual violence, facing actual flesh and blood African Americans during the rise of Jim Crow. As Leslie Dunlap has noted, white women "studiously avoided naming African American women as victims" of rape.[24] The social purity movement thus helped to lay the ideological and infrastructural groundwork for US overseas imperialism as a supposedly benevolent enterprise while it diverted attention from the troubling inconsistencies within US society.

"Lessons from India" in The Philippines

While American advocates of social purity unanimously criticized the British Empire and its policies on prostitution, they were divided over the question of whether the United States should acquire an overseas territorial empire. Bushnell and Andrew remained convinced that it should not, precisely because imperialism led to regulated prostitution. As early as 1893, Andrew had argued that the United States should not occupy and annex Hawai'i for that reason. Yet many WCTU members advocated the US acquisition of Hawai'i as a means of civilizing the Pacific. They believed the United States could chart a different course by preventing prostitution, encouraging sexual morality among Hawaiians, and prohibiting the sale of alcohol.[25] Although social purity activists differed in their stance on US empire, all articulated their fears and hopes about empire through its possible effects on sexual civilization.

When the United States went to war with Spain in 1898, these theoretical questions about US empire became more concrete. After fighting to end Spanish imperialism alongside Filipinos, Cubans, and Puerto Ricans, the US government quickly deemed itself in charge after the defeat of Spanish forces. Even though the Philippines declared independence after Spain's defeat and formed a provisional government, the United States annexed the archipelago, as well as Puerto Rico, and built US state power into Cuba's constitution. US troops would continue to fight a brutal war of conquest against Filipino nationalists and insurgents for a decade after the US government declared the war officially over in 1902.[26]

US colonial officials attempted to impose a sense of order to the islands' racial diversity, delineating Christian, Hispanicized Filipinos from "non-Christian" "savages" including adherents of Islam and forms of animism. Yet while mixed-race, Spanish-speaking Catholics could help the US officials to govern these less civilized peoples, Americans believed they could not fully govern themselves. And whenever it suited them, US soldiers and officials did not distinguish between the two groups at all, calling anyone from Hispanicized Catholics in the capital of Manila to the Muslims living in the southern archipelago "niggers."[27]

Social purity advocates shared the racist, civilizational framework articulated by the US government. They made sense of both the opportunities and dangers of an overseas empire through comparisons to British India.[28] After all, both places provided Anglo-Saxons with opportunities to civilize the uncivilized, but this very contact could also compromise the health of white soldiers and the metropole. "What will be involved for American soldiers thus brought in contact with, and control of, natives in those conquered islands, among whom the standard of morality is very low and licentiousness fearfully prevalent[?]," asked an article in the *Philanthropist*.[29]

Yet social purity activists remained hopeful. Social purity spokesman Aaron Macy Powell warned the United States to take "lessons from India." Learning from British mistakes, the United States could safeguard the "moral and physical health of our home population" by forbidding soldiers overseas to visit prostitutes. Methodist missionary Homer C. Stuntz, who had served eight years in India before moving to a new mission field in the Philippines, said that he had witnessed "similar social conditions" in the Philippines to those in British India. Yet, Stuntz claimed, the United States could bring eight million Filipinos "from the twilight of a belated civilization into the high noon of modern life" if it exercised "benevolent" rule, implementing policies that elevated the morals of Filipinos rather than degrading them as the British did in India.[30]

US military officials, too, understood their mission in the Philippines in terms of promoting civilized sexual morality. Ideas about race and gender saturated their conception of the civilizing process and shaped the ways they waged war and governed the country. US officials and the American popular press depicted Filipino men as childish and effeminate. At the same time, they portrayed them as rapacious and incapable of controlling their sexual urges, an echo of the myth of the Black rapist. They described Filipina women at times as feminine and alluring "dusky Venuses" in need of white American male protectors, and at other times as disgusting vectors of disease who threatened white men's health. US soldiers should "fuck all the women," as one soldier put it, but also, in the words of President William McKinley, "*protect the natives in their homes.*"[31]

Two images suggest the paradoxical portrayal of women of color in US territories in American popular culture. The postcard "Uncle Sam in the Philippines" (fig. 2.1) drew on a half-tone image, "His First Christmas in Hawaii," which first appeared in *Leslie's Weekly* magazine in 1898 (fig. 2.2). The postcard shifted the location from Hawai'i to the Philippines, but both depicted exoticized, hypersexual women of color who were the eager sexual partners of the occupying white American soldiers.[32] Both portrayed the women as sexually alluring, with large, bare breasts and short, feathered skirts over long, bare legs. Yet at the same time, both women's smiles verged on grotesque, with the Filipina woman's racial characteristics depicted similarly to caricatures of African Americans, emphasizing her broad nose and very dark skin. Both commented on the sexual discipline demanded of white US soldiers, yet winked at the impossibility of it for red-blooded American men in the tropics. Taken together, these two images demonstrate how conceptions of race and sexuality traveled between US colonial contexts and the mainland through print culture as well as debates over prostitution policy.

Military officials believed that healthy young white men should maintain control over their sexual urges, in contrast to Filipinos and to the African American soldiers who fought in the Philippines, whom white officials often portrayed as incapable of sexual self-control. But they also believed that virile white men needed appropriate sexual outlets. In the nineteenth century both European and American physicians espoused an idea of the spermatic economy that understood sexual energy as a powerful force within the male body. Forgoing intercourse could lead to excessive discharges of sperm through masturbation or, conversely, could cause a blockage of sperm. Lack of sex could cause men's genitals to atrophy but could also lead men to commit rape. Moreover, while military officials did not always make this concern explicit, the specter of same-sex intimacy led them to ensure that soldiers had access to women. Such assumptions shaped previous military policy during the US Civil War, when the Union army licensed individual prostitutes and inspected them for venereal disease.[33]

Shifts in tropical medicine at the turn of the century further heightened military physicians' concern over how to manage prostitution in the Philippines. At the turn of the century, physicians began to see tropical people and the diseases they supposedly harbored as a more pressing threat to white men than the tropical climate. Edward Lyman Munson, a member of the US Army

Medical Corps and author of an influential treatise on military hygiene, explained that in the tropics, men's "genital function appears to be increased," yet the climate made white men too lethargic to expend their excess energy through exercise. At the same time, they found themselves surrounded by "a large native population in which fornication is not regarded as a moral offence but as almost a legitimate calling."[34] Military officials warned of the "terrible danger" to soldiers of catching the "virulent form of syphilis" that existed in the Philippines and the potential of them spreading it to the US mainland.[35] Both social purity reformers and the military hoped the right approach to prostitution could protect soldiers and white families at home.

Regulated Prostitution in the Philippines

A commercial sex market already flourished in Manila in June 1898, when US troops arrived after their victory over Spain to keep Philippine Revolutionary forces out of the capital city. Spanish authorities had regulated prostitution in Manila since the 1880s, and in 1897 had implemented a more elaborate system, which required all prostitutes to register, submit to twice-weekly medical examinations, and pay monthly fees to cover the cost of examinations; mandated that brothel keepers register their houses; and created a special "vigilance" police force. Regulation continued briefly in the new Philippine Republic under Emilio Aguinaldo, expressly to demonstrate to the American occupiers that Filipinos could manage diseases themselves. When the United States declined to recognize the Philippine Republic, many Filipinos refused to trade one imperial ruler for another and immediately began to wage war against US occupying troops. In response, the US Army ramped up its force on the islands, with troop strength peaking at 74,000 in 1901.[36]

The influx of American soldiers reshaped the marketplace for commercial sex. While native Filipinas predominated in the sex industry under Spanish rule, the presence of tens of thousands of American soldiers with money to spend led women from across Asia, Europe, and the Americas to migrate to cities in the Philippines with an American troop presence. These women found in sexual labor a dangerous but potentially far more lucrative means of making a living than in other forms of employment available to them.[37]

Filipinas, too, faced an intensification of the factors that pushed and pulled them into sex work. The Philippines had waged war against Spain for two years prior to US arrival, and the US military's presence only compounded the social and economic upheavals Filipinos faced. Despite their rhetoric about

UNCLE SAM IN THE PHILIPPINES.

M. RIEDER, PUBL., LOS ANGELES, CAL. NO. 141

FIGURE 2.1. The image in the undated postcard "Uncle Sam in the Philippines" was also used in a postcard with the winking caption "A Test of Discipline." Image courtesy of Edward Delos Santos.

FIGURE 2.2. This cartoon, "His First Christmas in Hawaii," was published in *Leslie's Weekly* on December 15, 1898, just five days after the Spanish-American War ended.

"filthy" Filipina prostitutes, even US military officials recognized that poverty pushed young women into temporarily selling sex to support themselves and their families. As the US-appointed mayor of Manila noted, "it was almost the universal experience in Manila to find the native female who was leading a life of shame to be between fourteen and nineteen years of age. In many cases these young girls were induced to resort to this course of life to aid their parents."[38]

As Manila became the site of a bustling, international sexual marketplace, rates of venereal disease among US soldiers soared. Many soldiers arrived infected. An army official who sailed to the Philippines in 1898 reported that 480 men in a unit of 1,300 had been previously diagnosed with venereal disease. Yet army doctors quickly blamed the problem on prostitutes, and argued that Filipina women posed a special danger to the health of white men and the success of the US occupation. As military hygienist Munson explained, venereal infections seemed to "take place more certainly, and to assume a much more severe character, when relations are entered into between individuals of different racial characteristics than when both are of the same nationality; the aliens suffering, in this respect, to a greater degree than the resident populations."[39] In the Philippines, those vulnerable "aliens" were white US soldiers.

To manage such dangerous interracial sex, US administrators in Manila continued to regulate prostitution, elaborating on the existing Spanish system. As Warwick Anderson has argued, the Philippines became an important "testing ground" for US public health policies. In September 1898, the US military took over the Board of Health for Manila, created by the Spanish in 1883, and continued to rely on the police to enforce the registration of brothels and prostitutes and ensure that women submitted to regular examinations. Americans also followed the Spanish custom in financing the inspection and treatment of women through fees paid by women themselves. While the Spanish *Reglamento* had not explicitly mandated the confinement and treatment of infected women, US military physicians established a special ward at San Lazaro Hospital, founded by a Spanish religious order in 1578 to treat the poor and leprous, "for the proper isolation and treatment of all prostitutes found diseased." They also set up a clinic for the inspection of prostitutes, performed by a US military doctor rather than a local one.[40]

US officials often drew from other European imperial powers' methods as well as US municipal practices to formulate new policies. By 1899, the job of examining prostitutes had once again been turned over to a "native physician

(Spanish)" who made a "house-to-house inspection of all known brothels in the city" and examined women in their places of work rather than at a clinic. In addition, they reduced the examinations to weekly, rather than twice-weekly, as the *Reglamento* had stipulated. By 1900, officials required women to carry examination booklets that included their photographs in order to thwart the "many ways in which native women attempt to escape examinations and to substitute books."[41]

That same year, the US administration shored up its authority and once again replaced Filipino physicians and inspectors with white Americans, complaining that "native" physicians did not understand "modern methods of examination."[42] The new American staff, the administration reported, pursued prostitutes with vigor, increasing the number of registered prostitutes from 252 to 542 and the number confined to the hospital from 83 to 155 in just two-and-a-half months. While the records do not indicate their race, it is likely that Filipinas comprised the vast majority.[43] While they targeted Filipinas as disease vectors, US officials also positioned white American physicians as the only experts on hygiene, consolidating US authority over both the public health system and the bodies of Filipinas. In 1901, the US-controlled Board of Health instituted "the segregation of prostitutes in a certain part of the city, and a careful system of superintendence over them," creating a red-light district to make commercial sex less publicly visible, a method increasingly popular in mainland US cities.[44]

The US administration in Manila used the regulation system to uphold racial distinctions in a place where they could not legislate the kind of Jim Crow segregation found in the American South, since the US administration voiced a commitment to "benevolent assimilation." They based the fees a woman owed for inspection on her race. In Manila, Filipinas formed the majority of registered women, while Japanese women composed the largest group of registered foreigners. Yet officials also reported fourteen Americans, two "Europeans," one Spaniard, twelve Russians, three Romanians, one Hungarian, one Australian, two Italians, and one Turkish woman, all registered as prostitutes.[45]

As Eileen Scully has shown, white prostitutes in colonial spaces—and particularly American women in this case—could threaten the image of white female purity on which colonial racial hierarchies rested.[46] White women paid $4 for examinations conducted in their homes and $2 for examinations in the clinics, while Filipinas paid half of that. This practice likely reflected the higher price white women commanded for their services and may also have been a means of discouraging white women from selling sex in the Philippines.[47] Meanwhile, the women detained in hospitals were "almost entirely Filipinas, ranging in number from 20 to 90 daily," while white women avoided detention by seeking private treatment.[48]

Whereas Americans instituted the largest and most centralized system of regulation in Manila, US commanders elsewhere in the Philippines licensed prostitution in response to local conditions and concerns. US officials implemented a racialized scheme of regulated prostitution in Jolo, a Philippine island where the Moros, a Muslim ethno-religious group, had resisted imperial rule for hundreds of years, first by the Spanish and more recently by American troops. American commanders feared that sexual relationships between soldiers and Moro women would inflame the war.[49]

To ease tensions, Colonel Owen Sweet allowed thirty Japanese women, whom military officials saw as the cleanest and quietest Asian women, to work in three brothels designated for use by American soldiers, with sentinels stationed out front to prevent any non-Americans from entering. Sweet deported prostitutes found infected with "so-called Asiatic diseases" and initiated a campaign to drive out all prostitutes in order of the races he found most immoral, starting with Chinese women, then Moro and "objectionable" Japanese women, and finally Visaya and Filipino women. Eventually "only some twenty odd women remained."[50]

Indeed, Sweet saw his regulation system as a way to reduce prostitution to a bare minimum, conceding to male sexual necessity while at the same time disciplining women. Sweet argued that rather than encouraging prostitution, he had, "by his system of strict surveillance, exacting restriction, inspections, control and punishments and medical examinations . . . driven nearly all of these women out of the Archipelago."[51] Compared to methods in Manila, Sweet's methods of regulation in Jolo more tightly controlled the sexual relationships between women and US soldiers to in response to the heightened political tensions there.

This control extended to men's bodies as well. While Sweet focused much of his attention on controlling prostitutes, he also mandated that his men undergo regular inspections for venereal disease and detained those infected in a blockhouse a mile from the town.[52] Inspecting men had previously proven controversial for both British colonial military officials and purity reformers alike. The British, like Americans, singled out women as the vectors of disease; they assumed it unnecessary to examine men. Moreover, officials believed, they could not subject men to such forms of bodily control. In 1897,

World's WCTU vice president Lady Somerset had proposed examining British men in India as a means of equalizing the treatment of the sexes within the regulation system. But the British War Secretary rejected her proposal, arguing that genital examination "was regarded, and rightly regarded, by the men as a brutalizing and degrading practice." Meanwhile purity activists decried such a proposal for attempting "to make the sexes equal" through an "equality of unspeakable degradation for both."[53]

The exact genealogy of Sweet's decision to examine men is uncertain. In 1899, US military officials in Puerto Rico had recommended weekly inspections for unmarried men, but it is unclear whether they implemented this plan.[54] As Paul Kramer has shown, the examination of soldiers marked an American imperial innovation in the system of regulation. It soon became official policy: in May 1901, Military Governor General Arthur MacArthur, Jr issued an order mandating the inspection of US soldiers in the Philippines for venereal disease. In 1912, the War Department imported this policy to the mainland, issuing a general order to inspect all troops for venereal disease in US training camps.[55]

"The Un-American Certifying of Prostitutes by American Officers"

American social purity advocates' initial fear—that the expansion of US empire through military conquest would lead to sexual immorality—was soon confirmed. In 1899, the social purity press reported rampant prostitution in military training camps in the United States, where soldiers trained before embarking abroad. It reported an "appalling sight" near Camp Chickamauga on the Tennessee-Georgia border, where soldiers went for training before deployment: "The stage rooms were occupied without concealment by lewd women, while soldiers stood in line, waiting their turn of entrance" to meet with Black and white prostitutes. Such blatant—and interracial—prostitution at home could only mean that "the record of soldier vice in Cuba, Porto Rico and the Philippines is likely to be after the same order."[56]

Just as they viewed India as a warning to the United States, American purity activists also looked to India for solutions. Social purity spokesman Oliver E. Janney believed that Americans should follow the model set by Bushnell and Andrew in India, arguing "there is a great and immediate need of personal investigations in these new lands." In April 1899, Janney called for the establishment of a "bureau of information." Then activists could make "appeals" to "the government or to our people . . . upon a firm foundation of facts."[57]

In the spring of 1900, Chicago temperance worker and journalist William E. Johnson took up the challenge, travelling to the Philippines to investigate conditions there. He published a scathing report in the June 27 issue of the prominent prohibition newspaper the *Chicago New Voice*. "Far more of our boys . . . have met their deaths through bad women and drink than through the bullets of the Filipinos." Moreover, the military government encouraged their lust. In Manila, he reported, foreign prostitutes could pay a $50 "tip" to the customs house official and easily land. US officials even "imported destitute women" destined for the brothels of Manila and Jolo. Manila alone had 200 licensed houses of prostitution inhabited by 600 prostitutes "under the direct control of the military authorities."[58] That reformers did not discover the system of regulated prostitution in Manila until two years after its advent reflected both the difficulties they faced in places where they had little local knowledge, as well as the US military's ability to make the regulation scheme invisible.

Johnson indicted the US military for encouraging vice and even profiting from it. US officials required brothels to pay for liquor licenses and women, for their weekly examinations. While such fees supposedly funded venereal disease treatment for women, the American regulation scheme also made women pay for their time in the hospital. Where all this money went remained a mystery, though Johnson strongly intimated financial malfeasance on the part of US officials. A US commander ran the "department of prostitution," as Johnson termed it. This commander oversaw a "big staff of assistants, inspectors, doctors and flunkies." American men's desire for sex and alcohol had given entire neighborhoods over to "riot and lasciviousness." As visible proof of his findings, Johnson reproduced an inspection booklet as well as pictures of brothels draped in American flags.[59]

Johnson's exposé demonstrated to purity advocates that their nightmares had come true. Regulated prostitution had undermined the US government's ability to act as a civilizing and benevolent power. While the US government had created a modern bureaucratic state to administer hygiene and education, Johnson showed that it had a dark side in what he called "the military bawdy house department." In the red-light district, "there is scarcely a house of prostitution which is not decorated with American flags inside and out." The military authorities, supposedly representatives of "American 'Christian' civilization," in fact spread vice. Moreover, Manila's inhabitants associated Americans so closely with commercial sex that "while many of the inmates" of brothels "are Russians, Austrians and Roumanians, all vociferously declare that they are Americans." It was bad enough that Johnson discovered fourteen white American women selling sex in Manilla.[60] It was even worse to find brothels full of white women claiming American nationality. Both contradicted the image of pure white American womanhood central to selling US imperialism.

Johnson's report drew on tropes that Bushnell and Andrew had also used, setting up contrasts between heathen and Christian, savage and civilized, only to attempt to shock their audiences by showing that by regulating prostitution, civilized white countries acted like uncivilized countries inhabited by people of color. Such rhetoric powerfully raised the specter of degeneration and civilizational decline at a time when the American public and US officials feared "race suicide," a eugenicist theory that decried the replacement of white, middle- and upper-class native-born Protestants by Catholics, southern and eastern Europeans, East Asians, and African Americans.[61]

Newspapers across the country republished and excerpted Johnson's report. It generated numerous follow-up articles and investigations that decried "the un-American certifying of prostitutes by American officers."[62] Multiple overlapping but distinct constituencies latched on to the issue. Anti-imperialists used it to demonstrate that imperialism corrupted both the soldier's body and the American republican political tradition.[63] Suffragists denounced regulated prostitution in the Philippines because it "lower[ed] respect for all women," and thus harmed their cause.[64] The WCTU swiftly initiated a campaign of letter writing, petitions, and investigations to put an end to the "unspeakable conditions" in Manila.[65] Secretary of State Elihu Root complained that concerned citizens bombarded the War Department with letters "by the thousands."[66] Even the British social purity press covered the scandal. As Josephine Butler wrote, "I have observed with deep sorrow the action taken by authorities in the Philippines and Hawaii."[67]

In the wake of Johnson's report, social purity activists, temperance workers, and women's rights advocates assailed President McKinley with letters and petitions. Some of their rhetoric mirrored prior criticisms of regulation in India, though instead of criticizing the British government for unjust rule, they criticized their own. Regulation was "a most inexcusable wrong to helpless women," stated one memorandum.[68] Noted *The Philanthropist*, "our military rule in the Philippines means a social curse to the islands, and sexual slavery for many of their women, more appalling than the demoralization of our own soldiers, bad as that is."[69] Some even criticized the racism that made the inspection of Asian prostitutes possible, a practice "likely to be tolerated because the victims belong to a supposedly inferior race."[70]

At the same time, however, social purity reformers used language to describe Filipinas that stood in stark contrast to their consistent descriptions of the "timid Indian woman" and "our young Indian sisters" as the victims of the British government.[71] Instead, they worried about the danger Filipinas posed to white US soldiers and through them, the mainland. Aaron Macy Powell, for example, warned of the dangers to "our national life" of assuming control of "Cuba, Porto Rico and the Philippines, tropical islands with millions of natives, mainly ignorant and morally in a very low estate."[72] The American Purity Alliance wrote that regulated prostitution led to "moral degradation and physical disease among young men" and would thus "taint the moral atmosphere and threaten the purity of the home" when they returned to the United States.[73] No longer "sisters," prostitutes in the colonies now threatened white women in the metropole. Moreover, as US nationals, though not citizens, they might even come to the US mainland.

The "Filthy" Filipina

The US government initially denied the accusations of regulated prostitution, but in 1901, under growing pressure, General MacArthur admitted that the military inspected prostitutes for venereal disease as part of "sanitary regulations particularly necessary in the tropics," though he denied any form of licensing. Critics of regulation, MacArthur argued, "have a very imperfect information of general conditions in the Orient."[74] Yet social purity reformers saw themselves as quite knowledgeable about conditions in the Philippines. In fact, they shared many assumptions about Filipinos, and the islands themselves, with the US military.

The US administration justified regulated prostitution by using similar rhetoric that purity activists used to attack it, painting Filipinas as sexually immoral disease vectors who endangered white troops. While at home, white American men could exercise sexual restraint; in the tropics, it proved impossible. US soldiers were "in the prime of life," MacArthur wrote. Moreover, they found themselves "removed from the restraining influences that might be exercised over them by their home surroundings." The Philippines was a "low and debased society," Owen Sweet argued. "It is doubtful," Sweet argued, "if mortal man was ever created who can fully, and successfully, reform and purify the Oriental morals." Reported another soldier, Filipinas were "infected to a considerable extent with venereal diseases and have little regard for morality as far as sexual intercourse is concerned." Without licensing and examinations, these women would infect American soldiers.[75]

US military officials also pointed to the many American cities that regulated prostitution, as well as British-administered licensing in India, as evidence of its necessity in the Philippines. Such claims echoed purity reformers' fears that once state regulation took hold in one place it could spread to others. "In all cities throughout the world the police are familiar with the location of every house of prostitution; this is as true of Manila as of any city in the United States," MacArthur pointed out. MacArthur turned social purity complaints upside down: how could they point to regulation as un-American when it happened in their own backyards?[76]

In fact, MacArthur made a different kind of argument for American sexual exceptionalism, arguing that the US military in the Philippines had improved upon municipal and imperial regulation. In the Philippines, he noted, the US government had been "confronted with a problem which has vexed modern civilization in both Europe and America." Because of their methods, "no city in America or Europe, certainly not in Asia, can today vie with Manila in the good order and morality which have resulted from the practical measures adopted."[77]

Through such comparisons, US officials made two points: first, that their methods were superior to those of British and other European imperial powers, and second, that their system of regulating prostitution in the Philippines civilized rather than demoralized the islands. Thus, in contrast to the social purity party line, regulation did not thwart US goals in the Philippines, but rather promoted "benevolent assimilation," President McKinley's official policy in the Philippines.[78]

Both purity activists and the US government believed they had a duty to sexually civilize the Philippines, though they differed on how to bring it about. As MacArthur proclaimed, "the system of regulation and control" was "essential as a matter of protection" not only for the soldiers but also for "the community" around them. Army surgeon Charles Lynch wrote that regulation had helped to uplift "the lower class of Filipina in instilling some notions of cleanliness and personal decency." Commander Sweet framed his regulation system in Jolo as an "attempted reform in a recognized polygamous country, and the land of concubines and female slaves, and an almost wholly immoral woman community."[79]

Social purity reformers and US officials often expressed a shared disgust for Filipinos and depicted them as disease vectors. Pioneering physician

Dr. Elizabeth Blackwell wrote of US Caribbean and Pacific territories, "It seemed to me shocking to think of the forms of inveterate disease that the men will bring back from a licentious tropical country."[80] William Lloyd Garrison, Jr., son of the famed abolitionist, noted that "10,000 cases of syphilis afflicted the volunteers thus far returned from the Philippines to San Francisco," and questioned, "Who can estimate the ravages among our own people in consequence?"[81]

Purity activists also argued that regulated prostitution threatened America's global standing, particularly in comparison to European powers. It upended their vision of the United States' exceptional position as a supposedly abolitionist country by committing the "supreme evil of putting the United States Government in the position of *licensing* social vice, instead of *repressing* it."[82] The National American Woman Suffrage Association argued that regulation stood "contrary to the spirit of American institutions." "The United States should not adopt a method that Europe is discarding," it wrote.[83] Another suffrage journal condemned the US military for administering "the system of State-licensed vice which prevails in France and some other dissolute foreign nations, but which has never till now been authorized in connection with the American army," though this statement overlooked US military regulated prostitution during the Civil War.[84] Not only did regulation allow the "tropical" Asiatic toxin of venereal disease to "poison American society," according to the social purity press; it undercut the United States' sexual exceptionalism.[85]

Military officials and purity activists shared an ideological commitment to the United States' unparalleled ability to act as a benevolent, civilizing force in the Philippines. Thus, even after the revelations of US-regulated prostitution, many aligned with social purity continued to support the US military's presence. In November 1901, the WCTU tapped A. Lester Hazlett, a Methodist minister from Colorado, to study the "moral conditions" in the Philippines, now administered by a US-controlled civil government. What Hazlett discovered convinced him of the remarkable civilizing capacity of the US occupation, which uplifted the islands from the immorality of Catholic Spain and "tropical" savagery. In Manila, Hazlett noted, "the moral condition of the city is better than ever before since American occupation." Under Spanish rule, for example, priests had charged "exorbitant" fees for marriage, leading to cohabitation under the "querida system." But the US government broke up this system and insisted on marriage. "Many arrests had already been made," Hazlett proclaimed.[86]

Hazlett pointed to Filipinas as one of the most significant dangers to white men and to the occupation. As Hazlett wrote, "Probably in no other country in the world do white men become so degraded and demoralized, through associating with the natives, as in the Philippines, and nowhere else do they sink so quickly to the level of the native." The women who lived with US soldiers were "ignorant, lazy, and filthy in their habits, generally afflicted with some loathsome cutaneous diseases, and it is hard to comprehend that an educated American, decently brought up, can live among dirty, frowzy natives, who have not one redeeming quality."[87]

Hazlett's repugnance at Filipinas as ugly and riddled with venereal disease reflected the US administration's growing concern that any bodily contact across racial lines would lead to disease and degeneration for white soldiers.[88] Instead of placing the blame on the US administration or soldiers themselves, Hazlett painted white soldiers as victims of tropical women. Hazlett set out as an "ardent anti-expansionist," but he returned "a firm believer in the policy of the Administration." While regulated prostitution was a "reproach to our civilization," Filipinos were "but children" who could learn the "lessons of self-government" only from the American occupation.[89]

While white purity activists and military officials stressed the savagery of Filipinos as justification for the US presence, Black soldiers and purity activists articulated their own version of the civilizing mission. Many Black soldiers felt an affinity with Filipinos because of the racist treatment both received from white US soldiers, who commonly called Filipinos and Black soldiers "niggers."[90] T. Thomas Fortune, a prominent African American journalist and civil rights leader, argued that the sexual immorality and "race prejudice" of white Americans fundamentally threatened the United States' ability to civilize the Philippines.[91]

Yet while Fortune posited a solidarity between Black Americans and Filipinos, he remained staunchly pro-empire. In fact, he argued, respectable African Americans stood specially poised to do the work of uplifting the Philippines. Much of white men's sexual immorality resulted from the absence of white women, whose constitution made them unfit to live in the tropics: "the climate eats them up," as Fortune put it. In contrast, the African American men and women Fortune met on his travels throughout the Philippines felt "perfectly at home."[92]

Fortune critiqued the white supremacist sexual hierarchy that harmed women of color in the United States and spread abroad through imperialism. As he commented, "marriages between white American men and Filipino women are regarded with as much horror as marriages between blacks and whites in Tennessee." In one Manila neighborhood he saw a row of houses "occupied by ten white Americans, who are not married to the Filipino women" with whom they lived. White Americans simply "leave them when they tire of them." In contrast, the last house in the row was "occupied by a colored American, who is married to the Filipino woman."[93] In the Philippines, Fortune argued, Black men maintained the highest standards of sexual morality, which white men could not live up to.

The Black press, too, published letters from soldiers that reported the chivalrous behavior of Black soldiers toward Filipinas. One chaplain reported performing three marriages between Black soldiers and Filipinas. After the military recalled four African American battalions serving in the Philippines in 1902, around five hundred Black soldiers stayed, likely because of these marriages. In fact, a civil administrator's contention that Black men got along "too well with the native women" spurred the removal of African American troops from the Philippines. As he claimed, there was "a good deal of demoralization in the towns where they have been stationed."[94]

Although white officials intimated that Black soldiers' sexual exploits with Filipinas impeded their efforts at civilization, Black soldiers argued that the immoral sexual behavior of white troops jeopardized benevolent assimilation. When the white 3rd Infantry boarded a transport ship bound for the United States, reported one Black soldier, "fifteen deluded native women, their mistresses, turned away in tears as the Artillery band played "The Girl I Left Behind." As the soldier disparaged, "this is a daily example of how the army pacify and civilize the Filipinos, by deluding the females, and returning home to be worshipped as heroes."[95] Even high-ranking white US military officers participated in such relationships. John J. Pershing, whose military career ascended because of his "bravery" in the Philippines, lived openly with Joaquina Bondoy Ignacio, with whom he had two children, although he later denied it.[96]

Much like white US military officials and white social purity reformers, Fortune and the wider Black press also harnessed the power of the dual discourses of sexual morality and civilization. In Fortune's formulation, however, white Americans' sexual behavior marked them as uncivilized and thus unable to civilize others. Fortune pointed to the respectable and moral treatment of Filipinas by their African American husbands as evidence that African Americans, rather than white Americans, had a special role to play in the Philippines.

President Roosevelt, "A Good Friend"

At the start of 1902, social purity activists and the military faced a stalemate. Both agreed that "Oriental" prostitutes posed a danger to US troops and their families at home. Both believed that the United States had a duty to civilize

Filipinos from the influence of "native" custom as well as Spanish Catholic immorality. For the military, only regulated prostitution could address these concerns. For social purity advocates, regulation only further endangered American men and the US civilizing mission. The military defended itself against a continual onslaught of criticism by alternately denying and justifying regulation, yet the outcry by social purity advocates did little to change policy.

In February 1902, at a time when both the military and social purity organizations warned of the dangers posed by Filipina prostitutes, Margaret Dye Ellis, a WCTU worker and suffragist, seized on the Filipina child prostitute as an ideal victim who could generate sympathy and turn the tide firmly against regulation. The Filipino child proved a powerful figure for American social purity reformers. Indeed, military correspondence suggests that Filipina girls often sold sex to support their families, often through coercion from family members facing dire economic circumstances.[97] But the rhetoric of the Philippines itself as a childlike nation also proved crucial. Suffragists and other women activists argued that, as maternal figures, they had a special role to play in civilizing the Philippines, using the analogy of raising children from youth to adulthood as a metaphor for raising Filipinos from savagery to civilization. Both of these progressions required the cultivation of sexual morality. "To protect children at home and child races abroad is the expanded meaning of 'home protection' in the new century," proclaimed an article in WCTU organ *The Union Signal*. "And the first duty of our home defenders is to protect purity."[98]

The conflict between the military and social purity forces came to a head when Ellis delivered concrete proof of licensed prostitution: "the official registration-book issued by the U.S. authorities to one of the child prostitutes of the Philippines, whose name, translated, is 'Mary of the Cross.'" The booklet included her photograph for identification, depicting "a girl seemingly about twelve years old, with a childlike face and big, pathetic dark eyes." It contained "the official records of her regular examinations by a government surgeon, and his signature testifying to her state of health," intimating the horror that US officials had not only genitally inspected the girl with a speculum, but made her available for sex with US soldiers.[99]

After showing the book to her suffragist friends, Ellis left it at the White House for President Theodore Roosevelt himself, placed it in the hands of members of Congress, and published a circular including a facsimile of Mary's picture that she distributed to the homes of every member of the Congressional Committee on the Philippines, so that their wives might also see it. According to the suffrage and reform press, Ellis's circular led to such wide public outcry that it "swamped" the War Department, which had to hire ten clerks to answer all of the angry letters it received.[100] Leaving aside questions of the booklet's authenticity, including the almost impossibly perfect name "Maria de la Cruz," Ellis's campaign to save girls like Mary / Maria demonstrates that at the turn of the century the rhetoric of rescuing innocent victims and decrying dangerous prostitutes became increasingly intertwined as part of a flexible narrative about prostitution that could serve multiple political ends.

Ellis's campaign had greater effects than earlier investigations. Not only did it feature an ideal victim but its timing was right: President Roosevelt allied himself with the social purity movement far more than his predecessor William McKinley. Roosevelt held to a vision of white American masculinity that combined self-restraint and chastity with "strenuous" and often violent dominion over supposedly less civilized peoples.[101] As suffrage journal the *Woman's Column* reported, just two days after Ellis published her circular, Secretary of State Elihu Root sent an order to Manila to stop the practices of charging prostitutes for examinations and issuing certificates attesting to their disease status.[102]

In March 1902, Roosevelt issued an order to both officers and enlisted men in the army, "especially . . . those serving in the tropics." The "only really efficient way in which to control the diseases due to immorality," Roosevelt proclaimed, was "to diminish the vice which is the cause of these diseases." Attacking the doctrine of male sexual necessity, Roosevelt directed officers to teach their men "that venereal disease is almost sure to follow licentious living; that it is never a trivial affair, and that it is criminal folly to believe that sexual indulgence is necessary to health." Moreover, Roosevelt tied American national character and the United States' position in the world to a combination of masculine power and sexual restraint, asserting, "As a nation we feel keen pride in the valor, discipline, and steadfast endurance of our soldiers, and hand in hand with these qualities must go the virtues of self-restraint, self-respect, and self-control."[103]

Roosevelt's support of the social purity position reaffirmed for American purity advocates that the United States did not regulate prostitution, and thus charted a different course than European empires. An article in the *Philanthropist* termed Roosevelt "a good friend" to the social purity cause. "It ought to be a matter of satisfaction to be assured that there is in the Executive chair a man who can be reached, and who acts promptly, wisely and fearlessly."[104] Of course, while Roosevelt's order made clear his administration's stance against prostitution, it did not actually forbid US military physicians from inspecting women nor prohibiting men from visiting them.

In October 1902, reformers discovered that the civil government had continued to compel prostitutes to undergo medical examinations, though it had stopped collecting fees from women as a nod to ostensibly complying with Roosevelt's abolitionist stance. Purity activists charged the Secretary of the Interior of the Philippines, who oversaw the plan, with a "willful and wicked violation of both the spirit and letter of the president's order," which they lifted up as an "admirable preachment against the social evil."[105] According to their interpretation, as long as the US president stood firmly against any form of regulation, the United States could still be an abolitionist country, even if a US-controlled government licensed prostitution in the Philippines.

Conclusion

In battles about regulated prostitution in the Philippines, the US military triumphed over purity advocates. The war of 1898 gave the military a new opportunity to study tropical hygiene and to solidify conceptions of venereal disease transmission, with prostitutes, particularly women of color, as the primary vectors. The experience shored up the military's belief in male sexual necessity, especially for white men in the tropics, a logic that often excused assault and rape as much as it did prostitution.[106] US officials used the control of venereal disease and prostitution to consolidate US control over systems of public health in the Philippines, as well as other colonies.[107] Moreover, as they oversaw large numbers of troops and directed colonial governments, US administrators systematized formal policies around prostitution and venereal disease. Such policies had previously been piecemeal and up to the discretion of individual commanders.

Yet social purity advocates made significant gains because of their wartime campaign. By publicizing regulated prostitution in the Philippines, they galvanized American public opinion against regulation as an illegitimate and immoral way for a government to address prostitution, even in colonies. From that point forward, the military would have to carefully conceal regulated prostitution.

While purity activists focused their attention almost entirely on regulated prostitution in the Philippines, their continued pressure on the US government shaped prostitution policy throughout the United States' empire. As US officials in the Philippines worked to make regulated prostitution invisible at home, those in Cuba did the same, even as social purity activists paid less attention to the Caribbean. In 1901, US authorities placed Havana's municipal mayor in charge of regulated prostitution, rather than the US-appointed civil governor, who had previously overseen regulation. As Cuban physician Dr. Matías Duque rightly noted, "the government of military intervention wished to disassociate itself from this public service, which was abhorrent to North American customs, and thus relegated its administration to municipal authorities."[108] Due to the efforts of purity advocates, regulated prostitution had become un-American, even when Americans themselves oversaw it.

By 1903, Americans had largely turned to a new "social evil" in the Philippines, agitating against the US government's policy of regulating the importation, sale, and use of opium. When the Roosevelt administration considered a new regulation that further limited the importation of opium and restricted its use, thousands of people complained. They argued that such a regulation would incite opium use while pretending to limit it, much as regulating prostitution incited rather than suppressed it. The surge of public opinion against the bill led the Roosevelt administration to kill it.[109]

As the *Philanthropist* proclaimed, "Just as the inate [sic] moral sense of our people repudiates all schemes for regulating the social evil, so is it against taking any other vice under the tolerating and protecting wing of the government."[110] Reformers saw the demise of the bill as another victory in their crusade against government recognition of vice, proof that the fruits of their crusade against prostitution multiplied. To them, it served as further evidence that the United States could chart a new path from European countries as a benevolent empire, one that prohibited rather than accommodated vice.[111]

In practice, the US government regulated the opium trade until 1908. But that year the government implemented opium prohibition, building on a swell of popular support for prohibitionist approaches to immorality.[112] Indeed, such an approach had deep roots in American reform networks. In the 1880s, as the WCTU fought regulated prostitution in India, it also joined with other organizations in the United States to push for state and national alcohol prohibition, breaking with a more moderate movement that advocated enforcement of local laws to curb rather than prohibit drinking. The WCTU increasingly saw state and even federal law as the means to advance its causes.[113]

As activists—including many from the WCTU—decried regulated prostitution in the Philippines, their rhetoric began to sound prohibitionist. Avowedly feminist abolitionists like Josephine Butler and Katharine Bushnell wanted women—even "heathen" women of color prostitutes—to have bodily autonomy, free from state interference. But as the rhetoric of military officials and social purity activists converged in the Philippines around the figure of the dangerous Filipina prostitute, many began to argue that regulated prostitution endangered US soldiers by thrusting such women into their arms, in contrast to prior arguments claiming that regulated prostitution endangered women themselves.

This position had within it the seeds of a prohibitionist stance toward prostitution, one that believed the government's proper role was to actively prohibit prostitutes from having contact with soldiers, rather than to keep soldiers away from prostitutes or leave prostitutes alone altogether. In fact, such an approach was not wholly novel. For example, in the wake of Bushnell's and Andrew's investigation in India, the government began to prohibit and expel from cantonments any "disorderly" women and those who refused venereal disease treatment, so as not to appear to license prostitution.[114] Both abolitionist and regulationist approaches to prostitution, then, could move in a prohibitionist direction.

Even though social purity advocates could not overturn the military's policy of regulating prostitution, they laid the groundwork for future successes. Moreover, they gained the ear of the US government, particularly President Roosevelt, whom they saw as a key ally in their fight against sexual vice and drugs. Building on their supposed success of seeing "the evil abolished" in the Philippines, Margaret Dye Ellis visited the President to warn him "that many girls of foreign birth are lured to this country under false promises of employment." Drawing on their experience combating the dangers of regulated prostitution, social purity reformers stood ready to work with the government against a new danger: the "white slave traffic."[115]

3

"War on the White Slave Traffic"

CONSTRUCTING SEXUAL CITIZENSHIP
IN THE EARLY TWENTIETH CENTURY

BERTHA CLAICHE STROLLED into her small apartment after a long night of work in New York City's Tenderloin district. On tiptoe, she approached Emil Gerdron, tall, mustachioed, and asleep. Clutching her purse, lighter than she wished, she reached out to gently tweak Emil's ear. Leaping to his feet, Emil wrapped his hands around her neck before she could jump away. "Where is my money?"

Bertha made it to the corner of Seventh Avenue and 125th Street the next day for an appointment with two former clients. But Emil appeared again, locking his eyes on Bertha and walking toward her. As the two men sunk back into the doorway of a saloon, Emil reached for her throat. But the men moved faster. Locking their hands around Emil's arms, they jerked him away. Slipping a hand into her purse, Bertha brought out a pistol and fired three shots into Emil's back, watching silently as he fell to the ground, dead.[1]

That was the cinematic version of the story. The motion picture *Bertha Claiche: The Lovers*, played up the supposed romance between Gerdron and Claiche. One theater advertised it with life-sized wax figures of him choking her mounted at the door, suggesting the entertainment value of violence against women.[2] But there were many other versions. After 1905, when a woman named Bertha Claiche actually did shoot a man named Emil Gerdron on the streets of New York City, Americans consumed her tale through a range of media. Newspaper accounts revealed a particularly shocking aspect: the two men who helped Claiche entrap Gerdron were police officers. They repeated Claiche's claim that at least fifty police officers regularly demanded bribes from her and other French women who worked on the streets.[3]

From New York City, to Norfolk, Virginia, to Santa Fe, New Mexico, Americans followed Claiche's trial, her imprisonment in the Tombs, her release, and the many proposals of marriage that followed.[4] Newspapers reported that Claiche was "lured into a mock marriage" by Gerdron, who took her from France to New York and forced her into prostitution. According to some accounts, Gerdron had threatened to "make a similar white slave" of her younger sister.[5] In many ways, Claiche represented an archetypical white slave; beautiful, young, French, and forced by her cruel foreign pimp to come to the United States to sell sex. Yet she also embodied another side of the white slavery narrative, as a dangerous, cunning, foreign woman who killed a man in cold blood.

At the turn of the twentieth century, the campaign against "white slavery" ushered in a phase of anti-prostitution reform focused explicitly on mobility. White slavery narratives such as Claiche's spread in popular culture through lurid novels, titillating films, and journalistic exposés. But social purity reformers, working alongside government officials, developed the narrative's form through their undercover investigations, which they believed provided the foundation for formulating effective laws. The common definition of white slavery involved movement across state and national borders, suggesting a new legal framework for combatting commercial sex. Legislation such as the 1910 "White Slave Traffic Act," also known as the Mann Act, and the 1910 Immigration Act offered the federal government a role in policing prostitution—historically under the jurisdiction of states and municipalities alone—through border control.[6]

In the nineteenth century, "new abolitionist" social purity reformers had directed their ire at governments that regulated prostitution and charged them with failing to protect women. Americans conducted investigations in British India and in the Philippines, a US territory, and accused both governments of shirking their civilizing duty by overseeing systems of licensing and inspection. In the early twentieth century, however, the American anti–white slavery movement came to see the government as an ally and federal laws as the most powerful means of stopping trafficking. In less than a decade, American social purity reformers shifted from waging publicity campaigns against the US government for licensing prostitution in the Philippines, to working closely with it to formulate legal strategies to punish anyone involved in the white slave traffic.

The white slavery narrative incorporated a paradox. It portrayed prostitutes as powerless victims, tricked or forced to sell sex, often by swarthy foreigners or African Americans, and thus in need of rescue. It positioned the sexual enslavement of white women as exceptional—almost a contradiction in terms—and more terrible than the enslavement of African Americans under chattel slavery. At the same time, it painted women—particularly foreign women and women of color who sold sex—as a threat to the United States. The concept of white slavery also placed the blame for the ills of prostitution onto greedy and exploitative third parties—pimps, panderers, traffickers, madams—creating a new set of crimes and criminal identities. In doing so, it ignored the structural push and pull factors that shaped women's migration and involvement with commercial sex, such as their economic and social vulnerability and lack of political rights, particularly if they did not hold citizenship.[7]

While in Europe, governments tended to distinguish between willing prostitutes and victimized white slaves, US white slavery law made no such distinctions, labeling anyone who migrated and engaged in commercial sex as a white slave and anyone who aided or profited from prostitution as a trafficker. Both US officials and American anti–white slavery reformers declared that the United States was an exceptional country because of the vigor with which it attacked white slavery, specifically through migration control and criminalization. Taken together, these approaches focused state attention on the sexual behavior of women, African Americans, and immigrants, particularly those from Asia and Southern and Eastern Europe.[8]

Federal white slavery laws provided a new means of policing sexuality and upholding racial divisions across a range of jurisdictions. They applied in the case of state and international borders, but also in the District of Columbia, inside the boundaries of Indian reservations, and within US territories and colonies. The Panama Canal Zone, a leased zone under US government control, emerged as a key location in debates over white slavery. By policing the moral and geographical borders of the "greater United States," the movement to stop white slavery made a gendered and racialized vision of sexual morality central to constructions of US citizenship and nationhood.[9]

Making White Slavery

In the late nineteenth century, concerns over the traffic in women linked native-born white Americans' fears of non-white immigrants, unfree labor, and deviant sexuality. Often, Americans imagined the traffic in white women as a foreign phenomenon, even when it happened in the United States. Newspapers and magazines detailed the sale of white Eastern European women to the harems of the "heathen East." Reports on the traffic in women also blamed the presence of foreign "others" within the United States, as newspapers published accounts of Mormons luring unsuspecting white immigrant women to polygamous Utah.[10]

In the 1870s, many white Americans targeted Chinese laborers to express their anxieties over the social and economic effects of immigration, as they had their fears about slavery and contract labor earlier in the nineteenth century. On the West Coast, reformers decried the "yellow slave traffic" of Chinese women brought by Chinese men to fill brothels that served both Chinese and white men. While women missionaries spearheaded efforts to rescue Chinese women, their plight did not prompt transnational organizing on the same scale as did the traffic in white women.[11]

By the mid-1880s, American and European reformers wrote increasingly of the traffic in European and American women, using the term "white slave traffic" to describe not only the sale of women's sexual services but also their movement for the purpose of prostitution, either from the countryside to the city or from one country to another. But it continued to retain its other meanings, encompassing any form of prostitution, not only forced prostitution. White male laborers, too, continued to speak of white slavery to criticize capitalism until the early twentieth century.[12]

At the turn of the twentieth century, new patterns of immigration and migration shifted the demographics of American cities. Immigrants from Southern and Eastern Europe, often Catholic or Jewish, brought with them customs and family structures that seemed sexually suspicious to native-born middle-class white reformers. As African Americans from the South moved to northern cities in larger numbers, white middle-class reformers viewed Black prostitutes in red-light districts as signs of crime and squalor, while Black clients visiting white prostitutes raised the specter of the Black rapist. Single women increasingly migrated to cities both from abroad and from within the United States. For example, in New York City close to 29 percent of employed women lived in lodgings apart from their families by 1900.[13] White slavery narratives warned of the perils of cities full of unprotected young women and unrestrained young men, free from the watchful eyes of families and communities with a shared sense of identity.

Fears over white slavery both responded to and caused shifts in the structure of the urban commercial sex industry. In the late nineteenth century, most large American cities had bustling commercial sex districts where brothel-based and street prostitution flourished. At the turn of the twentieth century,

anti-vice reformers advocated the closure of brothels, or at times their reloca-
tion to Black and immigrant neighborhoods. As scholars have shown, commercial sex became recasualized, as vice raids pushed women out of brothels.
At the same time, new forms of wage labor and growing urban entertainment
districts pulled women into new forms of sexual exchange, including practices
of treating, in which women exchanged sexual favors for meals and entertainment, as well as supplementing wage labor with sex for pay.[14]

Indeed, commercial sex proved lucrative in comparison to other work. In
1900, domestic workers in Chicago earned an average of $4.28 per week, while
women in New York City's garment industry earned $6–12 per week.[15] As
one department store clerk and occasional sex worker told an investigator, she
would happily lead an "honest" life if her employer raised her salary from $6 a
week to $15. While some women experienced prostitution as a grueling form
of physical labor, others proclaimed it to be an "easy life." And the money could
not be matched. In New York City, women working in concert saloons reported
making up to $30 in an evening, while streetwalkers made as much as $50.[16]

While the anti–white slavery movement took the term "white slave" from
anti-slavery abolitionism, anxieties about the commercialization of sex and
women's mobility led it to the term "traffic." At first reformers used "traffic" as
a general term for prostitution, in the sense of a sale or transaction rather
than movement from one location to another. This usage tied the anti–white
slavery movement to broader unease over capitalism and the way that sexuality, idealized as part of the private domain of the home, had become a com-
modity in the marketplace.[17] Anti–white slavery reformers also borrowed it
from the temperance movement, which exhorted individuals, cities, and nations to end the traffic, or sale, of liquor. But members of the temperance
movement had also realized that the traffic, in the sense of movement across
political boundaries, offered them new ways to attack alcohol. Assailing the
"traffic" in liquor, transported between states and imported from abroad, allowed them to take up the issue at a national level, rather than simply fighting
local saloons or individual drunkards.[18]

The fight against white slavery, like that against state-regulated prostitution,
played out through transatlantic networks. A flurry of highly publicized investigations by British reformers in the 1880s had initially alerted Americans to
the problem.[19] The British reformer and journalist William T. Stead's 1885 se-
rialized exposé, "The Maiden Tribute of Modern Babylon," confronted the
Anglo-American public with the sexual vulnerability of young girls. Stead
completed the purchase of Eliza Armstrong—a poor, young virgin, he

highlighted—for five pounds, paid to her alcoholic mother and indifferent father. The trade in young girls occurred in London, he warned, right under the noses of a supposedly civilized populace.[20]

Americans quickly followed with their own inquiries. In her first of many investigations around the world, WCTU worker and former missionary Dr. Katharine Bushnell studied the "horrible White Slave Trade" in logging camps in Wisconsin and Michigan in 1888. Bushnell visited sixty "dens of degradation" reportedly run by "foreigners or those of foreign extraction" and collected information on 577 "American born and bred" women held as prostitutes. Reform newspapers around the country published Bushnell's vivid depictions of the dens surrounded by walls twelve feet high and guarded by packs of huge Spanish bloodhounds used to track down and even kill women who attempted escape.[21]

White slavery exposés quickly gain popularity far beyond social reform circles. As Progressivism swept the United States, journalists as well as social purity reformers saw the undercover investigation as a key method for bringing to light injustices, while the newspaper industry used salacious stories of imperiled white women as a means to sell more papers. In 1907, journalist George Kibbe Turner published a series of articles about white slavery in Chicago in the popular muckraking periodical *McClure's*, which had already helped to launch other national reform campaigns.[22] Turner estimated that ten thousand prostitutes plied their trade in Chicago and that organized prostitution yielded gross revenues of $20 million annually, mainly controlled by Russian Jews.[23]

Fueled by such reports, reformers founded new anti-vice organizations to address the sexual immorality that they believed led to rampant white slavery in American cities. These organizations grew out of the work of older social purity organizations, but no longer emphasized ending regulated prostitution, rescuing women, and uplifting the sexual morals of society. Instead, they targeted prostitution through investigations and agitated for new laws to criminalize a growing range of activities related to commercialized sex, particularly the participation of third-party profiteers. A new generation of professional reformers—both men and women—began to work for anti-vice organizations as well as the government, taking positions as district attorneys, immigration inspectors, social workers, and investigators as a means of confronting white slavery.[24]

New York City, a hub of immigration and migration as well as sexual commerce, emerged as a key site of anti-vice, anti–white slavery, and public health activism. Aaron Macy Powell based his New York Committee for Prevention of State Regulated Vice (reorganized as the American Purity Alliance in 1895) in New York City, where it published its reform journal the *Philanthropist*. Prominent New Yorkers founded the Committee of Fifteen in 1900 to investigate and legislate against prostitution and gambling. In 1905, physician Prince Morrow established the Society of Sanitary and Moral Prophylaxis, with the goal of combatting venereal disease. The Society worked alongside the American Purity Alliance to advocate for moral, educational, and legal measures to improve sexual morality and end regulation. That same year another citizen group, the Committee of Fourteen, came together to combat prostitution and alcohol. Similar committees organized in cities across the United States, with Chicago serving as the midwestern center of the anti-vice movement.[25]

In 1906, Oliver E. Janney, the American Purity Alliance President, reorganized many of its members into the National Vigilance Association, a group dedicated to rooting out white slavery.[26] The Association comprised prominent reformers who reflected the growing professionalization of social reform in the early twentieth century. While its leadership included those previously involved in social purity reform such as Grace Hoadley Dodge, the founder of the Working Girls Society and head of the Traveler's Aid Society, and Reverend Anna Garlin Spencer, a Unitarian minister, it also attracted James Bronson Reynolds, a social worker and special investigator for the Roosevelt administration, as well as Dr. Morrow.[27]

The National Vigilance Association placed "the social" over the individual. In addition to representing a moral outrage, trafficking posed legal, social, and public health problems, best addressed through law and policy.[28] While the organization acknowledged the investigative efforts of previous social purity reformers, it credited its members with "raising these investigations to the plane of scientific sociology and sound social reform" and leading the movement for sexual reform in a rational direction.[29]

Upon its founding in 1895, the American Purity Alliance had listed its aims as the "repression of vice, prevention of regulation by the state, the better protection of the young, the rescue of the fallen, and . . . to maintain the law of purity as equally binding upon men and women."[30] In contrast, in 1907 the National Vigilance Association stated its goals as "to break up the international white slave traffic by attacking its sources; to act as an auxiliary to the United States Government, and as an ally to similar associations in foreign countries . . . to prosecute the offenders."[31] Social purity reformers had hoped to transform American morals through religious and moral suasion. Now, as anti–white slavery advocates, they drew on Progressive faith in the power of government, using law to remake American sexual morality.

Immoral Immigrants

As fears about white slavery swept the country in the early twentieth century, reformers and government officials debated over how to understand the immigrant women they found selling sex: were they innocent trafficking victims or blameworthy, mercenary prostitutes?[32] Federal immigration law had targeted migratory prostitution from its inception, using it specifically as a means of barring East Asian immigrants. In 1875, Congress passed the Page Act, which excluded Asian contract laborers, felons, and all women who worked as prostitutes or who came to the United States "for lewd and immoral purposes."[33] As Marion J. Sims, president of the American Medical Association and famed gynecologist, warned, the "Chinese slave" prostitute "breeds moral and physical pestilence," promoting the increasingly common idea that Chinese people carried more serious forms of disease that endangered white people.[34]

Congress soon passed legislation to exclude an increasingly broad range of immigrants suspected of immoral sexual behavior. The Immigration Act of 1882 banned those "likely to become a public charge," whose poverty might force them to engage in prostitution, and the Act of 1891 excluded those guilty of crimes of "moral turpitude." Immigration inspectors easily placed women whom they viewed as sexually suspicious into these categories.[35]

Anti–white slavery reformers from private organizations had conducted investigations to root out the white slave traffic since the 1880s. The government adopted many of their techniques at the turn of the century. As immigration soared in the early twentieth century, particularly from Southern and Eastern Europe, government agencies set up investigative bodies to study the problem of sexually immoral immigrants and propose new laws to keep them out. An 1898 Industrial Commission investigation recommended the exclusion of prostitutes and procurers; the 1903 Immigration Act banned both categories.[36]

In response to figures showing that more than a million people had entered the United States in the 1905 fiscal year, President Roosevelt asked Congress to "keep out all immigrants who will not make good American citizens."[37] Congress responded by passing the 1907 Immigration Act, which expanded on the 1903 Act to exclude people suspected of a far broader range of prostitution-related offenses. In addition to banning alien women and girls entering the country for the purpose of prostitution or for "any other immoral purpose" and those who "imported" them, it called for jail time and fines for anyone who harbored an alien prostitute within three years of her entry into the United States. It also mandated the deportation of any woman who practiced prostitution "at any time" within three years of entering.[38]

The Immigration Bureau soon launched its own series of investigations of white slavery. The Bureau tasked Marcus Braun, a Hungarian Jewish immigrant, with conducting two of the most influential. His language skills and political connections had helped to secure him a position as a "special investigator" for the Bureau. Braun's prior investigations for the Bureau focused on a different kind of "white slavery," the flow of European contract laborers to the United States. But by 1908, as historian Gunther Peck has demonstrated, "white slavery" had been narrowed and feminized, exclusively signifying women trafficked for prostitution.[39] As Braun himself pondered, "what is the clandestine importation of a few hundred Chinese or Japanese, or a gang of men under contract to perform certain labor . . . in comparison to the importation of Daughters of Eve, the sex of Mother, Wife, Daughter, Sister for the purpose of Prostitution?"[40]

In the summer of 1908, Braun conducted undercover investigations in more than twenty US cities and two in British Columbia. Braun's preferred tactic involved hiring an immigrant prostitute, enticing her into a car, and then driving her directly to an immigration office to face arrest.[41] Despite his small-scale methods, Braun reached dramatic conclusions: more than 50,000, perhaps even 100,000, foreign-born prostitutes and at least 10,000 pimps and procurers resided in the United States.[42]

Braun focused on French, Belgian, and Eastern European Jewish prostitutes, whom he painted as both greedy criminals and innocent victims of dangerous third-party profiteers. "An international band of scoundrels" imported "the fallen women of European Cities with the allurement of making money fast." But they also seduced "thoughtless, innocent, inexperienced girls with false, deceitful lying promises for a brighter future." Although he noted that Japanese prostitution posed a growing problem on the West Coast, he primarily worried about women he considered white. At a time when Jewish people held a tenuous claim to whiteness, Braun, himself Jewish, rendered Jewish women racially white through the discourse of white slavery.[43]

Ambivalence toward immigrant women marked Braun's final report. Prostitutes transported by procurers represented one out of every thousand women brought to the United States, and two of every thousand became prostitutes after landing, "lured over under the promise of some lucrative employment," he argued. The trafficking of such women stood as a "crying shame upon our much boasted 20th Century Christian Civilization" and would make a man's "blood boil with horror and indignation." At the same time, however, Braun's assimilationist politics left little room for sympathy for the "undesirable element," immigrants he labeled "paupers, criminals, exconvicts," and "prostitutes."[44]

Based on his findings, Braun recommended the creation of a special white slave squad to surveil, arrest, and deport sexually immoral immigrants. In March 1909, the Immigration Bureau did just that, dispatching officers experienced in investigating prostitution to various sections of the country to "canvass actively" for non-citizen prostitutes and pimps to arrest and deport. It directed officers to find naturalized citizens who had been of "immoral character" at the time of their naturalization, making it subject to cancellation. During the dragnet's first month, officers arrested seventy-five people and deported thirty-three. By June 1909 the deportations had more than tripled, including all but one of the 103 people arrested that month.[45] Even as Braun's report professed deep sorrow for the victims of white slavery, then, the immigration policies he successfully advocated deported all alien prostitutes without distinguishing between forced and free migration. While not intended for public consumption, the National Vigilance Association circulated and publicized the report, further stoking public concern over white slavery.[46]

At the same time as Braun studied the white slave traffic, the Dillingham Commission, a congressional investigative body created by the 1907 Immigration Act, also conducted an extensive inquiry. In November 1907, a team of male and female undercover immigration investigators visited New York, Chicago, San Francisco, Seattle, Portland, Salt Lake City, Ogden, Butte, Denver, Buffalo, Boston, and New Orleans, and collected information on women "of different races and nationalities and living under different conditions." The Dillingham Commission came to conclusions that largely mirrored Braun's, though it emphasized the dangers of Japanese immigration. It called for stricter immigration laws and state laws against prostitution, as well as broader federal policing power and legislation to criminalize transporting a woman across state and national lines for immoral purposes.[47]

The Dillingham Commission report painted a less sympathetic picture of women than Braun's report. Most immigrant prostitutes, it found, had come to the United States of their own volition to earn more money for their sexual labor, calling into question whether they fit the definition of white slaves. The commission recommended that the Immigration Bureau give inspectors the authority to "arrest on sight" any alien prostitute and to imprison those who had previously been deported for prostitution. The report posited a deep divide in sexual character between the Old World and the United States. In European nations, it argued, "the feeling regarding sexual immorality is much less pronounced than in the United States . . . and the women . . . have not the consciousness of degradation from their fallen condition that in some instances causes the American girl her keenest suffering."[48] It emphasized that sexual morality defined American identity: even if a few American girls worked as prostitutes, they had the decency to feel shame.

At the same time, the report pointed to pimps, procurers, and brothel owners as the true criminal masterminds behind white slavery and called for their arrest and deportation. Jewish and French (and thus likely Catholic) immigrants comprised the majority, whose religious and national backgrounds rendered them doubly foreign.[49] When discussing such traffickers, the report adopted a strikingly different tone from other passages, painting women as innocent victims of these foreign third-party profiteers, rather than as greedy and willing prostitutes. Without irony, the report argued that strict laws against prostitution could further harm women by driving them into "the clutches of pimps," even as it simultaneously recommended arresting and deporting prostitutes.[50]

Both the Braun and Dillingham Commission reports found that, contrary to reformers' assumptions, trafficking did not solely involve virginal, and thereby virtuous, white women brought to the United States against their will. Drawing selectively on their data, investigators confirmed the problem of white slavery by defining the term more broadly, to encompass all migratory prostitution. The figure of the white slave could thus serve a wide range of ideological purposes. As a hardened and perverted alien prostitute, she endangered the nation's health. But she could also take the form of an innocent European girl looking for a better life, an Asian woman sold into prostitution by a man of her own nationality or, even worse, an American girl entrapped by a foreign man who deserved to pay for his crimes. Even as the reports proclaimed sympathy for victims, they recommended the exclusion, arrest, and deportation of all immigrant prostitutes, regardless of the circumstances that led them to sell sex. Under the guise of protecting women and the United States itself, the two reports advocated for broad federal powers to police and punish immigrant women.[51]

An International Campaign

As American reformers waged a war against white slavery in the United States, they participated in a larger movement that extended across the Atlantic. But the American movement developed its own contours. As Jessica Pliley has shown, the American narrative of white slavery reframed the British model, in which British women were kidnapped and sold to Continental brothels. Instead, Americans feared immigrant brothel keepers who lured innocent American girls, as well as immigrant girls, to their ruin.[52] Moreover, European reformers and governments generally distinguished between women who chose to migrate and sell sex and those who did so through force or coercion. In Britain, for example, officials could only charge a man with procuring if the victim was a previously virtuous woman.[53] In contrast, the American definition of white slavery came to encompass the figure of the innocent victim as well as the avaricious prostitute, and to criminalize as a trafficker anyone who aided or profited from her migration or work, even indirectly.

In the late nineteenth century, two major groups spearheaded the international anti-trafficking movement, both with their roots in England. Josephine Butler's International Abolitionist Federation had an explicitly feminist bent. It prioritized the rights of women and viewed regulated prostitution as a problem that both reflected and caused women's inequality: trafficking was merely a symptom. In contrast, the International Bureau for the Suppression of the White Slave Traffic, headed by William Alexander Coote, who had previously founded the British National Vigilance Association, emphasized the protection of virginal young women. Coote and his organizations focused on the foreign prostitute, particularly Jewish women, as a threat to the nation. Thus, the International Bureau worked with governments to make anti–white slavery policy that aligned with state interests, even if that meant tolerating regulated prostitution.[54]

In Europe the two organizations remained separate, with very little overlapping membership; they differed over whether working with regulationist governments could effectively stop the traffic in women or whether such capitulation to state interests undermined the integrity of the movement.[55] In contrast, the American anti-trafficking movement remained largely unified, containing within it the tensions that had split the Europeans. After all, American reformers maintained, the US government did not regulate prostitution (despite ample evidence that it had done so in the Philippines). Thus, to their thinking, the US government remained more moral than regulationist European governments, a better partner in the fight against white slavery. At the turn of the century, the American Purity Alliance had close ties with both the Abolitionist Federation and the International Bureau, combining the former's distaste for government support of prostitution with the latter's emphasis on working with and for the benefit of the government to stop white slavery.[56]

The US government initially expressed less enthusiasm than its European counterparts about preventing the white slave traffic. In 1899, the International Bureau hosted the International Congress on the White Slave Trade to lay the groundwork for an international agreement. While eleven European governments sent representatives, the United States did not, deeming white slavery a largely European problem. Eight American reformers attended as private citizens, including members of the American Purity Alliance and the New England Watch and Ward Society, as well as prominent Quaker peace and women's rights activists.[57]

Representatives of the same governments met again in 1904 and ratified the International Agreement for the Suppression of the "White Slave Traffic," which established a central authority in each government to coordinate information; charged governments with surveillance of ports and railway stations; asked governments to ascertain the nationality of foreign prostitutes and repatriate those who wanted to return; and recommended that governments regulate employment agencies, which often served as a front for procurers. The US State Department again declined to participate, arguing that the United States could not sign the agreement because it had "no national system of police" and thus could not comply with the treaty obligations.[58]

In the face of the State Department's refusal, American and British reformers pushed the US government into action. In 1907, the US National Vigilance Association solicited a visit from Coote, whose International Bureau held to a paternalist vision of anti–white slavery activism. Coote met with the police commissioner of New York, Secretary of State Elihu Root, officials from the Department of Commerce and Labor, and President Roosevelt himself to promote the international agreement. On June 6, 1908, Roosevelt complied. Reformers on both sides of the Atlantic felt overjoyed that the US government had fallen "in line" with European states in the fight against white slavery.[59]

American reformers and officials hoped that the agreement would help them pursue international traffickers and bring them to justice in the United States. In the summer of 1909, the Immigration Bureau sent Marcus Braun to Europe to investigate the sources of white slavery and the networks of traffickers who profited from it.[60] Braun planned to secure the help of European officials in carrying out his inquiries. After arriving in France, however, his expectations of cooperation were swiftly crushed.

Braun met with Félicien Joseph Louis Hennequin, the French official charged with upholding the 1904 Agreement, who told Braun that he had no right to conduct investigations on French soil. Moreover, Hennequin objected to Braun's definitions of white slavery and the policy of the US government to suppress it. French officials and much of the public understood licensed prostitution as necessary for the health of society, a means for men to release sexual energy while keeping their wives and children safe from the dangers of rape and venereal disease.[61]

As Hennequin informed Braun, "prostitutes have a perfect right to travel and to circulate freely from and into France." He had no obligation to enforce US immigration laws, laws with which he was "not at all in sympathy." Finally, Hennequin accused the United States of violating the 1904 Agreement by deporting women who had been lured there under false pretenses. "We must give such a woman protection," he argued, repatriating her only at her request.[62] French officials interpreted the treaty in ways that drew sharp ideological and legal distinctions between prostitutes who migrated of their own volition and unwilling victims of white slavery.[63]

Braun felt disappointed but undeterred. He continued to conduct investigations in France in what he termed "an absolutely inoffensive way," by "acting merely the part of a tourist" and visiting the places where "questionable women" congregated. While investigating the case of a missing girl, however, Braun overstepped his bounds and French officials accused him of violating the penal code. He departed before they could file charges, leaving the US ambassador to repair the strained diplomatic relations that resulted.[64]

This affair accentuated the conflict between European and American understandings of white slavery. In a letter to the Commissioner of Immigration Daniel Keefe, Braun complained that although European officials helped in cases of "the white slave traffic proper," they refused to assist in cases of "trafficking in prostitutes." "The conception of what constitutes a 'white slave' is quite different in Europe than it is in the United States," he wrote. No European country had laws preventing the "free circulation" of prostitutes between countries, nor did European governments share the same definition of "what constitutes an immoral person," so they would not assist in US efforts to limit their mobility. Braun concluded that "the 'white slave' agreement is very faulty and incomplete."[65]

Others concurred with Braun's assessment. Keefe informed the Senate that the international agreement stood as "practically worthless . . . in preventing the migration of alien procurers and prostitutes." The international agreement solely prevented the trafficking of "innocent women and girls," which the Immigration Bureau had "seldom, if ever" seen.[66] American reformers and the US government, in contrast, defined white slavery to encompass all women who sold sex, whether free or coerced, and sought to prevent their immigration as a means of policing the moral and physical borders of the country.

"For Any Other Immoral Purpose"

While reformers and legislators employed federal immigration legislation as the primary means of protecting US borders from international trafficking, they also sought to harness the federal government's resources to prevent domestic trafficking. But constitutional limitations on federal power obstructed their efforts.

In 1909, the Supreme Court hampered immigration officials in their quest to stem white slavery when it struck down Section 3 of the 1907 Immigration Act, which had allowed for the arrest and deportation of anyone keeping or harboring an alien woman for immoral purposes within three years of her arrival. Yet the decision included a suggestion for future action. The majority opinion stated that only through a treaty with a foreign power did Congress have authority to protect immigrants after arrival. Suddenly the 1904 International White Slave Treaty looked more appealing to those who had dismissed it. By late 1909, Congress was debating two new bills to stop white slavery. Both exploited the ambiguity of the American white slavery narrative to their advantage. The first, an Immigration Act, emphasized the dangers sexually immoral foreigners posed to the United States. The second, the Mann Act, focused on the federal government's duty to protect innocent white women from traffickers. The Mann Act seized upon the power of treaties to expand the federal government's ability to police immigration and sexuality.[67]

Proponents of what came to be known as the 1910 Immigration Act sought to amend and strengthen the 1907 Immigration Act after the Supreme Court had weakened it. The 1910 Act included many of the proposals suggested by the Dillingham Commission. It called for the deportation of non-citizens found selling sex or deemed procurers or pimps, no matter how long they had been in the country. It made deportable any non-citizen found to benefit from the earnings of prostitution, even indirectly, including those employed in dance halls and places of amusement "habitually frequented by prostitutes." Returning to the United States after being excluded or deported for prostitution became punishable by up to two years in prison.[68]

The bill also removed the gendered language of the 1907 Act, making it a crime for "any alien" to work as a prostitute or procurer.[69] While this change allowed courts to prosecute madams (as some indeed did), it likely represented a response to a discovery Braun made during his investigations in Europe. Writing to Keefe of "a new species of undesirable immigrant," the male prostitute "afflicted with 'Homosexuality,'" Braun warned of "frequent cases of 'shipment' to the United States."[70] Congress passed the immigration bill and President Taft signed it into law on March 26, 1910.

The debates and publicity surrounding the immigration bill helped pave the way for the domestic-focused "White Slave Traffic Act," called the Mann Act after its author, James R. Mann (R-Illinois), who chaired the Interstate and Foreign Commerce Committee.[71] Experienced lawmakers, Mann and his co-authors made savvy use of the Interstate Commerce Clause of the US Constitution to intervene into arenas expressly or implicitly reserved to the states. In designing the bill, Mann worked closely with Clifford Roe, an Illinois Assistant State Attorney and author of the Illinois Pandering Law, the first state law to criminalize the transportation of women into or out of the state for the purpose of prostitution.[72] If reformers could show that traffickers took women across state and national borders to sell sex, they could bring the force of federal law to bear on prostitution and procuration, both of which previously fell under state jurisdiction.

Mann drew on the sympathetic aspects of the white slave narrative to plead for help for young immigrant women and American girls "enticed away from their homes in the country to large cities." Mann met with President Taft several weeks before the bill's introduction to gain his support for federal government action, which Mann proclaimed was "the only authority strong enough to cope with this evil." Taft threw his support behind the bill, stressing the "urgent necessity" of legislation against "The White Slave Trade."[73]

Mann put before Congress a far-reaching bill to stop white slavery, and indeed, sex outside of monogamous marriage, which built on a range of previous legislation to achieve its goal. The bill made it illegal to transport or aid in the transportation of a woman or girl across state or national lines for prostitution or "for any other immoral purpose," mirroring the language of the 1907 Immigration Act. The clause "any other immoral purpose," which the Supreme Court had previously upheld, criminalized even consensual, non-commercial, extramarital sex if the parties crossed borders. In a nod to age of consent laws, Mann's bill stipulated harsher penalties for coercing a woman under the age of eighteen to travel across state or national lines for the purpose of prostitution.[74] For the first time, the federal government could police the sexual lives of its citizens, as well as immigrants.

Mann's bill exemplified the creative attempts of anti–white slavery activists and lawmakers to extend federal power in the face of constitutional limitations and political opposition to federal intervention.[75] Strategically invoking the president's treaty-making power, Mann based his bill in part on the 1904 International Agreement. He could thus claim federal authority over prostitution in ways "not possible to reach directly under the Constitution."[76] Based on the 1904 Agreement's call for countries to share information, the Mann Act required anyone who harbored a foreign-born prostitute within three years of her arrival to file a report with the Bureau of Immigration. Those who failed to do so faced jail time and fines; those who submitted a report faced possible arrest on state and local white slavery charges.[77]

In congressional debates over the bill, Mann exploited the contradictions contained in the Dillingham and Immigration Bureau reports to his own ends. While Mann and his colleagues worried about European women trafficked to the United States, their deepest concern remained the protection of white American women. Rather than targeting foreign prostitutes, as the Immigration Act did, the bill aimed to punish traffickers. To depict traffickers as villains, their victims had to be innocent. Selecting useful examples from the reports, Mann argued that most women did not choose prostitution. Instead, "the inmates of many houses of ill fame are made up largely of women and girls whose original entry into a life of immorality was brought about by men who are in the business of procuring women." The women were "practically slaves in the true sense of the word," Mann claimed.[78]

Ironically, Mann had adopted the European definition of "white slave," the very definition that rankled Braun, the Immigration Bureau, and the Dillingham Commission, going so far as to quote the treaty's definition of the term in his report. Like European states, Mann limited "white slavery" to women "unwillingly forced to practice prostitution." Moreover, while nothing in the text of the bill specifically mentioned race, Mann named it the "White Slave Traffic Act," adopting the European phrasing in a way that emphasized the primacy of white women.

At the same time, Mann vastly widened the definition of "white slave" by arguing that a woman's consent was immaterial; a woman was a white slave if transported across state or national lines "with or without her consent." By combining the European concept of the white slave as unwilling victim with a conception of trafficking that sidestepped the issue of consent, Mann solidified a new American legal definition of sex trafficking that rendered all women who traveled to sell sex as white slaves, into whose lives the state had a duty to intervene.[79]

Opposition to Mann's bill came primarily from Southern congressmen, who argued that the states alone had the right to govern and police "the health and morals of the people." The "Views of the Minority," authored by three Southern congressmen, contended that with "just such legislation as this bill proposes, under the plea of the reform of vice and morals, . . . Congress can establish a dangerous precedent that will gradually change our wise and successful federal system to a consolidated government."[80] Moreover, the bill challenged many white Southerners' conviction that white male heads of household held the responsibility to protect the sexual respectability of their wives and daughters by whatever means necessary.[81] Federal anti-trafficking law, then, impinged on a duty regarded as the sole purview of white men.

Yet many Southerners supported the bill. After all, who could argue against government protection of white womanhood? When he took the floor in defense of the Mann Act, Representative John Burnett (D-Alabama) told the House, "I am a strict constructionist of the Constitution, but God forbid that I should construe it so strictly as to say that we must sit by with hands folded and let this cankerworm gnaw at the moral vitals of our Republic." If the bill did not pass, Burnett warned, the fathers of the nation would have to tell their virtuous "mothers and wives and daughters" that "we live in a republic where members of their sex may be transported from State to State to be sold into a slavery worse than death itself."[82]

Southern congressman Gordon D. Russell (D-Texas) played on racist tropes to win Southern support for the bill. In defending the bill to his fellow Southerners, he recounted the case of John Frankling, a Black man from Tifton, Georgia, who had purchased a white wife in Chicago, chosen from among a group of twenty-five white women. According to Russell, Frankling claimed he had purchased three white women in this manner.[83] By raising the specter of Black men preying on white women, debates around the Mann Act promoted the myth of the Black rapist. Just as the white slavery narrative alternately portrayed women as innocent, native-born, white victims or hardened foreign prostitutes, so too could the trafficker change shape to fit peoples' racial fears, as an East Asian, Southern European, or Eastern European immigrant or an African American man. Mann's bill passed by voice vote on June 25, 1910, the final day of the congressional session, and President Taft immediately signed it into law.[84]

The Mann Act and 1910 Immigration Act worked together to police both state and national border crossings involving individuals deemed sexually immoral.[85] As Jessica Pliley has argued, the Mann Act represented a significant step in the growth of the federal government in the early twentieth century. Enforcing the Mann Act required a federal squad to police the conduct it criminalized. Only the Department of Justice's Bureau of Investigation, later called the Federal Bureau of Investigation (FBI), could perform this function, so the government expanded it. Through the Mann Act, the federal government policed areas of life that had never been subject to federal surveillance, particularly actual or even attempted consensual sex that involved crossing state lines. The Mann Act's enforcement led to the growth of federal prisons, especially women's prisons, since, contrary to its framers' expectations, women themselves transported other women and profited from their sexual labor.[86]

The 1910 Immigration Act made the Bureau of Immigration a more active participant in combatting prostitution. In 1906, it had rejected only thirty women at the border for being prostitutes and two people for being procurers; in 1914, it rejected 380 women for being prostitutes and 254 people for being procurers. It also deported 345 prostitutes and 61 individuals "supported by the proceeds of prostitution."[87] Between 1902 and World War I, women labeled as prostitutes comprised the second most deported category of immigrants. Immigration officials deported women deemed "likely to become a public charge" in the largest number, a category often used to deport women suspected of prostitution because the charge required less evidence.[88]

To be sure, many more women who sold sex successfully migrated to the United States than faced debarment or deportation. Marcus Braun reported that deported women often reentered the United States "in the most brazen fashion" and "laugh at the efforts of the Immigration Officials" to stop them.[89] Both immigrant and native-born women continued to sell sex as a means of supporting themselves, often to supplement a meager wage or unreliable income.

Nonetheless, white slavery laws marked a striking incursion of the federal government into the sexual lives and practices of people living in and attempting to enter the United States. The laws drew ideological boundaries around who belonged to the nation, whom the federal government had a duty to protect, and whom it should punish. Immigrants who sold sex or worked in the sex industry could face deportation no matter how long they had been in the country, marking sexual morality as an important indicator of fitness for citizenship. The laws labeled single women, particularly immigrants, as potential prostitutes who required surveillance, making gender an increasingly significant category in the policing of US cities and borders. Native-born white girls who perfectly fit the description of guileless victim remained harder to come by than officials had expected. But the idealized figure of the white girl lured to her ruin by a dark man justified federal laws policing sexual morality and persuaded white Americans of their humanitarian character.

White Slaves and Colored Maids

As the discussions on the Senate floor presaged, federal laws designed to prevent and punish white slavery, particularly the Mann Act, could serve as a powerful means of maintaining racial hierarchies. Kevin Mumford has argued that the Mann Act "constructed a racialized subject worthy of uplift—the white slave—and in the process erased the black prostitute."[90] The flexibility of the American white slavery narrative, exemplified by the ambiguity of the Mann Act's definition of trafficking as transporting a woman for "any other immoral purpose" "with or without her consent," allowed federal officials to apply anti–white slavery laws in ways that reflected their own prejudices. As enforced, the Mann Act rendered Black women who experienced sexual coercion or violence at the hands of white men undeserving of protection, while Black men who had consensual relationships with white women faced prosecution under it.

While anti–white slavery activists noticed Black prostitutes in vice districts, they did not discuss them in their analysis of the white slavery problem. White reformers often regarded Black women as immoral and hypersexual and thus did not see Black women in commercial sex as unnatural in the way they did white women. Instead, they portrayed Black women in sexual commerce not as endangered victims, but as a danger to respectable citizens. Most often, Black women appeared in studies of white slavery as the "colored maid" who helped to run the brothel and thus bore some responsibility for the entrapment of white women.[91]

Indeed, African American women disproportionately worked in domestic service because most industries excluded them from employment. Of the documents created by white reformers, only a Chicago Vice Commission Report reflected on the reasons that Black women often labored as servants in brothels. Cities often located their vice districts in or near African American communities, it noted. Moreover, "prejudice" against young African American women meant that employment agencies ignored their needs, and many "respectable homes" would not employ them as domestics, leaving brothels as one of few options.[92]

White reformers used the presence of Black maids to stress the unnatural—and un-American—role of white women in prostitution. One of the many treatises on white slavery, published by members of the Illinois Vigilance Association, included photographs to illustrate the plight of white slaves. In one, a white prostitute sat in squalor, while a Black woman, captured in profile standing in the doorway, supposedly prevented her from leaving the brothel (fig. 3.1). The image presented a double inversion of American social order, which upheld the supremacy and sexual purity of white women and, conversely, the inferiority and sexual promiscuity of Black women. It rendered the white woman as the "slave," with the Black maid as her overseer, if not her mistress. The trope of the colored maid not only held up white women as ideal victims, but effaced the poor wages and vulnerability to violence—including sexual violence—that Black women experienced as domestic workers.

As Cynthia Blair has shown, while African American reformers spoke out against the trafficking of innocent Black women and the movement of urban sex industries into their neighborhoods, they largely overlooked the challenges faced by the majority of Black women who sold sex.[93] These women's "wayward lives," as Saidiya Hartman has demonstrated, exceeded the constraints and stereotypes that both middle-class Black and white reformers attempted to place on them. Yet state violence consistently marked their lives, as law enforcement variously targeted them as criminals and ignored them as victims, and state governments and white citizens enforced racial segregation, making it harder for them to access decent housing, jobs, and education.[94]

Middle-class Black activists, like their white counterparts, hoped to secure the protection of women through anti-trafficking legislation and viewed the state as a potential ally. Black reformers worried about problems faced by African American women migrating north, a problem the racialized language of white slavery rendered invisible to white officials and audiences.[95] Before Mann's bill passed, David Newton E. Campbell, a Jamaican-born pastor and medical doctor in Baltimore, wrote to the Secretary of Commerce expressing his concerns. Campbell believed the white slave traffic was one of the most pressing issues facing the country. Yet he urged the government to reconceptualize it, pointing out that, "among the foreign and domestic victims entrapped

FIGURE 3.1. The caption of this photograph from the 1910 book *Fighting the Traffic in Young Girls, Or, War on the White Slave Trade*, read, "'The Gilded Life' As It Really Is" and reported that "all the fresh air these poor slaves get is in the back yard of the dives, which is full of refuse, and where they are watched by colored attendants." Note the Black woman in the doorway.

in this dragnet traffic, may be enumerated the Caucasian, Negro, Japanese, and Chinese. Since all these women are not 'white', why should the subject of their enslavement be designated 'White Slave Traffic'?"[96]

Campbell called attention to Black women's acute vulnerability. "More colored women and girls are lured and enticed from the Southland as 'helps and servants' to large Northern cities, under guise and promise of 'better wages, more pay, permanent position,' than the public would believe," he remarked. Using the social scientific currency of the day, he suggested that the Secretary of Commerce look at statistics compiled by African American women's groups as evidence of the problem. Echoing the rhetoric of government reports and white activists, he decried that such a traffic happened in a "Christian and highly enlightened country." While Immigration Commissioner Keefe responded to Campbell's letter informing him that his suggestions had been "carefully noted," there is no evidence that Keefe acted on them.[97]

African American reformers created their own narrative of sex trafficking that highlighted white men's sexual exploitation of Black women. Chicago African American newspaper the *Broad Ax* proclaimed, "The Laws on the 'White Slave' Traffic Should Protect the Women of all Races." The article described "immoral houses filled with Colored women for the entertainment of white gentlemen," a narrative that inverted the popular image of brothels filled with white women visited by Black men. Yet, the paper charged, "the reformers and the advocates of the strict enforcement of the white female slave traffic have never paid attention to these glaring facts."[98] African American reformers pointed out white reformers' hypocrisy in lamenting the sexual enslavement of white women but ignoring sexual violence that white men enacted on the bodies of Black women. They decried the violence committed by the state in refusing to protect Black women. At the same time, middle-class Black reformers did not always recognize the violence that state intervention, as well as neglect, wrought upon poor and working-class Black women.[99]

In the first decade of the Mann Act's enforcement, the *Broad Ax*'s assessment stood largely correct. I have found only one account of a white man convicted of violating the Mann Act for trafficking a Black woman, but officials charged him alongside a Black woman, named as his co-conspirator.[100] Courts found George Savage, a white real estate dealer, and Alice Jackson, a Black madam, guilty of transporting Frankie Allen from Chicago to St. Paul for immoral purposes, with Savage sentenced to five years in prison. The *Broad Ax* reported on the conviction with approval, saying, a "few more convictions . . . and this traffic will be stopped among Negro women, who feel that they were on account of their color immune from this law."[101] Although Savage appealed, the judge affirmed the conviction.[102] Since the FBI rarely, if ever, charged white men with Mann Act violations for trafficking Black women, it is likely that Savage's association with Jackson led to his conviction.

Federal agents and judges did occasionally pursue Mann Act cases against Black men accused of trafficking Black women, often as a means of closing brothels. When cities lacked statutes prohibiting prostitution, police could use the Mann Act as a workaround. For example, as part of a crackdown against prostitution in Laporte, Indiana, police raided a brothel and arrested twenty-five people. Asserting that they had "indisputable evidence of a traffic in colored girls between Laporte and Chicago and Chicago and Michigan City," the police charged Ben Davis of Chicago and Dick Johnson from Michigan City with violating the Mann Act.[103] Federal officials charged Guy Hart and Jay Chavis with Mann Act violations for inducing Ruby Scott and Maxine Gordon to come from Tacoma, Washington to Butte, Montana to "enter upon a fast life." Even as Scott and Gordon were purportedly the victims in the case, however, a local newspaper called their innocence into question.[104]

The FBI more often employed the Mann Act to make an example out of Black men who had relationships with white women. Such relationships had previously been policed extralegally through lynching but, increasingly, state anti-miscegenation laws in both the North and South also banned them. The Mann Act's racialized enforcement lent federal support to state legal prohibitions on relationships between white women and Black men.[105]

The most high-profile Mann Act case targeted famed African American boxer Jack Johnson, making headlines for nearly a decade. On July 4, 1910, Johnson defeated white boxer Jim Jeffries in a highly publicized fight. Race riots broke out across the country, as white men attacked Black men celebrating Johnson's victory. Many white Americans felt even more incensed when they discovered that Johnson openly had relationships with white women, including several marriages.[106]

In 1912, authorities saw an opportunity to punish his racial and sexual transgressions, arresting Johnson for a Mann Act violation for taking Belle Schreiber, his white girlfriend, across state lines. While Schreiber's previous work as a prostitute rendered her an imperfect victim, Johnson's race transformed her into a woman worth defending. The sentencing judge remarked that Johnson "is one of the best-known men of his race and his example has been far-reaching," making explicit the concern that Johnson's racial and sexual transgressions would encourage other Black men to act similarly, as well as the hope that punishing him would warn others.[107] He sentenced Johnson to one year in prison and ordered him to pay a thousand-dollar fine. Johnson himself called the charges "a rank frame-up," and African American newspapers decried Johnson's treatment as the result of race prejudice. Johnson fled to Paris to avoid incarceration and traveled between Europe, Mexico, and South America in exile until 1920, when he returned to the United States to serve his sentence. After his release he continued to enter the ring, but never again attained his previous levels of success.[108]

Federal officials charged other successful but less well-known Black men with Mann Act violations for consensual relationships with white women.[109] Newspapers around the Midwest reported the Mann Act charge brought against Halbert Grant, a Black pianist. Federal agent J. M. Bowen arrested Grant at a hotel in Minneapolis, found in the company of Lottie Grant, a seventeen-year-old white woman from a prominent Detroit family. The couple claimed they had recently married in Canada. Two months later, officials released the Grants from custody. The *Crisis*, the newspaper of the National Association for the Advancement of Colored People edited by W.E.B. Du Bois, reported on the falsity of the charges, as the Grants had "been married a number of years and had lived respectably in Detroit."[110]

Johnson's and Grant's arrests show one of the multitude of purposes that white slavery legislation could serve: the federal policing of relationships across the color line. Even though the federal government charged relatively few Black men with Mann Act violations for their relationships with white women, these cases showed all Black men that the government could and would punish them for such an affront to white supremacy. Moreover, its enforcement made clear who merited the state's protection and who fell outside of its concern. For example, the Bureau of Investigation did not pursue the case of Mary Lee Bolden, a fifteen-year-old girl taken from her home by a man who seduced her, likely because both parties were Black, even though it focused particular attention on similar cases involving young white girls.[111] These disparities sent a clear message to African American communities that the sexual abuse of young Black girls did not matter, while sexual exploitation of white women posed a national concern.

Canal Zone Traffic

The Panama Canal Zone loomed large in the sensationalist press coverage of white slavery in the United States. In 1910, an investigation in Boston uncovered the workings of the "Panama Gang," which supposedly shipped young women to brothels in the Canal Zone.[112] The consequences of new white slavery legislation also played out on the Isthmus of Panama. In addition to reinforcing racial hierarchies on the US mainland, anti–white slavery laws provided the US government with a new means of policing the crossing of racial, gendered, and jurisdictional borders everywhere it exercised authority. Such powers became increasingly important as the United States escalated its economic and military interventions in Latin America.

There were stark differences between the US government's anti–white slavery policy and rhetoric in colonies versus on the mainland. In the unincorporated territories of Puerto Rico, Hawai'i, and the Philippines, US officials oversaw red-light districts, even as on the mainland they enforced anti–white slavery laws that defined all migratory prostitution as white slavery and punished a wide range of figures in the sex industry as traffickers. The gap between mainland and colonial prostitution policy, and their intersection with federal white slavery laws, made clear the ambiguous status of territorial inhabitants. For example, immigration authorities prevented Isabel Gonzalez, a supposedly sexually immoral Puerto Rican woman, from entering the continental United States: as a territorial resident, but not a US citizen, they declared her inadmissible.[113] While US officials licensed women working in prostitution in Puerto Rico, if so-called immoral Puerto Rican women came to the mainland, immigration officials deemed them undesirable.

In the Panama Canal Zone, a leased Zone controlled by the US government, US officials used anti–white slavery law in unique ways in comparison with other overseas jurisdictions. Because US officials imagined the Canal Zone as a white settler colony rather than an administrative colony, they enforced white slavery laws as a means of replicating the continental United States' racial, gendered, and sexual hierarchies. Such legislation gained greater significance because it purportedly set the Zone apart from the neighboring Republic of Panama, whose inhabitants white Americans often portrayed as hypersexual and ridden with venereal disease.[114]

In the Canal Zone, then, white slavery legislation served as an example of the ability of the United States to civilize and tame Latin America and claim it for white Americans. "The Marvelous Cleaning Up of the Canal Zone Means Occupation of the Tropics by the White Race," announced a 1912 article in the *New York Times*, suggesting the significance of the Zone for broader American imperial ambitions.[115] As on the US mainland, policing white slavery in the Canal Zone acted as a project of national identity formation, accentuating the benevolence of the US government, which protected white women and purified the racially darkened lands it ruled from sexual vice.

The US government carved out the Panama Canal Zone in 1903, determined to reap the economic and military benefits of a path between the Atlantic and Pacific. Under duress, the Republic of Panama leased the zone to the United States, ceding control of the profits of the canal and a twenty-mile zone of territory around it, where the US government could enforce its own laws. The Canal Zone transected the Republic, cutting it into two noncontiguous parts; crossing the Zone provided the only land route from one side of the Republic to the other. The major Panamanian port cities of Panama and Colón remained under the jurisdiction of the Republic, though they directly bordered the Canal Zone.[116]

In many respects, US rule in the Canal Zone followed patterns established in other colonies, where officials enforced racial hierarchy and protected US

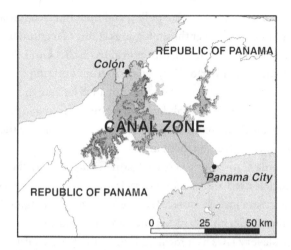

MAP 3.1. The Panama Canal Zone, created by the United States in 1903, bisected the Republic of Panama. Map courtesy of the Smithsonian Tropical Research Institute.

commercial interests. Building a canal required a massive workforce: men to undertake the physical labor of construction and women to perform the domestic, reproductive, and care labor of feeding, cleaning, and comforting. The US administration in the Canal Zone divided workers into two classes based on race—white American "gold roll" employees, and "silver roll" laborers predominantly from the West Indies. US officials upheld gold and silver roll distinctions in wages, housing, health care, and recreation. They also attempted to enforce white middle-class sexual decorum in the Canal Zone, a stark reversal from the usual colonial policy of regulated prostitution and an effort to turn the Canal Zone into an embodiment of white American scientific progress, morality, and discipline.[117]

In the early years of the Canal's construction, the US officials worked to establish an American-style social order based on racial hierarchy and stable, marital family units, as well as prevent the spread of diseases that had hampered prior French attempts to build a canal. A 1905 ordinance forbid cohabitation without marriage, a common family pattern among native Panamanians and workers from the Caribbean, making it punishable with a fine and jail time. Canal Zone officials threatened to fire white employees who cohabitated with "native and colored women," a surprising affront to white male sexual prerogative.[118] They punished adultery with jail sentences of up to a year.[119] US officials and white Canal Zone residents alike believed that excluding prostitutes—particularly Black prostitutes—from the Zone was a means of protecting white American women tasked with maintaining respectable families there.[120] At the same time, US officials also worked to keep white American prostitutes out of the Canal Zone, because their presence threatened the image of pure white American womanhood.[121]

US officials admitted that the large number of single men in the Canal Zone posed a problem and assumed that they required sexual release. They encouraged men to seek it over the border in the Republic of Panama, part of a larger pattern of US control of the licit economy in the Canal Zone, making the Republic's economy dependent on providing illicit goods and services.[122] A common adage on the Isthmus, according to one journalist, held that "the Republic of Panama is the Redlight District of the Canal Zone."[123]

Legislation to stop white slavery provided Canal Zone officials with a new means to control the sexuality and mobility of people on the Isthmus, while proclaiming the civilizing influence and protective nature of the United States' presence. The US Canal Zone administration's official newspaper, the *Canal Record*, as well as local newspapers, reported that the Mann Act and 1910 Immigration Act applied in the Canal Zone. Officials emphasized that they would strictly enforce the laws.[124]

Preventing white slavery justified increasing US control over immigration to the Republic of Panama as well as the Canal Zone. The US government appointed an officer to work with US quarantine officials, as well as the Panamanian government, to forbid "undesirables" from entering the Republic, even though Panamanian officials licensed prostitution. Through his efforts, the officer reported, "a number of white-slave dealers and notorious prostitutes were thereby turned back and not permitted to debark and yet others were deterred from attempting to come into the Republic."[125] Canal Zone officials also monitored the Panama Railroad trains for women traveling through the Zone to destinations in the Republic of Panama or other countries for "immoral purposes" in violation of the Mann Act.[126]

Isthmian newspapers intended for American readers regularly detailed the arrest, incarceration, and deportation of those engaged in white slavery. Articles remarked that French and South American traffickers preyed on innocent girls: "in almost every case, these girls are of tender years, and frequently have been led away from their homes by promises of good positions here."[127] The details that emerged from white slavery cases, however, often belied the Canal Zone government's vision of swarthy South American men kidnapping white European women. For example, an American couple was arrested after landing in Colón and traveling across the Isthmus to Panama City, where the woman entered a brothel in the Republic of Panama. Both were released after the woman testified that she had entered the brothel of her own will, while her companion had attempted to stop her.[128] Yet the narrative of protecting innocent young white women exploited by South Americans justified US officials' right to carefully monitor the borders of the Canal Zone and the Republic of Panama.

As in the continental United States, the sympathy extended to presumed victims of white slavery did not extend to Black women. In the fall of 1911, police accused ten Black Jamaican women of practicing prostitution and arrested them for vagrancy. Such a charge, leveled at anyone who "wandered around without visible means of support," provided justification for policing the bodies of Black women on the mainland, as well as in other places under US control.[129] The ten women, police argued, lived in the Republic but crossed into the Canal Zone to sell sex after canal workers' monthly payday, with the help of pimps who arranged for their travel. The courts sentenced the women to serve fifty-five days in jail and pay a fine of $25, then ordered them deported to the Republic. According to a US official, the women proved "a source of unusual trouble and are responsible for a great many of the most serious crimes committed on the Canal Zone."[130]

Alongside the women's deportation orders, the Chief of Police directed a police sergeant to assemble the women and read them a 1911 executive order issued by President Wilson, which made reentering the Canal Zone after imprisonment and deportation a crime punishable by a year in the penitentiary. The criminalization of reentry posed particular hardships to both migrants and Panamanians, many of whom held employment in the Zone. But Canal Zone officials remained determined to ensure that these disorderly women would not return.[131]

The more vigilant policing of prostitution and women's migration stimulated by the new federal laws likely played a role in the incarceration and deportation of these ten women, even though they were not arrested under them. Although officials admitted that pimps brought the women to the Canal Zone to sell sex, a crucial part of the white slavery narrative, there is no evidence that police pursued the pimps or considered the women victims. Policing prostitution through the racialized categories of white slavery and vagrancy in the Canal Zone enforced gendered white supremacy. While US officials expected white men to go to the Republic to find the sexual release supposedly necessary for their health, women who sold sex, particularly Black women, faced arrest and deportation for crossing into the Canal Zone. Relegating Black prostitutes to the Republic, where they could not disturb the Black-white color line that US officials adamantly upheld in the Canal Zone, made the claims of moral purity in the Canal Zone possible. It provided outlets for male sexual desire outside of US-controlled territory, creating the stark separation between white American civilization and "colored" South American vice.

The Mann Act, 1910 Immigration Act, and the white slavery narrative served important purposes for the US government in the Canal Zone. They provided new ways to police prostitution and immigration under the banner of protecting white women and bringing civilization to an uncivilized tropical place. They thus justified the US government's involvement in controlling not only the Canal Zone, but also the borders of the Republic of Panama, a sovereign nation, as well as the sexual labor of women there. These interventions would become even more pronounced with the outbreak of the First World War.

Conclusion

The American narrative of white slavery consolidated a broad range of anxieties into a single issue. It called for a defense of white womanhood from lurking danger, at a time when women increasingly lived on their own and entered the paid workforce, but often faced low wages and poor working conditions. It upheld white, middle-class, Protestant sexual morality, based on reproductive heterosexuality and monogamy, at a time when urban sexual commerce thrived and millions of immigrants with seemingly unfamiliar family structures and sexual practices arrived in the United States. It emphasized that illicit sexuality, and prostitution in particular, offended American morals and precluded individuals, especially women, from citizenship. It promoted the myth that African American men preyed on white women and denied Black American women the right to state protection it afforded white women, despite African Americans' efforts to foreground the sexual abuse of Black women by white men in white slavery discourse. In the context of US colonialism, it promoted the image of the United States as an exceptionally sexually moral—and white—country that had a duty to civilize others.

The 1910 Immigration Act and the Mann Act were written to encompass all of these concerns and enforced in ways that targeted them selectively. They could variously protect and police women, aims at once contradictory and complementary. The laws seemed contradictory because they led to the arrest and deportation of the very women they claimed to rescue. Yet they complemented one another because both policing and protecting warranted government intervention into the lives of anyone suspected of involvement in the sex trade, whether victim or perpetrator.

Putting an end to white slavery became an important justification not only for controlling women, but also for policing state and national borders and arresting and excluding those whose sexual practices transgressed the boundaries of white racial hierarchy and monogamous heterosexuality. The enforcement of anti–white slavery laws forged closer ties between conceptions of racial darkness, foreignness, and sexual deviance on the one hand, and American national identity, whiteness, and sexual morality on the other. In this framework, trafficking no longer constituted a crime against an individual woman, but a crime against the United States itself, punishable by an ever-expanding body of law.

4

Policing Women, Protecting Soldiers

THE AMERICAN PLAN ON THE
WORLD WAR I HOME FRONT

IN AUGUST 1917, Mamie Stapleton and Hattie Smith were arrested for vagrancy in Atlanta, Georgia, and placed in the county jail awaiting trial, caught up in the federal government's war against prostitution. Incarcerating such women, US army officials believed, protected soldiers at a nearby training camp. At the jail, Maude Miner, a prominent prison reformer working for the federal government, interviewed Stapleton and Smith. The white sixteen-year-olds sported stylish, short blond hair, and told Miner that they had been "travelling" together for the past two months, selling sex to men who could pay. Both hailed from small towns, and Stapleton had left a husband behind. Neither woman had ever worked in a brothel, though Stapleton admitted she had been "kept" by a man for a while. For a time, the two worked at Fulton Bag and Cotton Mill, but left their jobs a month prior. Minor reported that Stapleton "lisps" and Smith "looks to be mentally defective." Police had previously arrested and fined both women multiple times under Atlanta's municipal crackdown on vice.[1]

How did these two young, white, native-born girls, who might have been deemed vulnerable white slaves just a few years prior, end up jailed as dangerous prostitutes? In fact, Stapleton and Smith were not outliers. While police had long used vagrancy laws to target women they deemed sexually suspicious, the federal government had never attacked prostitution to such an extent.[2] During World War I, the federal government estimated that it arrested and incarcerated at least thirty thousand women. Officials arrested more—likely tens of thousands more—but held them in local reformatories and county jails, much like Stapleton and Smith, and thus omitted them from federal statistics.[3]

Significant shifts in both the ideology and political standing of anti–white slavery crusaders led to this moment. The "war on the white slave traffic" had caught the attention of billionaire financier John D. Rockefeller, Jr., just as he was refashioning himself as a philanthropist.[4] In 1913, Rockefeller, Jr., founded two organizations that promoted "social hygiene." These organizations could cooperate with the government, much as anti–white slavery organizations had. A broad movement, social hygiene put sexuality at the center of individual and national health, uniting the earlier social purity and anti–white slavery movements. Social hygiene had both a public health and a carceral bent. Its advocates worked to prohibit prostitution and eradicate venereal disease, building on the momentum of the alcohol prohibition movement, which similarly hoped to purify the nation through social control.[5]

Rockefeller's social hygiene organizations got the chance to test their methods during the border war between the United States and Mexico in 1916. Social hygiene investigators toured border towns and found both US military–regulated prostitution and rampant venereal disease. Such a discovery was, on the face of it, nothing new. Social purity reformers had encountered a similar situation when they visited the Philippines in 1900, but the military had ignored their pleas to stop inspecting women and running brothels. In 1917, however, the US military listened.

With Progressive-minded men in key positions, the military stood ready to create better soldiers through social engineering.[6] When the United States entered WWI in April 1917, the military placed social hygiene reformers from Rockefeller's organizations in charge of formulating and executing official military policies on prostitution and venereal disease. With more than 4.7 million men serving in the military before the Great War's end, social hygienists believed that their new ideas could transform the broader citizenry as well.[7] Social hygiene reformers no longer just worked in partnership with the state, as they had when fighting white slavery: they now held positions within it.

The stakes of maintaining the United States' sexual exceptionalism during wartime felt high to social hygienists and government officials because, they believed, white male sexual self-discipline anchored the global spread of American-style democracy.[8] In a letter to soldiers, President Woodrow Wilson charged, the eyes of all the world will be upon you, because you are in some special sense the soldiers of freedom. Let it be your pride, therefore, to show all men everywhere not only what good soldiers you are, but also what good men you are, keeping yourselves fit and straight in everything, and pure and clean through and through. Let us set for ourselves a standard so high that it will be a glory to live up to it, and then let us live up to it and add a new laurel to the crown of America.[9]

Freedom and democratic governance at home and abroad, as well as America's place in the world, rested on American soldiers' sexual self-control.

Despite the rhetoric of pure American manhood, US prostitution policy focused on controlling women. Social hygiene reformers eventually termed the policy they developed the "American Plan," a reversal of previous US military policy and a marked contrast with the supposed "European Plan" of state-regulated prostitution.[10] To social hygienists, it proved the United States' sexual exceptionalism: all other belligerents regulated or tolerated prostitution. "Law enforcement" stood as a pillar of the plan. It involved criminalizing and prohibiting prostitution, and in fact any extramarital sex between soldiers and women. Under the American Plan, officials could arrest any woman whom they suspected of carrying a venereal disease and force her to undergo treatment. The American Plan gave social hygiene reformers the power not only to study women like Stapleton and Smith, as they had previously done, but to incarcerate them and commit violence on their bodies in the name of treatment.

Incorporating Reform

John D. Rockefeller, Jr., felt frustrated. Along with twenty-three other respectable citizens, he had given six months of his life to a comprehensive grand jury investigation of white slavery in New York City, spending $250,000 to bankroll the project.[11] The only son of one of the wealthiest men in the United States, Rockefeller had made his debut in reform society by serving as the grand jury's foreman. Supplementing the city's budget, he paid the salaries of fourteen full-time investigators in the spring of 1910. The final report found "no evidence of an organized traffic in women for immoral purposes," but also concluded that "trafficking in the bodies of women does exist."[12] Much to Rockefeller's dismay, city officials actively suppressed the report.

A consummate institution-builder, Rockefeller founded two new philanthropic organizations devoted to solving the supposed crisis of sexual morality facing the United States. The Bureau of Social Hygiene, incorporated in 1913, conducted scientific research on sexuality and social problems. Its sibling, the American Social Hygiene Association (ASHA), incorporated in 1914, translated the Bureau of Social Hygiene's research into concrete policy proposals to deal with prostitution at the state, federal, and international levels. These organizations built upon Rockefeller's interest in public health projects, such as eradicating hookworm. Through previous public health efforts, Rockefeller-funded organizations had already worked both at home and abroad, and cooperated—both formally and informally—with the US government.[13]

To create the ASHA, Rockefeller united the two most powerful anti-prostitution reform organizations into a single, more efficient association. The American Vigilance Association, formed in 1912, had brought together the anti–white slavery National Vigilance Association and the more broadly focused American Purity Alliance. With Chicago anti-trafficking crusader Clifford Roe at its helm, the American Vigilance Association used legal means to suppress prostitution and the traffic in women.[14] Physician Prince A. Morrow led the American Federation for Sex Hygiene, which sought to reduce venereal disease by combating regulated prostitution and promoting sex education. As Morrow shockingly, and likely erroneously, proclaimed, at least 75 percent of adult men in New York City had gonorrhea, while syphilis rates stood at between 5 and 18 percent.[15]

Rockefeller used his personal ties and financial resources to persuade the leadership of the American Vigilance Association and the American Federation for Sex Hygiene to merge. Meeting at the home of veteran purity reformer Grace Hoadley Dodge, representatives agreed to form the ASHA. Members elected Charles W. Elliot, former president of Harvard University and a trustee of the Rockefeller Foundation, as president.[16] The new advocacy group integrated the religious perspective of purity reformers, who sought to replace the double standard of sexual morality with sexual continence for men as well as women and worked mainly through moral suasion. It also incorporated vigilance activists, who attempted to repress white slavery and prostitution through conducting investigations targeting prostitutes and pimps.

Medical and public health professionals, however, held the most sway in the ASHA. They focused on the cure and prevention of venereal disease, advocated the prohibition of prostitution, and labeled prostitutes as disease vectors and agents of social chaos. Drawing on eugenics, social hygienists believed in the power of human sexuality, which could improve the (white) race or cause its degeneration. Only marital, procreative heterosexuality could sustain conjugal families, the building block of American society. The ASHA conducted vice investigations, proposed laws and police measures to combat prostitution, developed sex education curricula, and fought venereal disease. Its inclusion of long established reformers helped it to appeal to a popular audience, while the experts in medicine and public health gave the group the imprimatur of modern science.

Rockefeller shaped the ASHA into an organization that reflected his belief in the rational and professional study of sexual problems, removing leaders he regarded as too moralistic.[17] These shifts constituted an implicit repudiation of the women who had built the social purity movement, along with its original feminist orientation. Social hygienists applauded the modern, detached, "scientific treatment" of prostitution and rejected the supposedly older, "undesirable sentimental method of viewing the problem," an approach that had been guided by the affective connections women reformers posited between themselves and supposedly "fallen" women.[18] Male public health professionals controlled the ASHA, including William F. Snow, a professor of hygiene at Stanford University and the secretary of the California State Board of Health.

Rockefeller's vision of morality and masculinity closely aligned with that of the Young Men's Christian Association (YMCA), whose efforts to inculcate sexual morality made it an important ally of the ASHA. A Protestant organization committed to molding the "whole man" by developing his "mind, body, and spirit," the YMCA expanded in the late nineteenth century as young single men flocked to cities. Building on the popularity of the physical culture movement, the YMCA offered physical education programs that imbued bodily exercise with spiritual meaning. By the 1880s, sex education had become a crucial component of such programs.[19] The YMCA and the ASHA worked closely together, printing and distributing each other's social hygiene pamphlets and posters. Through the language of social science, the ASHA secularized white middle-class Protestant sexual morality and made it into a public policy goal.

American Sexual Science

The studies Rockefeller commissioned from the new Bureau of Social Hygiene exemplified a policy-oriented form of sexual science. In the early twentieth century, American research on sexuality lagged far behind European scholarship. Many European sexologists, including Magnus Hirschfeld and Havelock Ellis, studied sexual behaviors often deemed abnormal or pathological, particularly same-sex attraction, and argued for a greater acceptance of sexual minorities and a broader understanding of sexuality.[20]

In contrast, the Bureau of Social Hygiene focused on "the study, amelioration, and prevention of those social conditions, crimes, and diseases which adversely affect the well-being of society, with special reference to prostitution and the evils associated therewith." American sexual science concerned itself with heterosexual prostitution and its relationship to crime.[21] Moreover, by the mid-1910s, Freud's concept of libido, the powerful sexual instinct driving all humans, had found its way into American popular culture, convincing more Americans that sexuality deserved rigorous study.[22] While they saw sexuality as powerful, however, social hygienists rejected the common axiom that men required sexual release for their mental, physical, and moral health.[23]

As one of the Bureau of Social Hygiene's first actions, it built a Laboratory of Social Hygiene at the Bedford Hills Reformatory, where reformers could teach women charged with prostitution in New York City to "live a good and useful life."[24] Katherine Bement Davis, an experienced activist with a PhD in economics, became director. Despite her academic credentials, male Bureau leaders often tried to undermine her.[25] By studying incarcerated women, she aimed to identify the physical, psychological, and social causes and results of prostitution.

Davis described many of the women at Bedford as feeble-minded, showing the deep influence of eugenic thought on social hygiene. Half of the white women had foreign-born parents, far in excess of their proportion in the general population. Similarly, African American women were disproportionately represented at Bedford, likely in part because police more aggressively targeted them and because few other institutions would accept "colored" women. Black women composed 13 percent of inmates, despite only making up 2.4 percent of the population of New York City in 1910. Most of the women at Bedford had fathers who worked as unskilled laborers and mothers who worked outside of the home. Most had toiled in unskilled jobs or domestic service themselves. More than one in five reported that their first sexual experience had occurred by force.[26]

To Davis and the Bureau of Social Hygiene, the data suggested that African Americans and the daughters of poor and working-class immigrants sold sex more often than native-born, middle-class white women. Davis did admit that police disproportionately arrested these women because they solicited on the street, while higher-class women worked out of sight in hotels. Yet, she argued, her data accurately reflected the realities of prostitution. To social hygienists,

Davis had proved that their anti-prostitution efforts should target poor, working-class, and African American women.[27]

Since the Bureau could not study policies to combat prostitution in a laboratory setting, comparative studies gave the best approximation of the scientific methods to which the Bureau of Social Hygiene committed itself. In the winter of 1911, Rockefeller hired Abraham Flexner, the brother of a trusted venereal disease researcher, to conduct a comprehensive investigation of prostitution in twelve European countries.[28] Flexner embraced a broad definition of prostitution. In Europe, police usually defined only registered women—or clandestine women they hoped to place on the registry—as prostitutes. But Flexner included a far broader range of women: "Prostitution will, therefore, in these pages be construed to mean more or less promiscuity—even transient promiscuity—of sex relationship for pay, or its equivalent."[29]

Despite Flexner's and Rockefeller's emphasis on scientific objectivity, both men's commitment to state repression of prostitution, rather than licensing, was evident in their correspondence. While in Paris, Flexner claimed: "I believe—and I can, I think, demonstrate—that *reglementation* [regulation] in Paris not only fails, but has practically collapsed."[30] Published in 1914, Flexner's *Prostitution in Europe* received widespread acclaim.[31] Regulation, Flexner argued, increased the supply of and demand for prostitutes, contributed to the spread of venereal disease, led to police corruption, and incited the traffic in women.

Perhaps most harmful, Flexner claimed, regulation perverted the proper role of government. "The modern state . . . is an organization charged with the positive duty of securing and promoting conditions which make for the welfare, happiness, and usefulness of every member of society." Although the state could not entirely eliminate prostitution, he conceded, the "whole weight of the state's power and influence, direct and indirect, must be thrown against [it] as wasteful, demoralizing, and infamous." In addition to demonstrating the socially destructive nature of regulation, *Prostitution in Europe* proclaimed it "by far the main factor in the spread of venereal disease."[32] For social hygienists, Flexner's work solidified the opposition between corrupt governance, regulated prostitution, and venereal disease on the one side, and Progressive governance, the repression of prostitution, and public health on the other.

Flexner's book amplified the long-standing American perception of Europeans as sexually immoral and backward. European countries, Flexner argued, placed far too few restraints on male sexuality. In his formulation, men possessed strong, dangerous sex instincts: the state should help to constrain and channel them into socially productive outlets, rather than toward the "perverse indulgence" of the brothel. The regulation of prostitution, he wrote, came from Europeans' lax attitude toward men and their "disregard of woman's dignity."[33] For Flexner, the government had a duty to keep sex within the bounds of marriage and family.

Arguing that a strong police force could aid the fight against prostitution, Flexner convinced Rockefeller to commission a study of the organization and methods of police in European cities. Flexner found them more effective than their American counterparts, with the notable exception of the morals police who oversaw prostitution.[34] To conduct the study, Rockefeller chose Raymond B. Fosdick, a lawyer and experienced vice investigator and brother of the famous liberal minister Harry Emerson Fosdick. Fosdick's commitment to social reform and desire to rid New York City of municipal corruption made him one of Rockefeller's long-term allies.[35] After visiting twenty-one European cities, Fosdick acknowledged that, although regulated prostitution often led to corruption, European police were "an excellent piece of machinery."[36] Together, Flexner's and Fosdick's books framed prostitution as a problem of public order rather than private morality: modern police forces should thus suppress rather than license it.

Immediately, the ASHA put the Bureau of Social Hygiene's findings into action, promulgating new laws suppressing prostitution and ensuring their enforcement. The ASHA first targeted the country's remaining red-light districts. During the height of the war on white slavery, municipalities and states had adopted red-light abatement laws to eradicate commercial sex districts. While they did not criminalize prostitution itself, they fined the owners of buildings where prostitution occurred, particularly those selling alcohol and renting rooms. Such laws increased the surveillance of people and places social hygienists considered sexually immoral. Soon after its founding, the ASHA became a major force behind spreading these laws throughout the country.[37]

San Francisco's Barbary Coast stood as one of the country's most visible remaining red-light districts. In early 1915, the ASHA dispatched its assistant counsel, lawyer Bascom Johnson, to attack it. Johnson posed as a potential customer to gather evidence and helped a local resident bring a suit against the owner of a brothel for violating red-light abatement laws. Within two years, Johnson won between fifteen and twenty suits against brothels in the Barbary Coast.[38] Through its publications, policy recommendations, and investigations, the ASHA's national influence grew in the years before US entry into World War I, promoting a national consensus against both licensed prostitution and spatially segregated red-light districts.

"Vice Conditions" on the Border

As Europe descended into war, a military conflict closer to home gave social hygienists an opportunity to reshape US military prostitution policy. In 1916, the US military entered a border war with Mexico after the popular revolutionary leader Pancho Villa attacked Columbus, New Mexico. Secretary of War Newton Baker sent Brigadier General John J. Pershing, who had served in the Philippines, to lead troops into the Mexican state of Chihuahua in pursuit of Villa. The expedition brought 12,000 regular soldiers to the border, along with multiple national guard units.[39] On the border, Pershing followed the policy codified in the Philippines—tolerated and regulated prostitution—albeit in ways largely invisible to the American public. Regulated prostitution remained the safest way, he and other military officials believed, to protect US troops from Mexican women, while allowing them to achieve necessary sexual release.

Indeed, Pershing's own personal life illustrated the assumptions on which military policy rested. While in the Philippines, he had lived with a Filipina mistress, as many soldiers did, based on the idea that men required sexual intercourse and female companionship. The relationship produced two children. Pershing's experience thus demonstrated another rationale behind regulated prostitution. Regulation alone provided sexual outlets for men without the threats posed by longer term relationships, particularly interracial ones.[40]

But keeping regulated prostitution invisible proved difficult, particularly when it occurred on the US side of the border. Soon rumors circulated that "vice conditions," including prostitution, proliferated around military camps. Representatives from the ASHA and the YMCA met with Secretary of War Baker. As mayor of Cleveland, Ohio, Baker had mounted a campaign against dance halls, so he sympathized with their concerns. Baker appointed Raymond Fosdick to investigate the situation, and Dr. Max J. Exner of the YMCA went as well.[41]

As Fosdick reported, prostitutes were "flocking" to border towns. In San Antonio, which had a large military base, he saw 500–600 soldiers in the red-light district; on payday the number rose to 1,500. Fosdick visited thirteen towns in Texas, Arizona, and New Mexico, where each military officer imposed his own rules. In Laredo, Texas, for example, the commander made local authorities examine the women in the red-light district for venereal disease. In Douglas, Arizona, both military and town officials issued licenses to women who submitted to two examinations for venereal disease. The military collaborated so closely with the sex industry in Douglas that soldiers regularly worked as pimps and bartenders to make money on the side.[42]

Fosdick and Exner found that commanders instituted racialized forms of regulated prostitution, as they had in the Philippines. In Columbus, New Mexico, military officials "set aside two restricted districts, one for Black and one for white soldiers, located on the edge of the encampment."[43] This policy addressed concerns that equal access to prostitutes would subvert racial hierarchy. In contrast, at his headquarters near Colonia Dublán, Pershing allowed a Chinese man to build shacks inside the camp to house Mexican prostitutes. Since Pershing's camp included white, Black, Native American, and Japanese men, anyone could visit these Mexican women without crossing the highly charged black-white color line. Pershing ordered his men to surround the shacks with barbed wire, leaving only one way in and out. As men exited, physicians gave them "prophylaxis," the military's term for preventative treatment soon after exposure to venereal disease.[44] Although individual commanders shaped their own policies, all regarded interracial sex as a temptation and danger to white men.

Social hygiene reformers, too, believed that interracial sex on the border was dangerous to white soldiers and their families. In Brownsville, Texas, Fosdick reported the presence of one thousand clandestine Mexican prostitutes "afflicted with a virulent form of syphilis known among the troops as 'Indian syphilis,'" reflecting the common conception that people of color harbored disease.[45] If the military continued its practice of tolerated vice on the Mexican border, Exner warned, "not only will these men bring back . . . a vast volume of venereal disease to wreck the lives of innocent women and children, but they will bring back . . . other influences, attitudes, and practices which will destroy homes, cause misery, and degenerate society."[46] During the militarization of the US–Mexico border, white US officials increasingly understood Mexicans as racial others.[47] Social hygienists' fears about the dangers of prostitution were built on racialized stereotypes of Mexican women as dirty and dangerous, transmitting corrupt sexual practices as well as venereal diseases to soldiers and, ultimately, threatening their white wives.[48]

Fosdick's and Exner's reports employed older tropes about the sexual dangers of women of color, visible in turn-of-the-century military and social purity rhetoric about Filipinas. Yet they signaled significant changes in Americans' arguments against regulated prostitution. The two professional men stated their opposition on "scientific" rather than moral grounds. Fosdick condemned the medical examination of prostitutes as "crude and unscientific," rather than as a violation of women's bodies, as women reformers at the turn of the century characterized it. In keeping with other Progressive reformers, Fosdick believed that the military needed a "uniform policy" developed by men of "modern training and scientific spirit." Both Exner and Fosdick worried about the minds and bodies of men, stressing the "demoralizing" effects of encounters with prostitutes on young men's health and sexual development.[49] The reports used the language of social and medical science to recast moral convictions about the ills of prostitution in terms of military preparedness, racial strength, and masculinity.

In contrast to the conflict between the reformers and the military in the Philippines, during the border war military officials at the highest levels shared reformers' concerns. Although Fosdick's report remained confidential, Exner published his report in the ASHA's *Journal of Social Hygiene* in April 1917. Exner recounted the response it aroused: "Numerous organizations and individuals all over the country brought pressure to bear at Washington. . . . with letters urging action."[50] Public outrage, combined with effective lobbying, spurred a revolution in military attitudes toward regulated prostitution on the eve of US entry into the Great War.

The Mexican border investigations solidified two key premises of US military prostitution policy. First, it recognized women, particularly foreign and racialized women, as the primary disease vectors. Second, it proclaimed sexual continence as the healthiest option for men. As Exner argued, military policy "must be based on the assumption that sexual indulgence is unnecessary."[51] The presence of prostitutes, he claimed, actually created demand for sex, rather than the reverse. By bringing together an older vision of women as sexually dangerous with a new vision of male sexual continence, reformers articulated a new approach to prostitution. Instead of controlling women through regulated prostitution, safeguarding troops required removing "the artificial excitations surrounding prostitution" by eliminating the prostitutes themselves.[52]

Presciently, Fosdick realized that a new military policy on prostitution could have effects beyond the armed forces. While many people still saw prostitution as a necessary evil of military life, "a strong word from the War Department would help to remove this impression and stimulate the growth of a healthier public opinion." Citizens in border towns repeatedly told Fosdick that they would fight prostitution if it helped the war effort. With the military leading the way, social hygienists believed, the war could initiate a national crusade to stamp out the sex trade entirely.[53]

Keeping "Fit to Fight"

The war in Europe had already raised Americans' concerns over sexual morality and venereal disease, as European militaries reported staggering infection rates. The rise of sexual science in Europe had spurred new research into sexually transmitted diseases and their dangers. German researchers had identified the bacterial cause of syphilis, *Spirochaeta pallida*, in 1905, and a year later a German scientist had developed the diagnostic Wasserman test, although it had a high incidence of false positives. In 1909, researchers developed the arsenic compound Salvarsan as an effective treatment for syphilis, but its toxicity caused painful side effects and the medical community did not universally accept it until the 1920s.[54]

In addition to leaving soldiers unable to fight, venereal diseases caused immense suffering among civilians. Syphilis and gonorrhea not only harmed those infected, leading to paralysis, dementia, sterility, and even death, but could also cause stillbirth, as well as blindness and severe cognitive impairment in children born to infected parents. Anti-vice campaigners expressed outrage that "innocent" wives and children suffered from venereal diseases contracted by "profligate" men.[55]

For social hygienists to achieve their goal of prohibiting prostitution and creating a sexually moral soldiery, they would have to seize control of military policy. In the spring of 1917, as the government prepared to enter the war in Europe, Secretary Baker asked Raymond Fosdick to study conditions in and around Canadian training camps, in operation since 1914. Drawing on his observations in Canada and Mexico, Fosdick suggested a policy whose object was "two-fold: it would try to keep the territory surrounding the camps but outside the jurisdiction of the military authorities decent and respectable, and it would promote recreation facilities which would draw the soldiers away from questionable and unhealthy amusements." A national commission would ensure "a definite policy for all camps . . . not left to the judgement and discretion of the individual camp commander."[56] A fortnight after the US declaration of war, Baker created the Commission on Training Camp Activities (CTCA) and appointed Fosdick as its chairman.

Two provisions in the Selective Service Act shaped the Commission's campaigns against prostitution. As the Senate Military Committee drafted the Act, Fosdick went before it to attest to the terrible conditions he found in training camps during the Mexican border war.[57] The Committee responded by including Sections 12 and 13 in the Act, which gave the President the power to prohibit alcohol and prostitution near military encampments. Wilson placed the CTCA in charge of enforcement. The Act prohibited keeping a brothel within a five-mile zone around army camps. Congress soon extended Sections 12 and 13 to apply to naval bases as well, and then expanded the zone of prohibition to a ten-mile radius.[58] These zones served as new jurisdictional spaces in which CTCA officials could prohibit and police prostitution, a task that previously fell under the purview of state and local officials.

The ASHA quickly took advantage of this unparalleled opportunity. William F. Snow encouraged every male member of the ASHA staff to enlist in the military so they could join the war against prostitution and venereal disease.[59] Fosdick filled the CTCA with well-known Progressive reformers. On the recreation side, Fosdick appointed YMCA leaders. To address the problems of prostitution and venereal disease, Fosdick chose men who were active in the ASHA. He placed Snow in charge of the Social Hygiene Division, which would inform the military and civilian population about the dangers of venereal disease, while Bascom Johnson headed the Law Enforcement Division, tasked with eliminating prostitution (fig. 4.1). In addition to prostitution, the CTCA targeted alcohol, claiming drink led to sexual promiscuity.

The Commission also facilitated cooperation among military officials, civilian reformers, and local governments to implement the military's social hygiene program. As an army officer remarked, since "civil officials are loath to take action upon request of military officials, . . . civil persons by cooperating with the Army could aid materially in getting rid of many of these undesirables surrounding camps."[60] Such cooperation also gave national and local private anti-vice and social hygiene organizations new power to advance their anti-prostitution agendas.

Fosdick's close relationship with Rockefeller shaped the CTCA's programs. The Rockefeller Foundation funded its initial activities and continued to donate money to the ASHA and the Bureau of Social Hygiene throughout the war. Although private organizations like the YMCA had cooperated with the US military before, private philanthropy had never financed such a robust military-civilian partnership. Fearing controversy, military officials attempted to keep the source of this money under wraps. William C. Gorgas, the army's surgeon general, did "not wish the Social Hygiene Association to permit it to be generally known that gifts of this kind are being directly and fully applied to government activities." He assured them, however, that he felt "deeply appreciative of this cooperation" and "of the value of the measures which may be taken both inside and outside the Army, for the control of the venereal

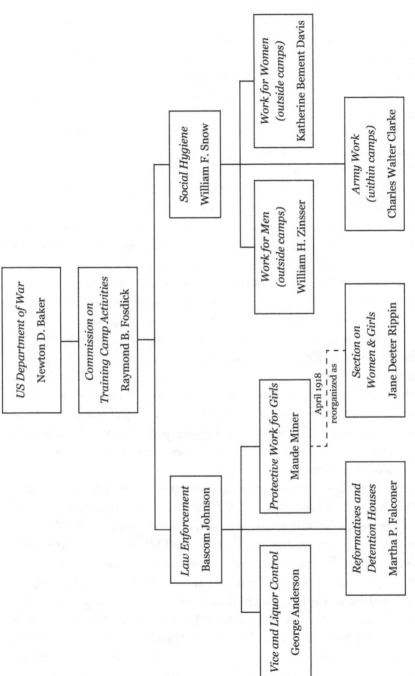

FIGURE 4.1. The leadership of the Commission on Training Camp Activities included many members of ASHA.

diseases."[61] Rockefeller funding underlay much of the coordinated attack on prostitution mounted by the CTCA and the ASHA.

To prevent soldiers from having any sexual contact with women, the Commission had to revolutionize older conceptions of military masculinity, which assumed men physiologically required sex. Moreover, it had to counteract concern that, without prostitutes, men would turn to rape, masturbation, or to other men for sexual release.[62] Before the First World War, the US military did not single out homosexual contact for punishment, considering same-sex intimacy as one of many "perverse" sexual acts it penalized.[63] The army's *Manual for Courts-Martial* listed sodomy as an offense for the first time in 1917, but defined it as anal penetration by a man of a person of either sex.[64] Masturbation, medical officials believed, similarly expended men's limited energy by unhealthy means. Using language at once euphemistic and graphic, one military lecturer told men to avoid illicit intercourse and "save every drop of your strength and manhood."[65]

As the first large-scale draft began in fall 1917, physical examinations of conscripts put venereal disease rates at 357 cases per 1,000, revealing the prevalence of disease among the civilian population.[66] In the spread of venereal disease, many white Americans saw their fears of "race suicide" coming true. The CTCA's new doctrine of male sexual self-control did not deny white American men's virility; instead, it saw men's sexual energy as a powerful force to discipline and direct toward military and nationalistic ends. Sexual contact could maintain or threaten racial purity. Performed correctly, it made respectable wives and mothers, but if conducted illicitly it made prostitutes; through it, future generations could progress or degenerate. Men's morals and bodies both were at stake.[67]

Education was the first step toward creating sexually continent men. The thirty-two new training camps across the country, whose populations could swell to more than 50,000 each, allowed CTCA officials to easily reach millions of soldiers.[68] The Army Surgeon General issued the booklet *Keeping Fit to Fight* to all troops. "The only sure way to escape venereal diseases is to keep away from loose women," it decreed.[69] Soldiers received pamphlets with titles like "Hello, Soldier Sport, Want to Have a Good Time?" (fig. 4.2) and a cover that featured a drawing of a pretty woman with a come-hither look, but inside declared, "IT'S A 90 TO 1 SHOT THAT SHE'S POISONED." As the pamphlet noted, "A German bullet is a damn sight cleaner than a whore."[70] The ASHA also issued the image as a placard to hang in training camps, positioning white American women as potential enemies of soldiers and of the broader war effort.

"Hello, Soldier Sport, want to have a Good Time?"

FIGURE 4.2. ASHA produced many pamphlets and posters that portrayed women as both alluring and dangerous. Image courtesy of the Social Welfare History Archives.

The military employed a range of tactics to convey their message. In training camps, men attended lectures declaring the "purpose" of the "sex impulse" was "marriage and reproduction," while "continence" was "healthy and not unmanly."[71] They watched the film *Fit to Fight*, which chronicled the experiences of five enlisted soldiers: two remained fit for deployment, while the other three found themselves hospitalized with venereal disease, alongside other "useless slackers."[72] They viewed traveling hygiene exhibitions mounted by the ASHA, which included graphic images of syphilitic lesions.[73] In just one week in May 1918, 177,050 men received pamphlets while 66,314 attended lectures.[74] To provide men with wholesome ways to release excess energy, Commission officials promoted basketball and boxing.[75]

Commission on Training Camp Activities officials did not put the same energy into molding "fit" Black soldiers as they did white soldiers. For "colored troops," the Commission provided "no constitutive social hygiene work, no lectures nor exhibits . . . no recreations . . . no athletic contests nor games . . . no reception tent for visitors."[76] Indeed, as historians have shown, the US military replicated the racist hierarchies of American society, at a time when lynch mobs across the country terrorized Black men because of their alleged sexual desire for white women, while Jim Crow laws stripped African Americans of fundamental rights.[77] In the US Army and National Guard, men served in segregated units. War Department policy consigned Black men to menial positions in the navy, with the marines open only to white men. Nevertheless, nearly 400,000 African Americans served in the military during WWI.[78] In the face of official neglect, African American communities near training camps provided what services and entertainment they could.[79]

The CTCA gave Black soldiers a "Colored Edition" of "Keeping Fit to Fight." While similar to the standard edition, this version presented more graphic information about what could happen to a man's penis if he contracted a venereal disease. The appeal to fear aligned with the Commission's strategy of preparing pamphlets for "a particular class of men," presumably Black, working-class, and immigrant men, whom officials believed could only be reached by "the frankest kind of appeal."[80] The "Colored Edition" drew on respectability politics to urge Black men to uplift their race through self-control: "Won't you do your part to make the world free and your race noble by living straight?," it implored.[81]

Such statements dangled the promise of racial equality—a reason many Black men did join the army—to encourage them to remain sexually self-restrained. Moreover, this emphasis on respectability dovetailed with the rhetoric of the African American professional class about military service. In publications and speeches, they portrayed Black soldiers as moral, healthy, and brave, emphasizing what scholar Khary Oronde Polk terms the "sanitized" Black soldier as part of their claims for rights.[82]

In addition to these public campaigns of education and healthy recreation, the CTCA quietly expanded the military's program of venereal disease prophylaxis. The procedure consisted of cleansing the penis with bichloride of mercury and injecting a solution of silver salt into the urethra, after which the soldier pinched his urethra closed to retain the medicine for five minutes. The last step of the procedure involved rubbing the penis with greasy calomel ointment and wrapping it in a napkin.[83] The military constructed prophylaxis stations within or near most camps, and military orders required men to seek treatment after visiting a prostitute. Many soldiers found prophylaxis an unpleasant experience and avoided it. Moreover, it did not always prevent disease.[84] To find hidden cases, military medical officials continued their biweekly inspections of soldiers for venereal disease, a practice they initiated in the Philippines in 1901 and subsequently imported to mainland camps.[85]

Social hygiene reformers knew prophylaxis remained controversial; some considered it a means of "making vice safe."[86] Secretary of the Navy Josephus Daniels agreed and banned the construction of naval prophylactic stations.[87] The majority of social hygienists, however, were convinced that the goal of a "clean" army required this medical measure. Although proper white masculinity rested on sexual self-control, they acknowledged the sometimes overwhelming temptation posed by prostitutes. As YMCA physician Max Exner argued, many soldiers had only reached adolescence, when "desire is strong and the will is weak." Moreover, he worried, the training camps thrust white, middle-class men into contact with working-class, immigrant, and African

American men, which might degrade their morals.[88] Prophylaxis, social hygienists believed, could at least keep these men free of disease, even as it revealed the fallibility of their self-control.

Military officials used prophylaxis as a core strategy to reduce disease rates among African Americans, whom they deemed sexually uncontrollable. Moreover, white officials believed that many, if not most, African Americans harbored venereal disease, particularly syphilis.[89] This opinion stood in marked contrast to the white medical establishment's previous consensus that African Americans had immunity to tropical diseases such as yellow fever, which made them valuable soldiers in tropical climates.[90] White officials backed up their assumptions about Black sexuality with statistics showing far higher rates of disease among Black troops, with six out of ten diagnosed with a venereal disease compared to one out of ten white troops. These statistics likely reflected officials' own biases, as well as the deliberate effects of military policies. Conscription boards often allowed African American men with syphilis to join the military but rejected white men with the same illness. Moreover, the poor or non-existent health care available to most African Americans contributed to higher rates of disease.[91]

Based on their vision of African American soldiers as hypersexual and syphilitic, some training camps began to institute mandatory prophylactic treatments for Black soldiers returning from leave, regardless of exposure. If African American men could not uphold civilized sexual morality, then only prophylaxis could keep them from acquiring venereal disease. As historian Nancy Bristow has argued, the white leaders of the CTCA did not believe that they could transform African American men into sexually moral and self-controlled citizens.[92]

Eradicating the "Prostitute Herself"

For young women like Mamie Stapleton and Hattie Smith, whose story opened this chapter, the Great War created new opportunities and dangers. Much like hundreds of thousands of other Southerners in the period—both Black and white—the two women migrated from a rural area to a larger Southern city.[93] With men in training camps and overseas, more women entered the paid labor force in mills and factories. Yet this work paid meager wages.

Thus, to support themselves and their dependents, many women living near military encampments sold sex to the men stationed there, both to supplement factory and domestic work and in place of it. While officials did not record Stapleton's or Smith's rates for sex, white women in Atlanta often charged between $3 and $5 for a single sex act, making prostitution a lucrative occupation compared to $7 for a week of nine- or ten-hour days at the mill where the two women had worked.[94] That they traveled together, and repeatedly faced arrest together, suggests the strong attachments young women who faced social and economic precarity could form with one another as they attempted to make lives for themselves.

But social hygiene reformers did not see young women like Stapleton and Smith as vulnerable workers struggling to make ends meet. Instead, they argued, such women threatened the war effort. Publicly, social hygienists stressed their "positive" programs of education and recreation, offering an optimistic view of their ability to mold moral soldiers. More surreptitiously, they touted the scientific advances they had made in venereal disease prophylaxis. But many believed that only punitive legal measures aimed at women could curb prostitution and venereal disease.

By December 1918, the US government called for the "eradication from the field of the prostitute herself."[95] Social hygienists blamed prostitutes for most cases of venereal disease. As one US Public Health Service official estimated, "about 90 per cent of infections are due to women, and 10 per cent to men." For such women, "Law enforcement is the only method though which they can be reached, and if the law enforcement were strict enough, venereal disease could be wiped out."[96] As a result of these "law enforcement" measures, women became the exclusive targets of the CTCA's most punitive and carceral approach to venereal disease.

The Commission's Law Enforcement Division based its fight against prostitution on the ASHA's methods and hired experienced ASHA workers. It employed investigators to speak with local officials, as well as undercover agents who attempted to blend in and learn about the sexual economy firsthand. CTCA officials used their findings to recommended new state and municipal laws to police prostitution more effectively, based on models drawn up by the ASHA. After such laws went into effect, the Commission determined whether the laws worked and drew attention to failures in enforcement, generating a cycle of investigation and legislation.[97]

The CTCA's series of investigations in Hattiesburg, Mississippi, near Camp Shelby, typified its law enforcement work across the country. In July 1917, the Commission dispatched undercover investigator Paul Kinsie to Hattiesburg. His reports included detailed descriptions of individual women he labeled as prostitutes, including renditions of his dialogues with them, which he wrote in "Negro" dialect. The vice district, located in a Black neighborhood termed "Jungle Town," contained four white brothels that serviced white men and six "negro shacks which cater to black and white trade." Kinsie expressed such disgust at the "filthy condition" of the "negro houses" that he did not inspect them. Walking around one evening, however, Kinsie was solicited by three Black women "who offered to take me into an alley-way for twenty-five cents," but saw only one policeman on duty who did not interfere.[98]

CTCA officials often faced an uphill battle in implementing the American Plan. Many seasoned military men balked at the idea of preventing troops from having sex. The commander of Camp Shelby believed that regulated prostitution conserved men's health.[99] Moreover, Camp Shelby, twelve-and-a-half miles from Hattiesburg, stood outside the zone in which the Commission could enforce the federal ban on prostitution. In such cases, Commission officials had to work more closely with local governments. When local officials did not cooperate in closing red-light districts, a frequent occurrence, the Commission threatened to move the military camps, depriving towns of a valuable source of jobs and revenue.[100]

In Hattiesburg, the municipal government proved cooperative—or at least aware of its self-interest. A month after Kinsie's investigation, Bascom Johnson arrived in Hattiesburg and suggested new measures to prohibit prostitution. The brothels Kinsie saw had disappeared, but now individual women walked the streets selling sex. Johnson particularly worried about the "elusive automobile prostitute," who conducted her trade in a car. Johnson adopted a strategy from earlier anti-vice campaigns: targeting behaviors closely associated with prostitution. At his suggestion, the town's commissioners passed a curfew law, tightened vagrancy ordinances, and enacted ordinances specifically forbidding prostitution in rooming houses and automobiles. The commissioners increased police presence on the streets and added a woman police officer to the force.[101]

In September the CTCA sent a third investigator to Hattiesburg to observe the city's progress. He reported succinctly: "Excellent from every point of view." He found little evidence of houses of prostitution. "The former restricted district . . . is in utter darkness." Yet now soldiers traveled to Gulfport, Mississippi, about eighty miles away, in search of sex and alcohol. He therefore recommended an expansion of the Commission's work to Gulfport.[102]

The example of Hattiesburg illustrates larger trends in wartime prostitution policy across the country. President Wilson had given the CTCA broad powers, which investigators and officials exercised forcefully. Investigators penned hundreds of reports about conditions around camps. Within the exclusion zones, they arrested women on federal charges.[103] Commission officials also attempted to create new exclusion zones by finding small training corps in or near cities and claiming they technically constituted camps, where the five-mile zone applied.[104]

Commission officials recognized the limitations on their power to control prostitution outside of the exclusion zones and the difficulties of rooting out clandestine prostitution. They thus dramatically increased the surveillance of women. Weekly reports on conditions near Camp Custer in Michigan, for example, included a daily log of whether any prostitutes had been seen by day or night, if anyone had been arrested, and if any rooms had been rented to unmarried soldiers with female companions.[105]

This surveillance gained teeth through new municipal and state "model laws" that the ASHA attempted to implement across the country, much as they did in Hattiesburg. These laws reconceptualized prostitution, defining it to "include the giving or receiving of the body, for hire, or the giving or receiving of the body for indiscriminate sexual intercourse *without hire*." Thus, any woman whom officials deemed promiscuous or who engaged in extramarital sex could also face arrest as a prostitute. The ASHA also recommended municipal and state laws to make "a single act of fornication" a misdemeanor. The model laws criminalized owning or occupying a "place," "structure," or "conveyance" for the purposes of "prostitution" or "lewdness," allowing the police to cast a far wider net.[106] Such laws provided federal officials and local police with more opportunities to interrogate and arrest people they suspected of being involved in prostitution.[107] When women whom Commission officials termed sexually suspicious moved elsewhere, Commission officials followed them, even if they went far from bases. Many cities and most states eventually adopted the ASHA's model laws, ensuring consistency across the country.[108]

Yet as CTCA officials worked to suppress vice, women who sold sex continued to evade them. They moved from brothels to rooming houses, hotels, and automobiles, and solicited on the street.[109] Although physically and mentally difficult, as well as dangerous, commercial sex provided a chance for women to earn far more money in far less time than in almost any licit employment. While native-born white women with native-born fathers earned an average of $7.91 per week in industrial work, many women with whom Commission officials spoke could earn the same amount in less than a day through selling sex.[110] Even as much of their profits often went to brothel keepers, hotel owners, and other go-betweens, women repeatedly told investigators that they sold sex because they needed to make money.[111] In Hattiesburg, for example, Kinsie found white women charging $3 for sex.[112] In Vallejo, California, two white women stated their prices as $10 for all night, $2 for "a short time."[113]

The kinds of sex on offer also changed over the course of the war. During the First World War, more men began to demand—and more women began to offer—oral sex, which investigators termed "perversion," as an alternative to vaginal intercourse.[114] In Hattiesburg, Kinsie reported, a brothel owner offered him "Lottie, a very young inmate, as a pervert" at one of the white houses.[115] For women, oral sex allowed them to service more customers and avoid pregnancy. For men, it presented an opportunity to engage in a salacious practice, often associated with the image of French brothel culture and seen as taboo within normative marital relations.[116]

Racialized Sexuality and Commercial Sex

As the example of Hattiesburg illustrates, race profoundly shaped the sex trade and attempts to suppress it. Brothels across the country remained segregated by race, with Black men denied entry to brothels reserved for white clients. In many brothels, white men had sexual access to Black women, while Black men could face violence for any sexual relationship with a white woman. As the CTCA's American Plan criminalized an increasing range of sexual activities, they pushed commercial sex into African American neighborhoods, such as "Jungle Town," just outside Hattiesburg. Moreover, the closure of red-light districts forced Black women into streetwalking, while white women could work more discretely and safely out of hotels or rooming houses.[117] The Commission's policies thus reinforced conceptions of Black criminality and created the very conditions they pointed to as evidence of Black inferiority.[118]

White social hygienists perceived Black women as inherently hypersexual, dirty, and diseased. One military physician characterized African Americans as "a notoriously syphilis-soaked race."[119] At the same time, however, many white citizens saw Black women as natural prostitutes by virtue of their supposed promiscuity. As Anne Grey Fischer has shown, this racial logic could lead state officials to variously target and neglect Black women.[120] At times, white officials arrested Black women for prostitution in disproportionately high numbers. For example, over the course of a year, the detention hospital in Newport News, Virginia held 160 African American women and forty-eight white women. After their release, officials apprehended and re-incarcerated twenty-three African American women, compared with two white women.[121] In Kansas, Black, working-class women made up one-third of women incarcerated even though African Americans represented 3 percent of the population.[122]

Yet in Southern cities in particular, many white citizens understood the brothel and the red-light district as an important tool of white supremacy.[123] The dictum of white men's sexual necessity, white women's sexual purity, and Black women's sexual availability often led local officials to selectively enforce the anti-prostitution ordinances decreed by the CTCA. The police in Macon, Georgia, wrote investigator Charles Walter Clarke, "do not give attention to men frequenting the negro section" of the city.[124] By tolerating the purchase of sex by white soldiers from Black women in Black neighborhoods, white officials attempted to keep white women safe from rape or solicitation. Indeed, despite the demand for sex created by nearby military training camps, a Macon official blamed Black women for the prevalence of prostitution: "holding down the social evil to a minimum is complicated in the South, when you consider the large percentage of our colored population, on account of the well- known high percentage of immorality that exists among the colored women."[125]

In fact, white soldiers sought out Black women for sex specifically because they charged less money than white women and had less control over their working conditions. On a night when "scores of negro prostitutes" walked the streets, investigator Paul Kinsie spoke with several white soldiers "looking for negros." As one told him, "a white Jane is all right on pay day, but dark meat is all we can get for two bits (25c). Many of these yellow gals never get the quarter either. After we ---- if she aint just nice, hit her a bust in the mouth and let her lay for dead in the alley."[126] The soldier's horrific comments to the investigator suggest an assumption that the military would not punish him for committing such violence. The men's pursuit of "yellow" women, indicating light-skinned Black women, spoke to such women's long-standing sexualization through institutions such as the fancy trade and quadroon balls, as well as the long history of white men raping enslaved and free Black women with impunity, often leading them to give birth to lighter-skinned children.[127]

Segregation both in and outside the South pushed and pulled Black women into the commercial sex industry. Before WWI, employers excluded Black women from higher paying, less strenuous jobs in factories, which they reserved for white men and women, instead relegating Black women to dangerous and dirty work.[128] Even after the start of the war, when more jobs became available to Black women, they received lower pay than white women for the same work. As Tera Hunter has shown, Black women protested these conditions collectively, with domestic workers in Atlanta organizing to demand fair wages. Although many Black and white wage workers won higher wages during the war, wages of most domestics did not increase.[129]

Sex work paid more than other kinds of employment and provided Black women one of the few paths out from under white employers' control. It permitted a greater degree of autonomy and offered more flexibility, allowing women to sell sex by night to supplement meager earnings from the labor they performed by day. Those advantages could particularly benefit Black women who juggled wage earning and childcare.[130] As in all forms of wage labor, Black women in commercial sex earned less than their white counterparts. For example, while white women in Hattiesburg brothels charged $3 for sex, Black women working on the street charged 25 cents.[131] In Northern cities the disparity also held. In the red-light district of Atlantic City, New Jersey, white women in the most expensive houses charged $5, while Black women charged $1.[132]

Still, Black women, like white women, could earn more money through sexual labor, in less time, than in the highest paying jobs available to them. During the war, unionized Black laundresses on government contracts earned $7.50 per week, an arrangement providing better wages and conditions than other work. Yet if a Black woman charged 25 cents per sex act, she needed only four customers per day to make the same amount of money as a unionized laundress would make working nine-hour days of hard physical labor, six or seven days a week.[133] Black women had to weigh the risks of abuse at the hands of a factory overseer, the white master or mistress of a household, and a male customer; and of dangerous labor in factories, backbreaking toil in white homes, and sex work in brothels and on the streets.

Black men also worked in the illicit sexual economy to supplement the low wages they earned in service jobs. In Atlanta, for example, Black hotel porters often solicited customers for white women who sold sex out of hotel rooms, in exchange for a portion of their earnings. As Kinsie explained, "by this method, of the clerk not admitting knowledge of what is going on in the hotel, it seems that in case of a police raid the porter would be held responsible for procuring the women. This method compares favorably to the shifting of responsibility from the Madam of a disorderly resort to her colored maid, in the event of a raid upon the place." In this way, the CTCA's attack on prostitution criminalized Black men as well as women. Although Black men risked arrest for their role in the commercial sex industry, Kinsie found many men participating in it.[134]

As CTCA investigators looked for signs of prostitution in African American and interracial neighborhoods, they also found other kinds of sexual vice, including evidence of same-sex prostitution. In Atlanta in 1919, Paul Kinsie scrutinized the Five Points neighborhood, home to Black and mixed-race dance halls and notorious for providing other forms of illicit entertainment.[135] According to Kinsie, "a number of homo-sexualists . . . nightly walk Peachtree St. They pick on the uniformed men. Several soldiers whom I had engaged in conversation admitted having pervert acts performed upon them by these fellows."[136] Since Kinsie did not mention the men's race, they were likely white.

But Kinsie took particular note of one man: "The most notorious of 'fairies' in town is a negro chef. . . . He is hailed by his clan as 'Black Pattie,' and has a nation wide reputation. Black Pattie in addition to his activities with soldiers and sailors is, according to admissions from prostitutes, a bi-sexualist."[137] In the early twentieth century, the terms bi-sexualist and fairy were largely interchangeable, both indicating a man with feminine characteristics, as well as someone who had sex with men and women.[138]

In pointing to Black Pattie's Blackness and perverse sexual appetite, Kinsie tied the myth of Black hypersexuality to same-sex sex, a perversion of "normal" sexuality he regarded as similar to prostitution.[139] As George Chauncey has shown, before World War II, working-class and African American culture often tacitly accepted gender and sexual fluidity. In fact, Black Pattie's moniker suggests a kind of celebration of race, gender performance, and sexual prowess. Black Pattie likely borrowed their name from famed Black opera singer Sissieretta Jones, nicknamed "the Black Patti," who performed throughout the United States and Canada.[140] That Black Pattie took the name of the highest paid African American female entertainer in the early twentieth century points to a proud self-fashioning and transgression of white middle-class racial, gendered, and sexual norms, as well as those espoused by Atlanta's Black middle class.[141]

"Detention Houses and Reformatories"

As the war went on, the CTCA expanded its focus from professional prostitutes to all women and girls who might have sex with soldiers, including white girls whom they had previously viewed as sexually innocent. Fosdick created the Committee on Protective Work for Girls in September 1917, responding to fears that "young girls are flocking to our camp towns, attracted by the khaki." Henrietta S. Additon, the assistant director of the Commission's programs for women and girls, observed a new and "unusual type of prostitute" who "spring[s] up in time of war." She recounted: "One such girl said that she had never sold herself to a civilian but she felt she was doing her bit when she had been with eight soldiers in a night."[142] Some women also exchanged sex for gifts and nights out on the town, leading reformers to term them "charity girls."[143]

Commission officials realized they needed more authority to reach these women and girls. At their urging, Congress expanded the scope of federal oversight when it unanimously passed the Chamberlain-Kahn Act in July 1918. The legislation extended the Commission's jurisdiction from the five-mile zones around military encampments to the entire country. It created the Interdepartmental Social Hygiene Board and empowered the War Department to adopt new measures to confine and treat civilians who carried venereal disease.[144]

The Commission also expanded the policing of prostitution, continuing to push state and local governments to enact the ASHA's model laws, which criminalized all consensual, extramarital sex, even if not for pay.[145] By 1920, thirty-two states had adopted portions of the ASHA's model laws, while ten states had passed them as written.[146] Women had little recourse after an arrest. While courts occasionally overturned these American Plan laws, most upheld them, affirming the police powers of the state.[147]

If all women were potential prostitutes, they were also possible vectors of venereal disease. The Commission encouraged state legislatures to pass laws requiring the detention and medical inspection of anyone "reasonably suspected" of carrying venereal diseases and making them subject to arrest and quarantine for treatment.[148] Many states also criminalized the act of exposing another to venereal disease. By the end of 1918, forty-two states had passed laws with such provisions.[149] If a physician diagnosed a woman with venereal disease, often through a rudimentary examination, he could detain and treat her using injections of arsenic-based drugs as well as mercury.[150] One public health official estimated that detention houses and reformatories admitted 16,943 women and girls, 15,520 of whom received venereal disease treatment. Detention houses held women for an average of 140 days, while reformatories held them for an average of one year.[151]

The expansion of federal and state public health boards combined with the criminalization of a broad range of sexual acts and behaviors worked together to give the government vast new powers over women's bodies. A range of state agents—from federal and state public health boards, to local police, to military officials—could arrest and detain any woman they deemed sexually suspicious. These arrests rested entirely on the discretion of the arresting official.

Eugenicist conceptions of poor white and Black women as "feeble-minded," and thus sexually immoral, drove officials to arrest such women in large numbers. Researcher Elizabeth S. Kite worked with the Commission on Train-ing Camp Activities to "clean up" several towns in New Jersey. At her sugges-tion, local officials arrested multiple female relatives of the white, sexually promiscuous, "mental defective" Millie Norcross, with plans to commit them to state detention homes. Kite did not mention any specific charges leading to the arrest of thirteen-year-old Esther Cramer, Millie's distant cousin, but de-clared, "it is in her blood to be bad." While she noted the death of Cramer's mother, leaving her to care for her father and baby sister, it did not seem a significant causal factor. Kite, and officials working with her, assumed that they could recognize sexually promiscuous and mentally defective women and girls simply by knowing their family tree or examining their faces. They arrested girls and placed them in detention homes on this basis.[152]

Indeed, poverty, more than any other factor, determined whom officials decided to arrest for prostitution. Case records showed that many women detained as prostitutes had left school and gone to work at or before the age of fourteen. Many women reported their earliest "sex experience" at or before the age of fourteen. Two reported that they had been seven, suggesting that the American Plan actually targeted particularly vulnerable women and girls with histories of rape and sexual abuse.[153]

Public health officials trumpeted their success at rounding up more than 30,000 sexually immoral women through the wartime American Plan.[154] In comparison, US officials arrested approximately 6,000 people for pro-German sentiments, suggesting the importance the government placed on anti-prostitution work.[155] The American Plan saw the detention of some men, yet only in small numbers. In Michigan, for example, over the course of a year officials incarcerated 1,072 women and forty-nine men for venereal disease treatment.[156] Although, CTCA officials pointed out, both men and women "passed through the same medical mill," an article in the Social Hygiene Bulletin explained the imbalance: "as infected men are more frequently wage earners and infected women often economic parasites, it is often found desirable to put men on parole."[157]

Women in detention houses faced harsh treatment, including spoiled and inadequate food, corporal punishment, cold-water baths, physical restraints, hard labor, and solitary confinement.[158] Doctors charged with overseeing treat-ment administered painful injections of mercury and arsenic compounds that left women's arms swollen and sore and could lead to loose teeth, liver failure, and death. Doctors swabbed women's urethras and cervixes with caustic chemi-cals and inserted tampons soaked in irritating disinfectants into their vaginas.[159]

SLEEPING VERANDA FOR WHITE GIRLS AT LIVE OAK FARM,
SAN ANTONIO, TEXAS

FIGURE 4.3. Photographs published in the *Journal of Social Hygiene* allowed readers to see inside detention houses and reformatories. These images should also be understood as propagandistic efforts to convince the public and the government to fund such facilities.

Barbed wire surrounded many facilities and guards ensured women could not leave.[160] Cities without a detention hospital or reformatory held women in jails.

Detention house officials enforced racial segregation, in part because they feared Black women would seek lesbian relationships with white women. Living conditions for white women were far better than those of African American or Mexican American women.[161] An article by Jane Deter Rippin, director of the Law Enforcement Section on Women and Girls of the CTCA, included photographs of detention centers. Such photos likely served, at least in part, as a call for increased federal government funding for detention facilities. The images emphasized the cleanliness and home-like accommodations for white women (fig. 4.3). In contrast, the only photograph to depict women's faces showed African American women housed in a former jail (fig. 4.4). In the

THE FORMER PRISON AT SPARTANBURG, S. C.

FIGURE 4.4. Black women and girls, as well as white women, were at times housed in city and county jails rather than reformatories or detention houses. The overcrowded conditions captured in this photograph from the *Journal of Social Hygiene* are a marked contrast to the more comfortable setting depicted in fig. 4.3.

foreground women lay two-to-a-bunk, with one woman sitting on a floor littered with debris. In the middle ground the bars separating the cells reinforced the punitive nature of the space.[162]

Incarcerated women forcefully protested their mistreatment. For example, an incarcerated woman set fire to City Farm, a detention hospital in Houston, Texas, and one year later the institution burned again.[163] Women at City Farm refused to work, rejecting the household tasks that would supposedly reform them. Women often attempted escape, sometimes successfully. At City Farm, fifty-three of 450 women escaped in a single year, while seventy-six women escaped from the Jacksonville, Florida detention house over a year and a half. Officials pursued these escaped women with vigor. At San Francisco's City Hospital, they recaptured seven of the nine women who escaped.[164] Some women even brought court cases over the state's violation of their rights. With the assistance of wealthy and middle-class women, women who had been incarcerated filed lawsuits against local health officials and detention house supervisors. As Scott W. Stern has shown, these rarely succeeded.[165]

The CTCA's single-minded focus on incarceration brought middle-class white women into leadership positions to oversee detention facilities. They also formed the rank and file of the Commission's Committee on Protective Work for Girls, scouring cities and towns for potential prostitutes.[166] In fact, many suffragists aligned themselves with this "protective" work.[167] Social hygienists often advocated women's suffrage because they believed women would support their program with their votes.[168]

Yet the Commission's protective work largely excluded Black women and girls. Working through their own infrastructure, then, African American clubwomen took up protective work for Black women to protect them from soldiers' sexual advances.[169] At the same time, however, middle-class Black women called for the arrest of African American prostitutes, proving their own respectability and refuting the stereotype of Black promiscuity.[170]

As the CTCA's measures became increasingly punitive toward women, some women in leadership positions grew uneasy. Maude Miner, appointed to head the Commission's Committee on Protective Work for Girls in 1917, initiated a broad program providing moral education for white women and girls. Additionally, she created a new force of female "protective officers," who patrolled the streets for wayward girls in need of assistance. As the war progressed, however, officials incarcerated girls rather than enrolling them in recreation programs or sending them home. In April 1918 Miner resigned, explaining that she could no longer "see the girls' interests entirely subordinated to the interests of the soldier."[171] Many other women Commission officials, including Katherine Bement Davis, did not share her concerns and continued to oversee women's detention centers.[172]

With her protest, Miner echoed the older generation of American and British feminist abolitionist reformers who had decried the American Plan from the start, terming it "neo-regulation."[173] After all, they pointed out, under the new US policy, much like the French and British systems, officials could detain and genitally inspect any suspected prostitute, and subsequently incarcerate and forcibly treat her. Longtime feminist abolitionist reformer Dr. Katharine Bushnell argued that the American Plan violated two key principles of the abolitionist movement. First, "the person of no woman, good or bad, shall ever be compulsorily examined, for any purpose whatsoever—by either man or woman doctor." Second, "prostitution . . . cannot be usefully punished by law. . . . The punishment for the dual offense always falls on the woman."[174] Moreover, this policy fell hardest on poor, working-class, and African American women. As Bushnell rightly pointed out, the American Plan replicated the logic of regulation, calling for the sacrifice of some women's civil rights to supposedly keep men and "respectable" women safe.

The feminist abolitionists who had initiated the first major campaign to abolish state-regulated prostitution argued that it stripped women of their civil liberties and placed the sexual desires of men above poor and working-class women's welfare. In contrast, social hygiene reformers in the Commission on Training Camp Activities opposed regulated prostitution on the grounds that it harmed men, regarding it as unscientific, unhygienic, and the cause of venereal disease and moral decay among soldiers. During the war, social hygiene reformers' fight against regulated prostitution turned into a US government attack on any woman suspected of prostitution, who had to endure genital inspection and detention for the good of society as a whole.

Despite the violation of women's bodies in the name of curing disease and protecting soldiers, the CTCA's efforts did not crush the commercial sex industry. Instead, they often sent it underground, making women's lives more precarious and dangerous. The prevalence of prophylactic treatment given to men, coupled with the Commission's ongoing campaign against prostitution, suggest the Commission's efforts did not prevent soldiers from having sex. But they did succeed in empowering local, state, and federal officials to exert new and far-reaching control over women.

Conclusion

The status of the ASHA as a professional organization, funded by John D. Rockefeller, Jr., a powerful businessman and philanthropist, solidified the partnership between reform-minded experts and the state. This alliance facilitated the movement of reformers into official civil and military positions during the war. World War I, Christopher Capozzola has shown, transformed popular understandings of the obligations of citizens to the state.[175] During the war, the private sexual activities of soldiers and civilians became a matter of public concern. The state became the rightful entity to fight venereal disease, prostitution, and sexual immorality of any kind, lest it harm the war effort and the country. The expansion of federal authority and the massive troop mobilization during the wartime emergency gave social hygienists a degree of control

previously unimaginable. Now they had the power to impose their most restrictive and punitive policies on women, particularly poor, working-class, and
Black women.

To social hygienists, the American Plan provided clear evidence of American sexual exceptionalism. In the words of one public health worker, the
American Plan was "the answer of a young, idealistic, essentially clean-thinking
nation to a problem that has baffled civilization for centuries. It is America's
contribution to a public health question of international scope."[176] Indeed, the
US government took a uniquely prohibitionist approach to prostitution: all
other militaries expected soldiers to visit prostitutes. Moreover, the populace
willingly embraced such policies. In Britain, for example, popular protest led
to the swift repeal of a wartime regulation making it illegal for a woman infected with a venereal disease to solicit or have intercourse with a soldier,
though laws against solicitation remained on the books.[177] In the United
States, in contrast, police could arrest any woman whom they suspected of
having a venereal disease and hold them for testing until the 1970s.[178] And
prostitution prohibition is still the law everywhere in the United States save
ten counties in Nevada.

The US military also stood out for its restrictions on prophylactic technolo-
gies, providing only post-intercourse treatment for men. British, German, Australian, and New Zealand militaries all distributed rubber condoms to their
troops. In the United States, in contrast, the manufacture and interstate transport of condoms remained illegal under the Comstock Law until January 1918.
In fact, American rubber-goods manufactures provided an important, though
surreptitious, supply of condoms for Allied militaries. Still, in the eyes of many
US military officials and members of the ASHA, condoms or treatments administered before rather than after sex only encouraged immorality.[179]

Despite the CTCA's efforts, popular sexual culture in the United States
became increasingly permissive during the war, and would grow even more so
in the 1920s. As scholars have shown, the commercial sex industry did decline
in decades after the war, but only because Americans engaged in more premarital and non-marital sex, rendering the exchange of sex for money less
necessary.[180] The postwar period also brought a new recognition of female
sexual desire, a double-edged sword for women under a legal regime that considered any "loose" woman as a potential prostitute and disease vector.[181]

Even with the advent of what scholars have termed the "first sexual revolution" in the 1920s, the wartime crackdown on prostitution had lasting effects.[182] Alongside the ongoing policing of prostitution, the racist legacy of the

CTCA's programs continued in the government's supposedly scientific studies of venereal disease. Significantly, the creators of the Tuskegee syphilis study had worked in various positions overseeing and enforcing the fight against venereal disease during and after the war. This infamous study, initiated in the 1930s, purposely denied African American men treatment for syphilis, instead using them as an experimental control group, without their knowledge.[183] The logic of the American Plan remained visible in the study: federal, local, and state officials had the right to control the bodies of those whom they believed incapable of self-control to improve the health of the nation, regardless of the harm caused to those individuals.

When social hygiene reformers evaluated the success of the American Plan, they compared US cities to foreign ones. "Looking abroad, . . . vice conditions in Paris, Berlin, London, Bucharest, Madrid, and elsewhere make Washington stand out as far and away the cleanest capital in the world."[184] In fact, feminist abolitionist reformers in Europe feared that Americans would spread "neo-regulation" to Europe and around the world, a reversal of the standard American narrative that dangerous prostitution policy emanated from Europe. As British suffragist and reformer Alison Neilans wrote, "America's influence on international problems is enormous and carries with it great responsibilities, and in no direction is this more marked than in international public health." She begged European reformers "to be careful that they do not even inadvertently strengthen States and Governments in their fatal designs anywhere by joining in demands for increased police powers over women."[185] As US troops traveled around the world during World War I, social hygiene reformers and US officials tried to do just that.

5

The Caribbean Laboratory

THE AMERICAN PLAN AND US EMPIRE

ON DECEMBER 11, 1920, police arrested Florencia Michel in San Pedro de Macorís, Dominican Republic, "for being a prostitute," a crime under a law recently imposed by the US military government. A native of the British West Indies, Michel was fined $25 and released from custody, but "immediately reconfined awaiting deportation." US authorities had mandated deportation for all migrant women who sold sex, a policy that targeted Black Caribbean women. Michel's re-imprisonment precipitated a conflict between US officials and Dominican judges over who had the right to police the moral and physical borders of the Dominican Republic. When the judges issued a writ of habeas corpus demanding Michel's release, US officials overruled them based on the US military government's power to enforce immigration law. In January 1921, after she had spent over a month in government custody, the military government deported Michel.[1]

During and immediately after World War I, US military and civilian officials in the Caribbean used the control of women's bodies as a crucial tool of empire. In debates over prostitution and venereal disease, US officials drew on modernizing discourses about public health and the protection of women.[2] First, US officials marshalled these discourses to enforce systems of state-regulated prostitution, in stark contrast to the American Plan of prostitution prohibition in place on the mainland. Yet just a year later, they would use these same discourses to implement the American Plan in the Caribbean, arresting and deporting women for prostitution—as they did Florencia Michel—and sometimes committing medical violence on their bodies.

US military officials—particularly medical officials—saw the Caribbean as a laboratory for testing American Plan. Most obviously, they enacted a policy experiment. Yet they did not follow the "colonial laboratory" model, in which governments tested policies in colonies and then imported them to the mainland.[3] Rather, US officials wanted to know if a policy designed for the US mainland, which they envisioned as a white, temperate space, could work in places they framed as racially dark, tropical, and less civilized. They also conducted a medical experiment. US military medical officials used local women as test subjects for venereal disease treatments. They sought to understand the supposed particularities of racially dark "tropical" bodies: could the American Plan "civilize" such people?

The implementation of the American Plan outside of the mainland was not a foregone conclusion. After the United States entered WWI on April 4, 1917, the American Social Hygiene Association (ASHA) had swiftly worked with the government to develop and implemented the American Plan on the mainland. Yet US officials in the Caribbean remained committed to licensing, not prohibiting, prostitution. They assumed that white men in the so-called tropics needed sexual release, and that all women there carried disease. They argued that the American Plan, designed for white US citizens, could not work in tropical climates inhabited by people of color. And they expressed concern that, without access to prostitutes, soldiers would turn to rape, masturbation, and same-sex contact, all of which threatened the image of white US soldiers' superiority to those they ruled.[4]

By late 1917, however, high-ranking military officials began to consider the American Plan's potential efficacy beyond the mainland. US officials first tested it in Puerto Rico, an unincorporated territory under US federal control, which they viewed as the most civilized of their Caribbean colonies. By the summer of 1918, US officials attempted to spread the Plan across the Isthmus of Panama, in both the Panama Canal Zone, a leased zone under US control, as well as in the Republic of Panama, a sovereign country where US officials had some jurisdiction over public health and exerted informal but coercive power over the government. By spring 1919, they implemented it in the Dominican Republic, a US-administered area under military authority. The US military also closed long-standing red-light districts in the Philippines and Hawai'i during the war. But in the Caribbean, US officials enacted a far-reaching policy experiment across different types of jurisdictions, inhabited by what they understood as different kinds of Latin American populations.[5]

US officials justified the American Plan in the Caribbean by arguing that it would morally and physically improve US soldiers and bring progress to colonized peoples of color. On the mainland, the Plan had more ambitious goals than prohibiting prostitution and arresting prostitutes. It also provided healthy recreation to curb soldiers' sexual urges (though for white troops only), specified that all soldiers receive venereal disease treatment, and offered programs to protect and reform supposedly wayward girls. It aimed to create, from an increasingly heterogenous population, upstanding American citizens.[6]

When US officials applied the American Plan in the Caribbean, however, they largely omitted its recreational and protective aspects. US officials in the Caribbean focused primarily on incarcerating women who sold sex, and on treating them—and soldiers—for venereal disease. Although the United States claimed the right to govern people in Puerto Rico, the Isthmus of Panama, and the Dominican Republic, it limited their rights and abnegated responsibility for their welfare.[7] US officials could thus enforce the carceral provisions of the American Plan far more strictly, subjecting women not only to mass arrest but to medical experimentation and sterilization.

Just as the US government advanced its interests through dictating prostitution policy, social and political elites in Puerto Rico, Panama, and the Dominican Republic used debates over prostitution to pursue their own projects of maintaining racial, ethnic, national, and class differences. At the same time, working people, including women who sold sex, used these debates to shore up solidarities. Whether they decided to embrace, resist, or be co-opted by US prostitution policy, people in each country did not simply react to US rule; they exerted political will and self-determination.

While the United States made itself an increasingly important force in the region, other dynamics profoundly shaped the Caribbean. Workers traversed long-standing inter-Caribbean routes of migration. Black migrants from the former French and British West Indies, and Chinese and South Asian labor migrants, traveled to South and Central America to work on plantations and construct the Panama Canal. The legacies of European imperialism and slavery marked the region. So did traditions of republican governance and nationalism. Pan-Africanist politics, West Indian organized labor movements, and Latin American traditions of science, eugenics, and public health flowed across political borders.[8]

Many valuable scholarly accounts of US imperialism in the Caribbean focus on the perspectives of people in Puerto Rico, the Isthmus of Panama, and the Dominican Republic.[9] While this chapter draws on that body of work, it says more about white, middle-class, US American constructions of sexuality, race, and civilization than it does about the people who lived under US colonialism. It shows how, by 1918, the ASHA members who created the American Plan had shaped a distinctive vision of sexual governance, which increasingly dictated US policy around the globe. It also demonstrates how local cooperation and resistance shaped US officials' policy successes and failures.

Although US officials claimed to civilize the Caribbean, they worried that this mission endangered the physical fitness and moral health of the largely white American soldiers who carried it out. The US military had encouraged African Americans to serve in Puerto Rico and Cuba at the turn of the twentieth century specifically because military medical officials believed they could better handle tropical climates. But during WWI, US military officials tended to imagine troops from the mainland as "fair-haired young" men from the "temperate zone."[10]

US officials argued that uncivilized men and women of color living in the tropics, particularly those of African descent, had high rates of venereal disease and could not control their sexual urges, while civilized white men from temperate regions possessed sexual self-control and had lower rates of disease.[11] But US officials were haunted by a suspicion that civilizational hierarchies might be mutable. Military medical doctors had moved away from the earlier presumption that white men could degenerate simply from being in a tropical climate, replacing it with a conviction that communicable disease caused degeneration. They labeled tropical peoples, particularly women of African descent, as its vectors. As Yale professor Ellsworth Huntington argued in 1915, "any young man of European race with red blood in his veins is in more danger of deteriorating in character and efficiency because of the women of the tropics than from any other single cause."[12]

US-Regulated Prostitution in the Caribbean

After the United States acquired Pacific and Caribbean territories following the War of 1898, US military and civilian officials oversaw systems of state-regulated prostitution in all of them. Even as Theodore Roosevelt, in 1902, proclaimed the US military's commitment to soldierly "self-restraint" in matters of vice, US officials continued to tolerate and regulate prostitution—albeit less detectably from the mainland—in US colonies. In each place, though, regulated prostitution took on different forms, shaped by local politics as much as by US goals.

US control of prostitution in Puerto Rico dated to 1898, after the US military occupied the country following its victory over Spain, despite many Puerto Ricans' claims to independent nationhood. At the time, Puerto Ricans were already debating how to manage prostitution as a means of maintaining social, racial, and gendered order. Puerto Ricans configured racial hierarchy based on factors including class status and family history, as well as skin color. As Eileen Findlay has shown, sexual respectability played a central role in constructing racial status.[13] In the 1890s, Puerto Rican elites successfully pushed for stricter registration and licensing requirements, aiming to protect bourgeois white women and families from ostensibly sexually suspicious working-class Black women. Regulating prostitution, in other words, helped distinguish Blackness from whiteness.[14]

In Puerto Rico, as in the Philippines and other former Spanish colonies, US officials initially continued the Spanish system of regulated prostitution with few alterations. In 1905, in the capital city of San Juan, Puerto Rican and US officials opened a "Special Hospital for Women" to inspect and treat prostitutes. Women received a "yellow ticket" that allowed them to legally practice prostitution so long as they reported to a women's hospital for regular pelvic examinations for venereal disease. Between July 1916 and June 1917, physicians at the Special Hospital for Women examined 1,540 women for venereal disease. If "clean," they could continue to sell sex. During that period, physicians administered a total of 46,858 outpatient and 13,907 inpatient treatments for venereal disease.[15]

Maintaining regulated prostitution in Puerto Rico marked the island as a racially dark and sexually immoral place to US officials and mainland US observers. A US medical official explained the high rates of venereal disease there by characterizing Puerto Ricans as the "offspring of the Spanish settler, his black slave, and mixture of the two races to all degrees. These men were born under the tropical sun."[16] Yet US officials had high hopes for their ability to civilize Puerto Ricans. Unlike the Cuban and Filipino people who had resisted US occupation, many Puerto Ricans—from elites to the working class—initially embraced US rule as a pathway toward liberation from Spanish colonialism. US officials used the supposedly hygienic regulation of prostitution and scientific treatment of venereal disease to legitimate US imperialism.[17]

While US officials understood Puerto Rico as standing midway between mainland civilization and tropical savagery, US officials set up the Isthmus of Panama to embody those two extremes. When they created the Canal Zone in 1903, US officials had taken a markedly different approach to prostitution from other US colonies at the time: they strictly prohibited the practice within the Zone's limits. They envisioned the Panama Canal Zone as a white American settler colony in the midst of the racially mixed Republic of Panama. As Julie Greene argues, many Americans saw the opening of the Panama Canal in 1914, just as Europe descended into war, as "a symbol of America's contribution to world civilization." Within the Zone, US officials upheld Jim Crow racial hierarchies by dividing workers into "gold roll" employees (largely white Americans) and "silver roll" laborers (primarily from the West Indies). Gold roll employees earned more money and had better housing, transportation, recreation, and health care.[18] US officials in the Canal Zone focused their attention on preventing the spread of diseases they believed harmed white people more than people of color, particularly syphilis.[19]

Just over the Canal Zone's borders lay the red-light districts of the two terminal cities of the Canal—Panama City and Colón. They remained part of the Republic of Panama (map 5.1). US Canal Zone officials believed that workers and soldiers in the Zone needed sexual release and viewed the red-light districts of Panama City and Colón "as a sort of safety-valve" that allowed men to blow off sexual steam while preserving the Zone's moral and racial purity.[20] US officials and civilians described the Republic as a place where "brown-eyed 'cholitas'" tempted Anglo-Saxon men, a "mongrel" place with a racial mix of "the original Indian substratum, the Spanish conquerors, Chinese railroad laborers, French colonials, Jamaicans, Barbadians, and other West Indian Negroes, Hindu coolies, Portuguese, Americans, British, and many others."[21] Canal Zone health officials' encouragement of prostitution in the terminal cities reflected a previously popular strategy on the mainland: pushing vice outside of city limits, often into poor, African American, and immigrant neighborhoods. In this way, Canal Zone officials shaped geographies of commercial sex to enforce racial segregation.[22]

While the border between the Republic and the Zone was porous, policing prostitution in the Zone made it more consequential. The many Afro-Caribbean women who migrated to the Isthmus to work as domestics, laundresses, seamstresses, and street vendors—some of whom engaged in sex for pay—stood out as particularly visible to US officials.[23] They termed these women "the worst and filthiest type," mirroring the language white Americans used to describe women who sold sex in Puerto Rico.[24] In 1912, Canal Zone officials had expelled so-called native settlements from the Zone, displacing the inhabitants of long-standing Black Panamanian and West Indian towns into the Republic. Since West Indian women could no longer live in the Zone, they had to cross the border each day as they traveled to work.[25] Moreover,

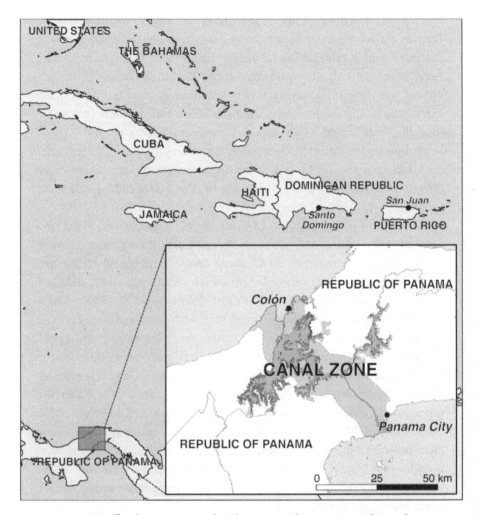

MAP 5.1. US officials experimented with enacting the American Plan in the Caribbean.

the flow of US men crossing into Panama in search of sex exacerbated tensions with the Panamanian government, demonstrating the extractive and exploitive nature of the larger US–Panama relationship.[26]

Although the US-controlled Canal Zone government exercised extensive administrative powers in Panama City and Colón, including exclusive control over "sanitary" issues, the Panamanian government retained police power, curbing US officials' ability to enforce prostitution policies.[27] Addressing prostitution in Panama City and Colón thus required diplomatic maneuvering, even for the powerful US government. Panamanian officials maintained the borders of the district, registered prostitutes, and mandated medical inspections. As US officials complained, though, they often enforced such regulations leniently.[28]

From the perspective of Panamanian officials, red-light districts were vital for maintaining racial and social order. Elite Panamanians argued that prostitutes shielded "decent Panamanian women" whom soldiers might rape if they could not access commercial sex. They also argued that immigrant Afro-Caribbean prostitutes protected "Panamanians of the lower classes" who otherwise might end up selling sex to US soldiers themselves.[29]

While US officials had to engage in coercive diplomacy to shape prostitution policy in the Panama Canal's terminal cities, they held more absolute control in the Dominican Republic. The Dominican Republic had been independent since it pushed out Spanish colonizers in 1865.[30] But the United States escalated military interventions in the region in the early twentieth century: in 1915, just a year prior to landing in the Dominican Republic, the US Marines had occupied Haiti, the other country on the island of Hispaniola.[31] In May 1916, the US government sent its all-white Marine Corps to occupy the Dominican Republic under the pretext of restoring "internal order" and in November placed the country under control of a US military government, headquartered in Santo Domingo. Dominicans across the social spectrum, from intellectual and political elites to poor workers in the sugar industry, hotly contested the invasion.[32] While US officials initially assured Dominicans that US rule would not destroy their sovereignty, in 1917 they suspended elections, abolished the legislative and executive branches of government, and appointed US military officers to administrative positions previously held by Dominicans.[33]

The US military government attempted to establish its legitimacy by promoting itself as the guardian of public health and women's rights. US military officials argued that Dominican racial and cultural heritage contributed to poor control of prostitution and venereal disease. The 800,000 occupants of the country, officials noted, comprised "a mixture of Spanish, Indian, and African, the negro element predominating and are noticeably Spanish in language, traditions and customs." "The women of this country," proclaimed a US military government publication, "are in need of a protection against the lust of men, which the law does not now afford."[34]

US officials worried about maintaining the health of troops stationed in the Dominican Republic, even though they numbered far fewer than in the Canal

Zone. When marines arrived, most cities maintained small red-light districts; others did not restrict or regulate prostitution.[35] As historian April J. Mayes has shown, Dominican elites used public health measures to control an increasingly racially and ethnically diverse population of workers. Cities such as San Padro de Macorís, the center of the sugar industry, instituted measures to confine prostitution to red-light districts located near Afro-Antillean and Puerto Rican neighborhoods.[36]

In addition to complaining about Dominican methods of policing red-light districts, US military physicians noted that Dominican physicians did not use modern medications and scientific methods in their venereal disease treatments.[37] US officials claimed that syphilis affected 70 percent of the population and led to criminal behavior and insanity. They pointed to the paucity of public health laws, including ones regulating prostitution, as evidence of the occupation's necessity.[38]

But they worried most about the safety of their own troops. Malaria and tuberculosis sickened and killed far more Dominicans than did syphilis, but US officials prioritized venereal diseases because they saw them as particularly harmful to white soldiers and, by extension, the white mainland population.[39] Regulated prostitution allowed white US Marines to satisfy their supposedly natural sexual urges with local women in a way relatively unlikely to lead to venereal disease, long-term partnerships, or mixed-race children.

Across the Caribbean, then, US military and civilian officials solidified their power by proscribing the forms that prostitution should take. They justified their presence by claiming that only their policy visions could protect women and improve public health. By enforcing state-regulated prostitution in Puerto Rico and the Dominican Republic; encouraging a particularly restrictive version of it in Panama City and Colón; and prohibiting prostitution altogether in the Panama Canal Zone, US officials constructed a civilizational ranking of the places they governed.

"The Porto Rican Experiment"

The unstable ground of global politics during World War I also shifted the US government's relationship to its colonies. In March 1917, as the United States stood poised to enter the war, Congress passed the Jones Act, which granted US citizenship to Puerto Ricans—or, as Puerto Ricans who advocated independence argued, imposed it upon them.[40] Puerto Ricans still did not have representation in Congress or the right to vote for President.

When it came to addressing public health, military officials had focused first—during the initial occupation of the island in 1898—on the health of occupying soldiers. Once the US entered the war, however, they became concerned with venereal disease rates among Puerto Ricans, now provisional citizens and potential soldiers, whose actions reflected on—and could harm— the mainland.[41] The territory was now "one of our own back doors," a Red Cross worker claimed, "and the back doors of our homes are the places where the germs come in."[42] The United States had to purify Puerto Rico if it did not want the mainland to become infected with the sexual disorder of its new citizens.

US officials used venereal disease statistics to depict Puerto Ricans as racially distinct from mainlanders, and distinctly dangerous. Initially, the US military drafted 12,000 Puerto Rican men and sent them to a camp near San Juan for training.[43] Herman Goodman, the US military medical doctor in charge of preventing venereal disease in wartime Puerto Rico, claimed that an astonishing 56 percent of men had syphilis, in comparison to 16 percent of white enlisted men and 36 percent of "colored" men on the mainland.[44] Such dramatic differences resulted from the US military's policies: the military instructed conscription boards in Puerto Rico to draft men even if they had syphilis. (Mainland boards also often accepted Black but not white men with syphilis.) US military physicians generally assumed most people of color had syphilis, but the military needed their bodies for the war effort.[45]

As the United States entered the war, US military physicians in Puerto Rico continued to oversee inspections at the Special Hospital for Women. After six months, as venereal disease rates rose, they began to argue that Puerto Ricans' lack of sexual self-control threatened the war effort. The US military must morally and physically remake Puerto Ricans to take part in "the great fight for civilization, liberty, and democracy," proclaimed Howard Kern, the US-appointed attorney general of Puerto Rico.[46] In October 1917, at the behest of military and civilian officials in Washington, officials in Puerto Rico stopped licensing and inspecting prostitutes in an attempt to reduce venereal disease among the island's troops.[47] When officers inspected cities, however, they found that women still openly sold sex.

In July 1918, Attorney General Kern initiated a campaign to "exterminate prostitution" on the island, based on plans from Bascom Johnson, the Commission on Training Camp Activities Director of Law Enforcement.[48] As on the mainland, the WCTU and Red Cross enthusiastically supported it. This campaign marked the start of what Goodman would later call the "Porto Rican

Experiment."[49] Applying the American Plan set Puerto Rico apart from other places in the Caribbean and emphasized the island's status as a part of the United States. At the same time, it also reiterated Puerto Rico's "subordinate status"—a form of what the scholar Yen Le Espiritu terms "differential inclusion."[50]

While US officials modeled the American Plan in Puerto Rico on the mainland policy, on the island they could enforce its harshest provisions more easily: first, because in the territory they had more power, unencumbered by state or local officials; and second, because Puerto Ricans had fewer rights than mainland citizens. Kern sent a circular to all the judges and district attorneys on the island. He demanded increased policing and stricter sentencing of prostitutes; reminded judges of their duty to fully enforce laws against prostitution, adultery, and alcohol; and threatened to fire those who did not comply. Kern went so far as to declare that anyone who opposed the incarceration of prostitutes committed treason, likening such opposition to support for Germany.[51] By enforcing the American Plan, Kern implied, elite Puerto Ricans could escape such infamy and demonstrate their status as patriotic Americans, worthy of the full rights of citizenship that they lacked but hoped to gain.

The American Plan of prostitution prohibition fell hardest on Puerto Rican women from the "poorer laboring classes."[52] Between July 1918 and January 1919, courts convicted 824 women of practicing prostitution, with sentences averaging eight to nine months.[53] Records listed slightly more than half of the women as white, the next-largest number listed as mulatto, and a smaller number as negresses, though those racial classifications likely reflected Puerto Rican, rather than US mainland, conceptions of race. Moreover, in the Puerto Rican context, where sexual respectability delineated racial status, being labeled as a prostitute could render a woman racially darker.[54] Because prostitution had previously been regulated in Puerto Rico, "the police in most of the towns know every house of prostitution and every prostitute, and have a list with the names, ages, and more or less of the personal history of the inmates of such houses."[55] What had once been a legal form of labor suddenly became a crime.

The scale of the arrests of women in Puerto Rico illustrates the intensification of the "Law Enforcement" program of the American Plan when applied outside of the mainland. As Red Cross director Gavin L. Payne excitedly wrote, "the confinement of so many women at one time was unparalleled elsewhere,—at least to my knowledge,—in the federal domain, if indeed the world." On the mainland, the US government incarcerated at minimum 30,000 women to protect more than four million US troops. In proportion to the island's population and in comparison to number of soldiers present, US officials arrested far more Puerto Rican women. "Porto Rico was cleaned up to protect a camp of fifteen thousand soldiers," Payne explained. "For every fifteen soldiers one woman was sent to jail for a long period. . . . If the same course of action were logically applied elsewhere, a quarter of a million would have been under lock and key strictly as a war measure."[56]

US officials also began an educational campaign aimed at molding Puerto Rican soldiers into self-controlled men capable of winning the war and worthy of US citizenship. The campaign mirrored the Commission on Training Camp Activities' efforts, which intended to turn a heterogenous group of soldiers on the mainland—particularly immigrants or the children of immigrants—into "real" American men, with the moral values and physical virtues that such status supposedly entailed. The American Social Hygiene Association translated its pamphlet "Sexual Hygiene for Young Men" into Spanish and the military distributed it to literate men, instructing them to read it to their fellow soldiers. Puerto Rican officers received lectures on the "dangers of illicit intercourse," "the advisability of continence," and "the true value of medical prophylaxis."[57]

When it came to Puerto Rican women, though, US officials did not replicate mainland programs of education and recreation, instead preferring simply to incarcerate women. As part of the plan to impose "cleanliness" on their minds and bodies, officials believed incarcerated Puerto Rican women should learn "honest" work while in jail, including "sewing, cleaning, cooking and gardening." Such work would prepare them for acceptable forms of reproductive and care work as domestic laborers, mothers, and wives.[58]

Dr. Goodman, the architect of the anti-venereal efforts for the military in Puerto Rico, described the American Plan as a "test-tube experiment" for venereal disease control methods in the tropics. He deemed it a success.[59] It had dramatically reduced venereal disease rates, he claimed. The first venereal disease report for the camp at San Juan showed the highest rate of admissions for venereal disease of any US military camp, but boasted the third lowest rate by the end of 1918. Moreover, the American Plan had led to the incarceration of more than one thousand women between February 1918 and January 1919.[60] And the "rape of innocent women," which proponents of regulation had worried would occur with prohibition, did not happen, according to Goodman.[61]

As Goodman proclaimed, "the Porto Rican experiment" had "definitively proven," once and for all, that "the main source of infection is the prostitute." Through her "isolation" and incarceration, he argued, "new cases of syphilis among the men of the community, and from these to the women and children, cease." Even more significantly, the experiment had proven that prohibition could work in tropical places among people of color. Goodman believed that Puerto Rico could eventually become "the example to all the world as the test-tube experiment which proved that syphilis need not be," a showcase of US imperial prowess.[62] Scholars have shown that US policymakers in the post–WWII period saw Puerto Rico's potential as a "hemispheric object lesson," one that could demonstrate the benefits of American-style capitalism to the rest of Latin America.[63] The testing of the American Plan in Puerto Rico during WWI suggests that the US government construed the island as a strategic springboard for US policy far earlier.

Fit to Fight Across the Caribbean

As officials in Puerto Rico began to experiment with applying the American Plan in the fall of 1917, those in the Canal Zone and the Dominican Republic intensified their efforts to regulate prostitution through licensing and policing red-light districts. They believed providing soldiers with safe sexual access to women was a crucial means of preventing disease and maintaining morale.

When the United States mobilized for war, US troop strength in the Canal Zone swelled to 15,000, with rising venereal disease rates to match. Canal Zone officials blamed the Panamanian government, arguing it did not properly enforce the licensing and examination of prostitutes in the terminal cities.[64] To protect US soldiers and sailors, Canal Zone officials proposed taking over supervision of the red-light districts, applying the US colonial policy of regulation in a sovereign state.[65] Under pressure, Panamanian President Ramón Valdes issued a decree, drafted by Canal Zone officials themselves, to implement a stringent system of state-regulated prostitution.[66]

US military officials and Panamanian health officials worked together to police the red- light districts. US officials placed some restrictions on male customers, requiring them to undergo medical examination and take prophylaxis when leaving the district. Yet they focused most of their efforts on surveilling prostitutes, including 456 registered prostitutes in Colón and 406 registered and 302 clandestine prostitutes in Panama City.[67] In Colón, US military police forced all registered prostitutes to move into the city's red-light district and reduced its size from six square blocks to one.[68] Physicians then diagnosed most of them with venereal disease, taking the women to a hospital for mandatory treatment at the expense of the Panamanian government.[69] US officials pushed all known clandestine prostitutes out of the city.

US officials also deported foreign prostitutes—including women from the US mainland, Jamaica, and other places throughout the Caribbean—from the two terminal cities. Their strategy involved arresting women and charging them a $100 fine, which they would refund if the women left. This method allowed US officials to circumvent the Panamanian government, which was reticent to deport the foreign prostitutes whom they believed shielded Panamanian women.[70]

Meanwhile, within the Canal Zone—a place they imagined as inhabited by white families, with white wives and mothers, who anchored the settler colony—US officials instituted even stricter methods of prostitution prohibition. In June 1918, Richard M. Blatchford, Commanding General of the Panama Canal Zone Department, issued a dramatic new order: "It shall be unlawful for any person who heretofore has been, who now is, or who may hereafter be practicing prostitution or pandering, or who heretofore has been, who now is or who may hereafter be registered or licensed as a prostitute, to enter upon or pass through the territory or waters of the Canal Zone."[71] Blatchford's order expanded the definition of prostitute, effectively granting US officials the power to arrest any woman entering the Canal Zone.

In the Dominican Republic, the issue of prostitution also came to the fore as the United States entered the world war. US military officials criticized the methods Dominican officials used to administer prostitution and public health. Santo Domingo, which housed the largest contingent of marines, did not have a clearly defined red-light district. Its city council expressed its reluctance to create one. "What right do we have to convert a part of the city into a zone of scandal?" asked one member.[72] In the summer of 1917, however, under pressure from US officials, the council passed measures creating a "zone of toleration" in the Barahona neighborhood. The US military government required all prostitutes to live in the zone, mandated that women submit to registration and examination for disease, forbade the sale of alcohol, and punished infractions with fines and jail time.[73] Any registered prostitute who wanted to leave Barahona had to obtain permission from the police and a certificate from the medical examiner.[74]

Marines both policed and patronized the district. In the estimation of two Marine Provost Guard members who patrolled Barahona, between half and three-quarters of the marines regularly frequented the area for sex.[75] US military government medical officials saw the district as a means of keeping their men free of disease and thus strong enough to rule over the Dominicans, who engaged in near-constant protests against the occupation.[76]

Thus, at the same time as US officials in Puerto Rico rejected state-regulated prostitution as a scientific and moral failure, it remained a bulwark of US governance on the Isthmus of Panama and in the Dominican Republic. By mandating prohibition in the Canal Zone and administering regulation in the terminal cities of the Canal, Canal Zone officials ensured that US troops would have safe sexual access to women without disturbing the respectable white women and families of the Zone. In Santo Domingo, the US military government regulated prostitution to maintain the image of healthy white marines and a benevolent US occupation.

Coercive Diplomacy in Panama

As the world war continued, justifying US oversight of state-regulated prostitution outside of the mainland became more difficult. By the summer of 1918, battles over prostitution policy on the Isthmus of Panama came to a head. Officials based in Washington increasingly announced their support for prostitution prohibition, even in places like Panama where they had previously believed it impossible. Commander Blatchford noted that US involvement in regulating prostitution in Colón and Panama City explicitly contradicted War Department orders, which pronounced the American Plan the only acceptable policy. When regulated prostitution continued unabated, Blatchford closed the two cities to the US Army and Navy to prevent men from visiting the red-light districts. The two terminal cities, he claimed, were a modern-day "Sodom and Gomorrah."[77]

Pro-regulation Canal Zone officials answered such criticisms by emphasizing the dangers that uncontrolled prostitutes, particularly Black West Indian women, posed to US soldiers. Arthur T. McCormack, the Chief Health Officer of the Canal Zone, proved the most vocal. A Columbia University–educated physician, McCormack had previously inspected men for disease during the US invasion of Mexico and directed the Rockefeller Commission for the Eradication of Hookworm Disease in Kentucky.[78] To defend himself, McCormack sent a packet of documents and photographs to officials in Washington, DC.

McCormack included materials that supposedly illustrated the successes of his strict methods of regulation and justified his non-compliance with prohibition policy. The caption of a photograph showing "a group of prostitutes with acute syphilis and gonorrhea" stated that such women had been "infecting American soldiers and civilians for years" (fig. 5.1). "Had the segregated district been abolished by law these highly infectious women would be at large multiplying their victims," it warned. Other photographs in the packet

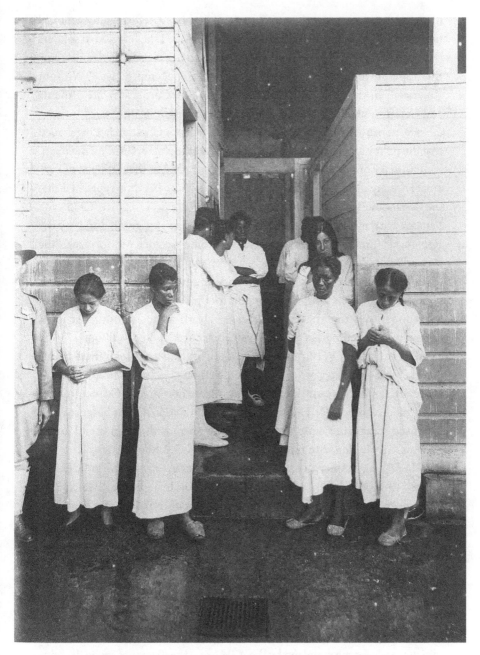

FIGURE 5.1. The photograph's caption terms these women "a group of prostitutes with acute syphilis and gonorrhea." Image courtesy of the US National Archives and Records Administration.

depicted arrested women's genitals, which had been deformed by venereal infection. Officials recorded that one woman claimed she "catered to soldiers only," while another "stated seven men were with her in 24 hours," reinforcing the trope of women of color as sexually voracious temptresses.[79] Without Americans in charge of regulated prostitution, McCormack wrote, Panama and Colón would remain "centers of vice and its resulting disease."[80]

In response to McCormack, Canal Zone Governor Chester Harding argued that the policy of prohibition had produced "remarkable results" on the mainland: Canal Zone health officials should thus apply it in the Republic of Panama. Directly disregarding Panamanian sovereignty, Harding suggested that the Canal Zone's Health Department should enforce prohibition in Colón and Panama City, even if doing so went beyond the powers granted to it by the Republic.[81] The US Army Surgeon General's office scolded McCormack: "the only policy which has been productive is repression. The Latin American can carry that out with just as much sincerity and honesty as he will the other policy."[82] US officials based their support for the American Plan in Panama on the conception that Latin Americans—both a racial and geographic category—could progress only through continued US intervention.

After the end of WWI, naval and merchant traffic through the Panama Canal rose, as did rates of venereal disease among US troops. Implementing the American Plan became more pressing. The Army Surgeon General's Office called medical officer Dr. Herman Goodman to the Canal Zone because of his supposed success in Puerto Rico, and charged him with bringing Colón and Panama City in line with official US military policy. Since Puerto Rico was "another Spanish-American and Tropical American community," policies that worked there should also work in Panama.[83] Goodman framed Puerto Rico as a crucial staging ground for the development of broader Latin American policy. Once Goodman had demonstrated the American Plan worked there, Americans could easily distribute the Plan across the region, given the supposed racial, climactic, and cultural similarities.

But US officials had more difficulty implementing the American Plan in the Republic of Panama, a sovereign country, than in a US territory like Puerto Rico. Goodman pushed his agenda through diplomatic and civil society channels, holding conferences with Panamanian elites and officials; screening films initially made for the mainland by the ASHA and the Commission on Training Camp Activities; and translating mainland social hygiene pamphlets into Spanish. US representatives urged Panamanians to revoke the decree regulating prostitution in Panama City and Colón. (They did not note the irony that

US officials had drafted it in the first place.) The representatives submitted copies of US federal and state laws as models.[84] They stressed that the modern state should not make itself "a partner to the business of prostitution" or recognize prostitution "as a legitimate manner of earning a livelihood." Jailing women who practiced prostitution and deporting foreign prostitutes best addressed the problem of venereal disease.[85] After "strenuous" debate, Panamanian officials agreed to end regulated prostitution.[86]

As agents of a sovereign country, however, Panamanian officials had some power to resist the American Plan. They continued to tolerate red-light districts in Colón and Panama City, minimally enforcing registration and inspection. When Canal Zone officials called for the deportation of all foreign prostitutes from the Republic in 1919, Panamanian officials appeased them, declaring that 124 women, primarily of Jamaican nationality, should face deportation as "persons of loose character" or "ill-fame." Yet the Panamanian government declined to provide funds for their deportation, so the women remained in Panama.[87]

In the face of Panamanian resistance, in the early 1920s US officials again tried to force the Panamanian government to prohibit prostitution. They threatened to prevent US sailors from visiting Panamanian cities when naval fleets came through the Canal, which would deprive the local economy of a major source of income.[88] They searched for loopholes in the treaty with Panama that would allow them, under the guise of sanitary control, to exercise police power in the two cities.[89] But eventually, US officials relented and accommodated state-regulated prostitution through registration, inspection, and segregation. They justified their ongoing participation in examining prostitutes for venereal disease as a means of modernizing public health in the Republic and protecting the safety of US citizens in the Canal Zone. Continuing to prohibit prostitution in the Canal Zone, while regulating it in the Republic of Panama and pushing the costs of regulation onto the Panamanian government, allowed US officials to exercise significant control over women in both places. Moreover, it made sexual vice a Panamanian rather than a US problem, even as Americans created increased demand for commercial sex.

Military Force in the Dominican Republic

In the summer of 1918, as Canal Zone officials argued over regulated prostitution versus prohibition, US military government officials in the Dominican Republic did so as well. The supposed success of the "Porto Rican Experiment" served as the catalyst. As in the Canal Zone, disputes in the Dominican Republic centered on differing ideas of how best to control white men's sexual contacts with women of color, whom US military government officials assumed carried venereal disease. But in the Dominican Republic, the US government had far greater powers than in the Republic of Panama to enforce policy however it pleased.

The debate in the Dominican Republic came to a head when the US military government held a hearing over complaints about the red-light district in Santo Domingo. The Reverend George L. Kerns, a recently arrived naval chaplain, testified that the district, which the US military government itself had essentially created, caused high rates of venereal disease and low morals among troops. As a solution, he proposed the American Plan, and provided newspaper articles from Puerto Rico and the mainland trumpeting the usefulness of incarcerating women.[90]

Rebutting these complaints, Naval Surgeon Reynolds Hayden, the chief sanitary inspector of Santo Domingo, argued that the red-light district protected men from disease, given the "general venereal conditions throughout the country." In fact, he claimed, "illicit sexual intercourse" was so widespread that US military police could not distinguish prostitutes from other women. In the red-light district, US officials could at least control sexual contacts; if they closed it, he argued, diseased and hypersexual women of color would inevitably have sex with marines and infect them. (At the same time, Hayden also admitted that many marines were already infected when they arrived.) Hayden proposed to increase the fee prostitutes paid for their weekly examination, giving the military government funds to confine them in the hospital for treatment.[91] Swayed by Hayden, the military government continued to regulate prostitution in Santo Domingo and consolidated public health work under Hayden himself.[92] That women should pay to for treatment for infections that, by Hayden's own admission, marines may have transmitted to them, demonstrated US officials' focus on the health of its men at the literal expense of local women.

By early 1919, however, top-level US military officials in Washington insisted on the American Plan as the only acceptable colonial policy, even in the Dominican Republic. The fact that the US military maintained regulated prostitution as long as it did may have been due to the relative autonomy granted to the Marine Corps.[93] In January 1919, the Chief Naval Medical Officer reminded Thomas Snowden, the Military Governor of Santo Domingo, that state-regulated prostitution had been "completely abandoned" by the US government and that any policy of venereal disease control must start with "the assumption that the practice is illegal." Every government in a foreign territory under US jurisdiction "should conform in this respect."[94]

US military medical officials worked to bring the military government in line with the American Plan and to standardize policy across the Caribbean. In the spring of 1919, Snowden sent Naval Surgeon Hayden to Puerto Rico to study its public health and sanitary organizations.[95] By fall, under Hayden's influence, the military government had reversed course and advocated prohibition. In October, Governor Snowden signed a law, drafted by Hayden, centralizing the control of public health under a national authority run entirely by US officials.[96]

The new law's provisions for the control of prostitution and venereal disease mirrored those in place on the mainland, in Puerto Rico, and within the Panama Canal Zone.[97] It declared prostitution "a fertile source of venereal disease" and criminalized it. It allowed health authorities to examine anyone suspected of carrying a venereal disease—naming prostitutes as particularly likely to harbor diseases—and to quarantine those infected. It defined a prostitute as "any woman or girl who publicly engages in lewdness, especially for profit, or who practices lewdness with anyone, or who has sexual relations for profit, or who prostitutes her body for profit."[98] The law thus marked all women as possible prostitutes whom the government could forcibly examine, incarcerate, and deport if they did not hold citizenship.

Policing and Medical Violence

Women across the US-governed Caribbean faced brutal treatment in the name of curing them of disease, uplifting their morals, and protecting soldiers from them. Under regimes of state-regulated prostitution as well as the American Plan of prohibition, officials regarded the bodies of incarcerated women as sites to test their hypotheses about how best to cure venereal disease and improve morality. In fact, women often experienced little difference in how US officials treated them under either regimes of regulation or prohibition, despite US insistence that the two policies were diametrically opposed to one another.

The history of US medical violence in the Caribbean is difficult to trace, given the existing sources. US officials left records of medical treatments that reflect their perspective, but not those of the women who received them. Yet it is clear that women did not have the right to choose: as prisoners, they could not reject treatment, regardless of its effects. The widely accepted venereal disease treatments at the time—administered to women and men alike—were painful and dangerous. They included injections of mercury and arsenic compounds, with side effects that ranged from nausea to fever to death.[99] Yet diseases such as syphilis, too, could cause severe illness and death. Such treatments, though harsh, offered the only cure according to the US medical community. At the same time, vital statistics from Caribbean territories demonstrated that tuberculosis and pneumonia killed far more local people than venereal diseases, suggesting that while US officials prioritized them as the most pressing threats to health, local people likely did not.[100]

In Puerto Rico, women incarcerated for prostitution under the American Plan lived in poorer conditions than those of incarcerated women on the mainland. For the care of detained Puerto Rican women, Attorney General Kern allocated only one-quarter of the average sum allotted per day at the all-white detention hospital in Houston, Texas.[101] An observer noted the Puerto Rican jails held "mere children of eleven, twelve and thirteen years of age," an age at which mainland officials did not usually incarcerate white girls.[102] US officials stressed that through incarceration they could provide women with the "best and most modern" treatment for venereal disease. But their primary goal was to render women "noninfectious" to soldiers.[103]

US officials used incarcerated women and Puerto Rican soldiers as subjects for their studies of venereal disease treatment and prevention. Dr. Herman Goodman established himself as an expert by publishing his research on Puerto Rican prostitutes and soldiers in major medical journals. A dermatologist and syphilologist from New York City, Goodman had graduated from Columbia University College of Physicians and Surgeons only one year prior to joining the Army Medical Corps. His wife Ruth, a dermatology nurse, joined him in Puerto Rico and helped to carry out treatments.[104] While little evidence exists of Ruth's activities, her presence suggests that some white American women, as well as men, advanced their careers through research on incarcerated Puerto Rican women.

Working alongside elite Puerto Rican physicians, Goodman used incarcerated women as test subjects for evaluating the efficacy of various treatment regimens for syphilis when completed under ideal circumstances. While "the physician in private practice is confronted with the fact that he cannot make a patient continue treatment persistently," wrote L. Yordán Pasarell, the physician at the Ponce jail, "we have been able to push the treatments to the utmost." Pasarell detailed the intensive regimens tested on two different groups: "a large group received intramuscular injections of mercury salicylate every six days and a small group cyanide of mercury every other day." Goodman described the regimen of invasive genital procedures at the Arecibo jail: "Daily and twice daily when necessary, irrigations were given. Local caustics were applied and tampons were inserted."[105] In addition to using established therapies in more intensive ways, Goodman also experimented with the timing of drug therapies. He injected Puerto Rican women who did not have syphilis with arsphenamine to see if it might work as a prophylactic treatment, rather than for treatment after infection as doctors customarily used it.[106]

Goodman used incarcerated Puerto Rican women, whom he termed "fountains of infectious disease," for research on so-called tropical diseases, including granuloma inguinale, a rare infection spread largely through sexual contact.[107] While other doctors had labeled granuloma a disease of "the colored races," Goodman concluded that it could spread to white people, even outside of tropical locations. He warned of "the increasing migrations between continental United States and Porto Rico, with the possibility of transferring the infection," and recommended "quarantine measures" for Puerto Ricans coming to the United States.[108] Goodman's research framed Puerto Rican women as dangerous, mobile vectors of diseases, who could infect otherwise healthy white mainlanders.

Goodman's access to the bodies of Puerto Rican women and Puerto Rican soldiers allowed him to develop new theories about the racial particularities of islanders. In an article devoted to the "genital defects" of Puerto Rican draftees, Goodman reported that hydrocele, or a swelling of the scrotum, "is almost an insular characteristic," because of its prevalence on the island. He noted that "the urethra of the Porto Rican is almost as subject to excessive scar formation as that of the negro."[109] He reported that, unlike on the mainland, the prevalence of venereal disease among Puerto Rican women remained consistently high across the racial categories of "white," "mulattos," and "negresses," suggesting the distinctiveness of islanders' sexual disorder, despite their differing degrees of visible African ancestry.[110] Enforcing the American Plan allowed military physicians to articulate long held stereotypes about the racial, sexual, and gendered differences between Puerto Ricans and white mainland Americans in terms of medical science.

On the Isthmus of Panama, US medical officials tested treatments on women through licensing and segregating prostitution, rather than prohibiting it. US medical officials at the Colón Hospital worked at "cleaning up" the redlight district: since they could not prohibit prostitution, they attempted to "remove the source" of infections, which they understood as women's bodies. Physicians even noted that some women who seemed well actually had "infected pus tubes" and "infected ovaries," reflecting the common conception in US tropical medicine that people of color could secretly harbor disease but not appear sick.[111]

Over the course of 1918, during the mandatory weekly inspections of prostitutes, physicians at the hospital opened the abdominal cavities of sixty women of "every nationality," the youngest only fourteen years of age, in order to discover hidden infections. They removed all ovaries and tubes they found diseased and "wherever practicable hysterectomy was performed." Doctors reported that the surgeries proved successful in two ways. First, they compared the sixty women on whom they operated with a group that did not receive operations: while surgery cured the women who received it, the hospital noted, the women who did not continued to remain infected and infectious. Second, doctors found that gynecological surgery acted as a form of moral uplift. As the hospital proclaimed, "the mental effect of having had the diseased portions removed led many of them to express the desire that they wished to leave the district and engage in an honorable calling."[112] Doctors saw no such change in women who did not undergo surgery.

In Colón, then, a US-run hospital took the violent logic of the American Plan to the extreme of sterilization, even though prostitution remained legal there. We do not know if doctors obtained women's consent. Indeed, Laura Briggs has shown that women in Puerto Rico at times turned sterilization programs to their own ends of fertility control.[113] But the phrase "wherever practicable" suggests that American doctors performed hysterectomies when they found it convenient, and as a means of transforming prostitutes into supposedly productive workers rather than as a means of disease treatment or birth control that women requested. In this light, gynecological surgery served as a labor policy as well as a public health policy, rendering former prostitutes fit for the domestic service, laundry, and marketing jobs that made the Canal Zone run.[114]

While US officials could not make Panamanians enforce the American Plan, their efforts led the Republic of Panama to institute increasingly punitive policies directed at women involved in the sex industry, particularly Afro-Caribbean women. Under pressure from US officials, the Panamanian government restricted gambling, dancing, and the sale of alcohol, and forbade women from running saloons, eliminating the forms of entertainment that had given women an opportunity to earn money.[115]

Moreover, Panamanian officials agreed with US officials that prostitutes, rather than men, spread venereal disease. Canal Zone health officials and Panamanian police cooperated in investigating every new case of venereal disease to "locate the source; when the origin can be found, the infected individual is rounded up by the police and held in the detention ward at the hospital for treatment."[116] US-operated hospitals detained 1,057 women for treatment in 1919 alone, and treated hundreds of women in subsequent years, though Canal Zone officials complained that the Panamanian police allowed prostitutes to evade inspections.[117] While US officials differentiated between state regulation and prohibition, they recognized that strictly enforced licensing and segregation enhanced the state's ability to manage women's bodies and delineate racial categories. If they could not make Panamanian officials enforce prohibition, they could help them to enforce regulation to attain the same goal of reducing prostitution to a minimum.

Meanwhile, in the Dominican Republic, the American Plan further expanded US control over the country. The US military government's 1919 public health law immediately consolidated its control of public health and escalated its policing of women. The military government charged the Guardia Nacional, a Dominican police force trained and supervised by US Marines, with enforcing the law, which spurred a "more general and complete rounding up of commercial and clandestine prostitutes."[118] Between 1920 and 1923 in San Pedro, prostitutes paid the vast majority of all health code fines.[119] As scholar Lorgia García-Peña has documented, the US military government incarcerated at least 953 women for practicing prostitution or carrying a venereal disease during the occupation.[120] These arrests represented a striking display of force, with one woman arrested for every two to three US Marines in the country.[121] But as Military Governor Snowden reported, "Because of the paucity of existent hospital facilities, the prisons in the various principal cities have been utilized for this purpose."[122] Despite arresting women, the US military government did not provide adequate funds for their housing or medical care, mirroring the situation in Puerto Rico and Panama.

Moreover, given the broad definition of "prostitute" US officials wrote into law, they could deem that all women who had sexual relationships with marines were prostitutes and punish them. US officials used this strategy to prevent cohabitation between white soldiers and Dominican women, which troubled the narrative of the US military as a benevolent occupying force. Indeed, when a US sanitary official reported that marines cohabitated with prostitutes, another official reproached him for repeating a "charge employed by Dominicans when seeking to discredit the forces of occupation." After an investigation, a sanitary official examined the four marines for venereal disease, while officials "apprehended" the women who supposedly lived with them.[123]

The case of Florencia Michel, which opened this chapter, shows how the law dealt harshly with women who could not prove Dominican citizenship. In the spring and summer of 1920, the US military government deported twenty-nine women for practicing prostitution, including seventeen Puerto Ricans. These women's presence reflected the US policy of encouraging Puerto Rican labor migration to the Dominican Republic, since officials believed that Puerto Ricans fell between mainland Americans and Dominicans in terms of civilization and culture.[124] Some may have come to sell sex after US officials criminalized prostitution in Puerto Rico. While women in the Caribbean had long migrated throughout the region for work, these women's arrival and deportation demonstrate that US occupations in the Caribbean created new demands and punishments for migratory sexual labor.

Women, Labor, and Protest

Despite the repeated violence committed against poor and working-class women under regimes of state-regulated prostitution and prohibition, women fought attempts to control their bodies and labor. Indeed, in Puerto Rico, the Isthmus of Panama, and the Dominican Republic, women's protests formed part of long-standing struggles against US rule as well as the injustices they faced from their elite compatriots. Working-class women drew on labor unions to fight their surveillance and incarceration. As Eileen Findlay has shown, US efforts to control prostitution in the Caribbean reflected broader US antagonism to organized labor, which threatened US business interests.[125]

In Puerto Rico, women loudly protested their arrests. They filed petitions for clemency, though in a five-month period, courts granted clemency to only 26 of the 156 women who applied for it. Women defended themselves in court and fought back once incarcerated. Official reports contain subtle evidence of daily resistance: "hysterical attacks were frequently treated" at Arecibo jail, likely putting a medical gloss on outbursts of anger, frustration, and pain.[126] When the director of the prison in Ponce prohibited visitors from bringing them food and cigarettes, more than three hundred women rioted and refused their treatments, "shouting at the top of their lungs and insulting the Red Cross, the Attorney General, and other officials." In another act of defiance, thirty-eight women set fires in the jail.[127]

Puerto Ricans across political parties, particularly Afro-Puerto Rican and working-class people, argued that the American Plan violated the protections the US Constitution purportedly offered them. The labor movement, in which women played a key role, included prostitutes as symbols of their larger battle against capitalist exploitation. Women labor organizers helped to publicize the case of Leonor Crespo, arrested by a police officer whose romantic advances she had spurned and who was then sentenced to thirty days in prison for prostitution. When the physician who examined Crespo pronounced her a virgin, newspapers as well as labor unions decried the abuses of power that US policies inflicted upon young working women.[128]

Organized labor also played an important role in the Isthmus of Panama, where prostitution remained state-regulated in the Republic and prohibited in the Canal Zone. These two policies worked together to place Afro-Caribbean women in the crosshairs as potential prostitutes as they crossed the border each day for work. For example, one night as Rosita Hall returned from her work in a Canal Zone laundry to her home in Panama City, a police officer apprehended her. Deeming her a prostitute, he took her to the venereal hospital, where medical officials performed a vaginal examination and blood test for syphilis, both of which came back negative.[129]

But Hall belonged to the West Indian Labour Union, which protested to the Canal Zone Board of Health. It argued that what happened to the "respectable" Hall had "many parallels" in the experiences of its Black Caribbean women members and asked Canal Zone officials to "use more discretion" so that such a thing would not happen again.[130] Working women confronted high stakes: if deemed prostitutes, they faced permanent exclusion from the Zone and thus from their places of employment. As the West Indian Labour Union protested Hall's treatment, they also protested US imperialism and the ongoing harassment of Black women under it, even as the Union also upheld divisions between "respectable" and sexually suspicious women.[131]

Women who sold sex in Panama also resisted US control of their bodies and labor. A weekly report from Panama City in the summer of 1918 found that only 49 of the 655 women registered as prostitutes reported to the hospital for examinations.[132] Even as Canal Zone officials performed some of the most violent documented medical procedures on prostitutes there, women who sold sex also demonstrated the limits of US-administered regulated prostitution: they simply refused to show up.

In the Dominican Republic, where the US military government maintained more absolute control, individual sex workers repeatedly filed complaints, doing so under regimes of US-regulated prostitution, as well as prohibition. In the spring of 1918, when marines regulated prostitution and patrolled Santo Domingo's red-light district, Carmen Valera brought a complaint to the military government. Three US Marines had visited her and demanded sex. "One, yes, and not with three," Valera told them, asserting her right to set the terms of her sexual labor. The angry men, who believed they should have unrestricted access to her body, set her bed on fire and hit her in the face with a stone. The military government let the men off with a warning and accused Valera of making a false accusation.[133] Such attempts to prevent women from speaking out against sexual mistreatment formed one aspect of the US military government's broader work to silence Dominican dissent.[134]

After the US military government enforced the American Plan in 1919, women accused of prostitution, now a crime, continued to protest their mistreatment. Rubersinda Herrdia wrote to the military government complaining that police falsely accused her of prostitution and "arbitrarily" sentenced her to twenty-five days in prison.[135] As in other parts of the US-controlled Caribbean, the US military government also deported foreign prostitutes. Though most women sentenced to deportation left, Melissa Madera has found several examples of women who successfully petitioned to remain in the Dominican Republic. Celina Ortiz, for example, explained that she had left Puerto Rico at age six, considered herself a Dominican citizen, and provided care for her child, mother, and sister. While officials initially denied her petition, they relented when her father wrote to the US military government promising to keep Celina away from "prostitution practices."[136]

Both Dominicans and the military government understood sexual violence as a material and symbolic concern, one that called into question the legitimacy of US rule. Women repeatedly filed complaints with the US military government, charging marines with assault and rape and demanding accountability.[137] Juana Facunda Cuevas wrote to the military governor to ask for compensation and medical support after several marines raped her twelve-year-old daughter, Gregoria. In the face of strong evidence, US officials agreed to send the girl to the military hospital for examination and treatment. Yet they accused Juana of having an "ulterior motive" in bringing forward Gregoria's case, noting it would make "splendid propaganda" for Dominicans' anti-occupation protests.[138] Even though US officials tacitly acknowledged that marines had raped Gregoria, they were more concerned about maintaining the image of US benevolence than about ensuring justice for her.

Across the Caribbean, women bore the brunt of the American Plan. For working-class women, Afro-Caribbean women, and women who sold sex, US efforts to both regulate and prohibit prostitution epitomized US rule, as US forces stripped countries of sovereignty and extracted resources while claiming to uplift the very people they harmed. At the same time, as scholars such as Lorgia García-Peña and Kamala Kempadoo remind us, women used sex as a strategy for survival, resistance, kin-making, and pleasure; their lived experience exceeded the constraints US military policy and elite rule placed on them.[139]

Caribbean Legacies of the American Plan

Working-class people, particularly women, vocally opposed US American methods of regulating and prohibiting prostitution. Elites and officials in Puerto Rico, Panama, and the Dominican Republic often maintained more complicated positions. At times they cooperated with US officials in spreading the American Plan because it furthered their own goals of controlling dangerous women, particularly migrant and Black women. Yet they also resented how US officials undercut their own authority, at times denouncing the American Plan as an illegitimate extension of US power.

In Puerto Rico, elites initially supported the American Plan, in no small part because the US government threatened those who objected. Yet the quest to make working-class Puerto Rican men and women into respectable citizens dovetailed with island elites' own long-term efforts at reform. Espousing and enforcing the American Plan allowed elites to shore up their authority, respectability, and whiteness. At a time of rising labor activism, repressing prostitution helped to subdue the poor and working classes, whom elites racialized as non-white.[140]

As they affirmed US officials' conceptions of Puerto Rico as sexually immoral, elite Puerto Ricans sought to play a central role in cleaning it up. Religious leaders, judges, and women's organizations wrote to US officials pledging their assistance.[141] The Rotary Club of San Juan resolved to work with authorities to make a "clean and safe city." Businessmen expressed concern that the capital had been placed off-limits to soldiers and hoped that their efforts would allow soldiers, and the money they spent, to flood back into the city.[142] As Laura Briggs has shown, elite Puerto Rican women gained political power and created a public role for themselves through anti-prostitution work.[143] The San Juan Woman's Christian Temperance Union, composed of "respectable" Puerto Rican and North American women, formed a Women's Police Reserve Corps, which performed "detective work" to collect evidence against suspected prostitutes.[144] They visited incarcerated women to reform them and proposed to open a day nursery for their children in the Arecibo jail.[145]

As the Great War went on, US officials' insistence on the mass arrests of prostitutes strained the Puerto Rican government's budget and exceeded the capacity of its jails, highlighting the power asymmetry between the United States and Puerto Rico. In fall 1918, twin catastrophes struck: a severe earthquake rocked Puerto Rico, destroying buildings and leaving people injured and homeless, and then the postwar influenza pandemic sickened thousands. Nonetheless, US officials continued to demand compliance with prostitution prohibition and insisted that the Puerto Rican government finance it. When the Puerto Rican legislature voted down an appropriation for women's jails, Attorney General Kern issued orders "reducing the rations for all prisoners to the very minimum consistent with the maintenance of life."[146] Rather than releasing women for whom the government could not afford to care, Kern insisted that they remain in jail, effectively holding the women hostage to US demands on the Puerto Rican government.

By early 1919, elite Puerto Ricans increasingly turned against Kern's antiprostitution crusade, arguing that it infringed on the rights of Puerto Ricans and demonstrated a fundamentally unequal relationship between the mainland and the island. In response to months of protests, a judge ruled that the federal court would hear prostitution cases and could prosecute women only within five miles of the military camp.[147] The Puerto Rican House of Representatives asked the US Senate not to reconfirm Kern as attorney general, and he left the position.[148] Although women remained incarcerated until the summer of 1919, police in Ponce began to respond to neighbors' complaints about prostitution by asking the women to move along, and a San Juan newspaper called on the mayor to reopen a special hospital for prostitutes.[149] Moreover, as demobilization came to a close, US officials cared less about enforcing the costly measures that had led to increasingly vocal conflict.

Yet the American Plan had lasting effects in the Caribbean, despite its relatively short life in Puerto Rico, the first place US officials tested it. It expanded Puerto Rico's bureaucratic state, equipping it to surveil the population through institutions such as jails, hospitals, and military camps and through scientific forms of knowledge such as medical research and statistics. As Laura Briggs has shown, it provided a foundation for continued policy and medical experimentation on the island, including early human trials of the birth control pill.[150]

On the Isthmus of Panama, even as local officials rejected the American Plan, they invoked its discourses of public health and disease prevention to justify the policing of Afro-Caribbean women. During the 1920s, Panamanian officials criminalized venereal disease itself, convicting many women of clandestine prostitution on the basis of a positive venereal disease test. Panamanian officials used public health campaigns to promote a new form of nationalism based on *mestizaje*, which advocated the creation of a singular Hispanic national identity and the elimination of Black and indigenous peoples from the body politic.[151] While US officials in the Panama Canal Zone used prostitution policy to implement their developmentalist ideas about racial and national order, Panamanians also employed their own vision of modern public health policy to challenge US imperialism and build a unified national and racial identity.

In the Dominican Republic, the American Plan lasted until the end of the occupation in 1924, and subsequent regimes adopted its tenets. US officials used public health work, including the prohibition of prostitution, to justify the occupation to other Latin American states as well as to the US public. Reynolds Hayden, who had overseen both the red-light district and the implementation of the American Plan, published an article arguing that "the time has not yet arrived, and will not arrive for some time to come, when [sanitary] work can be safely turned over entirely to the Dominicans." US control was "for the good of the Dominicans themselves."[152] US State Department officials championed Hayden's report as a way to counteract Latin American criticism of the US military government and to prove the munificence of the ongoing occupation.[153]

Elites in the Dominican Republic shared the military government's interest in controlling unruly women, despite fierce popular resistance to the American Plan. In a 1920 article on "modern" hygiene and sanitation, a Dominican official argued that prostitution prohibition prevented diseases that "contaminated mankind."[154] Scholars have shown that the occupation had lasting effects in the Dominican Republic. Lorgia García-Peña argues that it contributed to the disenfranchisement of Black women and the persecution of African cultural traditions.[155] As Melissa Medera has shown, by casting the repression of prostitution as part of modern governance and public health, the military government laid foundations that dictator Rafael Trujillo would build on to shore up his moral authority and solidify his brutal three-decade rule.[156]

Conclusion

The particular political circumstances in each country shaped how US officials carried out their American Plan experiments in the Caribbean. These experiments also reflected a broader shift in prostitution policy taking place throughout the US empire in mid-1919 based on a new imperial logic. Military officials contended that the success of the American Plan in Puerto Rico, even if short-lived, proved that a single, uniform prostitution policy could work everywhere the United States maintained its rule, both mainland and colonies.

Indeed, they believed it could work throughout Latin America. Through prostitution policy, Canal Zone health officers hoped to "awaken a public conscience" in the Republic of Panama, so that the "higher social standards" of the Canal Zone "may seem desirable to these allies and friends of ours."[157] In the Dominican Republic, the military government argued regarding prostitution prohibition, "there are no real grounds for the contention that such legislation is impracticable with tropical or Latin races." In fact, "the results depend entirely upon the authorities in charge of the administration of the law," it claimed, pointing to the ongoing need for US authorities' presence.[158] With help, US officials implied, other Latin American countries could also adopt a modern approach to prostitution. Such rhetoric portrayed US colonialism as concerned with the protection of women and public health, and thus as humanitarian, rather than imbricated with American economic, political, and military interests.[159]

While US officials framed the American Plan in the Caribbean as a form of civilizational uplift, their true concern was for the bodies of white men. A military doctor explained the high venereal disease rate among marines in the Caribbean: "the young American, anxious and eager for female companionship, finds none of his class nor color and he fails after so long a time to draw the color line."[160] If he could not draw it, the American Plan would draw it for him. Despite the discourse of white masculine self-control that developed during World War I, US officials in the Caribbean worked to control the bodies of women of color, particularly Afro-Caribbean women, to maintain the fiction of white American racial and gender superiority.

US officials used the wartime Caribbean as a site to experiment with their new methods of prostitution control. But Europe loomed even larger in their minds as the major theater of war and the original font of regulated prostitution. After all, social hygienists argued, despite the innate sexual immorality of tropical peoples, European colonizers held the responsibility for instituting regulated prostitution.

When Dr. Herman Goodman reflected on his time in Panama, he made connections between Europe and the Caribbean. Goodman lamented that US officials had been unable to make Panamanian officials enforce the American

Plan, observing that Panamanian ideas about sex "are a little closer to European customs" than American ones. Regulation in Panama, he noted, "was even more European than any system of regulation in Europe."[161] Bewilderingly, Goodman conceived of a regulationist prostitution policy drafted and executed by US officials as European, rather than American. His statements illustrate how prohibitionist prostitution policy had come to function as a crucial feature of US national identity during World War I. They also raised a tantalizing possibility: if the US military could test the American Plan in the Caribbean, could they do it in Europe, too?

6

A "Righteous Crusade"

TESTING THE AMERICAN PLAN IN FRANCE

IN THE SPRING OF 1919, US military police arrested Aline Legros in the town of Bourbonne-les-Bains, the location of the US National Guard's 29th Division. Gaetano Liberatore, a bugler with the 114th Infantry, had developed gonorrhea and pointed the finger at Legros as the source of his infection. A US medical officer examined Legros's internal and external genitalia but found no evidence of venereal disease. Outraged, Legros and her parents sent a petition to US headquarters. Legros wrote that she had been "the object of an injust [sic] and grievous inspection, made on the regrettable denunciation of disreputable persons." Her "dignity" had been "compromised in the eyes of her French fiancé," suggesting she experienced the procedure as a form of medicalized rape that had damaged her honor. In closing their petition, the Legros family entreated, "we want to stop the repeated attacks against us."[1]

The Brigade Commander investigated the family's claims. Despite Legros's clean bill of health, he found it "perfectly proper that this girl should have been examined." Moreover, if he saw her in the company of an American soldier in the future, "she would be subjected to the same rules as all other women" and examined again.[2] The commander's statement suggests that Legros was not alone in her experience. As on the mainland United States, the US military understood the rights of women—even white citizens of sovereign European countries—as secondary to their goal of maintaining soldiers' health.[3]

American social hygienists saw the Great War as a chance to transform the sexual morality and health of the United States and its colonies, and they extended their aspirations to Europe. John D. Rockefeller, Jr., the financial backer of the American Social Hygiene Association, proclaimed that the war provided "an opportunity for the United States to advance the standard of morality in the countries of the Allies not only among the men of the armies, but throughout these countries at large, such as under ordinary circumstances we could hardly have expected for years to come."[4] Members of organizations such as the ASHA, he believed, would have the chance to dictate sexual policy both at home and abroad. Wartime sexual reform would enhance the standing of the United States internationally and position it as the moral leader of the world.

Despite high hopes that the United States could eradicate prostitution in the European theater, social hygiene reformers, US officials, and American civilians feared the sexual temptations US soldiers would face there. Between June 1917, when the American Expeditionary Force began to arrive, and the end of the war on November 11, 1918, more than two million US soldiers landed in France.[5] The Commission on Training Camp Activities (CTCA), which set up recreational activities for "Doughboys," had tried to turn an ethnically and socioeconomically diverse (but racially segregated) group of recruits and draftees into self-disciplined soldiers, and its civilian officials did not want their efforts undone abroad. Controlled largely by members of the ASHA, the CTCA espoused the "American Plan" of prohibiting prostitution, demanding sexual continence, and mandating prophylactic treatment for soldiers who engaged in sex with local women in order to protect and control men's bodies.[6]

France loomed large in the American imagination as a place of sexual vice, danger, and freedom. Since the late nineteenth century, the "French" method had been slang for fellatio, syphilis was termed the "French pox," "French pictures" referred to pornography, and "French letters" was a euphemism for condoms.[7] The French institution of *réglementation*, or regulation, a state-controlled system of licensed brothels and prostitutes, influenced prostitution policy around the globe.[8] This system stood in stark contrast to the mass arrests of sexually suspicious women in the United States. During the war, through both diplomatic meetings and on-the-ground skirmishes, French and US officials clashed over opposing visions of sexual civilization.

US military officials felt more hopeful that the American Plan could work in Europe than in Puerto Rico, since they regarded the island's inhabitants and soldiers as nonwhite and morally inferior.[9] As Bishop Charles Brent, the Chief-of-Chaplains of the American Expeditionary Forces, wrote to a wary French official, "we are far from desiring to use France as an experimental station for the exploitation of new theories." Rather, Americans based their approach to prostitution on "the generally approved findings of science as confirmed by our own investigation and experience." As Brent disingenuously assured the French official, the US military would not think of "interfering in the domestic affairs of the French government or people." Rather, through enacting the American Plan in France, "we count it our privilege to safeguard your interests, where we may."[10]

As Brent's letter reveals, US officials brought a paternalist and imperialist logic to implementing the American Plan in France, as they had in the Caribbean. Despite their conception of France as a white, European country, US officials also saw French people as less civilized by virtue of their sexual morality, particularly their embrace of prostitution.[11] Although the American Plan purportedly uplifted US soldiers, US diplomats and military officials on the ground in France focused a large part of their campaign on controlling French women.

US officials' understanding of their superiority to the sexually degenerate French provoked conflicts with French officials, who resented being treated more like a colony than like a sovereign, allied, and imperial power. The attitudes and actions of both American and French officials had roots in an imperialistic sense of their role as civilized states that had the right to govern themselves and to civilize and rule others. For example, despite the US military's lack of experience in battle compared with the French and British militaries, President Wilson declared that American soldiers would fight as an independent army, serving only in units commanded by US military officers rather than in the amalgamated units that French and British commanders called for. Fighting as an independent army, Wilson believed, would allow the United States to control the terms of the peace settlement at the war's end, and would thus position the United States to become a leader on the global stage.[12] To French officials, such an insistence on maintaining an independent army, like their insistence on the American Plan, only proved the Americans' arrogance and naïveté.[13]

Americans' endeavors to impose a new form of sexual governance in France were intimately connected to their vision of a new postwar international political order.[14] As historian Ross Kennedy has argued, Wilson "was convinced that the United States was politically and morally superior to other nations and therefore had a duty to lead the world to a higher level of civilization."[15] Sexual morality formed a crucial part of that superiority. Wilson reminded US troops to keep themselves "fit and straight in everything, and pure and clean through and through" to show the world "what good men" Americans were.[16] Moreover, as the United States became more powerful on the global stage during the war, the US government and private citizen social hygiene reformers gained the power to enforce their vision of sexual civilization where they pleased.

US military officials explicitly linked the War Department's promotion of sexual continence to Wilson's charge that "the world must be made safe for democracy."[17] As Secretary of the Navy Josephus Daniels declared,

> We are fighting for the safety of democracy. It is our task to preach clean lives so as also to make democracy worth fighting for. We stand for a democracy which, while recognizing man's inherent right to self-government, insists that that right carries with it obligations to the State, most sacred in character. Those obligations require the individual to curb his passions and exercise self-restraint.[18]

US soldiers had to rule themselves, rather than seek out prostitutes, so that they could make others free and fit for self-rule. Daniels, among the loudest moralists in the military, expressed hope that the next generation might consider prostitution one of the "relics of barbarism" and pronounced the American war on prostitution a "righteous crusade." While the US government understood France as a sovereign nation, its embrace of regulated prostitution called into question its people's ability to properly govern themselves.[19]

US military officials justified their approach to prostitution in terms of controlling venereal disease and thus preserving military efficiency. Daniels proclaimed venereal disease as a more pressing threat to troops than the "bloody battlefield" itself, citing the high numbers of European troops under treatment for venereal disease.[20] Preventing men from contracting disease would guarantee enough healthy bodies to fight the war, as well as display to the world American men's self-control and the national character of the United States.

The presence of some 200,000 African American soldiers in France tested white officials' faith in the American Plan and soldiers' ability to remain "pure and clean." Daniels, an ardent white supremacist, understood sexual self-control in racialized terms, as did Wilson and many other white officials.[21] Sexual self-control characterized civilized white men; conversely, sexual profligacy characterized the inferior, more bestial, darker races. Men who could not rule their sexual urges could not rule their own countries. While US officials had high hopes that the American Plan would make white troops into moral and physical exemplars to the French, they expressed ambivalence that it could civilize African American troops, calling into question both the Plan's efficacy and ideology.

"Complete Continence Is Wholly Possible"

Members of the ASHA believed that the war was an opportunity to decisively shape the US government's prostitution policy and fought to ensure that the army's policies on prostitution in France reflected the American Plan. Many medical professionals who enlisted in the army promoted this point of view. Dr. Edward L. Keyes, a member of the ASHA's board of directors, became one of the architects of the US Army's overseas venereal disease prevention efforts.[22] Major Hugh Young, the head of urology at the Johns Hopkins Hospital who went on to join the ASHA's board after the war, became chief urologist for the army. Dr. George Walker, his colleague at Hopkins who had previously served as chairman of the Maryland State-wide Vice Commission, supervised urology at seaport bases in France and succeeded Young as the army's chief urologist in early 1919.[23]

But social hygienists worried that General John J. Pershing, the commander of US forces in France, would call for regulated prostitution, as he had in Mexico. "It would be most unfortunate to permit General Pershing to take his contingent to Europe with any possibility of his continuing that sort of policy," wrote YMCA physician Max Exner to Raymond Fosdick, the chairman of the CTCA and head of US military anti-prostitution and venereal disease efforts on the mainland.[24]

Military officials also looked to the ASHA for guidance. Social hygienists had a powerful ally in Secretary of War Newton Baker, who worked to convince Pershing that the US Army should play no part in regulating prostitution in France. When Pershing sailed for Europe, Major Young accompanied him. During the voyage, Young gave graphic lectures on venereal disease control in military and civilian contexts to the army's senior officers. Pershing read Abraham Flexner's steadfastly anti-regulationist *Prostitution in Europe*. By the time Pershing landed in Europe, he had been transformed from a proponent of regulation to one of its staunchest opponents.[25] As Pershing himself put it, "sexual continence is the plain duty of members of the AEF [American Expeditionary Forces], both for the vigorous conduct of the war and for the clean health of the American people after the war. Sexual intercourse is not necessary for good health, and complete continence is wholly possible."[26]

As troops began to land in France, US officials expressed confidence that Allied armies would adopt their superior methods of venereal disease control and "suppress vice itself," rather than addressing "only the consequences of vice."[27] Their hopes for French cooperation were quickly dashed.

"As soon as we arrived in France," wrote Young derisively, "we came face to face with the ancient institution of *réglementation de prostitution* [regulated prostitution], which the French consider the most scientific and effective method of combatting venereal disease."[28] For their part, French officials regarded US policy with disdain and alarm. French medical inspector Simonin found that "the strikingly original characteristic of the American theory is the repressive measure at the head of this program," whose object was "to prevent their soldiers from having sexual relations" through appeals to "religion and morals" as well as "violent physical exercise."[29] While the French military did suggest sexual continence as a healthful option for its soldiers, it was loath to involve itself too deeply in what it understood as the private lives of its men.[30]

Before the war began in 1914, France was home to a growing movement to abolish state regulation. As in the United States, French abolitionists took their name from anti-slavery activists, and the movement united feminists and moral reformers, as well as many medical doctors. When these physicians entered the military, however, most of them supported regulation as a military necessity, allowing soldiers to release their natural sexual urges in ways that maintained the purity of their homes, their wives, and their nation.[31] French officials distinguished between regulation, in which women worked in registered brothels and underwent regular examinations for venereal disease, and clandestine prostitution, in which women eluded registration, medical inspections, and the required fees. While French officials painted clandestine prostitutes as the primary vector of disease and disorder, only regulated prostitution, they believed, could effectively curtail venereal disease and uphold social order.[32]

US officials hoped to apply their own policy of prohibition in France in spite of their ally's policy of regulation. The US military dispatched an investigator to find out whether the five-mile zones around camps in the United States, in which the military could prohibit prostitution, might work in France. He concluded that under French law the US military could not implement such a policy by itself; legally, the United States had to depend on French authorities to control the sexual behavior of the civilian population.[33]

Since the US military could not impose American policy on French soil, US military officials first focused on keeping soldiers free from disease through other means. As troops arrived in Europe, General Pershing issued a series of increasingly strict General Orders aimed at controlling the conduct of his men. The first, issued on July 2, 1917, called for lectures on the dangers of venereal disease and regular genital inspections of soldiers. It mandated that soldiers who did have sexual contact—or who returned to camp intoxicated, which officials believed led men to seek out sex—report immediately to a prophylaxis station for treatment. To demonstrate the seriousness with which he approached the matter, Pershing made contracting a venereal disease punishable by court-martial.[34] A second General Order required venereal disease treatment to take place where troops were stationed, rather than in hospitals away from the dangers of the front.[35] As US medical official George Walker remarked, compulsory prophylaxis not only reduced rates of disease, but made "the average man associate in his mind the danger of disease with sex relation[s]."[36] By controlling soldiers' bodies through genital inspections and prophylactic treatments, medical officials hoped to make men internalize the sexual discipline they had been taught in the training camps back home.

The CTCA sent some of its best lecturers to France to persuade men of "the dangerousness of all prostitutes and other loose women."[37] The ASHA and the YMCA produced films, pamphlets, exhibits, and posters directed at soldiers that repeated this message (fig. 6.1).[38] At the same time as they warned of diseases, educational materials tied each man's sexual behavior to the fate of the United States. Lectures proclaimed that American "civilization" was "founded upon the family with but one wife and mother, the purity of blood and of family depending upon her chastity." "It needs no religious teaching to realize that to expose her to disease which would affect her children is not only unfair to her but is also a crime against civilization."[39] Such materials connected men's individual conduct to the country's war aims: soldiers who fought against barbaric Germans for the safety of democracy could not allow their base desires to degrade white American society from within.

The orders calling for education and prophylaxis initially appeared effective. During September and October 1917, medical officers reported declining venereal disease rates, from 80 men per 1,000 admitted to hospitals for venereal disease to 54 per 1,000. General Pershing expressed dismay, however, when rates quadrupled to 201 per 1,000 in early November. He sent Major Young to investigate conditions at the epicenter of the outbreak, St. Nazaire, a port city on the Atlantic.[40] Young found that US military officials there did not enforce Pershing's orders. Drunken US soldiers waited in long lines to visit prostitutes; one brothel owner told Young that her most popular girl had received sixty-five men on the previous day.[41] Some commanding officers, it seemed, did not trust the American Plan's efficacy, and preferred to employ long-standing military approaches to prostitution and venereal disease.

Remember

The Folks at Home—

They are waiting for you to come back with an honorable record.

Don't allow a whore to spoil the reunion

FIGURE 6.1. ASHA created several series of exhibition cards for military camps to warn troops of the dangers posed by prostitutes. These exhibition cards were also republished in the *Journal of Social Hygiene*.

When Young reported this "disgraceful" situation, an outraged Pershing rushed to St. Nazaire to attack regulated prostitution, which he saw as the source of venereal disease. On December 18, 1917, Pershing issued General Order No. 77, which ordered military officials to repress prostitution, if possible through cooperation with French authorities, but also through the use of a military secret service, which would locate houses, rooms, and neighborhoods where prostitution took place and declare them "off-limits" to US soldiers.[42] Realizing he could not fully control US soldiers' pursuit of sexual activity, Pershing and US military officials began to look for avenues that would allow them to control the women who sold sex, just as officials had done in the United States.

Diplomatic Debates

The St. Nazaire experience convinced US military officials that, even if they could not fully prohibit it, repressing prostitution provided the only effective means of combatting venereal disease in France. Moreover, venereal disease statistics from St. Nazaire bolstered their confidence that they could persuade the French to adopt their methods. For French officials, however, the episode at St. Nazaire caused a crisis. Keeping US soldiers out of brothels undermined the system of regulation and deprived local governments of the tax revenue brothels generated. As Prime Minister Georges Clemenceau argued, it increased the spread of venereal disease among French civilians, because soldiers would sleep with local women if they did not have access to prostitutes.[43]

In the spring of 1918, at the suggestion of American medical officials, French and US officials met for a series of conferences on venereal prophylaxis, each planning to convince the other side of the efficacy of their methods. Both sides shared the belief that prostitutes were the source of venereal disease, even as they differed on whether they should control women through regulation or repression.

During the meetings, French representatives appealed to their US counterparts on three fronts. First, they stressed regulated prostitution's efficacy in reducing venereal disease rates among soldiers. As one French police official reported, in Paris 60 percent of clandestine prostitutes had a venereal disease, but for registered women the figure stood at only one-half of 1 percent.[44]

Second, to assuage any moral concerns the Americans might have, they noted that the French military treated registered prostitutes well, and brothels did not cause any "white slave traffic" [*traite des blanches*]. One French military captain acknowledged that brothels seemed to provoke "repugnance" in Americans. Therefore, French officials could oversee the creation and control of brothels for US soldiers so US officials could keep their hands clean, a solution that showed how well French officials understood the problem of American public opinion.[45]

Third, they begged US officials to understand the human cost of repressing prostitution for respectable French women. "In many cities in France mayors themselves have asked for the creation of brothels," reported a military doctor. French representatives furnished a letter from the mayor of La Courtine as evidence. "American soldiers, during the night, went to a widow who has three little daughters, made shameful offers to her, and even wanted to do violence; the cries of this woman made the soldiers leave."[46] Without regulated brothels available to them, American soldiers harassed French women and girls.

The US side, represented by military doctors Edward Keyes, Hugh Young, and George Walker, refuted French officials' arguments, contending that the French employed unscientific and ineffective approaches to disease. When Young had accompanied a French doctor on his rounds in the brothels of St. Nazaire, he noticed that the doctor did not use modern diagnostic tools such as the microscope or the Wasserman test. "The women do not wash, such that their vagina becomes a veritable petri dish," Young lamented; soldiers actually spread infections to one another by means of the communal vagina, with individual women receiving forty to fifty men per day.[47]

Keyes argued that French statistics on venereal disease control rested on unsound methods; they compared only licensed to clandestine prostitution, rather than licensing to prohibition. In comparison, the declining rates of disease among US troops in St. Nazaire after Pershing declared brothels off-limits proved the salubrious benefits of repressing rather than tolerating prostitution. Moreover, as Young argued disingenuously, "for the American people, it is a question of morals but here we are among doctors and we speak only of hygiene. If there exists a method that reduces the risk of contagion, no consideration would prevent its adoption."[48] US military physicians used statistics to demonstrate the hygienic, as well as moral, benefits of prohibiting brothels.

In meetings and correspondence, US officials discounted French claims of rape. A US official in St. Nazaire reported that two women had accused US soldiers of rape before Pershing placed brothels out of bounds, and two women had done so afterward, illustrating that the policy did not lead to a rise in rape cases. When a woman in St. Nazaire reported an attempted rape to US officials, she could not tell them whether the soldier was "successful" or not since she had fainted. She claimed she had bit the soldier's finger during the attack, but when US officials looked for a soldier with a finger injury, they found none, which officials believed cast doubt on what they contended was an already questionable claim. As Young and Keyes wrote in a preparatory memo before the conference, French mayors expressed concern about brothel closures because of the loss of revenue for their towns, rather than because they cared about women's safety.[49]

The meetings laid bare the opposing assumptions that shaped French and American policy. As the French military doctor Major Gastou articulated it, "the genital need is indeed, for most men, a necessity. . . . When this appetite awakens the man lets himself be carried away by the first solicitation which he identifies." Since his "natural genital appetite" must be met, the brothel provided "maximum surveillance and minimum risk."[50] Not only did it reduce the spread of disease, but it also directed a man's sexual appetite toward the registered prostitute instead of the respectable women he might rape if his appetite became too enflamed. In contrast, Young argued that most US soldiers could practice "almost complete sexual continence," backing up his claims with statistics showing that within a division of 7,401 men, physicians had provided only 56 prophylactic treatments and only one soldier had contracted venereal disease. The war had exposed the fallacy "that the soldier must be a libertine in order to be a fighter," Young proclaimed. In the American formulation of male sexual desire, men could control their natural urges, but legalized prostitution, with both "unbridled street solicitation" and brothels, dangerously provoked these appetites.[51]

Moreover, French and American officials emphasized their differing conceptions of the relationship between the state and its citizens' sexuality. Gastou observed of the Americans, "these gentlemen do individual prophylaxis, and we do collective prophylaxis."[52] The French approach acknowledged the male sex drive and used the state to channel it into the regulation system, designed to keep the majority of men free of disease by providing them with access to inspected prostitutes, all without infringing on individual male liberties. Regulation protected respectable women from seduction or rape and protected wives and children from venereal disease, even if it did sacrifice some women for this collective good.

In contrast, US officials focused on keeping individual soldiers free of disease by inculcating self-discipline, preventing access to prostitutes, and mandating post-coital medical treatment for those who faltered. The state should make its male citizens capable of self-rule, the pillar of democracy, and channel male sexual energies into the family, the building block of a civilized nation. A civilized state had no business facilitating prostitution. As Young and Keyes argued, "from the moral point of view the licensing of prostitutes implies an alliance between the government and the pimp."[53] The state did, however, have the right to demand that its soldiers sacrifice individual sexual freedom for the good of the country, as US officials at the highest level repeatedly insisted.

After the conferences between the United States and France ended in a stalemate over the issue of regulating or repressing prostitution, US officials met with British and Dominion military and civilian government representatives in May 1918, with a second meeting in July 1918 that included French military doctor Henri Gougerot. US officials perceived these conferences as another opportunity to apply diplomatic pressure on the French and to convince the British to join them in repressing prostitution in France. The British had already faced public outcry over the high rates of venereal disease in the British and Dominion armies. In the spring of 1918, the British War Office put French brothels out of bounds for Crown troops to appease public opinion, but the move angered army officials, who feared it would only exacerbate the venereal disease problem. The War Office hoped that collaboration with Americans would demonstrate its commitment to tackling venereal disease to both the public and the British military.[54]

In London, British officials greeted the Americans with more comity than did the French. The British government expressed interest in American methods of repressing prostitution and promoting sexual continence. The Archbishop of Canterbury proclaimed the importance of American social hygiene for the war effort and beyond, quoting extensively from Abraham Flexner's 1914 book, *Prostitution in Europe*, the same book that turned Pershing away from regulation.[55] He attended the two conferences along with his friend Bishop Brent, the Chief-of-Chaplains of the American Expeditionary Forces. Despite both British and American militaries' insistence that they prioritized scientific rather than moral approaches to the problem of prostitution, a shared white Anglo-American Protestant conception of sexual purity wove through the meetings, as did a millennialist sense of the transformative possibilities of a global fight against prostitution. As Brent proclaimed, "This is the moment, the moment of the ages when we can take hold of this whole horrible thing in such a way as to make a cleaner and better world."[56]

At the meetings, US officials set themselves apart by their willingness to interfere in the domestic policies of allied countries. They pressed for British cooperation to suppress prostitution in France. US representatives asked British officials to prevent British troops from entering brothels in France and to pressure French officials to help enforce the policy. They also hoped to convince the British to strengthen their own domestic provisions against prostitution, such that British officials could arrest British women if they transmitted a venereal disease to a US soldier.[57]

Yet French officials stood firm in their position. At the second conference, Gougerot proclaimed that the majority of French military officials believed the regulated brothel alone could prevent disease. While he realized British and American officials had "scruples" about regulation, he begged them out of their "friendship toward France" not to put brothels off-limits, which would have "disastrous effects for our race."[58] In the face of French commitment to the brothel system, British officials feared that any attempts to weaken it would prove ineffective and strain relations with France. They would not ask the French government to close brothels and keep other Allied troops away from them.[59] Unlike US officials, they declined to jeopardize their diplomatic ties with an ally over what they understood as a matter of national policy.

British officials rarely prevented Crown soldiers from visiting brothels in France, despite the stated policy against it. When US medical officer George Walker found six British soldiers in a brothel in Cherbourg, he brought it to the attention of the British Provost Marshall, who informed him, "although these houses were officially out-of-bounds, he allowed the men to enter, because he considered it the better plan. When reminded of the order forbidding this, he simply shrugged his shoulders."[60] British officials, like Americans, aggressively policed women at home, arresting twenty thousand women in England and Wales for solicitation during a six-month period in 1918. Yet British military officials continued to believe that soldiers needed safe sexual release in France to protect respectable women at home, an idea with deep roots in British colonial policy.[61] Moreover, British officials remained committed to the diplomatic norms that US officials willingly flouted.

An "Unfortunate Intervention"

As US officials worked through diplomatic channels to convince British and French officials to adopt the American Plan and repress prostitution, officials on the ground were already fighting prostitution without regard for French law. When Pershing began to place brothels off-limits to US soldiers, his orders led officials to surveil French women using tactics developed at home.

A series of events in Blois, a small city in central France, demonstrated the increasingly punitive strategies US military forces used to control prostitution. They also illustrated the conflicts that arose over prostitution, both among US officials and between US and French officials. In mid-January 1918, US troops began arriving in Blois, where the US military had taken over old French army barracks and opened a hospital. At times, troop strength in the area reached ten thousand.[62] For the first two weeks men poured into the town's brothels, but the Provost Marshall quickly placed them out of bounds. Local authorities vocally protested his actions.[63]

Ignoring Pershing's orders, a US medical officer in Blois allowed one of the madams to keep her brothel open for the exclusive use of American soldiers, with a military police officer stationed at the door. US medical officers examined the women two or three times a week for venereal diseases, in return for a fee of five francs for the use of the room and five francs for "the services of the girl." While French officials supported the "American House," some of the town's residents expressed annoyance at its exclusivity. When a military policeman denied a Frenchman entry to the brothel one night, a drunken fight broke out and a US guard shot the man in the leg.[64] Despite top-down orders to keep men sexually continent, not all US military officials believed it possible.

Even as the medical officer in Blois flouted official US policy, high-ranking officers, including Pershing, grew more committed to prohibiting prostitution, demonstrating the dominance of social hygienists' ideas within the top levels of the military. In the aftermath of the shooting, an official sent General Pershing a report detailing the system of US military-regulated prostitution in Blois. In March 1918, Pershing reiterated the order declaring all brothels off-limits and instructed the military police to "use every effort to prevent clandestine prostitution," which they "rigorously carried out."[65] At the center of these renewed US military efforts to repress prostitution were the bodies of French women.

Hugh Young, dispatched to investigate the situation in Blois, described the American strategy:

The method now in vogue is that one of the military police meets each train, every woman going to Blois is observed, and if suspicious, a detail is sent to see where she goes and to watch her movements. If it is found that she is soliciting she is immediately reported to the French police and if not registered is always run out of town. If registered as a rule the French police turn her loose. The women found soliciting on the streets are arrested by the American military police and turned over to the French. As a rule they are turned loose again if they have cards, but they are promptly arrested again by the Americans and as a result of these frequent arrests most of them leave town. During the past month over 150 women have thus been forced to leave.[66]

The deliberate use of surveillance and harassment to force women to leave the locality reflected the tactics that the CTCA used in the United States. Across American cities, Commission officials arrested and harassed women for activities associated with prostitution but not in and of themselves illegal, including talking to soldiers or simply living close to a red-light district. Similarly, repeatedly arresting and harassing French women who had not committed a crime also suppressed prostitution through extralegal methods.

Moreover, in France, like at home, the US military articulated a far-reaching goal of reforming the country's sexual culture. As Young remarked, "there has been a tremendous transformation of vice conditions in Blois and the better French people have begun to appreciate it immensely." Repressing prostitution had a "wonderful effect not only in lowering the venereal rate but in improving the morality of the soldiers and also the civil population at Blois," although Young acknowledged that some politicians, as well as saloon and brothel owners, expressed outrage.[67] US officials saw the American Plan as more than a strategy for preventing venereal disease; in their eyes, it promised to inculcate and enforce a higher standard of morality and conduct.

Despite Young's sanguine pronouncements, French officials at the local and regional levels objected that the US military had far overstepped its bounds, with one terming the US military's actions at Blois an "unfortunate intervention." Not only had clandestine prostitution grown, they argued, but venereal disease rates also rose. Under pressure from US military officials, the chief official of the region cooperated with their request to clean up the disreputable hotels in Blois. As he complained, "But in addition to these measures which I already consider illegal, I am asked to carry out expulsions of all registered prostitutes en masse from the city, measures which I refuse to take because they are absolutely arbitrary and of a nature to cause scandals in the community."[68]

By enforcing the American Plan, which deliberately defied French laws and policies, US officials initiated a cat-and-mouse game, as US and French officials alternately arrested and released women accused of prostitution. While French officials felt angry at their loss of sovereignty, women faced the harshest consequences. By making and implementing its own rules in a sovereign country, despite the vocal protests of government officials, the US military acted more like an occupying force than an allied one.

US military officials used similar extralegal and illegal tactics to repress prostitution in cities across France. In St. Nazaire, one official reported, "the Provost guard have been constantly on the watch and when a house is discovered it is raided and the men kept out until the prostitutes of the closed house leave." When the women ended up in another brothel, it was "quickly discovered and raided again."[69] After US officials forced prostitutes to leave Void, a small town in northeastern France, French officials complained up the US Army chain of command about the "illegal acts of the American zone major."[70] In response to French complaints that the US military had illegally placed notices on brothels—the private property of French citizens—deeming them out of bounds, Pershing ordered US officials to seek permission before doing so. Yet US Military Police stationed in Ballon, more than two hundred miles south of St. Nazaire, placarded the residences of women whom they had examined and found diseased.[71]

French officials decried American attempts to repress prostitution and prevent soldiers from visiting prostitutes as an attack on the nation. In an investigation conducted by French officials, twenty-one mayors reported that Pershing's orders closing brothels to US troops proved "detrimental for public morality," and sixteen of them declared that it had an "untoward influence on the spread of venereal disease."[72] One police commissioner complained that clandestine prostitution now flourished in his town and that American soldiers were "not only seen with women, but with young girls of 14–16."[73]

After US officials placed brothels out of bounds and forbid French officials from opening a brothel for US troops in Guer, a local official reported the attempted rape of a ten-year-old boy. The baker's son "was busy picking strawberries in his garden when an American soldier, in a slight state of intoxication, entered the garden, took off his trousers, and proceeded to remove the boy's, offering him 50 francs." Although people arrived to stop him, the official noted that "frequently, similar facts were brought to my knowledge: several American soldiers were seen engaging in acts against nature on Algerians and young Spaniards."[74] The French sent a clear message: putting brothels off-limits prevented US soldiers from satisfying their sexual needs in a natural way and turned them toward rape, pedophilia, and same-sex activity. These kinds of acts, rather than sex with prostitutes, harmed both US soldiers and innocent French civilians.

In contrast, US officials pointed to the moral dangers that regulated prostitution posed to white American civilization. In France, George Walker discovered that "practically all of the prostitutes were perverts, and they encouraged the men to use of [sic] unnatural methods," indicating that they engaged in oral sex. American officials felt concerned enough to send an investigator to five French cities to study the problem. Of the 237 women he interviewed, only four denied engaging in "abnormal" intercourse. While Walker reported that American soldiers initially met these practices with "disgust and contempt," they soon "were indulging in perversions almost as willingly and as frequently as the French." From the "Anglo-Saxon viewpoint," Walker declared, sexual perversion "destroys the very fibres of decency." The hundreds of thousands of soldiers who would return to the United States "with these new and degenerate ideas sapping their sources of self-respect" could spread the "contagion."[75] For officials such as Walker, deviant forms of sexual contact in France raised the specter of white racial and national degeneration.

As a result of their growing fear that American men would become morally and physically infected through contact with French prostitutes, US military officials intensified their tactics after the armistice of November 11, 1918. The war's end brought new challenges for the American social hygiene program. Soldiers were granted long-awaited furloughs, traveling to cities such as Paris with thriving commercial sex districts. Rates of venereal disease rose dramatically. Not wanting to have its image tarnished or to have soldiers bring infections back with them, the US Army redoubled its efforts to repress prostitution and enforce prophylaxis, issuing an order that soldiers with venereal disease could not travel home with their battalions.[76]

In early 1919, CTCA official Bascom Johnson sailed across the Atlantic with a team of fifteen of his best law enforcement officers. In France, they were "instructed to apply, to as great an extent as possible, those measures which had proved effective in the United States."[77] While US officials had previously demanded that soldiers name the women who supposedly infected them, the practice of contact tracing seems to have intensified after Johnson's visit.[78] When disease rates rose in areas of France, Germany, and Luxembourg where US soldiers went on leave after the armistice, US officials "cross-examined" soldiers diagnosed with venereal disease for detailed information that could help the military apprehend suspected prostitutes (fig. 6.2).[79]

In spite of these conflicts on the ground between the US military, French officials, and civilians, the system of regulation and the American Plan had significant points of agreement, allowing for some Franco-American

Prostitution Record
In
Venereal Cases.

Name...........................Rank.........Org...........................

Diagnosis.......................Date of exposure.......................

Appearance of infection....................Prophylaxis............Time............

Where did you meet the woman who infected you, Specify exactly...................

What time of day was it.......................When you alone...................

Were you solicited by her...................Are any of the following places nea.

where you were solicited; Barracks, Church School or Public Square............. .

....
(Specify which)
To what place, (Hotel or Rooming house) did you go....................... .

Did you observe any other AEF, men about the premises?.......................

Were you required to register....................Was the woman...............

Price charged for the room...................By the Torai...................

Did the woman have herepolice card............How long were you together.......

Was the subject of venereal disease mentioned by the woman or you...............

Did the woman comment on civil or Military Police...........................

Have you seen the woman since exposure, if so where...........................

Here name and address if known...

Could you identify her if you see her again...................................

Do you know whether or not other members of the AEF were infected by her........

Remarks...

....

....

....

....

Signature...

FIGURE 6.2. This "Prostitution Record in Venereal Cases" form required
soldiers to disclose when and where they had sexual contact with a woman, her
name and address, as well as the price they paid. Image courtesy of the US
National Archives and Records Administration.

cooperation. French and US officials worked together to arrest clandestine prostitutes and quarantine prostitutes with venereal disease. In Bourbonne-les-Bains, for example, the mayor toured the town with a US military doctor while he inspected prostitutes and filed a report with the French military police for the "evacuation" of diseased prostitutes from the area. Such cooperation likely made it possible for US officials to arrest and inspect Aline Legros, whose story opened this chapter, and ensured that she had little recourse.[80] French authorities near Nice helped US authorities to suppress clandestine prostitution "as far as possible under their laws," forcing the "departure of approximately 800 women of questionable character from the area" within a single month.[81] While the French and American militaries differed dramatically over the issue of legal, regulated brothels, they fundamentally agreed that closer surveillance of and restrictions on women advanced both the war effort and public health.[82]

US military medical experts persuaded the French military to adopt their prophylactic methods, which French officials believed could work in tandem with the regulated brothel to reduce disease to the minimum.[83] In fact, US officials had modeled their program in part on the French military's use of new drug therapies, as well as the New Zealand and Australian Expeditionary Forces' extensive use of chemical prophylaxis.[84] In the fall of 1918, the French military began to construct prophylactic treatment stations, based on those built by the American Expeditionary Forces, where soldiers could seek treatment immediately after they had sex. Unlike the US military, however, French officials declined to make this treatment compulsory and did not punish soldiers who failed to receive treatment and developed venereal disease. Military doctors reported that few French soldiers used the system. Moreover, they observed that US soldiers who had developed venereal disease came to the French stations for treatment in an attempt to escape punishment by court-martial.[85]

The promising statistics that US officials presented to the French while promoting the American Plan's prophylactic methods initially won over some French officials. But by October 1918, a French military doctor argued that "the statistics so happily published by the Americans are entirely false."[86] To the French, the discrepancy between rhetoric and results provided further proof that the US military's methods had failed.[87] Moreover, the need for prophylactic stations—and the fact that US troops contracted venereal disease in the first place—demonstrated the falsity of American soldiers' supposed sexual self-restraint.

While the American Plan called for the total suppression of prostitution, its uneven application in France demonstrated that not all or even most soldiers and their superiors accepted its vision of masculinity or sexuality. George Walker's investigations revealed that many commanding officers did not enforce the orders declaring brothels off-limits and vocally complained that such measures did not work. After the armistice, Pershing toured the leave areas in France and found to his dismay that many commanders did not place brothels out of bounds, track down women suspected of spreading disease, provide prophylactic facilities, or court-martial officers who contracted venereal disease, and they provided little education on matters of hygiene.[88]

Even though Pershing personally asked commanding officers to enforce the court-martialing of officers, court-martial records suggest that they ignored his request. Very few men were court-martialed for contracting venereal disease or having sex with prostitutes. The records show that of the more than two million men in the American Expeditionary Forces, only thirteen faced court-martial for offenses related to contracting a venereal disease, while fifty-one faced court-martial for consorting with alleged prostitutes. As historian Andrew Byers argues, these cases involved another offense or created a public spectacle, suggesting that official concern lay less with men's actual sexual behavior and more with its appearance.[89]

A "Racial Quarantine":
The Limits of American Sexual Exceptionalism

While French and US officials could not agree on prostitution and venereal disease policy, both worked to uphold racial hierarchy and white supremacy as they sought to control soldiers' sexual contacts. The American Expeditionary Forces included 200,000 African Americans. While approximately 42,000 African American troops served in combat, the majority performed manual labor, including working as stevedores unloading ships.[90] Some 500,000 French colonial subjects served in Europe; known as *troupes indigènes*, they hailed from North and West Africa and Madagascar, as well as Indochina.[91] Both French and US officials saw Black and Asian men as hypersexual and diseased. Just as US officials claimed that African American soldiers had high rates of venereal disease, French physicians argued that colonial troops from Algeria, Morocco, and Senegal all carried syphilis.[92]

Although French and American officials both sought to manage relationships between white prostitutes and men of color, the tools available to them differed. The French principle of republican universalism forbade laws that explicitly discriminated based on racial identity. As Caroline Séquin has shown, because they could not set up an explicitly discriminatory system, French officials used the brothel as the primary means of maintaining racial order for Black troops stationed in France. African colonial soldiers must have access to white French prostitutes inside brothels, white officials believed, so they would not form relationships with or rape respectable white French women outside brothels.[93] Similarly, French officials expected that African American troops would visit white French prostitutes in brothels.[94]

The US military, in contrast, maintained racial segregation both in the United States and abroad.[95] While general orders placed brothels off-limits to all US troops, US officials expressed concern about sexual relationships between Black soldiers and white prostitutes. African American men visiting the same brothels as white men, staffed by white French women, smacked of a social equality that flew in the face of Jim Crow laws and the white supremacist convictions of many white soldiers and officials. Such experiences in France might make African American soldiers expect the same social equality when they returned home.[96] Moreover, the idea that white women could desire Black men subverted US racial logic, which portrayed Black men as rapists of innocent white women, rather than sexual partners they chose willingly.[97]

French officials regarded what they saw as the racially prejudiced American position with distaste. As one reported in a confidential memo to his superiors, "Americans are outraged at any public intimacy of white women with blacks." They had lodged "violent protests" against an engraving from a French magazine showing a white woman dining with a Black man, even though it clearly depicted a French soldier from Senegal. French officials and citizens, he argued, welcomed African American troops without prejudice. Yet in French settler colonies in Africa, he admitted, "intimate relationships between white women and black men are also deeply regretted by our experienced colonists, who see them as a considerable loss of prestige of the white race."[98] French officials worried that interracial sex, improperly controlled, posed a serious threat to white supremacy, even as they balked at Americans' methods.

The French and US governments' anxieties about the presence of African American soldiers demonstrated the high stakes of prostitution control for the two countries. By placing brothels off-limits to Black as well as white soldiers, US officials not only subverted French sovereignty and sexual order, they also undermined an important French mechanism of maintaining racial order. Yet for US officials, fighting a war in the name of American-style civilization and democracy, any consensual sex between white women and African American men laid bare the lie of pure white women, hypersexual Black men, and strong white male protectors on which the myth of American exceptionalism rested.

US military medical officials at the highest levels condemned interracial sex and sought to prevent it. In France, they were troubled by their observations that white French women would receive Black customers as readily as white ones.[99] US officials attempted to shape the behavior of African American troops with lectures and educational materials, although posters and films exclusively featured white men and white women. Hugh Young lectured the medical officers of the 92nd Infantry Division, the only African American military unit to serve in combat in Europe, on the "unsurmountable barrier between the two races" and "the necessity of leaving white women alone."[100]

The US military used far more punitive methods to prevent African American troops from having sex with white prostitutes than they did to control white soldiers. US military officials relied both on more restrictive policies for Black troops and on threats of extralegal violence. White soldiers became angry and even violent when they saw Black soldiers with white French women. Yet US officials laid the blame on Black men for crossing the color line. In St. Nazaire, George Walker reported the two thousand "negro stevedores" were "giving a great deal of trouble" because "they cohabit quite frequently with white women." When a group of white engineers "had trouble" with the stevedores, the engineers "armed themselves with clubs and went after them." After "order was restored" by white US Marines, officials searched the African American workers for weapons and presumably confiscated them.[101] Sexual contact between white women and African American men undermined the sexual prerogatives of white soldiers, already limited by army policy. Punishing African American men allowed white men to reassert their dominance.

White military officials were not alone in attempting to constrain Black men's sexual experiences during wartime. The Black professional class also discouraged men from sleeping with white French women, though they did so out of concern for the safety of soldiers and the violence they could face, as well as for their respectability. The Black press, Black clubwomen, and the few African American women who worked for the YMCA in France emphasized Black soldiers' faithfulness to their Black sweethearts at home and their love of African American women, rather than white French women. At the same time, as Khary Oronde Polk argues, Walker's complaints about the stevedores' behavior suggest that Black soldiers sought, and often found, willing white French women as sexual partners, transgressing the constraints that white officials, white soldiers, and the Black professional class attempted to place on them.[102]

US officials attempted to control the mobility of African American troops to keep them away from white women. After the scene Walker witnessed in St. Nazaire—Black and white troops fighting over access to white women—he advised: "It is very necessary that a suitable wire fence or wire entanglement be built around the stevedore encampment."[103] Military guards secured the entrance to the "stockade" to "afford total control of the men themselves."[104] This policy affected Black soldiers facing combat, as well as laborers. The military prohibited the 92nd Division from traveling more than a mile from its base and forbid the 368th regiment from visiting the village near their drill ground, instituting what a Black lieutenant termed a "racial quarantine."[105]

Despite these efforts to limit African Americans' access to white women, many US military officials believed Black sexual appetites were too strong to contain. In fact, some feared that preventing Black troops from visiting brothels would lead them to commit rape, echoing French arguments about the purpose of the regulated brothel. Brigadier General Walter Bethel, who had advocated the American Plan at the Allies' venereal disease conferences, wrote to Pershing with reports that one African American soldier in France had hanged for rape and two had faced trial. "I have considerable fear that the sexual instinct of the negro is going to embarrass us much. If they were grouped in one or two cities to the exclusion largely of other troops, I should hesitate very much to recommend the putting of houses in such places 'out of bounds.'"[106]

In Bordeaux, a commanding officer allowed five brothels to remain open for US troops, with three houses reserved for white enlisted men, one for white officers, and another for "colored" troops. While this plan rested on a broad conception of male sexual necessity, it also responded to particular concerns about Black hypersexuality. To keep African American troops away from the white women who solicited them on the street, the commanding officer placed military police in the vicinity to ensure that Black men visited only their designated brothel. While keeping Black troops from having sex with supposedly diseased clandestine prostitutes, it also enforced racial segregation and limited Black men's access to white women outside of the brothel, which corresponded with French practices.[107]

When French women accused Americans of rape, US officials often blamed African American men. In St. Nazaire, a US official recounted, "negroes" committed two of four attempted rapes, a fact Hugh Young and Edward Keyes termed "noteworthy" given the presence of 5,613 "colored troops" in the area. Moreover, they recounted, one attempt occurred when a negro "had been allowed to visit the home," attributing sexual assaults to French women's familiarity with African American men.[108] That so few rapes had been committed by sexually uncontrollable Black men demonstrated that the American Plan worked, Young and Keyes implied. When French women accused Black soldiers, however, the military punished them far more severely than white soldiers. It court-martialed and subsequently executed eight Black soldiers in France, in comparison to two white men, one of whom was also listed as "Indian?" [sic], calling his whiteness into question.[109] Other Black soldiers accused of rape faced execution without a trial.[110]

By calling attention to these rape cases, I am not suggesting that women always made false accusations or that Black soldiers never committed rape, though there is evidence that US officials tried to pin rape charges on Black men, even when women named white attackers.[111] What I want to point out is that white US officials used rape cases in France to uphold the myth of the Black rapist, making rape, to use historian Mary Louise Roberts's phrase, a "'Negro,' rather than 'American' problem," and thus to assert the role of white American men as protectors of civilization.[112] Lectures to troops proclaimed that "women and families of France and even of enemies should be protected."[113] Rape accusations against American soldiers undermined their role as protectors. Blaming and lynching Black men allowed white US officials to distance themselves from the accusations while also reaffirming the preeminent role of the United States and its American Plan in making the world safe for democracy.

For their part, French officials blamed African American troops for putting the French "in danger" as a means of challenging the American Plan. After Pershing put the brothels in St. Nazaire off-limits to Americans, the mayor wrote to the US commanding officer complaining about the "negro stevedores." The mayor presented him with three options: first "that three houses of prostitution be opened for the negros," second, "that negro women be brought over from the United States to serve as prostitutes for these men"; or, third, that "all of the negros be sent back to the United States."[114] The mayor's letter showed that he understood the threat of interracial sex as a pressure point for convincing US officials to allow soldiers to visit brothels. But it also reveals the profound threat interracial sex *outside* of the brothel posed to French officials' role as the protectors of respectable white French women and France's status as a white colonial power.[115]

While both French and US officials portrayed themselves as defenders of white women, US officials called French women's level of civilization into question. They repeatedly pointed out that only the "lower type of French women" associated with Black men, troubling their status as white women deserving of protection.[116] In Tours, Walker reported, the better brothels "did draw the line at colored soldiers, who were obliged to go to the eastern part of the city, where there were 'dives' of the most disreputable sort inhabited by wholly degenerate and perverted prostitutes."[117] By rendering these women as degenerate or perverted, adjectives with racialized connotations in both languages, US officials absolved themselves of their failure to fulfill their duty as white men to protect white women.

US military officials assumed that Black men contracted venereal disease more readily than white men. Medical officials forced African American soldiers to undergo prophylactic treatment every time they returned to their racially segregated camps, while only mandating it for white soldiers who admitted to having sex with a prostitute or who returned to camp drunk. During the treatments, a medical attendant injected a silver protein solution into the patient's urethra, which the patient had to retain for five minutes, and then refrain from urinating for four to five hours after treatment.[118] Since white officials did not believe they could inculcate self-discipline in African American men, white officials disciplined their bodies to keep them free of disease and to reinforce their subordination.

White US military officials acknowledged that African American men "objected strenuously to prophylaxis" and "regarded it with horrified suspicion."[119] While they repeated these claims to demonstrate Black soldiers' unruliness and ignorance, they also captured Black men's suspicion that prophylaxis did more harm than good and that white officials behaved negligently, and even violently, in providing such invasive medical treatment. Hugh Young related, as a supposedly humorous anecdote, the story of a Black orderly who asked his colonel for a transfer. When the colonel asked why he would give up his easy job of running 15–20 errands per day outside of the camp, the orderly replied that he received prophylaxis every time he returned and was thus "getting awful sore."[120] The orderly's experience and Young's retelling of it point to white officials' continued fixation with Black men's genitals as a place to enact violence as a means of control, a fixation they replicated in the United States and the Caribbean as well.[121]

Repeated, compulsory treatments may have actually spread venereal disease within African American battalions. One infirmary in the United States, where Black soldiers received medical care, listed 300 men under treatment for venereal disease even though only 174 had an infection. An educated observer noted incredulously that "the same syringes were used without any attempt at sterilization."[122] Such experiences in the United States would have made African American troops in France justifiably wary of prophylactic treatment.[123] Similar negligence likely occurred in France. In Tours, which had a large Black troop presence, an official reported "filthy and insanitary" prophylactic stations with "dirty syringes."[124]

Commanding officers had to justify themselves to General Pershing himself if they reported high rates of disease among their battalions. White officials relied on the stereotypes of Black men as diseased and hypersexual to place the blame on African Americans. Black battalions were often stationed in port cities, which already had high venereal disease rates due to such cities' substantial commercial sex trade. Moreover, African American troops had high rates of venereal disease before arriving in France, likely because conscription boards allowed African Americans with venereal infections to join the army, but excluded infected white soldiers.[125] When Pershing demanded an explanation of the high venereal rate at Camp Covington, near Marseilles, the Base Surgeon explained, "66.2% of camp inmates are negroes, these men go A.W.O.L., expose themselves to infection with the lower class of prostitutes, return to camp (over the wall) avoiding the guard and fail to take prophylactic for the fear of detection and punishment."[126] By attributing high disease rates to the presence of Black soldiers, commanding officers deflected criticism of their leadership, a practice that likely led to the overreporting of venereal disease among Black troops.

At the same time, white military officials trumpeted their ability to reduce venereal disease rates among Black troops as proof of the efficacy of US military medical technology. Medical officer Walker noted that the "magical" reduction in venereal disease rates among African American troops in five camps in France was "due almost solely to compulsory prophylaxis, for the men were allowed to go out from 5:30 to 9:30 and do whatever they pleased."[127] In a striking application of a racialized double standard, white officials interpreted low rates of venereal disease among white troops as proof that white soldiers exercised self-control, while citing low rates of venereal disease among Black troops as evidence that their scientific methods of prophylaxis could tame even the most recalcitrant and diseased bodies.[128]

While the rhetoric of the American Plan proclaimed American soldiers' remarkable capacity for sexual self-control as a symbol of the country's political, moral, and scientific progress, US officials feared that African American troops would undermine the image they stood determined to project. The US military disciplined and controlled Black soldiers' bodies to a far greater degree than those of white soldiers. In fact, US officials treated African American soldiers and sexually suspicious white French women in a notably similar way, regulating their mobility, forcibly inspecting their genitals, and subjecting them to invasive and painful medical intervention. They considered both groups uncivilized, a diagnosis they often articulated in the terms of sexuality. Moreover, sexual relationships between Black men and white French women, even lower-class and disreputable ones, threatened the racial and civilizational hierarchies that the architects of the American Plan wished to uphold.

Conclusion

US officials used a wide range of strategies to prevent soldiers from having sex in France, and, if that failed, to prevent them from contracting venereal disease. They worked through diplomatic channels to attack the French system of regulation itself. They educated, dissuaded, threatened, and shamed white soldiers and mandated prophylactic treatment for those who admitted to having sex. They used similar tactics on Black soldiers, but supplemented them with far more punitive measures, such as repeated and unnecessary prophylactic treatments, strictly limited mobility, and violence. Finally, they surveilled, harassed, arrested, and genitally inspected French women whom they believed to be prostitutes.

Through their efforts to repress prostitution and prevent the spread of venereal disease, US officials acted as imperialists in an Allied nation, infringing on both the bodies of French women and French sovereignty to protect the health of white US soldiers and the image of US troops as sexually moral and self-disciplined. The efforts of social hygiene advocates and US officials to implement the American Plan in France reflected their broader ambitions to assert the United States as a uniquely moral global power and to remake other nations in the United States' sexual image.

The American Expeditionary Forces based their approach to prostitution on an imperialist logic, evident in both the American Plan and in the ways many officials chose to ignore it. Military officials worked to control the bodies of French women and flouted French laws and policies to keep American men "clean." At the same time, many looked the other way and even encouraged the sexual conquest of French women by American soldiers. Both approaches circumvented the French system of regulation, a bulwark of French racial, gender, and social order. Moreover, because the American Plan demanded sexual continence from white soldiers (or at least the image of it through low rates of venereal disease), the policy had no means to address what was actually happening—sex between US troops and French women—and thus could not reduce or mitigate the harms that occurred.

Either through arresting women or sleeping with them, American soldiers and the US military asserted their dominance in France at a time when the United States began to stake its claim as a global power. The US military's approach to the sex lives of its soldiers in France during WWI thus lay an important foundation for the expansion of American power in the twentieth century. As historian Mary Louise Roberts has shown, in the aftermath of WWII, "the management of GI sex in France became a subtle but vital transfer point for the growth of American political power in Europe." By framing the United States as a moral, masculine protector and France as a feminized, prostituted nation, officials naturalized the United States' right to direct the post–WWI order.[129]

In many ways the American Plan in France failed. It did not prevent soldiers from having sex or contracting venereal disease, and it did not convince other militaries to follow suit. But in other ways, its powerful rhetoric prevailed long after the war's end. Social hygiene advocates, elevated to official positions in the US military, saw the American Plan as evidence of the country's sexual exceptionalism, which rested on women's chastity and men's self-restraint.

In the assessment of William Snow, the CTCA's Social Hygiene Director and the ASHA Secretary, the American Plan in France succeeded admirably: "The general impression both among Americans and foreigners is that the A.E.F. [American Expeditionary Forces] has a lower venereal rate than the other great armies." But more important than the low disease rate was how the US military achieved it. As Snow interpreted his data, "continence," followed by "factors which limit or repress prostitution," and then "medical prophylaxis" let to the Plan's success.[130] Prophylaxis almost certainly played a far greater role than Snow would have liked to admit: a contemporary army researcher found that 71 percent of American soldiers had sexual intercourse while in France.[131] But the use of prophylaxis did not fit easily with social hygienists' conception of a new American masculinity. It proved an important last resort for weaker men, but unnecessary for the majority—particularly those who were white.

The war served as a large-scale policy experiment, which American social hygiene reformers viewed as proof that civilized countries should prohibit prostitution rather than license it. The US government had granted members of the ASHA, including those who worked as civilians as well as those who joined the military, extraordinary powers to dictate US prostitution and venereal disease policy, both at home and everywhere that US troops were stationed. After the war, as social hygienists returned to their careers in government, higher education, and private organizations such as the ASHA, their wartime experience prepared them to take up their work on a new scale.

As ASHA officials proclaimed, "War in three years advanced social hygiene a decade.... [ASHA] has come out of the war, with its working staff increased in numbers, and enjoying a large experience gained thru intimate association with governmental agencies."[132] The ASHA reported that it had corresponded with 13,000 people from sixty-three countries, including US colonies, between mid-1919 and mid-1920.[133] After the war, the same social hygienists who carried out the American Plan would continue to act as agents of state power masquerading as citizen reformers as they attacked prostitution from a new angle: eradicating the international traffic in women.

7

"A World-Wide Influence"

AMERICANS AND THE LEAGUE OF NATIONS

IN EARLY 1925, American Paul Kinsie visited Marseilles, France, to conduct an undercover investigation of the traffic in women. He described its streets as "literally honeycombed with the vilest, filthiest, and most degraded prostitutes whom I have ever had the opportunity of meeting." Not only did they aggressively solicit men, but they even dragged them into their "filthy huts." Kinsie emphasized their diverse origins: "All nationalities along the Mediterranean are represented. Prostitutes from India, Greece, Italy, Egypt, Turkey, North Coast of Africa, Spain, together with the native French and Belgians are to be found here." Accentuating these women's benightedness, as well as the illicit appeal of exoticism, he noted, "some of these women wear their native costumes and do not attempt to conceal their nationality." Yet Kinsie found that local authorities officially registered such women as prostitutes, despite the fact that they were foreign.[1]

For Kinsie, it was of little consequence that Marseilles, a Mediterranean port city, was known for its racial, ethnic, and national diversity even before the war. In the war's aftermath, economic crisis and ongoing geographic displacement led more women to migrate there for sexual commerce.[2] To Kinsie the mere presence of foreign prostitutes, particularly in licensed brothels, provided clear evidence of the thriving international traffic in women.

While Kinsie's activities in Marseille were similar to those he carried out as an ASHA investigator and employee of the Commission on Training Camp Activities during WWI, in Marseilles, Kinsie represented the League of Nations. An intergovernmental organization forged as part of the WWI peace process, many countries hoped that the League might prevent future wars and foster international cooperation on pressing issues, such as trafficking. Yet the

United States declined to join the League, despite it being the brainchild of US President and social hygiene ally Woodrow Wilson, making Kinsie's role as a League investigator especially striking. Even though the US government remained formally absent from the League's work, Americans acting as private citizens involved themselves in League activities, particularly around causes deemed "social" and "humanitarian." In fact, John D. Rockefeller, Jr., funded the League's international trafficking investigations through the Bureau of Social Hygiene, much as he funded the ASHA's domestic ones.[3]

By establishing the landscape of trafficking using social scientific investigation, the ASHA inserted its agenda—one focused around criminalizing commercial sex and restricting migration—into the League's anti-trafficking work. Between 1924 and 1927, a team of American investigators working for the League of Nations Enquiry into Traffic in Women and Children traveled to 112 cities in 28 countries and conducted 6,500 interviews with government officials, local voluntary organizations, madams, prostitutes, traffickers, and pimps, whom investigators usually termed "souteneurs," using the French word for procurer. In consultation with members of the League of Nation's Committee on Traffic in Women and Children, the investigators compiled their findings in a thick, two-part report, published in 1927 and widely publicized by major newspapers.[4] As a result of this success, three years later the League conducted an Enquiry into Traffic in Women and Children in Asia, which they termed "the East." Funded by Rockefeller and led by ASHA personnel, a team visited seventeen countries, colonies, and mandates, publishing another report in 1932.

Onto the diverse social, political, and linguistic contexts of forty-five countries across five continents, each with distinct histories of migration, articulations of racial categories, and conceptions of gendered labor, American investigators projected their own visions of race, gender, class, and national identity. They forged these visions during their WWI anti-prostitution crusades, which disproportionately targeted poor and working-class women and women of color. The solutions that American social hygienists posed to combat international trafficking reflected those they had implemented on the mainland, as well as across places with US troop presence: abolishing regulated prostitution, prohibiting prostitution to the greatest extent possible, and limiting women's mobility.

The 1927 and 1932 reports established the "facts" of prostitution and trafficking upon which the League would formulate subsequent international policy. The reports defined trafficking to encompass all sexual labor, migratory or not, and regardless of consent. They then pointed to the many women whom investigators found selling sex around the world as clear evidence of widespread trafficking. They identified state-regulated brothels and third-party profiteers as the primary drivers of the commercial sex industry, rather than the economic issues of which women themselves spoke. They labeled all women who sold sex as both trafficking victims and a danger to society, in need of state surveillance and intervention for their own protection and to protect others from them. They thus imprinted the American definition of "the traffic in women," previously conceptualized in a range of ways, onto international politics.[5]

These investigations on behalf of the League advanced American social hygienists' wartime efforts, in the words of YMCA physician Max Exner, to "have a world-wide influence, not only in relation to armies but in the social life of the nations."[6] They hoped to do so by reshaping laws and mores about prostitution in order to make other countries fit for democracy and capitalism. Working to fight the traffic in women for the League of Nations thus gave the ASHA a new means to attack prostitution using the authority of an international organization. The investigations furthered a Wilsonian internationalism that extended the United States' power through methods of social control presented as moral improvement. The fight against trafficking advanced gendered, racial, and national hierarchies by articulating them in the language of protecting women, rhetoric that held power in the postwar moment. In formulating trafficking as a problem of women and sexual morality, the ASHA helped to brand anti-trafficking work as humanitarian, concealing its explicit political aims. The League investigations allowed ASHA officials to act as agents of US power on a global scale, in places where the US military and government could not exercise power directly.

Yet the structure of the League as an intergovernmental organization also curbed US power. Even as the American investigators brought with them money, scientific expertise, and political pull, they found themselves confronted by governments and transnational organizations who did not share US-specific conceptions of trafficking—particularly the French, who were still angry about the US military's attempt to undermine regulated prostitution during the war. At a time of growing nationalism, many delegates involved in the League's anti-trafficking work also saw it as an opportunity to advance their agendas and shore up their own visions of racial, gendered, and national order. Although American investigators produced the data, imbued with their own assumptions, that would form the basis of international policy, they could not control how others used this information for their own purposes.[7]

From the American Plan to the League of Nations

At the end of WWI, social hygienists hoped to build upon wartime improvements in prostitution and disease control. The Commission on Training Camp Activities' "law enforcement" activities moved to a new civilian organization, the Interdepartmental Social Hygiene Board.[8] But arresting, detaining, examining, and treating thousands of women was expensive, and the Board's budget fell short of what social hygienists hoped for. In 1919, John D. Rockefeller, Jr., donated $310,000 to the Board while waiting for Congress to appropriate more funds. But with the wartime emergency over, government priorities moved away from venereal disease control. In December 1920, Congress declined to appropriate money for the Board, and by 1923 it had dissolved.[9] Other Americans who wanted to control sexuality from an explicitly moralizing perspective also turned against some of the ASHA's most popular wartime work. The New York State Board of Censors banned the anti-prostitution and anti-venereal disease film *Fit to Fight* for obscenity, and other states outlawed any mention of venereal diseases in films.[10]

With its work at home curtailed, the ASHA increasingly looked abroad (fig. 7.1). As intercontinental travel resumed, governments and voluntary organizations worried that white slavery would rise once more. Reformers in North and South America feared the influx of supposedly sexually depraved European immigrant women, while those in Europe worried that poverty and social powerlessness would make their own women vulnerable to traffickers. It was this tension that the ASHA seized upon.

The war had catapulted the United States to new geopolitical prominence. Even though Senate Republicans had prevented the country from joining the League, President Woodrow Wilson's role in dictating the postwar international order gave Americans new access to international politics.[11] American social hygienists remained convinced of the superiority of their methods of fighting sexual vice. The regulated prostitution implemented by European governments was "a superstition of a primitive society," they argued.[12] As they had with the French during WWI, American social hygienists used civilizational terms that usually pertained to people of color to describe European governments. While European governments themselves used such terms as a rationale for imperial domination, American social hygienists used them to justify their imperialist attempts to mold the international prostitution policy to the shape of American policy.

Although the League did not have the power to enforce the agreements it adopted, termed Conventions, it could exert significant pressure on countries

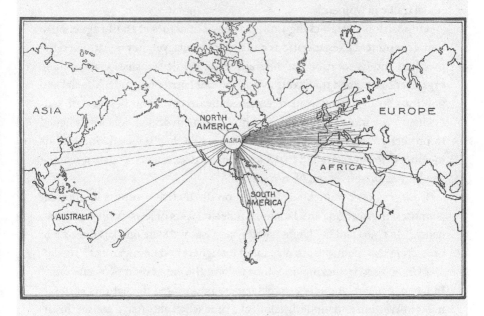

FIGURE 7.1. ASHA created a series of posters to depict their international reach. Image courtesy of the American Sexual Health Association.

through constructing and upholding international norms.[13] Multiple constituencies had an interest in how the League might address the traffic in women. Raymond Fosdick and William Snow, both former CTCA officials, met with President Wilson in Paris and convinced him to put an article on the traffic in women into the League of Nations Covenant. The feminist-oriented International Bureau also lobbied for its inclusion. Moreover, part of the League's purpose was to coordinate international agreements. By taking up trafficking, already the subject of two prior international conventions in 1904 and 1910, the League solidified its bureaucratic authority to oversee international policy.[14]

In its final form, the Covenant of the League of Nations included Article 23, which committed the League to supervising efforts to combat the international traffic in women.[15]

Opposition to trafficking united a range of actors at the League, both non-governmental organizations and governments, yet they constructed the problem and its solutions in different ways. While transnational women's organizations framed trafficking as a significant barrier to women's social and political equality, many women remained divided over how best to curb trafficking.[16] The International Council of Women advocated policies designed to protect young women from traffickers when they traveled. Some of its members, however, argued that such policies discriminated against women and limited their freedom of movement.[17]

Concerns over trafficking also took on distinctive contours in different countries. In Argentina and Poland, it reflected fears of Jews' supposed criminality.[18] In Cuba and the United States, activists and state officials linked it to protecting the country from unwanted foreigners and immigrants.[19] The Soviet Union used trafficking discourse to limit the emigration of its citizens.[20] In Japan, concern about sex trafficking communicated the nation's commitment to Western and modern values at a time when anti-Asian racism threatened its position in the League of Nations.[21] All agreed, however, that the "traffic in women" was a humanitarian issue as well as a crime.[22]

While the US government could not officially send a representative to the League's first conference on the traffic in women in 1921, the ASHA did send Bascom Johnson, the former CTCA Director of Law Enforcement whose work had led to the mass arrest of prostitutes. Johnson joined representatives from thirty-four countries, along with members of national and international voluntary organizations. There, representatives created an official Advisory Committee on Traffic in Women and Children (Trafficking Committee) and passed the 1921 International Convention for the Suppression of the Traffic in Women and Children, which called for states to collect information about trafficking and consider solutions.[23] While the representatives on most other League committees remained almost exclusively male, the Trafficking Committee always included multiple women among the nine national delegates and five representatives from voluntary organizations.[24]

At the conference, representatives replaced the term "white slave trade" with "the traffic in women" as a means of demonstrating the League's concern for women of color as well as white women. While in the late nineteenth and early twentieth centuries "white slavery" often applied to any trafficked women, it had racial connotations that the League wanted to shed. In practice, however, concerns over race shaped many member countries' conceptions of trafficking. France, Spain, Britain, and Japan declined to apply the Convention to their respective mandates, colonies, and territories, where imperial governments depended on both local and migrant women to provide sexual services for soldiers and workers. Many of the national representatives held implicit and often overtly racist views of women of Asian and African descent, as well as Jewish women, which continued to shape League debates over trafficking, despite the changing terminology.[25]

As the Trafficking Committee drew renewed international attention to the traffic in women, it also brought different factions of anti-trafficking activists together, each with their own approach. The regulationists, led by the French, called for measures to stop trafficking, so long as these measures did not interfere with states' rights to regulate and license prostitution as they saw fit. In contrast, the abolitionists, led by the British and Americans, demanded the abolition of state licensed prostitution as a central part of their anti-trafficking platform.

Yet the term "abolitionist" both glossed over the many differences among its factions and was also, in a way, inaccurate: the term referenced a policy they rejected, rather than asserting what, exactly, they desired. Feminist abolitionists, including representatives of women's voluntary organizations such as prominent French author and journalist Ghénia Avril de Sainte-Croix, as well as state representatives such as Uruguayan delegate Dr. Paulina Luisi, wanted to end regulation because they opposed any laws that specifically targeted women or prostitutes as a special class.[26] In contrast, paternalist abolitionists, such as the British and Dutch, advocated restrictions on women's mobility as a means to fight trafficking.[27] Taking this position a step farther, Americans opposed prostitution in any form and believed the state should criminalize and eradicate it, a more prohibitionist stance than their paternalist abolitionist allies. While each party called themselves abolitionist, they differed profoundly in their conceptions of the prostitution policy that should replace state regulation and licensing.[28]

The Anglo-American Abolitionist Alliance

On the Trafficking Committee, British and American representatives established a coalition that served both countries' political interests. Anglo-American political alliances played a crucial role in creating the League, and

Brits held many important positions. Rachel Crowdy, a nurse and longtime anti-white slavery reformer, headed the Social Section, the group that oversaw the issues of trafficking and child welfare. Concerned that France and other regulationist countries would seize power and shape the League's agenda, Crowdy sought to bring Americans into the Committee to shift the balance of power toward abolition.[29] Although he opposed US membership in the League, Wilson's successor, President Warren G. Harding, appointed Grace Abbott to the Trafficking Committee in an "unofficial capacity."[30] An important contributor to Progressive reform, Abbott headed the Children's Bureau of the US Department of Labor and was a member of the Executive Board of Rockefeller's Bureau of Social Hygiene.[31]

Abbott acted quickly. Even before she traveled to Geneva to attend Trafficking Committee meetings, Abbott and Johnson planned that she would advocate for an international investigation of trafficking and call attention to the benefits of US-style immigration restrictions for curbing it.[32] At the March 1923 meeting of the Trafficking Committee, Abbott proposed a multiyear, multinational study of the traffic in women.[33] Her definition of trafficking explicitly contrasted with international norms, established through the 1921 International Convention for the Suppression of the Traffic in Women and Children. The 1921 Convention outlined trafficking as transporting a woman from one country to another for "immoral purposes," which applied only to adult women taken by force or fraud to another country for the purpose of prostitution, and to all women under the age of 21.[34] For the purposes of the investigation, however, Abbott proposed to target women who "willingly and with full knowledge" traveled to sell sex, as well as those who did so by means of "force or fraud," reflecting the American legal dictum that a woman's consent was immaterial.[35] Although Abbott officially acted as a private citizen rather than a state representative, those lines often blurred.[36]

Similarly, Abbott proposed that the investigations employ the ASHA's undercover methods, using "agents of high standing with special training and experience to make personal and unofficial investigations."[37] Like Crowdy, she suspected that many European delegates were simply apologists for licensed prostitution, and that their governments might suppress information linking legal brothels to the traffic.[38] The Anglo-American alliance legitimized the controversial idea that Americans would conduct secret, undercover investigations without the full knowledge of local officials. In the face of French resistance to such methods, British representative Sidney W. Harris expressed his strong support for the idea. Pointing to the extensive investigations of prostitution the ASHA had carried out in the United States, Harris "doubted whether it would be possible to find elsewhere persons with the right sort of experience and qualifications."[39]

In response, the Trafficking Committee created a Special Body of Experts, with eight members from different countries charged with overseeing the investigation, for which Abbott secured a donation of $75,000 from the Bureau of Social Hygiene.[40] In gratitude for the money and in deference to Americans' expertise as investigators, the Committee appointed William Snow, former head of the CTCA Social Hygiene Division, as chairman of the study. Snow appointed his CTCA colleague Bascom Johnson as Field Director, supervising the day-to-day workings of the investigations. The investigation's leadership, then, was identical to that of the US military's anti-prostitution campaign during WWI.

Despite the power given to American investigators, conflicts between the factions—regulationists, feminist abolitionists, paternalist abolitionists, and prohibitionist Americans—continued to play out in the meetings of the Special Body of Experts as each group attempted to shape the study. French representative Félicien Joseph Louis Hennequin disagreed with any definition of traffic that discounted a woman's ability to consent to sell sex. As he argued, "many adult women go to Argentina, to Uruguay, or to Mexico. . . . They go whether spontaneously, because they are called by their friends, because they are promised a lot of money; it is not properly called traffic."[41] After all, the French regulationist system rested on the idea that prostitution was an essential if unfortunate profession that some women chose.

The Uruguayan representative, Dr. Paulina Luisi, offered a similar critique from a feminist abolitionist perspective. "It was necessary to distinguish between two classes of women, namely, those who were already prostitutes, and who passed from one continent to another in pursuit of their profession, and those whose good faith had been exploited and who had fallen into a trap," Luisi contended.[42] She suggested that investigators should contextualize their findings within broader immigration statistics to ascertain whether their data reflected the broader phenomenon of women's labor migration rather than trafficking.[43] Luisi remained wary of defining trafficking in ways that would curb women's rights and mobility.

Other conflicts revolved around the issue of scale. What distinguished international from national or local trafficking?[44] The French representative stressed that investigating prostitution within a single country fell outside the study's proper scope and would impinge on national sovereignty. His comments reflected broader French worries that an undercover investigation of trafficking done by prohibitionists, particularly Americans, would become an indictment of state-regulated prostitution, and thus a threat to French social order.[45] After all, during the war US officials had used both diplomatic and coercive, even illegal means to keep French women away from US soldiers.

Emboldened by the support of representatives from Britain, however, Snow and Johnson operated under an "extended" definition of trafficking, including "offences of procuring within national boundaries."[46] There was an irony to American support for a definition of trafficking that allowed an international organization to focus on domestic laws, since concerns over sovereignty had kept the United States from joining the League. But such a definition allowed Americans to attack their two most pressing concerns—state-regulated prostitution and unrestricted migration—on a national as well as international level.

Investigating "the Underworld"

Once Snow and Johnson took the reins of the League's study, they assembled a team of trusted investigators, men who had worked for the ASHA and CTCA, and who had spent more than a decade battling prostitution. George Worthington, Frank Whitin, and Charles Walter Clarke had served as long-time ASHA investigators and worked for the CTCA during WWI. Walter Brunet, a former lieutenant in the US Marine Corps, had traveled to the Dominican Republic, Haiti, and Cuba to suppress venereal disease among marines. Snow and Johnson tapped immigration and vice investigator Samuel Auerbach for his ability to speak Yiddish as well as several Eastern European languages. To spearhead the effort, they selected Paul Kinsie. While Snow and Johnson did not appoint women to official positions, three American women, Chloe Owings, Christina Galitzi, and Ruth Walkinshaw, conducted investigations that coincided with their work for other organizations, including the ASHA and the Young Women's Christian Association.[47]

Beginning in the spring of 1924, investigators traveled to European ports and boarded steamers bound for the Americas. Over the next three years, they crisscrossed the Atlantic, visiting cities in Europe, the Middle East and North Africa, and North and South America. While Snow and Johnson conducted interviews with officials, undercover investigators such as Kinsie infiltrated "the underworld," posing as pimps, traffickers, and clients.

FIGURE 7.2. Women outside an "official dispensary where prostitutes are examined" in Montevideo, Uruguay. Image courtesy of United Nations Archives at Geneva.

Investigators collected images, business cards, and documents, and took photographs as part of their survey (figs. 7.2 and 7.3). Such physical evidence marked their forays into commercial sex districts as social scientific studies rather than pleasure trips.

The investigators were plagued with difficulties finding what they understood to be reliable evidence. Official sources of information, they noted, underreported the traffic in women and downplayed the problems caused by regulated prostitution, particularly the prevalence of pimps. The study's leadership thus privileged evidence gleaned from undercover investigations over conversations with state officials and official statistics provided by governments. At the same time, Snow and Johnson remained wary of taking the testimony of those in the sex industry at face value. In Argentina, for example, investigators interviewed registered prostitutes, all of whom claimed to be

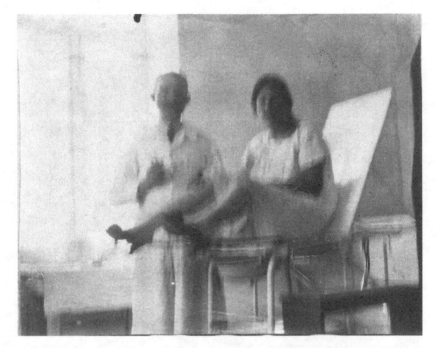

FIGURE 7.3. An examination room in Vourla, a segregated compound where prostitutes lived in Piraeus, Greece. The woman is in stirrups in preparation for a venereal disease examination. Image courtesy of United Nations Archives at Geneva.

over the minimum age to register and who stated that they had "voluntarily entered into a life of prostitution."[48] Even though they had no evidence of coercion, investigators assumed these women made false statements, since they believed that women could not truly consent to register as prostitutes. Of all the "underworld" characters, investigators seemed to have trusted male pimps and traffickers more than women. Kinsie often recorded their words verbatim, down to the dialect and colorful language they used.

Since they could not trust their interlocutors' words, investigators often interpreted visual evidence. They described the shape of women's faces, noses, and lips; the color of their hair, eyes, and skin; and the style, fabric, and color of their clothing. Such evidence could work as an unofficial identification document; moreover, in the context of the interwar interest in eugenics, it could also help investigators to determine a woman's innate sexual deviance and criminality.[49]

Accurately discerning a woman's race, investigators believed, allowed them to determine whether she was a trafficking victim. Investigators considered the presence of a woman of one race in a country where they assumed the populace to be of another as clear evidence of trafficking. Yet they had difficulty reading the bodies of women in Brazil, a society in which descendants of enslaved Africans, Indigenous peoples, Portuguese colonizers, and more recent European migrants had created a racially diverse population where racial categorization took on its own configurations.[50]

In Rio de Janeiro, one investigator estimated that foreign women made up 50 percent of all prostitutes, while another estimated the percentage at 70. Ultimately, they used a white American racial calculus to determine women's nationalities and thus discern their status as victims of international trafficking. As Johnson recorded, "if we consider all those who have half negro blood, and all those who are black, as native Brazilians, the percentage is probably . . . half foreign and half native." According to his calculations, any white woman found in a country whose population he assumed to be Black because of its admixture of "negro blood" provided evidence of international trafficking.[51]

Such conclusions betrayed investigators' focus on white women, rather than women of color, as the "true" victims of sex trafficking. Johnson's mapping of race onto nationality not only ignored the multiple gradations that Brazilians themselves used to describe race, but it also did not account for Brazil's significant influx of European migrants. Between 1890 and 1919, more than 2.6 million immigrants settled in Brazil, with the majority from Europe.[52] Yet finding white women in a country they constructed as Black led investigators to report large numbers of trafficked women in Brazil.

In Argentina, the investigators' concern with trafficked white women dovetailed with an anti-Semitic, nationalist trafficking discourse. Kinsie, who was himself Jewish, could speak Yiddish and gained access to Eastern European Jewish networks that stretched across the Atlantic. However, he could not speak Spanish, which prevented him from communicating with a significant portion of the population. Moreover, Jewish men and women, excluded from most jobs, were highly visible in Argentina's sex industry. Taken together, these factors led Kinsie to focus primarily on Jewish prostitutes and traffickers in his reports on Argentina. As Mir Yarfitz argues, the anti-trafficking crusade in Argentina "darkened" Jewish men as the swarthy traffickers of women, while simultaneously "whitening" Jewish women as their innocent victims.[53]

Despite investigators' claims that they needed to study local conditions to understand international trafficking, their focus on white European women often led them to purposefully ignore local women, particularly women of color. In Mexico City, Worthington described cheap brothels with "30 inmates in each place, mostly Indian and half-breed." Yet he decided that "inasmuch as the inmates seemed to be for the most part Indians, it seemed that very little would be gained by entering" these brothels; "places, such as these, while furnishing a market for local white slavery, are probably not directly connected with international traffic." While using "white slavery" as a generic term for prostitution, Worthington nonetheless disregarded women of color, even though he and other investigators repeatedly remarked on their exploitative labor conditions, as well as their lower pay and relative youth in comparison to white European women.[54]

Investigators looked for evidence of trafficking by trying to determine women's ages, since they believed young girls were particularly vulnerable. But when they looked for such girls in official records, they rarely found them. Investigators repeatedly reported that official documents did not accurately capture women's true ages. In most countries that regulated prostitution, women below a certain age could not register as prostitutes, and thus women lied about their ages when registering, pimps and madams lied about the ages of the women who worked for them, and complicit officials turned a blind eye. For the same reason, investigators noted, many women they interviewed also claimed to be older than their real age.

Reading women's bodies and faces became an important way for investigators to judge ages, but racial features again confounded them. In Rio de Janeiro, for example, Johnson reported the presence of many girls under the age of 21. "We were not always able to verify the ages of these girls, because very often, and particularly amongst those who have negro blood, they mature very young; girls who ordinarily would be supposed to be 35, or at least 20, are in reality only 14 or 15."[55] As with their attempts to determine nationality, investigators' assumptions about racial characteristics profoundly shaped the ways that they perceived and reported evidence of trafficking. Repeating the racist trope that young Black girls looked like sexually mature women, investigators considered them less worthy victims than white European women.

At the same time, however, investigators worried that beautiful white women posed a special danger to men; French women were particularly arousing and thus threatening. As Elisa Camiscioli has shown, French women, and the concept of "Frenchness," gained particular "erotic cachet" in the global sex market of the early twentieth century.[56] In a high-end Havana brothel staffed by French women, Worthington salaciously described dancing with "the most beautiful girl I have ever seen in any house of prostitution anywhere . . . neck of gown was cut low; breasts exposed when she danced." Later that evening, there entered an "American boy who did not appear to be 20," who, according to Worthington, had come simply out of "curiosity." After dancing with a beautiful woman, "his passions had become too much aroused for him to control them, and they hurriedly departed for her room."[57] The trope of dangerous French women, exploited by the US military in WWI, continued on in the League investigations.

Investigators paid close attention to interracial sex as proof of trafficking, particularly white women having sex with Black or Asian men. Pointing to the prevalence of trafficking in the French port of Le Havre, Kinsie reported that the women there solicited sailors of all races, including "Negros, Chinese, Japanese."[58] In Mexicali, Mexico, Worthington reported, he spoke with an American woman who serviced "mostly Chinese" clientele.[59] In the red-light district of Montevideo, Uruguay, Kinsie found that women of multiple races freely and aggressively solicited customers. "Inmates in the cheaper places are required to entertain trade of all nationalities and races. Repeatedly I saw negroes enter white houses and select white inmates and accompany them into their bed rooms."[60] US white supremacist ideology held that such sex across the Black-white color line could only happen through force. Thus, these women were trafficking victims.

In his report, Kinsie linked the disruption of racial order he witnessed in Montevideo's red-light district to inversions of gendered and sexual order. In addition to interracial sex, investigators argued that trafficking led to "unnatural" sex acts. Much as the US military had worried about the effects of French oral sex on US troops during the war, Snow and Johnson feared that such acts "spread insidious corruption through the community, especially among the young men."[61]

Investigators catalogued the proliferation of sexual acts available at brothels around the world, suggesting how attempts to suppress trafficking created new discourses on sexuality. In Montevideo, Kinsie reported, "to encourage trade, the inmates wag their tongues, and also make a circle with their index fingers and thumbs, which is indicative of perversion and sodomy."[62] In Tampico, Mexico, Worthington spoke with two French women who offered to show him a "circus": "they immediately stripped and indulged in a series of pervert practices with each other which are too disgusting to describe."[63] Auerbach went to a house in Santander, Spain, where women did it the "French way." In addition, "while in the house I asked the 'Madame' whether 69 was being used there and she replied that it is practiced there."[64]

Moreover, investigators linked such heterosexual perversions to homo-sexuality, another form of perversion that social hygienists increasingly worried could endanger young men in the 1920s. As Kinsie noted, in addition to women who offered anal and oral sex, Montevideo's red-light district housed male homosexual and cross-dressing prostitutes, who "sit about in female attire and solicit men." These men charged the same price as women and performed "all kinds of pervert acts" for their customers. American investigators associated interracial sex with "perverse" sex, inversions of proper gender roles, and "disgusting conditions" in the streets.[65] They articulated their intersecting concerns about race, gender, sexuality, national identity, and migration through the idiom of trafficking, much as they had used the language of prostitution to articulate these concerns during the war.

"I Make Good Money Here"

Investigators attempted to capture verbatim conversations with the women they encountered. When read carefully, the investigators' notes tell a different story than the inquiry's final report, providing insight, albeit highly mediated, into women's experiences navigating migration and sex work.[66] They suggest that women's lives did not conform to the categories of prostitute and trafficking victim. They tell a story of migration in the aftermath of the First World War, women's limited economic opportunities in the wage labor market, and the racialized and gendered patterns of violence and labor exploitation that many working women faced.

The First World War had drastically curbed transatlantic migration for its duration but had also displaced millions of people.[67] Although specific data on migration remain sparse, in the years following the war the global movement of people once again skyrocketed to prewar levels, with more than three million people per year migrating by the late 1920s, and 1.2 million transatlantic migrants in 1924.[68] The war had broken up three empires, leaving hundreds of thousands of people stateless.[69] The economic recession that followed the war also created tremendous instability.[70]

The investigators' interviews demonstrate that women who sold sex acted much like other workers in an increasingly global capitalist economy, choosing the form of labor and the market where they could earn the most. In Mexico, George Worthington spoke with two French women who decided to emigrate because "after the American troops had been removed . . . it was so quiet in Western France that they could not make a living."[71] Other women took up sex work because it often paid far more than the other jobs available to women. As a Parisian souteneur told Kinsie of one of his "girls," "you ought to see her embroider!" "She has a regular trade, but it don't pay." Now "she makes over 100 francs a day."[72] In comparison, women in France's garment industry received an average of 1.52 francs per hour: it would require over 66 hours of work to make 100 francs.[73]

In Rio de Janeiro, which investigators considered a major destination for trafficked women from Europe, Kinsie reported that a prostitute could earn between 18 and 35 milreis in a day, with some making up to 150–250 milreis a week.[74] In contrast, adult women working for wages in Rio de Janeiro made an average of 4.60 milreis per day.[75] Ida, a US citizen working in Mexico, told Worthington that "Mexicali is a terrible place, but . . . she made a lot of money over there,—over 100 men a week at $3 per rapport."[76] In comparison, a woman working as a drawing-frame tender in a New York cotton textile mill made an average of 34.2 cents per hour, and a more highly skilled sewing machine operator could make 64.5 cents per hour.[77]

Although women emphasized the money they could earn, many expressed ambivalence about their work and spoke frankly about the difficult working conditions. Marussia Camick, a Russian-born woman who immigrated to New York City at a young age, related to Kinsie that she ended up at a cabaret in Panama with the help of a "booking agent." "The first few months I hated the place," she told Kinsie. When Kinsie asked, "Didn't you know what kind of a place it was?," she replied, "Yes, but I didn't think it was quite so rough." After a few months, however, the woman changed her mind: "Now, I like it; I signed my second contract the other day." After their conversation, she solicited Kinsie, requesting $20 for the night.[78] The investigators' notes indicate that economic concerns overwhelmingly drove women's labor and migration patterns. Both their movement and their labor were constrained and coerced, but primarily through economic and political circumstances rather than by nefarious individuals.

Women told investigators that sex work allowed them to control their time and labor conditions, something that domestic and factory work—and often marriage—did not afford. As Loretta Haims, a woman working as a streetwalker in Vienna, told Kinsie, "I make good money. I am my own boss. I can walk where I want. I can pick the men I want to, and I aint [sic] got anybody to answer to."[79] Although streetwalking posed its own dangers, it allowed more autonomy than brothel-based sex work or other jobs available to women.

While investigators attempted to draw a sharp boundary between the categories of prostitution and "respectable" employment, their notes show that for women, that distinction was rarely so clear. Miss Girendos, a Budapest-born woman working as a cabaret artist in Bucharest, Romania, told Kinsie, "I am a dancer, but you know it don't pay so well. I get my fare paid and a small salary. I pick up a few dollars from the drink money, and now and then I meet a nice man. I go to bed with him and that way I live."[80] Ruth Walkinshaw, one of the few women investigators, noted that in Brazil, the man of the house often expected his domestic servants to provide sex.[81] Domestic workers as well as women in factories faced assault and harassment at the hands of their bosses.[82] Thus, women who labored in supposedly respectable jobs often performed sexual labor and faced sexual violence, even as the League's investigation often tried to ignore this entanglement between sex and labor.[83]

The investigators did meet several women who fit a narrower definition of trafficking victim, transported to sell sex against their will. Nineteen-year-old Georgiana Lobos told Kinsie that a man and his wife brought her from Colombia to Panama under the promise of employment. When they arrived in Panama, however, "they forced her into a life of prostitution." Although she went to the police, they did nothing. As Kinsie reported, "at the present time, she is being treated for a disease, and wants to return home."[84] Such cases demonstrated young women's profound vulnerability as they sought work abroad, as well as the failure of public officials to assist them.[85]

Moreover, although women stated that they migrated and sold sex of their own volition, they reported exploitation by third parties, including pimps, procurers, and madams. Brothels and pimps often used systems of debt bondage, in which women owed more money for their lodging or their passage into the country than they could reasonably pay back. Elsie, a German woman working in Genoa, Italy, related that she had initially planned to stay there only a short time, but has "been there three years and I have been trying ever since to get out of debt." As she told Kinsie, she made "150 lira a day" but "I get 75; the madame gets 75. Then I must pay 25 for pension; that leaves 50; then 5 lire every day for the doctor."[86] Women recounted that they could not pay to travel to another country by themselves. They thus turned to third parties, usually men, to provide money for transportation and necessary immigration documents without foreseeing the difficulty of paying off such debts.[87]

Migration cost so much, in part, because state restrictions often generated systems of bribery and corruption. Both women and men repeatedly boasted about how they bypassed laws designed to curb prostitution, migration, and trafficking, but just as often lamented the cost. As Elsie recounted, "5 lire, or 150 lire a month, I must pay the police. . . . The policeman was around today and he wants to make me leave the country."[88] As her account shows, while madams and other third parties in the sex industry took much of women's earnings, government officials also took their money and played a role in keeping them in debt.

The investigators' notes demonstrate that rather than solving the problem of trafficking, restrictive immigration policies put women into precarious situations. In Panama, for example, Kinsie interviewed a French woman named Helene Ollier who had been detained by US authorities in the Canal Zone for practicing prostitution and who subsequently faced deportation. Ollier told Kinsie that she had "no living relatives, and does not know what she will do when she is deported to France."[89] Investigator Charles Walter Clarke met a woman born in Lithuania to Latvian Jewish parents. She had moved to the Free City of Danzig after marrying a Pole, but her husband abandoned her and their young child. Unable to legally work in Danzig, she also could not leave because no government would issue her a passport.[90] While investigators pointed out the violence of trafficking, they ignored women's complaints about the violence inflicted by state officials and border control regimes.

"A Traffic of Considerable Dimensions"

After two and a half years of investigations, Snow and Johnson produced a two-volume report, totaling more than 276 pages. In March 1927, the League published Part 1, an overview of the enquiry's findings, and nine months later issued Part 2, a detailed summary of each country. "A traffic of considerable dimensions is being carried on," it proclaimed. "Many hundreds of women and girls—some of them very young—are transported each year from one country to another for purposes of prostitution." Though some women had previously sold sex, "nearly always there was evidence that their movements were controlled by others, and many of them could not have realised the sort of life to which they would be subjected."[91]

The reports named "the attitude adopted towards prostitution" by the state as the leading cause of trafficking. Just as ASHA and US officials had hoped when they initiated the study, the report concluded that "we have definite evidence that licensed houses create a steady demand for new women and this demand is met by traffickers and causes both national and international traffic." According to their findings, the solution to trafficking clearly presented itself: the end of all state-regulated prostitution. Using the language of science and progress, the report argued that countries should recognize prostitution as "a public evil to be kept within the narrowest possible limits." Reflecting Bureau of Social Hygiene studies of prostitution that dated back to Abraham Flexner, whose study the report cited, the report argued that "the remedy lies in a sound and vigilant public policy."[92] Implicitly, Snow and Johnson proposed American-style prohibition as an international policy. After all, Johnson had long argued that "law is the foundation of all public-health efforts."[93]

Unrestricted migration, the report argued, also fueled trafficking. It applauded the countries "now taking steps to verify the qualifications and character of the intending immigrant in the country of origin before the journey is commenced."[94] This praise reflected the US policy of screening immigrants before departure, a crucial part of the growth of the United States' border control regime, which allowed US consular officials to police the borders of the United States from outside the country. As the report noted approvingly, "some countries make a practice of excluding, and in suitable cases, of deporting foreign prostitutes" as well as foreign *souteneurs*, madams, and traffickers.[95] As Adam McKeown has argued, in the twentieth century countries began to adopt strict immigration laws, including Asian exclusion laws, as a means of proving their modernity and commitment to international norms.[96] Immigration restrictions aimed at curbing the traffic in women operated in a similar way.[97]

Even though both women and men in the sex industry cited economic factors as their primary consideration, the report granted them less than half a page. It briefly acknowledged that women's low wages often led them to sell sex. The report gave more attention to the social and psychological profiles of prostitutes. It spent three and a half pages dissecting the different "kinds" of prostitutes, from the "professional" to the "semi-professional," the "complacent," the "artiste," and the "inexperienced."[98] As contributing factors, the report pointed to the greed of individual pimps, traffickers, and madams, whom the report termed "parasites who live on the body as well as on the soul of their host." According to the authors, "the unrestricted sale of alcohol" and the "trade in obscene books, photographs and other articles," inflamed men's desires and stimulated the traffic in women.[99] The movement of large numbers of men for military purposes, work, or tourism exacerbated the traffic, as did the low age of consent to sex in many countries.

The American investigators' findings and conclusions helped Snow and Johnson to fashion an international political framework for conceptualizing the traffic in women. This framework focused on illicit sex, particularly regulated and tolerated prostitution, as *the* problem, isolating migratory sex work from other forms of migratory labor, coerced labor, and coerced migration.[100] The report reaffirmed that the policy of regulated prostitution no longer constituted a national matter but an international problem that fell under the League's jurisdiction.[101]

While the League could not force its member nations to change their laws, it could exert real pressure through the international norms it developed and upheld.[102] The report stressed the abolition of regulation and the implementation of immigration restrictions as key solutions to the problem of trafficking. Although it did not call for criminalizing the sale of sex, as the ASHA had across the United States during the war, it named prohibition as the best method. Since this policy allegedly served the ends of combating trafficking and protecting women, the League's inquiry helped to code it as scientific, modern, and humanitarian.

Members of the Special Body of Experts agreed on the broad findings and solutions presented in Part 1 of the report, but bitterly disagreed over the detailed national reports in Part 2. Many representatives felt that the reports had portrayed Latin American countries unfairly, while glossing over others' faults. Belgian representative Isadore Maus attacked the investigators' methods and competence. The final report on Poland, Maus argued, reflected the investigator's "obsession with the flow of French and Polish prostitutes," which "absolutely distorts the overall picture." The American investigators could not speak most languages spoken in Poland and did not understand the "whole set of conditions," both social and political, from which prostitution resulted. Their ignorance and hubris, he argued, were "truly incomprehensible."[103]

Maus struck at the heart of the ASHA's claims to the universal applicability of its social scientific methods and its investigators' ability to conduct a multinational investigation. He framed trafficking not as a universally identical phenomenon, but as one deeply rooted in local as well as global circumstances. He struck out at the American arrogance that bothered many European and South American representatives. Moreover, in the context of postwar nationalism, members of the Special Body of Experts feared that countries portrayed critically in the report would publicly reject it, thus undermining the credibility of both the report and the League's anti-trafficking work. Maus delivered his critique of the report on Poland with such vehemence because it discussed state sanctioned anti-Semitism, an increasingly sensitive topic in Europe.[104]

Although many governments as well as the international press dismissed the details of the report, they largely accepted its broad framework.[105] At a time of rising nationalism, paternalist abolitionism and prohibitionism emerged as attractive strategies for state-building, much as regulation had served as an important empire-building strategy in the nineteenth century. Indeed, due to changing international norms, many countries that had previously adopted state regulation ended the system in the interwar period, including Argentina, Belgium, Czechoslovakia, Germany, Russia, Sweden, and Switzerland. Immediately after visits from League investigators, Cuba and Hungary issued new immigration restrictions on people in the sex industry, while Argentina, Uruguay, Poland, and Japan did so in the aftermath of the report's publication.[106]

Even as countries abolished regulated prostitution, fulfilling a long-standing goal of feminists, feminist abolitionism itself was eclipsed by the carceral, prohibitionist stance toward prostitution favored by Americans. Snow and Johnson shaped the report to advance their prohibitionist agenda, while the members of the Special Body of Experts shaped it to accommodate their own nationalist interests. The final report largely excluded the evidence investigators found of police and state corruption that made women more dependent on third parties to help pay bribes and navigate increasingly strict systems of border control.

A few women did speak out about this oversight. Uruguayan representative Paulina Luisi had long been critical of an approach to trafficking that seemed to privilege government interests over those of women. At one meeting of the Trafficking Committee, she declared that "after listening to some of the speakers, she wondered whether the task of this Committee was to defend society against prostitutes. She thought, on the contrary, that it was called upon to find means to contribute to the rescue of these women."[107] Additionally, by the late 1920s divisions between feminists became more pronounced. They argued over whether to compromise with regulationists and work toward the gradual abolition of regulated prostitution, or to reject any policy other than immediate abolition of licensed prostitution. Moreover, they disagreed over whether protectionist legislation would keep women safe or would merely limit women's mobility.[108]

The purposeful removal of women from domestic and international anti-trafficking organizations catalyzed the shift toward conceptualizing the prostitute as dangerous rather than endangered. In the late 1920s, male leaders pushed women—many of whom brought a feminist perspective to their work—out of positions of power in the League, as well as in the ASHA. In 1925, eugenicist and Executive Secretary of the ASHA Paul Popenoe essentially wrote women out of the organization's history, noting, "it is certain that women played little part in the suppression of legalized prostitution. It has been essentially a men's movement."[109] In 1928, the League's Secretariat renewed Rachel Crowdy's contract as the head of the Social Section for only one year, while renewing male heads for seven years. The following year two men took her position. In 1935, the Secretariat restructured the Social Section and reduced the role of non-governmental organizations, the primary way feminists had participated in the work of the Trafficking Committee.[110] As paternalist abolitionists sidelined feminist abolitionists, they also discarded the women's rights framework that had animated the abolitionist movement at its inception.

"Enquiry into Traffic in Women and Children in the East"

The supposed success of the first investigation for illuminating the problem of trafficking provided the ASHA the opportunity to expand its influence. As the 1927 report noted, the Japanese member of the Special Body of Experts had examined "conditions in the Far East" and found that "the international traffic in women is also met with in this part of the world," both in independent states as well as colonies.[111] Snow and Johnson recommended a second study to assess the extent and the sources of this traffic in the East. Satisfied with the success of the first study for raising the profile of the League's humanitarian work, the Trafficking Committee commissioned the "Enquiry into Traffic in Women and Children in the East."

Just as the first investigation had led to conflicts over the relationship between national sovereignty and international governance, the second study caused fierce contestation over the relationship between international governance and imperial rule.[112] The members of the Special Body of Experts believed that the second study would differ from the first because of the "differences of race, religion and custom" in the Far East.[113] In fact, the second study differed from the first because while the first surveyed sovereign states, the second occurred primarily in colonized countries.

As a result of the harsh criticism that Part 2 of the first report generated, both among government representatives and in the international press, the Trafficking Committee declined to offer William Snow the position of chairman and disbanded his team of American investigators. But once again, Rockefeller's Bureau of Social Hygiene funded the investigation, providing $125,000, no small amount given the ongoing economic depression. Thus, although tempered,

Americans still exerted their influence. The Trafficking Committee appointed Bascom Johnson to chair the investigation. Johnson, the Polish diplomat Karl Pindor, and the Swedish physician Alma Sundquist formed a three-person Traveling Commission, with Snow occasionally joining.[114]

The American leadership of the first investigation had seen regulationist Latin American and European countries as backward, in need of civilizing through American methods of prostitution prohibition and immigration control. But during the second investigation these hierarchies shifted in service of shoring up the division between West and East, "Occident" and "Orient." These supposed differences provided crucial ideological support for justifying the post–WWI international order—and ongoing imperialism—as a civilizing force.[115]

Between October 1930 and March 1932, the Traveling Commission visited major ports and cities throughout South and East Asia and the Middle East (fig. 7.4). In the wake of WWI, these regions experienced tremendous political upheaval. The swell of interest in self-determination had fueled struggles for national independence; many anti-colonial nationalist movements looked to the League as the arena in which to make their claims.[116] Indeed, as Julia Martinez has pointed out, the study of trafficking in the East coincided with anti-colonial demonstrations across Asia.[117] At the same time, the League had imposed the mandate system, which placed the former colonies and territories of the defeated states under the authority of the war's victors.[118]

US and European imperialism shaped the imagined geography of the second investigation. This investigation labeled Europe—including Russia—and the European settler societies in the American hemisphere as the civilized West. Such places stood in contrast to the Asian countries the investigation termed the uncivilized East. The European colonies in Asia, the Middle East, and North Africa hung precariously in the balance. Revelations of regulated prostitution in colonies and mandates, the League understood, threatened the legitimacy of the post–WWI imperial world order. Most ruling governments continued to regulate prostitution in their colonies and mandates, even when they had closed licensed brothels in the metropole. Such contradictory policies belied the supposed civilizing nature of the League's mandate system. As geographer Stephen Legg argues, in the Far East, the League's attempt to turn the imperial world into an international order threatened imperial sovereignty.[119]

Now, British representatives deemed the American leadership's broad definition of trafficking and their undercover methods unsuitable, despite their previously vocal support. The British government feared that such methods would invite criticism at a time when it hoped to shore up its authority. The issue of India remained particularly thorny, given the presence of regulated brothels and the growth of independence movements, which the government often met with brutal repression.[120] As Johnson complained of his former allies, "they tried in the meeting to define International Traffic very strictly and to shut off undercover investigations altogether."[121] Officials within the British Home Department debated whether the Commission should visit India at all, though they finally allowed it.[122] The Home Department deemed sites other than major port cities irrelevant to the "international aspect of the problem" and forbade the Commission from making "secret" or undercover inquiries in India without the permission of the local governments.[123] The Traveling Commission thus had to rely on government officials for information, allowing states more control over the narrative of trafficking.[124]

The Far East study demonstrated the limitations of the ASHA's vision of prostitution prohibition in the imperial world, where it fit less easily with governments' reliance on commercial sexual labor. During the Far East investigation, ASHA officials confronted the disadvantages of using an international governing body to implement their vision of sexual civilization, particularly when they no longer had British support. Furthermore, as the global economic depression deepened in the 1930s, funding for the ASHA, the Bureau of Social Hygiene, and the League itself was cut, suggesting another set of limitations American reformers faced in trying to advance their agenda through nongovernmental and international organizations. If the League amplified US power in the first inquiry, it curbed it in the second.

"The Recognized Standard of Morality in the World"

The final report on the "Far East" used international governance to uphold imperialist geopolitical distinctions between West and East. The League released the hefty document in December 1932, while Johnson published a summary of it in February 1934. "In the countries of Europe, North and South America, the traffic in women is banned, both by law and by public opinion, thus becoming a criminal offence," Johnson noted. "But in the East, such is not the case."[125] Johnson and his colleagues had drawn on Orientalist tropes of Eastern sensuality and depravity to argue for the investigation, and their findings corresponded with their expectations. They recorded 17,000 foreign women, almost exclusively of Chinese and Japanese nationality, registered in state-authorized brothels in the cities they visited.[126]

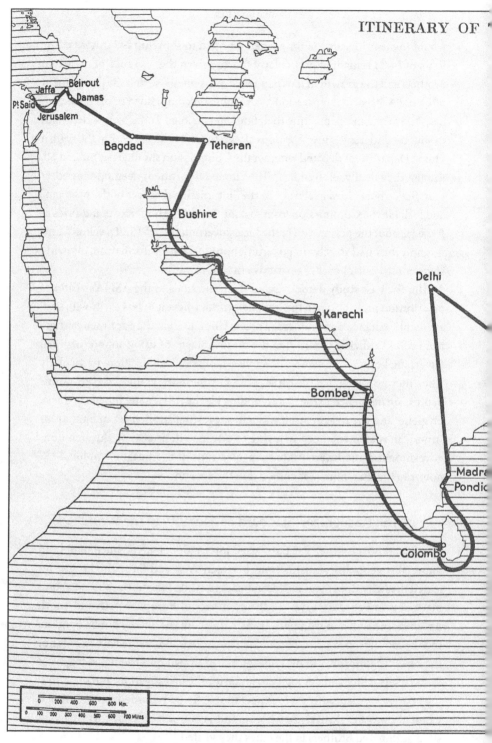

FIGURE 7.4. The "Commission of Enquiry into Traffic in Women and Children in the Far East" primarily visited locations under colonial rule. Image courtesy of United Nations Archives at Geneva.

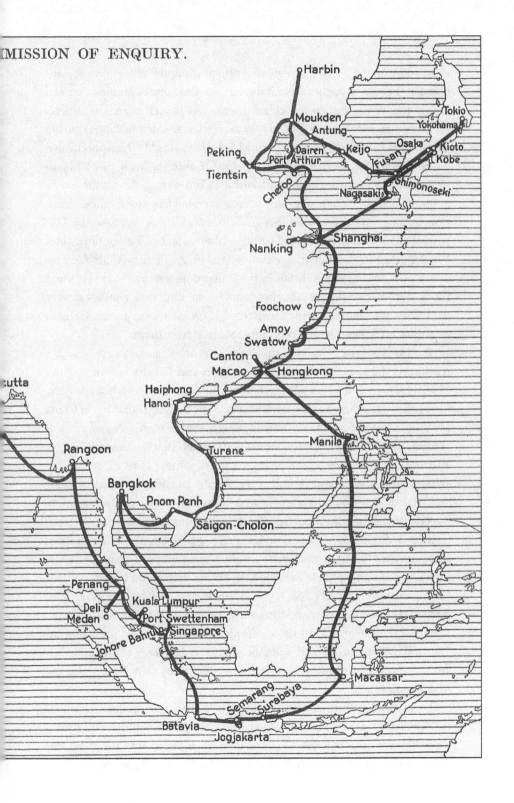

In addition to abolishing regulated prostitution, the report also recommended that governments expand their abilities to control immigration and emigration. While the first report had recommended such migration controls for all women, in the Asian context they assumed a new significance, given the global spread of anti-Asian immigration laws in the 1920s.[127] The report lauded governments that surveilled and "subjected to interrogation" any Chinese woman departing from a major port, curbing Chinese migration at the source in the name of anti-trafficking. It also recommended US-style Chinese exclusion, noting that the Philippines had little trafficking because the US-controlled government excluded Chinese laborers and all foreign prostitutes and deported anyone violating immigration law. As Johnson's summary reported, US immigration officials in the Philippines deported nine hundred Chinese women in the previous five years.[128] Echoing earlier yellow slavery discourses, the report presented such restrictions as a way to protect Chinese victims of trafficking, as well as protect countries from them.

The Far East report—and particularly Johnson's summary of it—further reinforced the global division between West and East by identifying the "Social Structure" and "Family System" of the East, particularly among the Chinese, as a significant cause of trafficking.[129] By framing trafficking in China as a problem of culture, the report willfully ignored the economic and political contexts that fundamentally shaped women's sexual labor and migration. After all, to attend to economic and political factors, rather than a facile sense of culture, would have revealed similarities rather than differences between East and West. It also would have implicated European, American, and Japanese imperialism as a significant driver of migratory commercial sex.

Indeed, despite the report's emphasis on the problem of Chinese culture, it documented bustling commercial sex districts in European-controlled commercial ports and Japanese-occupied territories, with 4,000 Chinese prostitutes in Hong Kong and 5,000–6,000 in British Malaya. The Traveling Commission reported that, of 17,000 total trafficked women they found in the East, 10,000 of them worked in British colonies. Yet they blamed the figure on "demand by Chinese abroad," and indeed praised the recent efforts of British authorities to close brothels and prevent prostitutes from landing on the Malay peninsula.[130]

The report drew further divisions through its discussion of white "Occidental" Russian refugee women in China. The Bolshevik revolution had driven many Russians into exile in China, and in its wake, Soviet authorities denaturalized some 1.5 million citizens living outside the USSR, rendering them stateless.[131] Although far smaller in number than Asian victims of trafficking—the report counted 140 Russian women in brothels and another 1,000 who served as dancing partners and waitresses—their plight generated the most interest and activity of any part of the study. As one British journalist explained, "the appearance of white women in such disgraceful capacity as that of prostitutes among the natives of the lowest class, *affects very deeply the prestige of the Western nations in the Orient."*[132]

Moreover, the report explained the prevalence of white Russian women in prostitution through their "precarious economic situation," unlike the cultural and racial explanations it used to explain the traffic in Chinese women. In fact, their economic straits supposedly resulted from Oriental greed. According to the report, Russian men living in China could not find work to support their families, while debt bondage to greedy Chinese landlords forced respectable Russian women into prostitution.[133]

If, as the report argued, cultural backwardness regarding hygiene, sex, gender, and the family formed the root of the problem of sex trafficking in the Far East, then its solutions involved modernization, a concept by which Euro-American powers justified their attempts to control the economic, political, and social life of other countries.[134] The report recommended that governments should appoint central authorities in charge of collecting and exchanging information about trafficking with the League of Nations, building the bureaucracy and governing capacity that were considered hallmarks of supposedly modern states. It called for Eastern governments to cooperate with Western missionaries and private organizations, who could improve the position of women and "disperse deplorable superstitions" about sex.[135]

As in the first report, the Far East report also pointed to state-regulated prostitution as a significant cause of trafficking. But in the context of colonialism in Asia and the Middle East, the fight to abolish regulation took on a different significance. In the nineteenth century in parts of the British, Spanish, French, Dutch, and US empires, colonial officials had instituted regulated prostitution as a way to manage the sexual contacts between white soldiers and local women of color. Regulation also purportedly modernized these colonies through public health measures, while still accommodating the allegedly inherent sexual immorality of local peoples as well as the bodily needs of white troops. Now, the report suggested, empires could civilize and modernize countries in the East by abolishing regulation.[136]

The second study thus shifted the geopolitical significance of trafficking. In the first study, the ASHA and its British allies employed anti-trafficking discourse to enforce a hierarchy of civilized, abolitionist Anglo-Americans against backward, regulationist European and Latin American governments. In the second, they used anti-trafficking work to mark a distinction between West and East. By locating the regulated brothel as the key institution that drove trafficking, the Far East report depicted prostitution as a problem of badly administered imperial governance, but not a feature of empire itself. In fact, in the nineteenth century some feminist abolitionists had warned that regulated prostitution and trafficking represented some of the inherent evils of colonialism and militarism.[137] But by the 1920s, and particularly as men pushed women out of positions of authority within the Trafficking Committee, few representatives voiced such a critique. The report's singular focus on state-regulated prostitution obscured the fact that empire-building relied on sexual labor, even as the Traveling Commission's observations themselves made this point clear.

Significantly, the move away from regulated prostitution toward an abolitionist, even prohibitionist, approach paralleled a similar shift in imperial opium policy in the early twentieth century. In the nineteenth century, imperial powers in Asia regulated opium. But in 1908, the United States implemented opium prohibition in the Philippines; by 1940, a global prohibitionist consensus emerged.[138] In both the cases of prostitution and opium, this policy change reaffirmed the authority of colonial bureaucracies to govern the everyday and the intimate.

Although American investigators set the terms of the League's trafficking discourse through the two reports, other representatives used this discourse for their own ends. Japanese officials well understood that anti-trafficking work, and particularly the abolition of regulated prostitution, served as an important marker of civilization. Japan was a charter member of the League, though European and American powers at times sidelined Japanese representatives, such as when they rejected Japan's proposal to include a clause about racial non-discrimination in the League's Covenant. Japan used the League to assert its standing as the preeminent East Asian power and to advance its policy of accommodation with Western powers, a policy it was beginning to discard in 1931 with the invasion of Manchuria.[139]

Prostitution policy had long been an important way that Japan signaled its status as modern to Western trading partners, as Maki Kumuri has shown. In the 1820s, Japan codified a system of regulation with licensing and inspections based on European models. As the tide began to shift against regulation in the twentieth century, Japanese elites promoted abolition as a means of shedding

FIGURE 7.5. The caption of this newspaper photograph read, "The League of Nations White Slave Commission Visits Geisha School in Japan." Bascom Johnson sits at center right, with Alma Sundquist and Karl Pindor to his left. Image courtesy of the *Sydney Morning Herald / Alamy*.

Japan's reputation in Europe and the United States as a premodern society. Japan promised to close its licensed houses following the first League Report.[140]

During the second investigation, the Traveling Commission noted approvingly that the governor of a Japanese prefecture told investigators he wanted to abolish state-regulated prostitution because it was "opposed to humanitarian ideas and the recognized standard of morality in the world."[141] In Tokyo, the committee visited a new geisha school, established "as a means of training geisha girls in modern methods of entertainment—ballet dancing, singing, English conversation, etc.," indicating that their work no longer included sex (fig. 7.5).[142] That the Traveling Commission and the Trafficking Committee lauded Japan's abolitionist efforts precisely when other League sections condemned its territorial expansion suggests that Japanese officials understood the central role that sex played in Western conceptions of a country's standing on the international stage. Japan used abolitionism as a form of humanitarian whitewashing, a way to bolster their own claims to modernity and the right to act as European empires did, invading territories under the pretense of stabilizing them.[143]

At the same time as the League debated modern trafficking policy, discourses about the relationship between sex and modernity proliferated. The 1920s witnessed what scholars have described as a revolution in sexual mores. The rise of the "Modern Girl," who eschewed traditional gender and sexual norms; the increasing acceptance of premarital sex, divorce, contraception, and dating; and the rise of a more visible homosexual culture and identity reverberated around the world.[144] The ASHA used the issue of trafficking to articulate an alternate vision of sexual modernity, one that reinforced key aspects of gender, class, and race relations that they perceived to be under threat via the loosening of sexual strictures during the 1920s, but that also employed the language of women's rights, freedom, and science. Their crusade against trafficking worked to keep sex within narrow bounds of normative marital heterosexuality. For ASHA members, and a growing number of countries, sexuality was central to political and economic life. Sexual self-control and a state that did not accept vice made for good democracy; a marketplace free of sex, contained instead within the heterosexual male-headed family, made for good capitalism.[145]

Conclusion

The League investigations represented the culmination of years of effort by ASHA and US officials to shape international trafficking policy, with a bent toward criminalization, prohibition, and border control. In the interwar period other countries, including Britain and the Netherlands, advocated the abolition of regulation as a means of increasing, rather than diminishing, state control of women's bodies, rejecting the feminism that had originally animated the abolitionist movement.[146] Although the United States was not alone in its orientation, it maintained a more explicitly carceral approach to prostitution and venereal disease than its closest allies. The British government, for example, never criminalized the act of selling sex, nor did it criminalize the status of carrying a venereal disease outside of wartime, even as it targeted some— those deemed prostitutes, delinquent girls, and paupers, for example—for compulsory treatment and incarceration.[147] Thus, while Americans were not alone in pushing for a carceral and paternalistic anti-trafficking regime, due to the ASHA's methods and Rockefeller's money, they stood poised to control the narrative.

The ASHA's investigative methods and findings reframed prohibitionist prostitution policy in the increasingly authoritative discourse of social scientific research.[148] By the 1920s, the ASHA had fully sidelined an older American investigative tradition, pioneered by women like Dr. Katharine Bushnell. Bushnell's investigations, spanning from India to China, Wisconsin to California, had sought to demonstrate women's right to bodily integrity, without government control, even if they sold sex. In 1920, Bushnell wrote to a colleague expressing her pessimism about "state rehabilitation homes or farms, managed by political influence as they will be. It will be a history of dividing the spoils among officers thereof, and the girls subjected to more or less mistreatment by officials who have no interest in anything much but their own salaries."[149] For Bushnell, the purpose of investigations was not to make new laws or justify the arrest of women, but to "[drag] into the light of public" all of the wrongs committed against women and demand they cease.[150]

Instead, the two League inquiries built on Abraham Flexner's 1914 study, the first to supposedly offer scientific proof of the failures of regulation. They used the ASHA's undercover methods to give "definite evidence," in the form of the investigators' observations and conversations with "underworld" figures, that regulation caused trafficking, and that prostitution and trafficking were one and the same. Government action against prostitution, then, provided the solution.[151]

Although the ASHA's power at the League of Nations waned in the 1930s, its influence continued through the two reports and the new international agreements that built upon them. The 1933 International Convention for the Suppression of the Traffic in Women of Full Age wholly erased the possibility of women's consent, along the model of the investigations. The 1933 Convention defined the offense of trafficking as procuring, enticing, or leading away "even with her consent, a woman or girl of full age for immoral purposes to be carried out in another country."[152] Thus, anyone who profited from migratory commercial sex became a trafficker and a criminal, and any woman who migrated and sold sex became a trafficking victim. Both statuses necessitated state surveillance and intervention. Some representatives, such as the Danish physician Dr. Estrid Hein, warned that such an approach infringed on "the liberty of action of adults," which "should be respected."[153] Yet the Trafficking Committee overruled this objection.[154]

The next agreement, outlined in 1937, defined trafficking to encompass prostitution that happened within a single country, again echoing the definition employed by ASHA investigators. In fact, the 1937 draft Convention for Suppressing the Exploitation of the Prostitution of Others wholly mirrored the definition of trafficking in US law—with or without consent, regardless of age, and whether or not a national boundary was crossed, making all prostitution evidence of trafficking.[155] While the Second World War halted the League's anti-trafficking work, after the armistice the United Nations, which replaced the League, adopted the 1937 draft Convention's broad definition of trafficking. It explicitly cited the 1927 Report as evidence that state-regulated prostitution caused trafficking.[156]

Somewhat ironically, in this post–WWII moment, as the United States emerged as a superpower, the US government largely lost interest in international anti-trafficking.[157] But by supposedly proving that prostitution and trafficking were one and the same, the ASHA's investigations had already framed attacking prostitution as the key to preventing international trafficking. Thus, US influence could be felt at the UN even in the absence of US government or private organizational involvement.

The final form of the first UN anti-trafficking agreement, the 1949 Convention for the Suppression of the Traffic in Persons and of the Exploitation of the Prostitution of Others, targeted prostitution as the cause of trafficking and sought to abolish both. The 1949 Convention termed prostitution a menace to society, "incompatible with the dignity and worth of the human person." Its preamble argued that prostitution and trafficking "endanger the welfare of the individual, the family and the community." It advocated the abolition of licensed houses and called for the criminalization of a broad range of activities related to commercial sex. States should "punish" anyone who "procures, entices or leads away" another person for purposes of prostitution, regardless of consent, as well as those who benefited in any way from the profits of prostitution. It called for scrutiny of "persons who appear, prima facie, to be the principals and accomplices in or victims of such traffic," framing the surveillance of women immigrants and emigrants as a means of protecting them.[158]

Despite the shifts in sexual cultures taking place around the world in the interwar and postwar periods, criminalizing commercial sex and restricting migration ultimately prevailed in international anti-trafficking policy. Americans did not promote such policies solely on their own: they succeeded because of the powerful support of the British government, along with the growing abolitionist consensus in the international community. But the two investigations embedded American perspectives into international governance and provided seemingly concrete evidence of the ills of regulated prostitution. Investigators' assumption that women could not consent to migrate and sell sex led them to overlook the factors that shaped when, why, where, and how women sold sex, making these constraints invisible. They largely disregarded the broader contexts of migratory labor in which women's sexual labor was deeply embedded, setting apart trafficking, which they equated with prostitution, as a unique problem, decontextualized from questions of labor, economics, gendered violence, and empire.

Indeed, the League's two studies drew no distinctions between the experiences of Marie, the entrepreneurial French woman whom Kinsie observed in Rio who asserted her financial independence and planned to open her own brothel; Elsie, the German woman Kinsie met in Genoa who had been trying to work off her debts to the brothel owner for the past three years; the unnamed "Indian" and "half-breed" women in Mexico City's brothels whom Worthington did not deign to visit; and the unnamed Chinese women selling sex to male laborers in the British-occupied Malay Peninsula.[159] These women became not individuals but statistics, just as trafficking became a problem of sex, and its solution, the control of women's bodies—a solution with striking parallels to the very regulation system that Americans so often decried. There were other ways to frame these women's labor and experiences, but the League reports collapsed them into the problem of trafficking. This framing is still evident in international policy today.

Conclusion

IN THE LATE NINETEENTH CENTURY, many reform-minded Americans believed that the United States had a special role to play in sexually civilizing the world, and in the twentieth century it gained the power to do so. Americans' ability to impose their own sexual morality abroad resulted from a powerful alliance between the US state and American private organizations. The government gave private reform organizations a platform from which to advance their anti-prostitution agenda. In exchange, the involvement of private organizations helped to conceal and soften what were, in reality, drastic expansions of state power into seemingly private life. Reformers provided moral and scientific legitimacy to the US government's campaigns to prohibit prostitution and restrict immigration by framing them in terms of public health, humanitarianism, and the protection of women.

Proclaiming these values was a way for Americans to jockey for position on the global stage. They insisted that the United States was a uniquely benevolent and sexually moral empire. In this view, hypersexualized people of color required US intervention, but so did sovereign states and imperial governments, because those that regulated prostitution showed themselves to be uncivilized. To sustain this flattering picture of themselves, Americans needed to insist that the United States never tolerated prostitution, even though it often did. So, when US officials licensed prostitutes, both the government and reformers described it as an aberration or European import: a distinctly un-American policy.

The ideology of American sexual exceptionalism was thus self-reinforcing. It insisted on America's exceptional sexual morality, and it set the eradication of prostitution as the standard of civilization. But to reach its own standard, the government had to enact harsher anti-prostitution and anti-trafficking laws. The harsher these were, the more the United States displayed its supposed leadership, which in turn justified its interventions into prostitution and trafficking policy abroad.

Reform-minded citizens and governments thought about prostitution in a range of ways in the late nineteenth century. In the 1870s, two groups were the most visible: medical doctors, who argued for a regulationist system with licensing and inspection, and feminist abolitionists, who argued that the government should make no laws that violated women's bodies and rights. But by the 1910s and 1920s, American reformers and the US government helped to solidify a framework that equated all prostitution with trafficking. This framework viewed all commercial sex as evidence of a crime, and those involved required either state punishment or protection depending on whether officials believed a woman was forced to sell sex or had chosen to do so (even though American conceptions of trafficking held that a woman's consent was immaterial). Although positioned as oppositional, punishment and protection often looked quite similar, involving police harassment, arrest, forcible genital inspections, and restrictions on mobility.

This framework for conceptualizing commercial sex and migration, set more than a hundred years ago, is still the basis of US policy. During the "unilateral moment" at the turn of the twenty-first century, when the United States exerted global power on an unprecedented scale, the US government seized the opportunity to shape the direction of international anti-prostitution and anti-trafficking work once again. It has justified intervening into other countries to dictate public health and prostitution policies by invoking the protection of women. And it has used private organizations, now known as nongovernmental organizations (NGOs), to enact anti-prostitution efforts both domestically and globally. As in the past, such partnerships have allowed the US government to exert its policy aims internationally even in the absence of direct US intervention.

Protective Violence and US Empire in the Twenty-First Century

Domestic and global shifts in the 1990s set the stage for the resurgence of trafficking as a key international political issue, much as it had been in the early 1900s and the interwar period. Deregulation and globalization accelerated the cross-border migration of people for work around the world and made it more visible. Meanwhile, in the United States, the marriage between evangelicals and political conservatives brought questions of sexual morality to the fore.

Much like previous anti-trafficking movements, the movement of the 1990s united activists with a broad and often contradictory range of commitments. Socially conservative Christians concerned with global justice and evangelization, feminists committed to an anti-prostitution framework, and both liberal and conservative politicians joined to fight trafficking, working through non-governmental organizations as well as through government channels.[1]

Building on this momentum, anti-prostitution and anti-trafficking became major policy goals of the George W. Bush administration. The Bush administration articulated a new vision of American sexual exceptionalism for the twenty-first century. It sought to contain sex strictly within heterosexual, marital, conjugal households and punish those whose practices, identities, and labor placed them outside these rigid norms. It married prostitution prohibition with the prohibition of abortion and contraception, the promotion of abstinence-only programs, and an attack on LGBTQ+ rights, all framed around the United States' status as an exceptional, Christian nation that stood for the protection of women and families.[2] Prostitution is "inherently harmful and dehumanizing," Bush stated, and should not be treated "as a legitimate form of work for any human being."[3] Thus, "It should be the policy of the United States to eradicate such practices."[4]

Indeed, justifying US interventions abroad by claiming to protect women marked early 2000s US foreign policy more broadly. First Lady Laura Bush deemed alleviating "the plight of the women and children," about whom "civilized people throughout the world" were concerned, as a primary goal of the US invasion of Afghanistan in November 2001. As she proclaimed, "Because of our recent military gains, in much of Afghanistan women are no longer imprisoned in their homes," even as the war killed tens of thousands of Afghan civilians and led to economic, public health, and infrastructural collapse.[5]

A centerpiece of the Bush administration's anti-trafficking crusade was the anti-prostitution pledge. First enacted in 2003, it required any entity receiving US government funds for work on HIV / AIDS, tuberculosis, and malaria, as well as sex trafficking to have a "policy explicitly opposing prostitution and sex trafficking."[6] With the anti-prostitution pledge, the US government began to use infectious disease prevention and control, in addition to trafficking, as a means of advancing its agenda to eradicate prostitution.

The anti-prostitution pledge applies to both NGOs and governments. Indeed, in 2005 the national AIDS commissioner of Brazil, Pedro Chequer, rejected $40 million of US funding for HIV / AIDS work because he refused to comply with the anti-prostitution pledge. Sex work is legal in Brazil, Chequer argued, and sex workers are "partners" in implementing AIDS policy. "How could we ask prostitutes to take a position against themselves?" Chequer pointed to the pledge as an infringement on Brazil's sovereignty, declaring that "no country is supposed to decide what another country must do."[7]

International public health organizations and experts largely agree that including sex workers in policy development and implementation, rather than stigmatizing them through criminalization, is the most effective means of reducing disease transmission as well as forced sexual labor—that is, sex trafficking.[8] Still, the US government has enforced the anti-prostitution pledge, with what researchers have demonstrated are damaging consequences for sex workers. In May 2000, a group of NGOs, in collaboration with sex workers themselves, launched the Lotus Club, a drop-in center for predominantly Vietnamese migrant sex workers living and working in Svay Pak, Cambodia. This center provided health care, offered workshops on issues such as negotiating with clients, and worked to stimulate "collective action for improving work and living conditions, including reducing vulnerability to STIs, particularly HIV / AIDS."[9]

But as the US government shifted toward a more explicit anti-prostitution stance, the US Committee on International Relations labeled the Lotus Club as a case of "Foreign Government Complicity in Human Trafficking." Under increased scrutiny, the Club scaled back its work, including efforts to provide child sex workers with a safe place to rest, since the US government could construe such activities as supporting child prostitution and sex trafficking. Eventually it closed, hampered by the anti-prostitution pledge in its ability to respond to changes in the local sexual marketplace.[10]

The US government also enforces its prostitution prohibitionist stance globally by issuing an annual report that ranks countries into different tiers based on their response to the problem of trafficking. If a country ranks below a certain tier, they can no longer receive non-humanitarian, non–trade related aid from the United States. Tier rankings are based largely on the severity with which countries criminalize and punish commercial sex. While rankings take into account efforts to protect victims, they specifically exclude "developmental initiatives" that might focus on general poverty reduction, labor protection, and health care. Even though such initiatives are often what sex workers themselves call for to improve their safety, according to the US government they do not have "concrete ties" to the stated US goals of prosecution, protection, and prevention.[11] Indeed, many countries in Africa and Southeast Asia have prohibited prostitution and enacted laws that punish sex work and migration more harshly in an attempt to improve their tier ranking.[12]

Through the anti-prostitution pledge and the tier ranking system, the United States continues to position itself as the global arbiter of anti-prostitution and anti-trafficking policy. In doing so, it has at times superseded the work of the UN, which has increasingly moved away from prostitution prohibition and criminalization as means to address trafficking. According to legal scholar Janie Chuang, the tier ranking system and threat of sanctions "elevates [sic] U.S. norms over international norms by giving the former the teeth the latter so often lack."[13] In this way, the US government bends public health policy around the world toward prostitution prohibition.

The US government continues to partner with NGOs to enact anti-prostitution and anti-trafficking work, just as it did with the American Social Hygiene Association in the early twentieth century. The United States is now home to the largest number of anti-trafficking organizations of any country, the majority of which focus on sex trafficking, even as other forms of labor trafficking are more prevalent.[14] Anti-trafficking NGOs have become their own industry, with combined budgets in the billions, but with little transparency on how their money is actually spent.[15]

Reminiscent of the WWI-era closure of American red-light districts, today's NGOs partner with local and federal police agencies to conduct prostitution stings, which often target women of color. While NGOs and governments advertise these stings as missions to rescue sex trafficking victims, they often lead to the detention and arrest of women.[16] As Elena Shih has demonstrated, such methods support the "trafficking-deportation pipeline" of Asian women engaged in massage work in North America.[17] And while NGOs use the language of "modern slavery," as Lyndsey Beutin has argued, they elide the ongoing anti-Blackness that makes the lives of Black women, particularly Black trans women, more precarious.[18] Globally, contemporary anti-trafficking work "enables or supports racial and ethnic profiling" alongside discrimination, according to Shih and Kamala Kempadoo.[19] Anti-trafficking NGOs, in partnership with the US government, thus continue to target Black, Asian, and other women of color, much as they have for a century.

Despite the continuities between past and present US international anti-prostitution efforts, there are notable differences. Most obviously, the scale of global markets for cheap labor, including sexual labor, is vastly larger than in the early twentieth century. But the ideology driving American sexual exceptionalism has also undergone a shift. An explicitly evangelical Christian perspective drives much of contemporary US government and NGO anti-prostitution and anti-trafficking efforts. In contrast, the social hygiene movement of the early twentieth century consciously rejected the religious moralism it associated with the older social purity movement, instead framing itself as rooted in modern science, research, and data. Yet these social hygienists forged the carceral policy framework that the contemporary evangelical anti-trafficking movement continues to uphold. Such a framework abandons the vision of an earlier generation of evangelical feminists like Josephine Butler or Katharine Bushnell, who argued that "confinement and deprivation of freedom are not compatible with the development of morality, which grows in liberty, or not at all."[20]

"Sex Work Is Work": Another Road

Examining policy debates in the early twenty-first century demonstrates the lasting power of American anti-prostitution and anti-trafficking frameworks developed in the early twentieth century. It also presents a new opportunity to understand the perspectives of people in the sex industry. To glimpse the perspectives of sex workers in the late nineteenth and early twentieth centuries requires reading against the grain, using sources produced by police, reformers, and doctors, most of whom viewed prostitutes as the problem. Today, sex workers around the world are increasingly organized and vocal in articulating their perspectives; in their words, we also see important continuities.[21]

The US government's prohibitionist stance on prostitution—as well as its insistence on policies that conflate consensual sexual labor with forced sexual labor trafficking—ignore alternative conceptions of sexual labor long put forth by many people who sell sex. People who sell or have sold sex do not hold one, singular position. Sex workers are diverse; the fact that they have sold sex does not necessarily unite them. Yet over the last 150 years, many sex workers have argued that carceral policies aimed at protecting them—or protecting society from them—make their lives more precarious.[22]

This book has demonstrated the real harms that such protective violence— at the hands of the state through criminalization, or at the hands of reformers through supposed rescue missions—has wrought on the bodies of people who sell sex. Repeatedly, people who sell sex have framed sex work as work, even though they did not always use that phrase, and demanded their right to bodily autonomy and freedom of movement.

Indeed, in 1871, women incarcerated in the St. Louis Social Evil hospital critiqued the punitive methods of state licensing under which they labored, as chapter 1 recounted. These women were not representative of all sex workers; indeed, all were white and made very comfortable incomes. Yet their position reflected how harsh licensing and quarantine rules that specifically singled out sex workers could harm all women who sold sex. As a journalist reported, women told him, they "feel that they have no right to be used in any other way than such as they may desire, so long as it is compatible with sanitary principles. They are sensitive, and resent interference, and do not think the board of health has a right to meddle with their doctors or their steward, or their bill of fare. In fact, they ask no outside sympathy, and they want no outside meddling."[23] In essence, they asked to control their own living and working conditions and their bodies, free from interference by the state or private reform organizations.

Similarly, in 1924, Marie Biaggioni's conversation with a League of Nations investigator, which opened this book, demonstrates that she understood herself as a migratory worker, not a trafficking victim or trafficker. The investigator's notes capture Marie laying out a plan that she hoped would give her and her family economic stability. As she detailed to him, "she is making a lot of money here via prostitution; . . . she will gradually bring over several of her other sisters, and then she proposes to open a pencion [sic] herself, and after several years of this kind of work in Rio, she hopes to return with her sisters to France with a great deal of money saved up."[24]

We do not know if her plan worked. Marie's archival trail goes cold after she crossed paths with League investigators. But we do know that her road to Rio and her goal—to make money abroad so that she and her family could live a better life—made her much like millions of other people at the time, rather than an outlier because of the kind of labor she performed.[25]

Today, many sex workers around the world work together to push local, national, and international policy toward a rights-based and labor-based framework rather than a carceral one.[26] In the face of police violence, restrictive immigration policies, and lack of access to resources, they organize collectively, support one another through mutual aid, and advocate for legal change. In the words of Kthi Win, an organizer and sex worker from Burma, "The key demand of the sex worker's movement in Burma, in Asia and all around the world is simple. We demand that sex work is recognized as work."[27]

What does it mean to see sex work as work? Certainly, as many sex workers argue, it means freedom from police and community harassment, stigma against themselves and their children, and violence at the hands of clients. Yet sex worker activists also articulate a positive vision of a world in which sex work is treated as work, and they strive to make it a reality. They organize unions, much as other workers do to gain collective power. They call for access to quality health care, both primary care as well as prevention and treatment for HIV / AIDS. They claim the right to safe housing for themselves and their children. And they demand the ability to raise their own children, including the means to feed, clothe, and educate them. Indeed, in the absence of state support, sex worker collectives often provide many of these resources themselves. For example, the Indian sex worker organization VAMP runs HIV prevention programs, provides childcare, and hosts meetings for sex workers—men and women, transgender and cisgender—where they can discuss their particular concerns.[28]

Now, as in the past, American activists and the US government shape global definitions of prostitution and trafficking in powerful ways, predicated on a model that sees victims or villains, citizens or aliens, endangered "modern day slaves" or dangerous prostitutes. Thus, Marie Biaggioni could be either a sex trafficking victim or a nefarious trafficker attempting to entrap her younger sister. League investigators simply could not see, despite everything she told them, that she was a migrant, sister, mother, daughter, friend, survivor of intimate partner violence, and worker, enmeshed in a web of social connections and caught at the nexus of global political and economic forces, yet also able to make choices for herself. What might international policies on migration and sexual labor look like if they were more than governmental grandstanding? If, instead, they took seriously the perspectives of women like Marie?

ACKNOWLEDGMENTS

THIS BOOK WAS made possible by the generosity of so many people and I have felt overwhelmed by gratitude as I finished it. How do you thank the people who have been with you through births, marriages, deaths, and a pandemic, as well as the not-so-small task of writing a book? These acknowledgments are a start, but please know that I have not forgotten how many drinks, dinners, edits, and childcare swaps I owe so many of you.

At Harvard, I was lucky to find supportive advisers who helped give shape to the sprawling dissertation on which this book is based. My deepest thanks goes to Nancy Cott, who has continued to be a sharp reader since she first agreed to direct my dissertation. This book is much better for her intellectual curiosity and breadth of knowledge. Ann Braude has been my cheerleader and critic for well over a decade, and I would have foundered without her personal and intellectual support. Andrew Jewett has long been a perceptive reader and encouraging mentor. Erez Manela always pushed me to see the bigger stakes of my arguments, which has been crucial as I wrote the book.

I was so lucky to be part of the American Studies Program at Harvard. I'm not sure I could have done this project anywhere else. From the moment we met, my cohort in the program was brilliant, supportive, and so, so much fun. Sandy Placido, Brian Goodman, Theresa McCulla, and Collier Brown were a joy to do grad school with. It's been a pleasure to be part of their lives, to spend time with their partners, particularly Alison Hemberger and Brian Goldstein, and to meet all of their hilarious children. Arthur Patton-Hock made the program run, facilitated my numerous research trips, and more than that, was fantastic to chat with when I needed a break.

I owe so much to intellect and friendship of many of my grad school classmates, particularly Chris Allison, Rudi Batzell, John Bell, Colin Bossen, Carla Cevasco, Eli Cook, Holger Droessler, Marisa Egerstrom, Dan Farbman, Amy Fish, Maggie Gates, Altin Gavranovic, John Gee, Katherine Gerbner, Kyle Gibson, Balraj Gill, Cristina Groeger, Aaron Hatley, Hillary Kaell, Zach

Nowak, Scott Paulson-Bryant, Evander Price, Charles Peterson, Summer Sha-fer, Rebecca Scofield, and Stephen Vider. A meeting with Ann Marie Wilson sparked the entire project when she suggested I look at social purity reformers.

Many faculty members at Harvard also provided invaluable guidance, es-pecially Joyce Chaplin, Lisa McGirr, Marie Griffith, Jennifer Roberts, Charles Rosenberg, Allan Brandt, Leigh Schmidt, John Stauffer, and Laurel Thatcher Ulrich. Cliff Tabin's generosity made it possible for my family to live in the same place—even though I never worked with him directly, I have learned much from him about compassionate mentorship. I'm also grateful to Vonda Shannon for working out the details. Special thanks to Ericka Knudsen, who patiently helped me improve my French and shared her passion for new wave cinema with me.

Grad school workshops provided an early venue for testing out parts of this project. Liz Cohen's twentieth-century US workshop offered the perfect environment to work through sticky chapters. I'm grateful to its members, particularly Claire Dunning, Andrew Pope, Shaun Nichols, and Casey Bohlen. The Weatherhead Graduate Student Associate program kept me well-fed and surrounded by brilliant people. Special thanks to Clare Putnam, Margot Moin-ester, Lydia Walker, Erin Mosely, Mircea Raianu, Nancy Khalil, and Jessica Tollette. The North American Religions Colloquium provided a stimulating intellectual community throughout my time at Harvard. Spending alternate Tuesday evenings with its members taught me so much about being a gener-ous giver and receiver of feedback. Particular thanks to Deirdre DeBruyn Rubio, Kip Richardson, Elizabeth Jemison, Helen Jin Kim, Max Mueller, Brett Grainger, Kera Street, Cori Tucker-Price, David Hempton, David Holland, David Hall, Dan McKanan, Katherine Brekus, Healan Gaston, and Heather Curtis. The Gender and Sexuality Workshop at Harvard also gave thoughtful feedback on very early drafts. I'm particularly grateful to Afsana Najmabadi, Sarah Richardson, Elizabeth Katz, and Cara Fallon.

Early on in my academic career, Charles Hallisey, Jonathan Schofer, and Kathi Sell took a very earnest and eager undergraduate very seriously. By sug-gesting works that quite literally blew my mind and then generously discussing them with me during office hours, they laid the foundations that led me here. My friends from my master's program, including Karen Bray, Taylor Lewis Guthrie Hartman, Molly Housh Gordon, Tiffany Stanley, Becky Curtain, Ken-dra Goodson Plating, and Audrey Dickinson, have provided lasting support. The decades-spanning friendship of Nicole Capriccio has made life far more entertaining. Johanna Straavaldsen's travels took me across the Atlantic for the first time and helped me see a bigger world.

I was so lucky to have met Jessica Pliley at a conference many years ago. She has been a generous mentor and good friend from the first post-panel beer she bought me to the final round of comments she gave me on this book's introduction. She also played a central role in bringing me into a brilliant group of scholars writing about sexual labor and migration. It was through her that I met Elisa Camiscioli, whose feedback on this book has made it so much better, and whose presence in various iterations of our zoom writing group made writing a book during a pandemic far less lonely. I'm grateful to Julia Laite, Caroline Séquin, Sandy Chang, and Katie Hemphill, for being sharp interlocutors, careful readers, and good friends. Eileen Boris has been a steadfast supporter and provided brilliant commentary on intimate labor. Philippa Heatherington was one of the smartest people I've ever met, and, in her absence, I still find myself turning to old drafts of her writings for insights.

My next debt is to the many librarians and archivists without whom the book would not exist at all. My deepest thanks to Matthew Herbison at the Drexel University College of Medicine Legacy Center, the late Tom Rosenbaum at the Rockefeller Archives Center, Linnea Anderson at the Social Welfare History Archives, Ryan Bean at the Kautz Family YMCA Archives, Janet Olson at the Frances Willard Memorial Library, Jacques Oberson and Lee Robertson at the League of Nations Archives, David Sbrava at the Service Historique de la Défense, Dennis Northcott at the Missouri Historical Society Library and Research Center, and Diana Carey at the Schlesinger Library. Thanks are also due to the staff at the National Archives and Records Administration, the Women's Library at the London School of Economics, the Friend's Historical Library, Princeton University Rare Books and Special Collections, the Presbyterian Historical Society, the World YMCA Archives, the Geneva Library, the British Library, the Boston Public Library, Countway Library, Houghton Library, Harvard Interlibrary Loan, and the University of Mississippi Interlibrary Loan.

Research assistance from Margaret Polk, Henry Shah, and Lauren Cain allowed me to tie up loose ends. Sandy Placido generously took time out of her own fascinating research to photograph materials for me while she was at the Archivo General de la Nación. Asaf Elia-Shalev graciously shared his discoveries about the mysterious Paul Kinsie. Special thanks to Alexander Ward, who swiftly double-checked quotations and footnotes and saved me from several embarrassing errors. I am responsible for any that remain.

My research, and the time to write about it, was made possible by generous funding from the Drexel Women in Medicine Archives, Rockefeller Archives Center, the Center for American Political Studies and the Weatherhead Center at Harvard University, Princeton University Press, the University of Mississippi Department of History Neff Fund, and the University of Mississippi College of Library Arts. A Loeb Fellowship from Harvard gave me a year of uninterrupted time to start on the book manuscript.

The kindness of friends and friends-of-friends, who offered up spare rooms, couches, travel advice, meals, and plenty of wine made what could have been lonely and tedious archival research trips into adventures. In Geneva, Anca Cretu found me the one affordable place to stay and showed me around. The many late nights spent in John Clive and Michelle Newell's garden were highlights of my time in London. In Minneapolis, Katie Gerbner and Sean Blanchet kept me cozy and well fed during the polar vortex. In Princeton, post-archive evenings floating in the pool with Julian Ayroles and Sarah Kocher gave me the energy to keep digging.

The support of my current and former colleagues in the history department at the University of Mississippi has allowed me to finish this book. Deep thanks to Jessie Wilkerson, Shennette Garrett-Scott, Jarod Roll, Alex Lindgren-Gibson, and Peter Thilly, who have generously read my work. My gratitude to Mikaëla Adams, Garett Felber, Annie Twitty, Ted Ownby, Darren Grem, Jesse Cromwell, April Holm, Zack Kagan Guthrie, Graham Pitts, Robert Colby, Theresa Levitt, Susan Gaunt Stearns, Vivian Ibrahim, Frances Kneupper, Mark Lerner, Joshua First, Chiarella Esposito, Emily Fransee, Robert Fleegler, Joshua Howard, Bashir Salau, Paul Polgar, Isaac Stephens, Oliver Dinius, Douglass Sullivan-González, Jeff Watt, Nicolas Trépanier, and the late John Neff. And of course, who could forget Becky Marchiel? As department chairs, Noell Wilson and Chuck Ross offered generous financial support for a manuscript workshop, which made this book far better. Toi Parker, Kelly Brown Houston, Brittany Ellis, and Suneetha Chittiboyina helped make my research trips—and much more—actually happen.

So many people have provided feedback on parts of the book over the years, including Laura Briggs, Alexa Rodriguez, Jeongmin Kim, Marc Aidinoff, Laura Prieto, Matthew Guariglia, Allison Lange, Casey Riley, and Jeffrey Parker. I'm grateful to Jessica Pliley, Elisa Camisioli, Daniel Immerwahr, Julia Irwin, and Peter Thilly for reading the entire manuscript during my workshop. The members of the Delta Women Writers generously commented on several chapters and I'm thankful for the intellectual community they have provided. Grey

Osterud helped give the book shape and always had faith in it even when I was flailing. I was lucky to work with Bridget Flannery-McCoy, Alena Chekanov, and Theresa Liu at Princeton University Press, whose support and editorial eye improved the manuscript. Karen Verde's copyedits made the book far more polished.

It's safe to say I would not have made it through the height of the pandemic, which corresponded with the writing of this book, without my incredible neighbors. Wednesday evenings in the backyard with Joanna and Cyndii Jo, rain or shine, saved my sanity. Provisions of food, shelter, company, and child-care by Nicole and Jeff, Ariel and Tal, Susan and David, Frank and Amanda, Ari and Stephanie, Katie and Blake, Robert, and the midtown WHIPs kept us afloat. Teachers at NLS, MMS, and PTCC, as well as Sandy, Luz, Paty, Dean, and Rosie did the crucial work of educating and caring for Syd while I researched and wrote.

The Chronophages helped me over the finish line. Charles Peterson started it all. Amy Zanoni, Erin Hutchinson, and Dylan Gottlieb always seemed to be on when I needed them. Brian Goodman provided encouragement and excellent edits at the very end, not to mention introducing me to the perfect Czech ice cream sandwiches many years ago. Daniel Immerwahr helped me to write in my own voice, even if I had to get into character to do it.

Among the good friends I made in grad school, none have been a more lasting source of support, internet culture, dismal photographs, and Racine newspaper headlines than the crew of PSD. Tim McGrath and Tenley Archer provide just the right mix of science talk and spot-on impressions. Brian and Laura McCammack are always in for a Sunday night bourboning. I'm grateful for Virginia visits with Jack Hamilton and Annie Galvin and Cambridge updates from Derek Etkin. Brian Hochman's wisdom helped me through a tough time. Nick Donofrio's baseball enthusiasm and Verena von Pfetten's linguini clams have been summer highlights. George Blaustein correctly insisted that I remove all gerunds from my title. Pete L'Official's brilliant writing and sense of style were an inspiration long before we became friends, and now I am lucky to count Pete, Liz Munsell, and Viva as family. Maggie Gram was there at the very beginning, as I rambled about dissertation ideas in her living room, and she was there at the very end, as I finished final revisions at her dining room table. Her careful edits made much of the book more intelligible. I'm so grateful to have Maggie, Jen Touhy, Glory, and little Nan as part of our chosen family.

In Cambridge, my enological sisters have helped me direct my research skills in more hedonistic directions. Maura Smyth provided feminist insight and arepas. Shannon McHugh offered wit and perfect pronunciation. Meg Nesmith is a beautiful writer; I am so grateful for her edits. Brook Hopkins read the entire manuscript and prevented me from making shameful constitutional law mistakes. Rebecca Richman Cohen has been a fruitful conversation partner on carceral feminism. It has been a joy to count her, along with Leo and Nala, as our summer family.

My parents, Roger and Kathie, have always nurtured my inquisitive tendencies and I would not be who I am without their love and generosity. My brother Collin's pizza prowess sustained me for many of the years I was writing this book, as did Rachel's ability to make every place she has ever lived calm and beautiful. They hosted me on more research trips than I can count. Even though they now live on the other side of the world, Collin, Rachel, and now Asa, still always find ways to cheer me up. My mother-in-law Diane has been a welcome presence and an invaluable provider of childcare. For countless morning cups of coffee in bed, afternoon walks in the woods, and evening cocktails on the porch, I am indebted to Evan. I'm in awe of Sydney's boundless curiosity and energy. The two of them are simply the best.

NOTES

Introduction

1. The narrative of Biaggioni's life presented here is pieced together from the following sources from the League of Nations Archives, United Nations Archives at Geneva, Switzerland (hereafter LNA): Samuel Auerbach, "In Re. S.S. Valdivia," October 28, 1924, Box S181 / 36 / 4; Samuel Auerbach, "In Re. T. W. & C. Re: S.S. Valdivia," November 4, 1924, Box S181 / 36 / 4; Samuel Auerbach, "In Re Trip on S.S. Valdivia of the Frenchline from Marseilles to Buenos Aires, Argentina, S.A., April 30 to May 21, 1924," May 29, 1924, Box S181 / 36 / 4; Samuel Auerbach, "Passengers Mentioned in S.S. Valdivia Report as Having Debarked at Rio de Janeiro," July 25, 1924, Box S181 / 36 / 4; Paul Kinsie, "Rio de Janeiro, Brazil," July 12, 1924, Box S172 / 27 / 5. My method here is indebted to Julia Laite, *The Disappearance of Lydia Harvey* (London: Profile Books, 2022).

2. On women's labor in post–WWI France, see Laura L. Frader, *Breadwinners and Citizens: Gender in the Making of the French Social Model* (Chapel Hill, NC: Duke University Press, 2008).

3. Thaddeus Blanchette, "Rio de Janeiro," in *Trafficking in Women (1924–1926): The Paul Kinsie Reports for the League of Nations Vol. 2*, ed. Jean-Michel Chaumont, Magaly Rodríguez García, and Paul Servais (Geneva: United Nations Publications, 2017), 199. See also Elisa Camiscioli, *Selling French Sex: Prostitution, Trafficking, and Global Migrations* (Cambridge: Cambridge University Press, 2024).

4. "WWI Draft Card for Paul M. Kinsie," *World War I Selective Service System Draft Registration Cards 1917–1918*, M-1509, National Archives and Records Administration, Washington, DC, https://www.ancestrylibrary.com/imageviewer/collections/6482/images/005263042_00826?treeid=&personid=&rc=&usePUB=true&_phsrc=ojw1&_phstart=successSource&pId =71820024.

5. League of Nations, *International Convention for the Suppression of the Traffic in Women and Children*, Geneva, September 31, 1922. A.125(2)1921 IV, Article 5, 3.

6. "New York State Census, 1915," *State Population Census Schedules, 1915*, New York State Archives, Albany, NY, 23, https://www.ancestrylibrary.com/imageviewer/collections/2703/images/32848_B094060-00416?treeid=&personid=&rc=&usePUB=true&_phsrc=ojw3&_phstart=successSource&pId=13333505.

7. Jennifer Fronc, *New York Undercover: Private Surveillance in the Progressive Era* (Chicago: University of Chicago Press, 2009).

8. *Materials for the Report on Vice Conditions in the City of Lancaster, PA. 1913*, Affidavit No. 151 (Lancaster, 1913–1914).

9. "Paul Kinsie, 86, Ex-Investigator for Unit Fighting Spread of V.D.," *New York Times*, Obituary section, November 1, 1979, Section D, Page 23. Thanks to Asaf Elia-Shalev for sharing this information.

10. League of Nations and Special Body of Experts on Traffic in Women and Children, *Report of the Special Body of Experts on Traffic in Women and Children*, Part 1 (Geneva: League of Nations, 1927), 43.

11. Heather Berg argues that sex work is "a space both of exploitation and creative resistance." Heather Berg, "Reading Sex Work: An Introduction," *South Atlantic Quarterly* 120, no. 3 (July 2021): 489.

12. On French regulation see Alain Corbin, *Women for Hire: Prostitution and Sexuality in France After 1850* (Cambridge, MA: Harvard University Press, 1990); Jill Harsin, *Policing Prostitution in Nineteenth-Century Paris* (Princeton, NJ: Princeton University Press, 1985). I retain the term "venereal disease" to reflect my historical actors' belief that such infections were intimately tied to sexual morality.

13. In the antebellum period, anti-slavery activists were often involved in a range of reform causes, including women's suffrage, prison reform, temperance, and the rehabilitation of prostitutes. See Steven Mintz, *Moralists and Modernizers: America's Pre-Civil War Reformers* (Baltimore, MD: Johns Hopkins University Press, 1995). On the origins of the American "new abolitionists" see David Pivar, *Purity Crusade: Sexual Morality and Social Control, 1868–1900* (Westport, CT: Greenwood Press, 1973). British and American activists used "social purity" in different ways. See Pivar, *Purity Crusade*, 62–66. On broader nineteenth-century US sexual culture see Helen Horowitz, *Rereading Sex: Battles Over Sexual Knowledge and Suppression in Nineteenth-Century America* (New York: Vintage, 2003); John D'Emilio and Estelle B. Freedman, *Intimate Matters: A History of Sexuality in America* (New York: Harper & Row, 1988).

14. Judith Walkowitz, *Prostitution and Victorian Society: Women, Class, and the State* (Cambridge: Cambridge University Press, 1980); Karen Offen, "Madame Ghénia Avril de Sainte-Croix, the Josephine Butler of France," *Women's History Review* 17, no. 2 (2008): 239–255.

15. Josephine Butler, "Introduction," in *Women's Work and Women's Culture*, ed. Josephine Butler (London: Macmillan, 1869), xv–xvi.

16. Jessica R. Pliley, "Ambivalent Abolitionist Legacies: The League of Nations' Investigations into Sex Trafficking, 1927–1934," in *Fighting Modern Slavery and Human Trafficking: History and Contemporary Policy*, ed. Genevieve LeBaron, Jessica R. Pliley and David W. Blight (Cambridge: Cambridge University Press), 103; Stephanie Limoncelli, *The Politics of Trafficking: The First International Movement to Combat the Sexual Exploitation of Women* (Stanford, CA: Stanford University Press, 2011); On paternalist abolitionism in Britain see Pamela Cox, "Compulsion, Voluntarism, and Venereal Disease: Governing Sexual Health in England after the Contagious Diseases Acts," *Journal of British Studies* 46, no. 1 (2007): 91–115; Julia Laite, *Common Prostitutes and Ordinary Citizens: Sex in London, 1885–1960* (New York: Palgrave MacMillan, 2012). On debates over abolitionism at the UN see Sonja Dolinsek, "Tensions of abolitionism during the negotiation of the 1949 'Convention for the Suppression of the Traffic in Persons and of the Exploitation of the Prostitution of Others,'" *European Review of History: Revue européenne d'histoire* 29, no. 2 (2022): 223–248. The reformers I follow differed from those Mara L. Keire discusses, who advocated for strategically placed commercial sex districts, Mara L. Keire, *For Business and Pleasure: Red-Light Districts and the Regulation of Vice in the United States, 1890–1933* (Baltimore, MD: Johns Hopkins University Press, 2010).

17. Scott W. Stern, *The Trials of Nina McCall: Sex, Surveillance, and the Decades-Long Government Plan to Imprison "Promiscuous" Women* (Boston, MA: Beacon Press, 2018); David Pivar, *Purity and Hygiene: Women, Prostitution, and the "American Plan," 1900–1930* (Westport, CT: Greenwood Press, 2002); Nancy Bristow, *Making Men Moral: Social Engineering During the Great War* (New York: New York University Press, 1996).

18. Kristin Luker, "Sex, Social Hygiene, and the State: The Double-Edged Sword of Social Reform," *Theory and Society* 27, no. 5 (October 1998): 601–634; On the growth of the US federal government cooperation through cooperation with private organizations see Gary Gerstle, *Liberty and Coercion: The Paradox of American Government from the Founding to the Present* (Princeton, NJ: Princeton University Press, 2015). On alcohol prohibition see Lisa McGirr, *The War on Alcohol: Prohibition and the Rise of the American State* (New York: Norton, 2015). On opium prohibition see Anne L. Foster, "The Philippines, the United States, and the Origins of Global Narcotics Prohibition," *Social History of Alcohol and Drugs* 33, no. 1 (Spring 2019): 13–36.

19. On global anti-vice activism see Jessica R. Pliley, Harald Fischer-Tiné, and Robert Kramm, *Global Anti-Vice Activism, 1890–1950: Fighting Drinks, Drugs, and 'Immorality'* (Cambridge: Cambridge University Press, 2016). The connections between prohibitionist regimes is a topic ripe for future research.

20. On sex exceptionalism see Aya Gruber, "Sex Exceptionalism in Criminal Law," *Stanford Law Review* 75 (April 2023): 755–846. David A. Bell, "American Exceptionalism," in *Myth America: Historians Take on the Biggest Legends and Lies about Our Past*, ed. Kevin M. Kruse and Julian E. Zelizer (New York: Basic, 2022), 15.

21. Margot Canaday, Nancy F. Cott, and Robert O. Self, "Introduction," *Intimate States: Gender, Sexuality, and Governance in Modern US History* (Chicago: University of Chicago Press, 2021), 1–18.

22. Margot Canaday, *The Straight State: Sexuality and Citizenship in Twentieth-Century America* (Princeton, NJ: Princeton University Press, 2009).

23. Jessica R. Pliley, *Policing Sexuality: The Mann Act and the Making of the FBI* (Cambridge, MA: Harvard University Press, 2014); Cynthia Enloe, *Bananas, Beaches and Bases: Making Feminist Sense of International Politics*, 2nd ed. (Berkeley: University of California Press, 2014); Paul A. Kramer, *The Blood of Government: Race, Empire, the United States, and the Philippines* (Chapel Hill: University of North Carolina Press, 2006); Paul A. Kramer, "The Darkness that Enters the Home: The Politics of Prostitution during the Philippine-American War," in *Haunted by Empire: Geographies of Intimacy in North American History*, ed. Ann Laura Stoler (Durham, NC: Duke University Press, 2006), 366–404; Kristin L. Hoganson, *Fighting for American Manhood: How Gender Politics Provoked the Spanish-American and Philippine-American War* (New Haven, CT: Yale University Press, 2000); Laura Briggs, *Reproducing Empire: Race, Sex, Science, and U.S. Imperialism in Puerto Rico* (Berkeley: University of California Press, 2002); Eileen Suárez Findlay, *Imposing Decency: The Politics of Sexuality and Race in Puerto Rico, 1870–1920* (Durham, NC: Duke University Press, 1999); Tiffany Sippial, *Prostitution, Modernity, and the Making of the Cuban Republic, 1840–1920* (Chapel Hill: University of North Carolina Press, 2013); Joan Flores-Villalobos, *The Silver Women: How Black Women's Labor Made the Panama Canal* (Philadelphia: University of Pennsylvania Press, 2023); Mary A. Renda, *Taking Haiti: Military Occupation and the Culture of U.S. Imperialism, 1915–1940* (Chapel Hill: University of North Carolina Press, 2001).

24. Scholars of European imperialism have crucially shaped this approach. Ann Laura Stoler, *Carnal Knowledge and Imperial Power: Race and the Intimate in Colonial Rule* (Berkeley: University of California Press, 2002); Stoler, ed., *Haunted by Empire.*

25. Daniel Immerwahr, *How to Hide an Empire: A History of the Greater United States* (New York: Farrar, Straus, and Giroux, 2019). For a broad view of the effects of US colonialism on the metropole see Alfred W. McCoy and Francisco A. Scarano, eds., *Colonial Crucible: Empire in the Making of the Modern American State* (Madison: University of Wisconsin Press, 2009). On transatlantic progressivism see Daniel T. Rodgers, *Atlantic Crossings: Social Politics in a Progressive Age* (Cambridge, MA: Harvard University Press, 1998); Ian Tyrrell, *Reforming the World: The Creation of America's Moral Empire* (Princeton, NJ: Princeton University Press, 2010); Ian Tyrrell, *Woman's World / Woman's Empire: The Woman's Christian Temperance Union in International Perspective, 1880–1930* (Chapel Hill: University of North Carolina Press, 1991); Alan Dawley, *Changing the World: American Progressives in War and Revolution* (Princeton, NJ: Princeton University Press, 2003).

26. Tyrrell, *Reforming the World.* Paul A. Kramer, "The Military-Sexual Complex: Prostitution, Disease and the Boundaries of Empire during the Philippine-American War," *Asia-Pacific Journal* 9, no. 30 (2011): 1–35; Warwick Anderson, *Colonial Pathologies: American Tropical Medicine, Race, and Hygiene in the Philippines* (Durham, NC: Duke University Press, 2006).

27. See, for example, Kramer, *The Blood of Government*; Briggs, *Reproducing Empire*; Hoganson, *Fighting for American Manhood*; Findlay, *Imposing Decency*; Renda, *Taking Haiti.*

28. See Kristin L. Hoganson and Jay Sexton, eds., *Crossing Empires: Taking U.S. History into Transimperial Terrain* (Durham, NC: Duke University Press, 2020).

29. Paul A. Kramer, "Empires Exceptions, and Anglo-Saxons: Race and Rule between the British and U.S. Empires," in *The American Colonial State in the Philippines: Global Perspectives*, ed. Julian Go and Anne L. Foster (Durham, NC: Duke University Press, 2003), 43–91.

30. Gerstle, *Liberty and Coercion*; Brian Balogh, *The Associational State: American Governance in the Twentieth Century* (Philadelphia: University of Pennsylvania Press, 2015).

31. Gail Bederman, *Manliness and Civilization: A Cultural History of Gender and Race in the United States, 1880–1917* (Chicago: University of Chicago Press, 1995); Nayan Shah, *Stranger Intimacy: Contesting Race, Sexuality and the Law in the North American West* (Berkeley: University of California Press, 2012); Peggy Pascoe, *What Comes Naturally: Miscegenation Law and the Making of Race in America* (Oxford: Oxford University Press, 2009).

32. Benjamin Coates, "American Presidents and the Ideology of Civilization," in *Ideology in U.S. Foreign Relations: New Histories*, ed. Christopher McKnight Nichols and David Milne (New York: Columbia University Press, 2022).

33. Nancy F. Cott, "Passionlessness: An Interpretation of Victorian Sexual Ideology, 1790–1850," *Signs* 4, no. 2 (Winter 1978): 219–236.

34. Silvia Salvatici, *A History of Humanitarianism, 1755–1989: In the Name of Others* (Manchester: Manchester University Press, 2019), 9; Michael Barnett, *Empire of Humanity: A History of Humanitarianism* (Ithaca, NY: Cornell University Press, 2011), 12; Charlie Laderman, *Sharing the Burden: The Armenian Question, Humanitarian Intervention, and Anglo-American Visions of Global Order* (Oxford: Oxford University Press, 2019); Davide Rodogno, *Against Massacre: Humanitarian Interventions in the Ottoman Empire, 1815–1914* (Princeton, NJ: Princeton University Press, 2012); Fabian Klose, *In the Cause of Humanity: A History of Humanitarian Intervention in the Long Nineteenth Century* (Cambridge: Cambridge University Press, 2022).

35. Klose, *In the Cause of Humanity*, 208–236.

36. Hoganson, *Fighting for American Manhood*, 202.

37. Coates, "American Presidents," 57–58.

38. Salvatici, *A History of Humanitarianism*, 87–88. On the League's Trafficking Committee see Jean-Michel Chaumont, *Le Mythe de la Traite des Blanches: Enquête sur la Fabrication d'un Fléau* (Paris: La Découverte, 2009); Daniel Gorman, *The Emergence of International Society in the 1920s* (Cambridge: Cambridge University Press, 2012); Paul Knepper, "The Investigation into the Traffic in Women by the League of Nations: Sociological Jurisprudence as an International Social Project," *Law and History Review* 34, no. 1 (February 2016): 45–73; Stephen Legg, "'The Life of Individuals as well as of Nations': International Law and the League of Nations' Anti-Trafficking Governmentalities," *Leiden Journal of International Law* 25, no. 3 (2012): 647–664; Barbara Metzger, "Towards an International Human Rights Regime during the Inter-War Years: The League of Nations' Combat of Traffic in Women and Children," in *Beyond Sovereignty: Britain, Empire, and Transnationalism, C. 1880–1950*, ed. Philippa Levine, Kevin Grant, and Frank Trentmann (New York: Palgrave Macmillan, 2007), 54–79; David Petruccelli, "The Crisis of Liberal Internationalism: The Legacies of the League of Nations Reconsidered," *Journal of World History* 31, no. 1 (March 2020): 111–136. Pliley, "Ambivalent Abolitionist Legacies"; Magaly Rodríguez García, "The League of Nations and the Moral Recruitment of Women," *International Review of Social History* 57, no. 20 (2012): 97–128; Limoncelli, *Politics of Trafficking*.

39. Josh Lambert, *Unclean Lips: Obscenity, Jews, and American Culture* (New York: New York University Press, 2013), 3.

40. James P. McCartin, "Gender and Sexuality," in *The Cambridge Companion to American Catholicism*, ed. Margaret M. McGuinness and Thomas F. Rzeznik (Cambridge: Cambridge University Press, 2021), 216–230; Catherine McGowan, "Convents and Conspiracies: A Study of Convent Narratives in the United States, 1850–1870" (PhD diss., University of Edinburgh, 2009).

41. Michael L. Krenn, *The Color of Empire: Race and American Foreign Relations* (Lincoln, NE: Potomac Books, 2006).

42. Camiscioli, *Selling French Sex*.

43. Ernest Bell, cited in Tracy Fessenden, "The Convent, the Brothel, and the Protestant Woman's Sphere," *Signs* 25, no. 2 (2000): 465.

44. "Activities and Plans of the American Social Hygiene Association for the Year Ending September 30, 1914," 7–8, American Social Health Association Papers, Folder 01, Box 170, Social Welfare History Archives, Anderson Library, University of Minnesota, Minneapolis (hereafter ASHA).

45. Tracy Fessenden, *Culture and Redemption: Religion, the Secular, and American Literature* (Princeton, NJ: Princeton University Press, 2007).

46. On Britain see Walkowitz, *Prostitution and Victorian Society*; Walkowitz, *City of Dreadful Delight: Narratives of Sexual Danger in Late-Victorian London* (Chicago: University of Chicago Press, 1992); Antoinette Burton, *Burdens of History: British Feminists, Indian Women, and Imperial Culture, 1865–1915* (Chapel Hill: University of North Carolina Press, 1994); Philippa Levine, *Prostitution, Race, and Politics: Policing Venereal Disease in the British Empire* (New York: Routledge, 2003); Edward J. Bristow, *Vice and Vigilance: Purity Movements in Britain Since 1700* (Dublin: Gill and Macmillan, 1977); Edward J. Bristow, *Prostitution and Prejudice: The Jewish Fight against White Slavery, 1870–1939* (Oxford: Clarendon Press, 1982). Laite, *Common Prostitutes and*

Ordinary Citizens; Stephen Legg, "Of Scales, Networks and Assemblages: The League of Nations Apparatus and the Scalar Sovereignty of the Government of India," *Transactions of the Institute of British Geographers* 34, no. 2 (2009): 234. Mrinalini Sinha argues that the idea of Indian sexual degeneracy played a crucial role in justifying British imperialism. Mrinalini Sinha, *Specters of Mother India: The Global Restructuring of an Empire* (Durham, NC: Duke University Press, 2006). On France see Elisa Camiscioli, *Reproducing the French Race: Immigration, Intimacy, and Embodiment in the Early Twentieth Century* (Durham, NC: Duke University Press, 2009); Camiscioli, *Selling French Sex*; Caroline Séquin, *Desiring Whiteness: A Racial History of Prostitution in France and Colonial Senegal, 1848–1950* (Ithaca, NY: Cornell University Press, 2024). On Italy see Laura Schettini, *Obscene Traffic: Prostitution and Global Migrations from the Italian Perspective (1890–1940)*, trans. Karen Burch (New York: Routledge, 2023). For more on Western Europe, see Limoncelli, *Politics of Trafficking*; On Poland see Keely Stauder-Hustad, *The Devil's Chain: Prostitution and Social Control in Partitioned Poland* (Ithaca, NY: Cornell University Press), 3. On Russia see Philippa Heatherington, "Victims of the Social Temperament: Prostitution, Migration and the Traffic in Women from Imperial Russia and the Soviet Union, 1885–1935" (PhD diss., Harvard University, 2014). On Argentina see Mir Yarfitz, *Impure Migration: Jews and Sex Work in Golden Age Argentina* (New Brunswick, NJ: Rutgers University Press, 2019); Donna J. Guy, *Sex and Danger in Buenos Aires: Prostitution, Family, and Nation in Argentina* (Lincoln: University of Nebraska Press, 1991). On Cuba see Sippial, *Prostitution, Modernity*. On Mexico see Katherine Elaine Bliss, *Compromised Positions: Prostitution, Public Health, and Gender Politics in Revolutionary Mexico City* (University Park: Pennsylvania State University Press, 2010).

47. Thomas P. Lowry, *The Story the Soldiers Wouldn't Tell: Sex in the Civil War* (Mechanicsburg, PA: Stackpole Books, 1994), 76–87.

48. Cathleen D. Cahill, *Federal Fathers and Mothers: A Social History of the United States Indian Service, 1869–1933* (Chapel Hill: University of North Carolina Press, 2011); Anne M. Butler, *Daughters of Joy, Sisters of Misery: Prostitutes in the American West, 1865–90* (Urbana: University of Illinois Press, 1987), 13–14, 50.

49. Kramer, "The Military-Sexual Complex."

50. Immerwahr, *How to Hide an Empire*.

51. Kramer, "The Military-Sexual Complex."

52. Mary Louise Roberts, "The Price of Discretion: Prostitution, Venereal Disease, and the American Military in France, 1944–1946," *American Historical Review* 115, no. 4 (October 2010): 1002–1030.

53. Philippa Hetherington and Julia Laite, "Trafficking: A Useless Category of Historical Analysis?," *Journal of Women's History* 33, no. 4 (2021): 7–39.

54. Recent works that demonstrate this contention across a range of geographic and temporal contexts include Christina Elizabeth Firpo, *Black Market Business: Selling Sex in Northern Vietnam, 1920–1945* (Ithaca, NY: Cornell University Press, 2020); Liat Kozma, *Global Women, Colonial Ports: Prostitution in the Interwar Middle East* (Albany, NY: State University of New York Press, 2016); Johan Mathew, *Margins of the Market: Trafficking and Capitalism Across the Arabian Sea* (Berkeley: University of California Press, 2016); Kazuhiro Oharazeki, *Japanese Prostitutes in the North American West, 1887–1920* (Seattle: University of Washington Press, 2018); Yarfitz, *Impure Migration*. On the changing meaning of white slavery see Gunther Peck,

"Feminizing White Slavery in the United States: Marcus Braun and the Transnational Traffic in White Bodies, 1890–1910," in *Workers, the Nation State and Beyond*, ed. L. Fink and J. Greene (Oxford: Oxford University Press, 2011), 221–244; Sandy Chang, "Intimate Itinerancy: Sex, Work, and Chinese Women in Colonial Malaya's Brothel Economy, 1870s–1930s," *Journal of Women's History* 33, no. 4 (Winter 2021): 92–117; Anna Dobrowolska, "'Everyone Dreams about Leaving': Debates on Human Trafficking in State-Socialist Poland," *Journal of Women's History* 33, no. 4 (Winter 2021): 168–193; Pamela Fuentes, "'White Slavery' and Cabarets: Mexican Artists in Panama in the 1940s," *Journal of Women's History* 33, no. 4 (Winter 2021): 142–167; Julia Martinez, "The League of Nations, Prostitution, and the Deportation of Chinese Women from Interwar Manila," *Journal of Women's History* 33, no. 4 (Winter 2021): 67–91; Caroline Séquin, "Marie Piquemal, the 'Colonial Madam': Brothel Prostitution, Migration, and the Making of Whiteness in Interwar Dakar," *Journal of Women's History* 33, no. 4 (Winter 2021): 118–141.

55. Katrina Quisumbing King, "The Structural Sources of Ambiguity in the Modern State: Race, Empire, and Conflicts over Membership," *American Journal of Sociology* 128, no. 3 (November 2022): 768–819.

56. Anne Grey Fischer, *The Streets Belong to Us: Sex, Race, and Police Power from Segregation to Gentrification* (Chapel Hill: University of North Carolina Press), 7.

57. Stern, *Trials of Nina McCall*, 148–160.

58. Eithne Luibhéid, *Entry Denied: Controlling Sexuality at the Border* (Minneapolis: University of Minnesota Press, 2002); Martha Gardner, *The Qualities of a Citizen: Women, Immigration, and Citizenship, 1870* (Princeton, NJ: Princeton University Press, 2005).

59. Eileen Boris, Stephanie Gilmore, and Rhacel Parreñas, "Sexual Labors: Interdisciplinary Perspectives Toward Sex as Work," *Sexualities* 13, no. 2 (2010): 131–132. Heather Berg, "Working for Love, Loving for Work: Discourses of Labor in Feminist Sex-Work Activism," *Feminist Studies* 40, no. 3 (2014): 693–721; see also Brooke Meredith Beloso, "Sex, Work, and the Feminist Erasure of Class," *Signs* 38, no. 1 (September 2012): 47–70.

60. See for example Luise White, *The Comforts of Home: Prostitution in Colonial Nairobi* (Chicago: University of Chicago Press, 1990); Ruth Rosen, *The Lost Sisterhood: Prostitution in America, 1900–1918* (Baltimore, MD: Johns Hopkins University Press, 1982). There is also an important literature on sex as a form of anti-work. See L. H. Stallings, *Funk the Erotic: Transaesthetics and Black Sexual Cultures* (Urbana: University of Illinois Press, 2015); Kathi Weeks, *The Problem with Work: Feminism, Marxism, Antiwork Politics and Postwork Imaginaries* (Durham, NC: Duke University Press, 2011); Vanessa Carlisle, "Sex Work Is Star Shaped": Antiwork Politics and the Value of Embodied Knowledge, *South Atlantic Quarterly* 120, no. 3 (2021): 573–590.

61. Judith Walkowitz, "The Politics of Prostitution and Sexual Labor," *History Workshop Journal* 82, no. 1 (Autumn 2016): 189.

62. Laura Agustín, "The Disappearing of a Migration Category: Migrants Who Sell Sex," *Journal of Ethnic and Migration Studies* 32, no. 1 (2006): 39.

63. Elisa Camiscioli, "Coercion and Choice: The 'Traffic in Women' between France and Argentina in the Early Twentieth Century," *French Historical Studies* 42, no. 3 (2019): 483–507.

64. Grace Peña Delgado, "Border Control and Sexual Policing: White Slavery and Prostitution Along the U.S.-Mexico Borderlands, 1903–1910," *Western Historical Quarterly* 43, no. 2 (Summer 2012): 157–178.

65. See for example Cynthia M. Blair, *I've Got to Make My Livin': Black Women's Sex Work in Turn-of-the-Century Chicago* (Chicago: University of Chicago Press, 2010); Katie M. Hemphill, *Bawdy City: Commercial Sex and Regulation in Baltimore, 1790–1915* (Cambridge: Cambridge University Press, 2022); Flores-Villalobos, *The Silver Women*; Laite, *The Disappearance of Lydia Harvey*.

66. In the period I cover, I am specifically interested in the ways the discourse of protecting women operated to legitimize prostitution prohibition. It is important to note, however, that men and trans people have historically been involved in the commercial sex industry. On queer and trans commercial sexual labor see Andrew Israel Ross, *Public City / Public Sex: Homosexuality, Prostitution, and Urban Culture in Nineteenth-Century Paris* (Philadelphia: Temple University Press, 2019); C. Riley Snorton, *Black on Both Sides: A Racial History of Trans Identity* (Minneapolis: University of Minnesota Press, 2017), 59–66.

Chapter 1: The "New Abolitionists"

1. William Lloyd Garrison, "Speech of William Lloyd Garrison on the Movement for the Abolition of State Regulation of Vice," Leaflet, London, England, ca. June 29, 1877, Boston Public Library, Rare Books Department.

2. See Eric Foner, *Reconstruction: America's Unfinished Revolution, 1863–1877* (New York: Harper & Row, 1988).

3. Josephine Butler, *The New Abolitionists, a Narrative of a Year's Work: Being an Account of the Mission Undertaken to the Continent of Europe by Mrs. Josephine E. Butler, and of the Events Subsequent Thereupon* (London: Dyer Brothers, 1876).

4. Philippa Levine, *Prostitution, Race, and Politics: Policing Venereal Disease in the British Empire* (New York: Routledge, 2003), 6.

5. J. P. Gledstone, "A Greeting from Great Britain," *Philanthropist* 1, no. 2 (February 1886): 1–2.

6. See for example Maria Serena Mazzi, *A Life of Ill Repute: Public Prostitution in the Middle Ages* (Montreal: McGill-Queen's University Press, 2022); Ruth Mazo Karras, *Common Women: Prostitution and Sexuality in Medieval England* (Oxford: Oxford University Press, 1996); Elise van Nederveen Meerkerk, Lex Heerma van Voss, and Magaly Rodríguez García, eds., *Selling Sex in the City: A Global History of Prostitution 1600s–2000s* (Leiden: Brill, 2017).

7. Jill Harsin, *Policing Prostitution in Nineteenth-Century Paris* (Princeton, NJ: Princeton University Press, 1985), xv.

8. Alain Corbin, *The Foul and the Fragrant: Odor and the French Social Imagination* (Cambridge, MA: Harvard University Press, 1986), 17, 46.

9. Harsin, *Policing Prostitution*, 8–13

10. Harsin, *Policing Prostitution*, xvii; Alain Corbin, *Women for Hire: Prostitution and Sexuality in France After 1850* (Cambridge, MA: Harvard University Press, 1990); Ann Elizabeth Fowler La Berge, *Mission and Method: The Early Nineteenth-Century French Public Health Movement* (Cambridge: Cambridge University Press, 1992).

11. For a partial list of countries that implemented regulation, see Stephanie Limoncelli, *The Politics of Trafficking: The First International Movement to Combat the Sexual Exploitation of Women* (Stanford, CA: Stanford University Press, 2011), 24.

12. Levine, *Prostitution, Race, and Politics*, 17–18.

13. Durba Ghosh, *Sex and the Family in Colonial India: The Making of Empire* (Cambridge: Cambridge University Press, 2006); Levine, *Prostitution, Race, and Politics*; Ann Laura Stoler, "Rethinking Colonial Categories: European Communities and the Boundaries of Rule," *Comparative Studies in Society and History* 31, no. 1 (1989): 134–161; Ann Laura Stoler, "Sexual Affronts and Racial Frontiers," in *Tensions of Empire: Colonial Cultures in a Bourgeois World*, ed. Frederick Cooper and Ann Laura Stoler (Berkeley: University of California Press, 1997), 198–237.

14. David Arnold, *Colonizing the Body: State Medicine and Epidemic Disease in Nineteenth-Century India* (Berkeley: University of California Press, 1993), 83–84.

15. Judith Walkowitz, *Prostitution and Victorian Society: Women, Class, and the State* (Cambridge: Cambridge University Press, 1980), 51–52.

16. Levine, *Prostitution, Race, and Politics*, 38–39.

17. For a detailed account of this history see Walkowitz, *Prostitution and Victorian Society*; Levine, *Prostitution, Race, and Politics*.

18. Walkowitz, *Prostitution and Victorian Society*, 92–93. On Butler see Anne Summers, "Which Women? What Europe? Josephine Butler and the International Abolitionist Federation," *History Workshop Journal* 62 (2006): 214–231; A. Van Drenth and Francisca De Haan, *The Rise of Caring Power: Elizabeth Fry and Josephine Butler in Britain and the Netherlands* (Amsterdam: Amsterdam University Press, 1999); Jenny Daggers and Diana Neal, eds., *Sex, Gender, and Religion: Josephine Butler Revisited* (New York: Peter Lang, 2006).

19. Josephine E. Butler to Frederic Harrison, May 9, 1868, in *Josephine Butler and the Prostitution Campaigns: Diseases of the Body Politic*, ed. Josephine Elizabeth Grey Butler, Jane Jordan, and Ingrid Sharp (London: Routledge Curzon, 2003), 1:18.

20. Josephine E. Butler, "The Moral Reclaimability of Prostitutes," May 1880, quoted in *Josephine Butler and the Prostitution Campaigns*, 1:121–127.

21. Dr. James John Garth Wilkinson, *The Forcible Introspection of Women for the Army and Navy, by the Oligarchy, Considered Physically* (London: F. Pitman, 1870), 3–5.

22. Elizabeth W. Andrew and Katharine Caroline Bushnell, *The Queen's Daughters in India* (London: Morgan and Scott, 1898), 16.

23. Wilkinson, *The Forcible Introspection of Women*, 3–5; Walkowitz, *Prostitution and Victorian Society*, 56–57; Harsin, *Policing Prostitution*, 16–17.

24. Laura Briggs has argued that scholars have underrepresented the number of municipalities that briefly adopted regulated prostitution in the United States. See Briggs, "Familiar Territory: Prostitution, Empires and the Question of U.S. Imperialism in Puerto Rico, 1849–1916," in *Families of a New World: Gender, Politics, and State Development in a Global Context*, ed. Lynne A. Haney and Lisa Pollard (New York: Routledge, 2003), 252n31; Kristin Luker, "Sex, Social Hygiene, and the State: The Double-Edged Sword of Social Reform," *Theory and Society* 27, no. 5 (October 1998): 605. Women could be prosecuted for "lewdness," but only if it was public and notorious. Sharon E. Wood, *The Freedom of the Streets: Work, Citizenship, and Sexuality in a Gilded Age City* (Chapel Hill: University of North Carolina Press, 2005), 22.

25. Clare A. Lyons, *Sex among the Rabble: An Intimate History of Gender and Power in the Age of Revolution, Philadelphia, 1730–1830* (Chapel Hill: University of North Carolina Press, 2006), 10.

26. Barbara Meil Hobson, *Uneasy Virtue: The Politics of Prostitution and the American Reform Tradition* (Chicago: University of Chicago Press, 1990), 11–12.

27. Larry Whiteaker, *Seduction, Prostitution, and Moral Reform in New York, 1830–1860* (New York: Garland Publishing, 1997), 54–58; Timothy J. Gilfoyle, *City of Eros: New York City, Prostitution, and the Commercialization of Sex, 1790–1920* (New York: Norton, 1992), 63–65.

28. Gilfoyle, *City of Eros*, 59–70. Daily cost of living estimates derived from weekly estimates. Gilfoyle, *City of Eros*, 59.

29. Gilfoyle, *City of Eros*, 59.

30. Whiteaker, *Seduction*, 54–55; J. Shoshanna Ehrlich, *Regulating Desire: From the Virtuous Maiden to the Purity Princess* (Albany: State University of New York Press, 2014), 7–32; Nancy F. Cott, *The Bonds of Womanhood: "Woman's Sphere" in New England, 1780–1835* (New Haven, CT: Yale University Press, 1997), 225; Mark E. Kann, *Taming Passion for the Public Good: Policing Sex in the Early Republic* (New York: New York University Press, 2013), 10; Hobson, *Uneasy Virtue*, 75.

31. Gunther Peck, "Feminizing White Slavery in the United States: Marcus Braun and the Transnational Traffic in White Bodies, 1890–1910," in *Workers, the Nation State and Beyond*, ed. L. Fink and J. Greene (Oxford: Oxford University Press, 2011), 223.

32. Louise Michele Newman, *White Women's Rights: The Racial Origins of Feminism in the United States* (Oxford: Oxford University Press, 1999), 5.

33. Ronald G. Walters, "The Erotic South: Civilization and Sexuality in American Abolitionism," *American Quarterly* 25, no. 2 (1973): 177–201; Marc M. Arkin, "The Federalist Trope: Power and Passion in Abolitionist Rhetoric," *Journal of American History* 88, no. 1 (2001): 75–98; Kristin Hoganson, "Garrisonian Abolitionists and the Rhetoric of Gender, 1850–1860," *American Quarterly* 45, no. 4 (1993): 566–567.

34. Walters, "The Erotic South," 182.

35. "Moral Reform," *Liberator*, January 10, 1840, 7. See Walters, "The Erotic South," for numerous examples.

36. Pamela Haag, *Consent: Sexual Rights and the Transformation of American Liberalism* (Ithaca, NY: Cornell University Press, 1999), 74–82; Estelle Freedman, *Redefining Rape: Sexual Violence in the Era of Suffrage and Segregation* (Cambridge, MA: Harvard University Press, 2013), 6–8.

37. "Notes and Comments," *The Philanthropist* 2, no. 5 (May 1887): 1; Deborah G. White, *Ar'n't I a Woman?: Female Slaves in the Plantation South* (New York: Norton, 1985), 27–31.

38. Katie M. Hemphill, *Bawdy City: Commercial Sex and Regulation in Baltimore, 1790–1915* (Cambridge: Cambridge University Press, 2022), 10–11.

39. Cynthia M. Blair, *I've Got to Make My Livin': Black Women's Sex Work in Turn-of-the-Century Chicago* (Chicago: University of Chicago Press, 2010); Hemphill, *Bawdy City*; Emily Epstein Landau, *Spectacular Wickedness: Sex, Race, and Memory in Storyville, New Orleans* (Baton Rouge: Louisiana State University Press, 2013).

40. Hobson, *Uneasy Virtue*, 88–89.

41. See Hobson, *Uneasy Virtue*, 85–109.

42. Hobson, *Uneasy Virtue*, 111, 117.

43. Gilfoyle, *City of Eros*, 58.

44. Catherine Lee, "'Where the Danger Lies': Race, Gender, and Chinese and Japanese Exclusion in the United States, 1870–1924," *Sociological Forum* 25, no. 2 (2010): 255. On Chinese migration see Erika Lee, *At America's Gates: Chinese Immigration during the Exclusion Era,*

1882–1943 (Chapel Hill: University of North Carolina Press, 2003); Mae Ngai, *The Lucky Ones: One Family and the Extraordinary Invention of Chinese America* (Princeton, NJ: Princeton University Press, 2012); Mae Ngai, *The Chinese Question: The Gold Rushes and Global Politics* (New York: Norton, 2021). On connections between anti-Blackness and anti-Chinese sentiment see Najia Aarim-Heriot, *Chinese Immigrants, African Americans, and Racial Anxiety in the United States 1848–82* (Urbana: University of Illinois Press, 2003).

45. Lucie Cheng Hirata, "Free, Indentured, Enslaved: Chinese Prostitutes in Nineteenth-Century America," *Signs* 5, no. 1 (Fall 1979): 3–29.

46. US Congress. House. *An Act Supplementary to the Acts in Relation to Immigration (The Page Act)*. Section 141, 18 Statute 477 (March 3, 1875), 43 Congress, 2nd Session, introduced in House on February 18, 1875.

47. Martha Gardner, *The Qualities of a Citizen: Women, Immigration, and Citizenship, 1870* (Princeton, NJ: Princeton University Press, 2005), 52.

48. Peggy Pascoe, *Relations of Rescue: The Search for Female Moral Authority in the American West, 1874–1939* (New York: Oxford University Press, 1990), 13–17, 76–85.

49. Anne M. Butler, *Daughters of Joy, Sisters of Misery: Prostitutes in the American West, 1865–90* (Urbana: University of Illinois Press, 1987), 4–14; Jan MacKell, *Brothels, Bordellos and Bad Girls: Prostitution in Colorado, 1860–1930* (Albuquerque: University of New Mexico Press, 2007), 255–267.

50. Richard White, *It's Your Misfortune and None of My Own: A New History of the American West* (Norman: University of Oklahoma Press, 1991), 305.

51. Butler, *Daughters of Joy*, 55–60, 2.

52. Butler, *Daughters of Joy*, 100, 146.

53. Butler, *Daughters of Joy*, 9.

54. Ned Blackhawk, *The Rediscovery of America: Native Peoples and the Unmaking of U.S. History* (New Haven, CT: Yale University Press, 2023), 361.

55. Butler, *Daughters of Joy*, 9–12.

56. Gilfoyle, *City of Eros*, 92–116.

57. William W. Sanger, *The History of Prostitution: Its Extent, Causes and Effects Throughout the World: Being an Official Report to the Board of Alms-House Governors of the City of New York* (New York: Harper & Bros., 1858), 584, 452. There were 137,255 white women ages 15–29 in New York in 1860, Eighth Census, 1860, p. 322. https://www2.census.gov/library/publications/decennial/1860/population/1860a-26.pdf.

58. Sanger, *History of Prostitution*, 645.

59. Thomas P. Lowry, *The Story the Soldiers Wouldn't Tell: Sex in the Civil War* (Mechanicsburg, PA: Stackpole Books, 1994), 78–80.

60. Lowry, *Story the Soldiers Wouldn't Tell*, 81.

61. Charles R. Reynolds, "Prostitution as a Source of Infection with the Venereal Diseases in the Armed Forces," *American Journal of Public Health and the Nation's Health* 30, no. 11 (November 1940): 1277.

62. Stuart Creighton Miller, *The Unwelcome Immigrant: The American Image of the Chinese, 1785–1882* (Berkeley: University of California Press, 1969), 165.

63. Daniel Rodgers argues that during the period between the Civil War and World War II Americans were particularly open to European models and institutions. Daniel T. Rodgers,

Atlantic Crossings: Social Politics in a Progressive Age (Cambridge, MA: Harvard University Press, 1998).

64. "Social Evil Hospital," *Missouri Republican*, December 29, 1872.

65. The "social evil" also stood in contrast to the "solitary evil" of masturbation. See April Haynes, *Riotous Flesh: Women, Physiology, and the Solitary Vice in Nineteenth-Century America* (Chicago: University of Chicago Press, 2015).

66. John C. Burnham, "Medical Inspection of Prostitutes in America in the Nineteenth Century: The St. Louis Experiment and Its Sequel," *Bulletin of the History of Medicine* 45, no. 3 (1971): 206; *Missouri Democrat*, June 18, 1871, 4 quoted in Burnham, "Medical Inspection," 208.

67. Duane R. Sneddeker, "Regulating Vice: Prostitution and the St. Louis Social Evil Ordinance, 1870–1874," *Gateway Heritage* 11, no. 2 (Fall 1990): 26–27.

68. Briggs, "Familiar Territory," 252n31. Aaron Macy Powell, "An Open Letter to the President of the New York Academy of Medicine," *American Bulletin* no. 4 (May 1883). "Regulation Efforts in Indiana," *The Philanthropist* 1, no. 7 (July 1886): 4; F. S. Shepard, "Municipal Regulation in Davenport," *The Philanthropist* 9, no. 2 (February 1894): 5; Emily Blackwell, "It Will Endure While the World Lasts," *The Philanthropist* 4, no. 12 (December 1889): 1–3.

69. J. Marion Sims, "Address of J. Marion Sims," *Transactions of the American Medical Association* vol. 27 (Philadelphia: Collins, 1876), 108.

70. David Pivar, *Purity Crusade: Sexual Morality and Social Control, 1868–1900* (Westport, CT: Greenwood Press, 1973), 50–52.

71. George M. Gould, *Borderland Studies: Miscellaneous Addresses and Essays Pertaining to Medicine and the Medical Profession, and Their Relation to General Science and Thought* (Philadelphia: P. Blakiston's Son & Co., 1896), 123–4n†.

72. Sneddeker, "Regulating Vice," 41.

73. On evangelicalism and millennial Protestantism in the anti-slavery movement see Timothy Patrick McCarthy and John Stauffer, eds., *Prophets of Protest: Reconsidering the History of American Abolitionism* (New York: New Press, 2006); Douglas M. Strong, *Perfectionist Politics: Abolitionism and the Religious Tensions of American Democracy* (Syracuse: Syracuse University Press, 1999); John R. McKivigan, *The War Against Proslavery Religion: Abolitionism and the Northern Churches, 1830–1865* (Ithaca, NY: Cornell University Press, 1984); James H. Moorhead, *American Apocalypse: Yankee Protestants and the Civil War, 1860–1869* (New Haven, CT: Yale University Press, 1978).

74. "Great Meeting of Women at Plymouth," *The Shield* 17, June 20, 1870, 132.

75. Walkowitz, *Prostitution and Victorian Society*, 255–256. On contemporary resonances see Laura María Agustín, *Sex at the Margins: Migration, Labour Markets, and the Rescue Industry* (London: Zed Books, 2007).

76. Elizabeth Cady Stanton, Susan Brownell Anthony, and Matilda Joslyn Gage, *History of Woman Suffrage* (Rochester, NY: Charles Mann, 1886), 3:145–146.

77. Elizabeth Blackwell, "Rescue Work in Relation to Prostitution and Disease" (1881) in *Essays in Medical Sociology*, ed. Elizabeth Blackwell (London: Ernest Bell, 1899), 1:159; Aaron Macy Powell, *Personal Reminiscences of the Anti-Slavery and Other Reforms and Reformers* (New York: Caulon Press, 1899), 59, quoting letter from Garrison, n.d. French critics of abolitionism also termed it an "Anglo-Saxon" movement rather than a movement with domestic French roots as a means of discrediting it. Julia Christine Scriven Miller, "The 'Romance of Regulation': The

Movement Against State-Regulated Prostitution in France, 1871–1949" (PhD diss., New York University, 2000), 33.

78. Henry Joseph Wilson and James P. Gledstone, *Report of a Visit to the United States as Delegates from the British, Continental and General Foundation for the Abolition of Government Regulation of Prostitution* (Sheffield, UK: Leader and Sons, 1876), 14–32; Jesse Olsavsky, *The Most Absolute Abolition: Runaways, Vigilance Committees, and the Rise of Revolutionary Abolitionism, 1835–1861* (Baton Rouge: Louisiana State University Press, 2022).

79. Pivar, *Purity Crusade*, 68–73.

80. Pivar, *Purity Crusade*, 283–284.

81. Powell, "An Open Letter."

82. Helen Horowitz, *Rereading Sex: Battles Over Sexual Knowledge and Suppression in Nineteenth-Century America* (New York: Vintage, 2003), 5–9. They also diverged from a growing anti-vice movement that sought to confine commercial sex in red-light districts rather than eliminate it. See Mara L. Keire, *For Business and Pleasure: Red-Light Districts and the Regulation of Vice in the United States, 1890–1933* (Baltimore, MD: Johns Hopkins University Press, 2010).

83. Ian Tyrrell, *Woman's World / Woman's Empire: The Woman's Christian Temperance Union in International Perspective, 1880–1930* (Chapel Hill: University of North Carolina Press, 1991), 194.

84. "Social purity" had different connotations in the British and American contexts, in the former sometimes indicating a willingness to reform regulation rather than abolish it and to use state coercion. In the latter, it was usually synonymous with abolitionism, as well as a broader reform platform. Pivar, *Purity Crusade*, 62–66.

85. *Minutes of the National Woman's Christian Temperance Union, 1886* (Chicago: Woman's Temperance Publication Association, 1886), xlii.

86. On rape and age of consent see Estelle Freedman, *Redefining Rape: Sexual Violence in the Era of Suffrage and Segregation* (Cambridge, MA: Harvard University Press, 2013), 125–146; Ehrlich, *Regulating Desire*, 44–60.

87. Aaron Macy Powell, "Over the Ocean," *The Philanthropist* 4, no. 10 (October 1889): 1–3.

88. Walkowitz, *Prostitution and Victorian Society*.

89. Susan B. Anthony, "Social Purity" (1875) in *The Life and Work of Susan B. Anthony*, ed. Ida Husted Harper (Indianapolis, IN: Bowen-Merrill Company, 1898), 2:1008–1011. On slavery and US women's rights see Amy Dru Stanley, *From Bondage to Contract: Wage Labor, Marriage, and the Market in the Age of Slave Emancipation* (Cambridge: Cambridge University Press, 1998); Ana Stevenson, *Woman As Slave in Nineteenth-Century American Social Movement* (London: Palgrave Macmillan, 2019).

90. Aaron Macy Powell, *State Regulation of Vice: Regulation Efforts in America—The Geneva Congress* (New York: Wood & Holbrook, 1878), 9.

91. Josephine E. Butler, *The Constitution Violated: An Essay* (Edinburgh: Edmonston and Douglas, 1871), 12–21, 46–49, 29, 43, 156.

92. "The First Decade Meeting," *The Philanthropist* 1, no. 3 (March 1886): 3.

93. Emily Blackwell, "The White Cross Movement in Great Britain," *American Bulletin* 6 (June 1884): 2.

94. Blackwell, "The White Cross Movement," 2.

95. Christine Bolt, *The Women's Movements in the United States and Britain from the 1790s to the 1920s* (Amherst: University of Massachusetts Press, 1993). Bolt quotes a contemporary

observer who stated that the number of women physicians in the United States "was double that of France, England and Germany combined," 112. Ruth J. Abram, *Send Us a Lady Physician: Women Doctors in America, 1835–1920* (New York: Norton, 1985), 108. See also *Index File Cards of International Students*, Women's Medical College of Pennsylvania, Legacy Center Archives & Special Collections, Drexel University College of Medicine, Philadelphia, PA.

96. Blackwell, "Rescue Work in Relation to Prostitution and Disease,"150.

97. Rebecca C. Hallowell, "The Prevention of Prostitution," Women's Medical College of PA, Report of Proceedings of Annual Meeting, March 16, 1888 (Philadelphia: The JAS. B. Rodgers Printing Company), 37. Hallowell cites Blackwell's "Human Element in Sex," 39.

98. Josephine Butler to Henry Joseph Wilson and James P. Gledstone, July 11, [1876], 3HJW / E / 1 no. 416, The Women's Library, London School of Economics (hereafter TWL).

99. On degeneration and eugenics see Mark H. Haller, *Eugenics: Hereditarian Attitudes in American Thought* (New Brunswick, NJ: Rutgers University Press, 1963); Wendy Kline, *Building a Better Race: Gender, Sexuality, and Eugenics from the Turn of the Century to the Baby Boom* (Berkeley: University of California Press, 2001); Laura L. Lovett, *Conceiving the Future: Pronatalism, Reproduction, and the Family in the United States, 1890–1938* (Chapel Hill: University of North Carolina Press, 2009); Daniel J. Kevles, *In the Name of Eugenics: Genetics and the Uses of Human Heredity* (Berkeley: University of California Press, 1985). On the WCTU in particular see Riiko Bedford, "Heredity As Ideology: Ideas of the Woman's Christian Temperance Union of the United States and Ontario on Heredity and Social Reform, 1880–1910," *Canadian Bulletin of Medical History* 32, no. 1 (2015): 77–100.

100. Nancy Monelle-Mansell, "Heredity," *Medical Council* 1 (March 1896): 38.

101. William T. Sabine, "Social Vice and National Decay," in *The National Purity Congress: Its Papers, Addresses, Portraits. An Illustrated Record of the Papers and Addresses of the First National Purity Congress, Held Under the Auspices of the American Purity Alliance, Baltimore, October 14, 15 and 16, 1895*, ed. Aaron Macy Powell (New York: American Purity Alliance, 1896), 42.

102. Pivar, *Purity Crusade*, 88–92.

103. Pivar, *Purity Crusade*, 20–21. Charles H. Kitchell, *The Social Evil, Its Cause and Cure: A Paper* (New York: Beeken & Gerry, 1886), 20–21.

104. "Medical Declaration Concerning Chastity," *The Philanthropist* 10, no. 5 (May 1895): 3, 6; on Philadelphia see "Medical Declaration Concerning Chastity," *The Philanthropist* 11, no. 7 (July 1896): 8–11.

105. Hobson, *Uneasy Virtue*, 87.

106. William L. Barrett, "Prostitution in Its Relation to the Public Health" (St. Louis, MO: St. Louis Health Department, 1873), 7–8.

107. Barrett, "Prostitution in Its Relation to the Public Health," 9–10.

108. Barrett, "Prostitution in Its Relation to the Public Health," 12, 11.

109. "Social Evil Hospital," *The Missouri Republican*, December 29, 1872.

110. "Social Evil Hospital," *The Missouri Republican*, December 29, 1872.

111. "Social Evil Hospital," *The Missouri Republican*, December 29, 1872. Archeological evidence from other brothels also indicates that women working in brothels had better and more varied diets than their working-class neighbors. Donna J. Seifert and Joseph Balicki, "Mary Ann Hall's House," *Historical Archaeology* 39, no. 1 (2005): 59–73.

112. "Social Evil Hospital," *The Missouri Republican*, December 29, 1872.

113. Sneddeker, "Regulating Vice," 28.

114. "Social Evil Hospital," *The Missouri Republican*, December 29, 1872.

115. On the Guardian home see Martha S. Kayser, "Women's Christian Association," in *Encyclopedia of the History of St. Louis*, ed. William Hyde and Howard L. Conard (New York: The Southern History Co., 1899), 4:2533.

116. "Social Evil Hospital," *The Missouri Republican*, December 29, 1872, italics in original; Hobson, *Uneasy Virtue*, 95.

117. "Social Evil Hospital," *The Missouri Republican*, December 29, 1872.

118. Pliley, *Policing Sexuality*, 20–21. On sexual violence under slavery see White, *Ar'n't I a Woman?*; Thomas A. Foster, *Rethinking Rufus: Sexual Violations of Enslaved Men* (Athens: University of Georgia Press, 2019); Daina Ramey Berry and Leslie M. Harris, eds., *Sexuality and Slavery: Reclaiming Intimate Histories in the Americas* (Athens: University of Georgia Press, 2018).

119. Stanley, *From Bondage to Contract*, 218–219; Pliley, *Policing Sexuality*, 17. While more radical reformers like Mary Wollstonecraft argued that marriage was simply "legal prostitution," new abolitionist reformers did not take their critiques of prostitution or of marriage that far. See Carole Pateman, *The Sexual Contract* (Stanford, CA: Stanford University Press, 1988), 190; Nancy Cott, *Public Vows: A History of Marriage and the Nation* (Cambridge, MA: Harvard University Press, 2000), 70.

120. Josephine E. Butler, *Personal Reminiscences of a Great Crusade* (London: Horace Marshall & Son, 1896), 13.

121. As Gunther Peck has shown, reformers in the United States continued to use the phrase "white slavery" to criticize both prostitution and bad labor practices until the early twentieth century, when "white slavery" took on an entirely feminized and sexual meaning. Peck, "Feminizing White Slavery."

122. Powell, *State Regulation of Vice*, 29–30.

123. Sally Barringer Gordon makes a related argument about anti-polygamy reformers. Gordon, "The Mormon Question: Polygamy and Constitutional Conflict in Nineteenth-Century America," *Journal of Supreme Court History* 28, no. 1 (March 2003): 24.

124. Rev. H. B. Milner, "An Appeal from a Needy Mission Field," *The Philanthropist* 7, no. 12 (December 1892): 6.

125. "Notes and Comments," *The Philanthropist* 2, no. 5 (May 1887): 1.

126. Jane E. Dabel, *A Respectable Woman: The Public Roles of African American Women in 19th-Century New York* (New York: New York University Press, 2008), 85–86.

127. Eugene Harris, "Appeal for Purity in Negro Homes," *The Philanthropist* 13, no. 3 (July 1898): 7, 10.

128. "The La Crosse Conference," *The Philanthropist* 20, no. 4 (January 1906): 2. While middle- and upper-class Black women such as Terrell worried about sexual respectability, Saidiya Hartman has shown how poor and working-class Black women navigated sexuality and pleasure, as well as the violence they faced. Saidiya Hartman, *Wayward Lives, Beautiful Experiments: Intimate Histories of Riotous Black Girls, Troublesome Women, and Queer Radicals* (New York: Norton, 2019).

129. "The La Crosse Conference," 2.

130. Frances E. W. Harper, "Social Purity—Its Relation to the Dependent Classes," *The National Purity Congress: Its Papers, Addresses, Portraits* (New York: American Purity Alliance, 1896), 328–329.

131. "Negro Social Morality," *The Philanthropist* 19, no. 4 (January 1905): 6.

132. On the popularity of the single standard see John D'Emilio and Estelle B. Freedman, *Intimate Matters: A History of Sexuality in America* (New York: Harper & Row, 1988), 155–156. On the prevalence of prostitution in New York City in the 1890s see Gilfoyle, *City of Eros,* 197–223 and 337n11.

133. D'Emilio and Freedman, *Intimate Matters,* 139–140.

134. Powell, *State Regulation of Vice,* 44.

135. Frances E. Willard, "Social Purity, the Latest and Greatest Crusade," *The Philanthropist* 1, no. 6 (June 1886): 2.

136. J. P. Gladstone, "A Greeting from Great Britain," *The Philanthropist* 1, no. 2 (February 1886): 1–2.

137. Wilson and Gledstone, *Report of a Visit to the United States,* 32.

138. Wilson and Gledstone, *Report of a Visit to the United States,* 18.

Chapter 2: Purifying Empire

1. Elizabeth W. Andrew and Katharine Caroline Bushnell, *Heathen Slaves and Christian Rulers* (Oakland, CA: Messiah's Advocate, 1907), 3. Italics in original.

2. Andrew and Bushnell, *Heathen Slaves,* 3, iii.

3. Judith R. Walkowitz, *Prostitution and Victorian Society: Women, Class, and the State* (Cambridge: Cambridge University Press, 1980); Josephine E. Butler, *The Revival and Extension of the Abolitionist Cause: A Letter to the Members of the Ladies' National Association* (Winchester, UK: John T. Doswell, 1887); Kenneth Ballhatchet, *Race, Sex, and Class under the Raj: Imperial Attitudes and Policies and Their Critics* (London: Weidenfeld and Nicolson, 1980), 49.

4. National WCTU (NWCTU), *Annual Report* (1897), 107 quoted in Ian Tyrrell, *Woman's World / Woman's Empire: The Woman's Christian Temperance Union in International Perspective, 1880–1930* (Chapel Hill: University of North Carolina Press, 1991), 206.

5. Julian Go, "The Provinciality of American Empire: 'Liberal Exceptionalism' and U.S. Colonial Rule, 1898–1912," *Comparative Studies in Society and History* 49, no. 1 (2007): 74–108.

6. Tessa Winkleman, *Dangerous Intercourse: Gender and Interracial Relations in the American Colonial Philippines, 1898–1946* (Ithaca, NY: Cornell University Press, 2022), 6–7.

7. Genevieve Alva Clutario, *Beauty Regimes: A History of Power and Modern Empire in the Philippines, 1898–1941* (Durham, NC: Duke University Press, 2023); Nerissa S. Balce, *Body Parts of Empire: Visual Abjection, Filipino Images, and the American Archive* (Ann Arbor: University of Michigan Press, 2016); on American intimacy with Filipinos see Andrew J. Rotter, *Empire of the Senses: Bodily Encounters in Imperial India and the Philippines* (Oxford: Oxford University Press, 2019).

8. Emily Conroy-Krutz, *Christian Imperialism: Converting the World in the Early American Republic* (Ithaca, NY: Cornell University Press, 2018).

9. Dana L. Robert, *American Women in Mission: A Social History of Their Thought and Practice* (Macon, GA: Mercer University Press, 1996), 130.

10. Tyrell, *Woman's World / Woman's Empire.*

11. Tyrell, *Woman's World / Woman's Empire,* 197.

12. *Minutes of the NWCTU, 1886* (Chicago: Woman's Temperance Publication Association, 1886), xlii; "President's Address," *Minutes of the NWCTU, 1895* (Chicago: Woman's Temperance Publication Association, 1895), 347; P. T. Winskill, *The Temperance Movement and Its Workers* (London: Blackie and Son, 1982), 58; *Minutes of the NWCTU, 1891* (Chicago: Woman's Temperance Publication Association, 1891), 64.

13. Merwyn S. Garbarino, *Sociocultural Theory in Anthropology: A Short History* (Long Grove, IL: Waveland Press, 1983), 28–29; Joan Jacobs Brumberg, "Zenanas and Girlless Villages: The Ethnology of American Evangelical Women, 1870–1910," *Journal of American History* 69, no. 2 (1982): 349, 355, 363; Gail Bederman, *Manliness and Civilization: A Cultural History of Gender and Race in the United States, 1880–1917* (Chicago: University of Chicago Press, 1995), 121–169; Tracy Fessenden, *Culture and Redemption: Religion, the Secular, and American Literature* (Princeton, NJ: Princeton University Press, 2007), 161–180; Vron Ware, *Beyond the Pale: White Women, Racism, and History* (London: Verso, 1992); Louise Michele Newman, *White Women's Rights*.

14. Andrew and Bushnell, *Heathen Slaves*.

15. Mary Clement Leavitt, *Report Made to the First Convention of the World's Woman's Christian Temperance Union* (Boston: Alfred Mudge & Son, 1891), 277; Emily Brainerd Ryder, *The Little Wives of India* (Melbourne: Varley Bros., Printers, 1893), 7, 10, 233.

16. Philippa Levine, *Prostitution, Race, and Politics: Policing Venereal Disease in the British Empire* (New York: Routledge, 2003), 95–100; Katharine C. Bushnell, *Dr. Katharine C. Bushnell: A Brief Sketch of Her Life Work* (Hertford: Rose and Sons, 1932), 7.

17. Elizabeth W. Andrew and Katharine Caroline Bushnell, *The Queen's Daughters in India* (London: Morgan and Scott, 1898), 16, 25–31, 34, 42, 55, 102; Elizabeth Andrew, "The Inextinguishable Sentiment of Dignity in Eastern Womanhood," August 31, 1895, Archives de l'Association abolitionniste genevoise et de la Fédération abolitionniste international, CH BGE Ms. Fr. 5774, Geneva Library, Geneva, Switzerland.

18. "Proof of Mrs. Elisabeth Wheeler Andrew," 3AMS / C / 03 / 03, Bushnell and Andrew Journal report 1867–1893, Folder 3, TWL; Andrew and Bushnell, *Queen's Daughters*, Appendix B; See for example, "Licensed Vice in India," *New York Evening Post*, September 13, 1893, (New York, NY, United States), 1; Andrew and Bushnell, *Queen's Daughters*, 87–98; 106; Levine, *Prostitution, Race, and Politics*, 104–116.

19. Anna Garlin Spencer, "Women and Regulation," *The Philanthropist* 13, no. 2 (April 1898): 4; Andrew and Bushnell, *Queen's Daughters*, 73, 87–98, 103, 106.

20. Tyrrell, *Woman's World, Woman's Empire*, 211–212.

21. Andrew and Bushnell, *Queen's Daughters*, v. On the ideology of moral contagion see Tyrrell, *Woman's World, Woman's Empire*, 191–192.

22. Andrew and Bushnell, *Queen's Daughters*, v; "American Purity Alliance—Special Meeting," *The Philanthropist* 12, no. 1 (January 1897), 13; Bushnell and Andrew, *Queen's Daughters*, 42.

23. Joel Quirk, *The Antislavery Project: From the Slave Trade to Human Trafficking* (Philadelphia: University of Pennsylvania Press, 2011); Andrew and Bushnell, *Queen's Daughters*, 102.

24. Leslie K. Dunlap, "The Reform of Rape Law and the Problem of White Men: Age-of-Consent Campaigns in the South, 1885–1910," in *Sex, Love, Race: Crossing Boundaries in North American History*, ed. Martha Elizabeth Hodes (New York: New York University Press, 1999), 363.

25. "Annexation of Hawaii," *Union Signal* (February 16, 1893), 8; Tyrrell, *Woman's World / Woman's Empire*, 213.

26. On the Philippine-American War see Paul A. Kramer, *The Blood of Government: Race, Empire, the United States, and the Philippines* (Chapel Hill: University of North Carolina Press, 2006). On the US military's use of torture see Frank Schumacher, "'Marked Severities': The Debate over Torture during America's Conquest of the Philippines, 1899–1902," *Amerikastudien / American Studies* 51, no. 4 (2006): 475–498.

27. Kramer, *The Blood of Government*, 128–144.

28. Paul A. Kramer, "Empires Exceptions, and Anglo-Saxons: Race and Rule between the British and U.S. Empires," in *The American Colonial State in the Philippines: Global Perspectives*, ed. Julian Go and Anne L. Foster (Durham, NC: Duke University Press, 2003), 43–91.

29. "The War and After," *The Philanthropist* 13, no. 4 (October 1898): 12.

30. Aaron M. Powell, "Lessons from India," *Friends' Intelligencer*, March 25, 1899; Homer Clyde Stuntz, *The Philippines and the Far East* (Cincinnati, OH: Jennings and Pye, 1904), 5, 155–159. Stuntz drew upon President William McKinley's policy of "benevolent assimilation" in the Philippines.

31. Kristin L. Hoganson, *Fighting for American Manhood: How Gender Politics Provoked the Spanish-American and Philippine-American War* (New Haven, CT: Yale University Press, 2000), 137. On Filipinas' use of beauty and fashion to navigate their status see Genevieve Alva Clutario, *Beauty Regimes*; Hoganson, *Fighting for American Manhood*, 187; William McKinley's executive order to the Secretary of War, December 21, 1898, is best known as the "Benevolent Assimilation Proclamation." For the full text, see William McKinley, Executive Order Online by Gerhard Peters and John T. Woolley, The American Presidency Project, https://www.presidency.ucsb.edu/node/205913

32. C. F. Budd, "His First Christmas in Hawaii," *Leslie's Weekly* (December 15, 1898), 477.

33. Andrew Byers, *The Sexual Economy of War: Discipline and Desire in the U.S. Army* (Ithaca, NY: Cornell University Press, 2019), 89–91; Philippa Levine, "Gender, Sexuality, and the Empire," in *Gender and Empire*, ed. Philippa Levine (Oxford: Oxford University Press, 2004), 134–155; Timothy Verhoeven, "'Apostles of Continence': Doctors and the Doctrine of Sexual Necessity in Progressive-Era America," *Medical History* 61, no. 1 (2017): 89–106; Ben Barker-Benfield, "The Spermatic Economy: A Nineteenth-Century View of Sexuality," *Feminist Studies* 1, no. 1 (1972): 45–74; Thomas P. Lowry, *The Story the Soldiers Wouldn't Tell: Sex in the Civil War* (Mechanicsburg, PA: Stackpole Books, 1994), 78–86.

34. Edward Lyman Munson, *The Theory and Practice of Military Hygiene* (New York: William Wood and Company, 1901), 910.

35. Warwick Anderson, *Colonial Pathologies: American Tropical Medicine, Race, and Hygiene in the Philippines* (Durham, NC: Duke University Press, 2006); W.A. Nichols to Adj 23rd Infantry, March 10, 1902, filed with AGO Docfile 343790, Box 2307, RG 94, NADC.

36. For an overview see Paul A. Kramer, *The Blood of Government*; Andrew Jimenez Abalahin, "Prostitution Policy and the Project of Modernity: A Comparative Study of Colonial Indonesia and the Philippines, 1850–1940" (PhD diss., Cornell University, 2003), 60–73, 284–285; Thomas K. Deady, "Lessons from a Successful Counterinsurgency: The Philippines, 1899–1902" *Parameters* 35, no. 1 (Spring, 2005): 55.

37. Abalahin, "Prostitution Policy and the Project of Modernity," 287.

38. Brig. Gen. Robert P. Hughes to Adj. Gen., Feb 7, 1902, filed with AGO Docfile 343790, Box 2307, RG 94, NADC.

39. Ken De Bevoise, *Agents of Apocalypse: Epidemic Disease in the Colonial Philippines* (Princeton, NJ: Princeton University Press, 1995), 85; George W. Davis to Secretary to the U.S. Military Governor in the Philippine Islands, 29 May 1901, Enclosure 1, Report of Captain Albert Todd, May 16, 1901, filed with AGO Docfile 343790, Box 2307, RG 94, NADC; Munson, *Theory and Practice of Military Hygiene*, 828.

40. Anderson, *Colonial Pathologies*, 18; Abalahin, "Prostitution Policy and the Project of Modernity," 84; US Department of War, *Annual Reports of the War Department for the Fiscal Year Ended June 30, 1901, Report of the Lieutenant-General Commanding the Army, Vol. 5* (Washington, DC: Government Printing Office, 1901), 183–184.

41. George W. Davis to Secretary to the U.S. Military Governor in the Philippine Islands, 29 May 1901, Enclosure 1, report of Captain Albert Todd, 16 May 1901; George W. Davis to Secretary to the U.S. Military Governor in the Philippine Islands, 29 May 1901, Enclosure 2, report of Charles Lynch, 18 May, 1901, filed with AGO Docfile 343790, RG 94, Box 2307, NADC; US Department of War, *Annual Reports of the War Department for the Fiscal Year Ended June 30, 1901, Reports of the Chiefs of Bureaus* (Washington, DC: Government Printing Office, 1901), 709; on the rationale for segregation, see letter from Ira Brown, US Department of War, *Annual Reports of the War Department for the Fiscal Year Ended June 30, 1901, Report of the Lieutenant-General Commanding the Army*, 189–190.

42. Brown, *Annual Reports of the War Department*, 190.

43. George W. Davis to Secretary to the U.S. Military Governor in the Philippine Islands, 29 May 1901, Enclosure 2, report of Charles Lynch, 18 1901, filed with AGO Docfile 343790, RG 94, Box 2307, NADC.

44. George W. Davis to Secretary to the U.S. Military Governor in the Philippine Islands, 29 May 1901, Enclosure 1, report of Captain Albert Todd, 16 May 1901; George W. Davis to Secretary to the U.S. Military Governor in the Philippine Islands, 29 May 1901, Enclosure 2, report of Charles Lynch, 18 May, 1901, filed with AGO Docfile 343790, RG 94, Box 2307, NADC; US Department of War, *Annual Reports of the War Department for the Fiscal Year Ended June 30, 1901, Reports of the Chiefs of Bureaus* (Washington, DC: Government Printing Office, 1901), 709; on rationale for segregation see letter from Ira Brown, US Department of War, *Annual Reports of the War Department for the Fiscal Year Ended June 30, 1901, Report of the Lieutenant-General Commanding the Army*, 189–190; Mara L. Keire, *For Business and Pleasure: Red-Light Districts and the Regulation of Vice in the United States, 1890–1933* (Baltimore, MD: Johns Hopkins University Press, 2010).

45. A. Lester Hazlett, "A View of the Moral Conditions Existing in the Philippines" [n.d., investigations started in November 11, 1901], filed with AGO Docfile 343790, RG 94, Box 2307, NADC.

46. Eileen P. Scully, "Prostitution as Privilege: The 'American Girl' of Treaty-Port Shanghai, 1860–1937," *International History Review* 20, no. 4 (December 1998): 855–883.

47. See Scully, "Prostitution as Privilege," 872–873.

48. George W. Davis to Secretary to the U.S. Military Governor in the Philippine Islands, 29 May 1901, Enclosure 1, report of Captain Albert Todd, 16 May 1901, filed with AGO Docfile 343790, RG 94, Box 2307, NADC.

49. See Brian McAllister Linn, *Guardians of Empire: The U.S. Army and the Pacific, 1902–1940* (Chapel Hill: University of North Carolina Press, 1997); Memo for Colonel Andrews, February 18, 1902; Capt. Commissary H. G. Cole to Col. J. M. Thompson, March 12, 1902, filed with AGO Docfile 343790, RG 94, Box 2307, NADC.

50. R. R. Stevens to Adj 23rd Infantry, March 25, 1902; Owen Sweet to Adj. Gen., February 7, 1902, filed with AGO Docfile 343790, RG 94, Box 2307, NADC.

51. Owen Sweet, Memo for Colonel Andrews, February 18, 1902, filed with AGO Docfile 343790, RG 94, Box 2307, NADC.

52. Owen Sweet to Adj. Gen., February 7, 1902, filed with AGO Docfile 343790, RG 94, Box 2307, NADC.

53. Andrew and Bushnell, *Queen's Daughters*, 72, 108.

54. Military Government of Puerto Rico from October 18, 1898 to April 30, 1900, *Appendices to the Report of the Military Governor, Epitome of Reports of the Superior Board of Health and the Board of Charities* (Washington, DC: Government Printing Office, 1901), 126–127.

55. Paul A. Kramer, "The Darkness that Enters the Home: The Politics of Prostitution during the Philippine-American War," in *Haunted by Empire: Geographies of Intimacy in North American History*, ed. Ann Laura Stoler (Durham, NC: Duke University Press, 2006), 393; John Boyd Coates, ed., *Preventive Medicine in World War II, Volume V, Communicable Diseases Transmitted Through Contact or By Unknown Means* (Washington, DC: Office of the Surgeon General, 1961), 139.

56. "The New Army Perils," *The Philanthropist* 14, no. 2 (April 1899): 20.

57. "The American Purity Alliance, Twenty-Third Annual Meeting," *The Philanthropist* 14, no. 2 (April 1899): 6.

58. William B. Johnson, "The Crowning Infamy of Imperialism" (Philadelphia: American League, 1900).

59. Johnson, "The Crowning Infamy of Imperialism."

60. Johnson, "The Crowning Infamy of Imperialism."

61. Laura L. Lovett, *Conceiving the Future: Pronatalism, Reproduction, and the Family in the United States, 1890–1938* (Chapel Hill: University of North Carolina Press, 2009).

62. See, for example, "Vice Flourishes at Manila under Government Control," *Omaha World Herald* (Omaha, Nebraska), September 9, 1900, 18; Elnora M. Babcock, "The Disgrace of Our Nation—State Regulation of Vice at Manila," *The Daily Picayune* (New Orleans, Louisiana), September 12, 1900, 16; "The Philippine Opium Monopoly," *Christian Work and the Evangelist* 75 (July 11, 1903), 48.

63. Hoganson, *Fighting for American Manhood*, 187–193; Kramer, "Darkness that Enters the Home," 387–388.

64. Hoganson, *Fighting for American Manhood*, 191.

65. "Against the Canteen: W.C.T.U. Denounces the Sale of Liquor to Soldiers. Awful Vice in the Philippines," *Washington Post*, December 6, 1900.

66. Kramer, "Darkness that Enters the Home," 389.

67. "Voices from the International Purity Congress of 1901," *The Light* (May–June 1919): 57.

68. "Memorial of American Purity Alliance," *The Philanthropist* 15, no. 3 (October 1900): 5–6.

69. "Notes and Comments," *The Philanthropist* 15, no. 1 (April 1900): 1.

70. "An English Book with American Applications," *The Philanthropist* 15, no. 2 (July 1900): 5.

71. Elizabeth Blackwell, "The Responsibility of Women Physicians in Relation to the Contagious Diseases Acts," *The Philanthropist* 12, no. 4 (October 1897): 9; Rev. Anna Garlin Spencer, "Women and Regulation," 5.

72. "The American Purity Alliance, Twenty-Third Annual Meeting," 5.

73. "Memorial of American Purity Alliance," 5–6.

74. General MacArthur to Adj. Gen., February 4, 1901, filed with AGO Docfile 343790, RG 94, Box 2307, NADC.

75. General MacArthur to Adj. Gen., 4 Feb 1901 filed with AGO Docfile 343790, RG 94, Box 2307, NADC; Owen Sweet to Adj. Gen., February 7, 1902, filed with AGO Docfile 343790, RG 94, Box 2307, NADC; W.H. Sage to Adj. 23rd Infantry, March 13, 1902, filed with AGO Docfile 343790, RG 94, Box 2307, NADC.

76. General MacArthur to Adj. Gen., February 4, 1901, filed with AGO Docfile 343790, RG 94, Box 2307, NADC.

77. General MacArthur to Adj. Gen., February 4, 1901, filed with AGO Docfile 343790, RG 94, Box 2307, NADC.

78. William McKinley, "Benevolent Assimilation Proclamation," December 21, 1898.

79. Secretary of War to George B. Cortelyou, February 5, 1902, filed with AGO Docfile 343790, RG 94, Box 2307, NADC; George W. Davis to Secretary to the U.S. Military Governor in the Philippine Islands, May 29, 1901, Enclosure 2, report of Charles Lynch, May 18, 1901; Owen Sweet to Adj. Gen, February 7, 1902, filed with AGO Docfile 343790, Box 2307, RG 94, NADC.

80. "The War and After," *The Philanthropist* 13, no. 4 (October 1898): 12.

81. William Lloyd Garrison [Jr.], "Indictment by Mr. Garrison," *The Anti-Imperialist* 1, no.6 (October 1900): 38.

82. "Memorial of American Purity Alliance," 5–6.

83. "Memorial Against Regulation of Vice in Manila," *The Philanthropist* 15, no. 3 (October 1900): 6.

84. "A National Disgrace," *The Woman's Column* 13, no. 23 (November 17, 1900): 1.

85. "Legalizing Social Vice in the Philippines," *The Philanthropist* 15, no. 3 (October 1900): 4.

86. A. Lester Hazlett, "A View of the Moral Conditions Existing in the Philippines," filed with AGO Docfile 343790, RG 94, Box 2307, NADC.

87. Hazlett, "A View of the Moral Conditions Existing in the Philippines."

88. Anderson, *Colonial Pathologies*, 2.

89. Hazlett, "A View of the Moral Conditions Existing in the Philippines."

90. Willard B. Gatewood, Jr., *"Smoked Yankees" and the Struggle for Empire: Letters From Negro Soldiers, 1898–1902* (Urbana: University of Illinois Press, 1971), 243.

91. T. Thomas Fortune, "The Filipino: A Study in Three Parts," *Voice of the Negro* 1, no. 3 (March 1904): 93–99; T. Thomas Fortune, "The Filipino," *Voice of the Negro* 1, no. 5 (May 1904): 199–203; T. Thomas Fortune, "The Filipino," *Voice of the Negro* 1, no. 6 (June 1904): 240–146.

92. T. Thomas Fortune, "Morality in the Philippines," *Evening Post* (New York, NY), August 1, 1903, Saturday Supplement, 1; Fortune, "The Filipino," 243.

93. Fortune, "Morality in the Philippines."

94. Gatewood, *Smoked Yankees*, 303, 243.

95. Gatewood, *Smoked Yankees*, 315.

96. Ronald K. Edgerton, *American Datu: John J. Pershing and Counterinsurgency Warfare in the Muslim Philippines, 1899–1913* (Lexington: University of Kentucky Press, 2020), 15–19.

97. Brig. Gen. Robert P. Hughes to Adj. Gen., February 7, 1902, filed with AGO Docfile 343790, RG 94, Box 2307, NADC.

98. "The Next Great Battle for Home Protection," *Union Signal* (January 30, 1902), 4.

99. "Against 'Regulated Vice,'" *Woman's Column* 15 (May 3, 1902), 1.

100. "Against 'Regulated Vice,'" 1.

101. On Roosevelt and masculinity see Bederman, *Manliness and Civilization*, 170–216.

102. "Against 'Regulated Vice,'" 1.

103. "For Social Purity in the Army," *The Outlook* 70 (April 19, 1902): 944–945.

104. "For Social Purity in the Army," 944–945; "President Roosevelt on Army Health and Morals," *The Philanthropist* 17, no. 1 (April 1902): 1; "A Good Friend," *The Philanthropist* 18, no. 1 (April 1903): 4.

105. "More Trouble in Manila," *The Philanthropist* 17, no. 3 (October 1902): 4–5.

106. On rape committed by US soldiers in the Philippines see Hoganson, *Fighting for American Manhood*, 187; Richard E. Welch, Jr., "American Atrocities in the Philippines: The Indictment and the Response," *Pacific Historical Review* 43, no. 2 (May 1974): 234.

107. On Cuba see Tiffany Sippial, *Prostitution, Modernity, and the Making of the Cuban Republic, 1840–1920* (Chapel Hill: University of North Carolina Press, 2013); on Puerto Rico see Laura Briggs, *Reproducing Empire: Race, Sex, Science, and U.S. Imperialism in Puerto Rico* (Berkeley: University of California Press, 2002) and Eileen Suárez Findlay, *Imposing Decency: The Politics of Sexuality and Race in Puerto Rico, 1870–1920* (Durham, NC: Duke University Press, 1999).

108. Sippial, *Prostitution, Modernity*, 133–134, 140; Duque, *Medicina Cubana* 10:7 (August 1925): 480, quoted in Sippial, *Prostitution, Modernity*, 140.

109. Anne L. Foster, "Models for Governing: Opium and Colonial Policies in Southeast Asia, 1898–1910," in *The American Colonial State in the Philippines: Global Perspectives*, ed. Julian Go and Anne L. Foster (Durham, NC: Duke University Press, 2003), 92–117.

110. "Opium in the Philippines," *The Philanthropist* 18, no. 2 (July 1903): 6.

111. Anne L. Foster, "Prohibition as Superiority: Policing Opium in South-East Asia, 1898–1925," *International History Review* 22, no. 2 (June 2000): 253–273.

112. Anne L. Foster, "The Philippines, the United States, and the Origins of Global Narcotics Prohibition," *Social History of Alcohol and Drugs* 33, no. 1 (Spring 2019): 13–36.

113. Ann-Marie E. Szymanski, *Pathways to Prohibition: Radicals, Moderates, and Social Movement Outcomes* (Durham, NC: Duke University Press, 2003), 3; Tyrrell, *Woman's World / Woman's Empire*.

114. Levine, *Prostitution, Race, and Politics*, 118–119.

115. "A Good Friend," 4.

Chapter 3: "War on the White Slave Traffic"

1. This narrative is compiled in "Bertha Claiche: The Lovers" (1905), Douglass Crockwell collection, Box 18, Subject 3074-A, American Mutoscope and Biograph Company, Accession No.: 1974:0023:0018, George Eastman Museum, Rochester, New York (the second reel is missing); Kemp R. Niver, *Early Motion Pictures: The Paper Print Collection in the Library of Congress*, ed. Bebe Bergsten (Washington, DC: Library of Congress, 1985), 28.

2. "Forming New-York Children's Taste," *New York Daily Tribune*, Sunday, January 21, 1906, part V.

3. "Names Policemen as Blackmailers," *New York Herald*, Thursday, March 8, 1906, 5.

4. "Wealthy Farmer Wants to Wed Bertha Claiche," *Norfolk Journal of Commerce and the Twice-a-Week Virginian Pilot* 4, no. 26 (March 9, 1906): 6.

5. "Once in Limelight," *Richmond Palladium* 42, no. 226 (August 3, 1917): 10.

6. On white slavery in the United States see Jessica R. Pliley, *Policing Sexuality: The Mann Act and the Making of the FBI* (Cambridge, MA: Harvard University Press, 2014); David J. Langum, *Crossing Over the Line: Legislating Morality and the Mann Act* (Chicago: University of Chicago Press, 1994); Gunther Peck, "Feminizing White Slavery in the United States: Marcus Braun and the Transnational Traffic in White Bodies, 1890–1910," in *Workers, the Nation State and Beyond*, ed. L. Fink and J. Greene (Oxford: Oxford University Press, 2011); Brian Donovan, *White Slave Crusades: Race, Gender, and Anti-vice Activism, 1887–1917* (Urbana: University of Illinois Press, 2006). On federal law and morals regulation see Gaines M. Foster, *Moral Reconstruction: Christian Lobbyists and the Federal Legislation of Morality, 1865–1920* (Chapel Hill: University of North Carolina Press, 2002). On border control and sexuality see Peña Delgado, "Border Control and Sexual Policing: White Slavery and Prostitution Along the U.S.-Mexico Borderlands, 1903–1910," *Western Historical Quarterly* 43, no. 2 (Summer 2012): 157–178; Eithne Luibhéid, *Entry Denied: Controlling Sexuality at the Border* (Minneapolis: University of Minnesota Press, 2002); Martha Gardner, *The Qualities of a Citizen: Women, Immigration, and Citizenship, 1870* (Princeton, NJ: Princeton University Press, 2005).

7. Julia Laite, "Traffickers and Pimps in the Era of White Slavery," *Past & Present* 237, no. 1 (November 2017): 237–269.

8. On immigration and sexuality see Luibhéid, *Entry Denied*; Gardner, *The Qualities of a Citizen*. Prior to 1875 states had broad leeway to enforce their own immigration policies. On US immigration policy broadly see Roger Daniels, *Guarding the Golden Door: American Immigration Policy and Immigrants Since 1882* (New York: Hill and Wang, 2004); Mae Ngai, *Impossible Subjects: Illegal Aliens and the Making of Modern America* (Princeton, NJ: Princeton University Press, 2004); Daniel Kanstroom, *Deportation Nation: Outsiders in American History* (Cambridge, MA: Harvard University Press, 2010); Donna R. Gabaccia, *Foreign Relations: American Immigration in Global Perspective* (Princeton, NJ: Princeton University Press, 2015).

9. Daniel Immerwahr, *How to Hide an Empire: A History of the Greater United States* (New York: Farrar, Straus, and Giroux, 2019).

10. See, for example, "White Slaves for the East," *New York Times*, May 30, 1886, 4. "The Mormon Question," *San Francisco Chronicle*, May 5, 1881, 3; Frederick K. Grittner, *White Slavery: Myth, Ideology, and American Law* (New York: Garland Publishing, 1990), 23–26.

11. The 1899 International Congress on the White Slave Traffic did not mention Asian women. National Vigilance Association (Great Britain), *The White Slave Trade. Transactions of the International Congress on the White Slave Trade* (London: Office of the National Vigilance Association, 1899). On white women's rescue work for Chinese prostitutes see Peggy Pascoe, *Relations of Rescue: The Search for Female Moral Authority in the American West, 1874–1939* (New York: Oxford University Press, 1990).

12. Peck, "Feminizing White Slavery."

13. Cynthia M. Blair, *I've Got to Make My Livin': Black Women's Sex Work in Turn-of-the-Century Chicago* (Chicago: University of Chicago Press, 2010);; Timothy J. Gilfoyle, *City of Eros: New York City, Prostitution, and the Commercialization of Sex, 1790–1920* (New York: Norton, 1992), 290.

14. On New York see Gilfoyle, *City of Eros*, 197–250; Elizabeth Alice Clement, *Love for Sale: Courting, Treating, and Prostitution in New York City, 1900–1945* (Chapel Hill: University of North Carolina Press, 2006), 212–239. On Baltimore see Katie Hemphill, *Bawdy City: Commercial Sex and Regulation in Baltimore, 1790–1915* (Cambridge: Cambridge University Press, 2022), 228–256.

15. Alice C. Hanson and Paul H. Douglas, "The Wages of Domestic Labor in Chicago, 1890–1929," *Journal of the American Statistical Association* 25, no. 169 (March 1930): 48; Gilfoyle, *City of Eros*, 287

16. Gilfoyle, *City of Eros*, 290–291, 287.

17. Mara L. Keire, "The Vice Trust: A Reinterpretation of the White Slavery Scare in the United States, 1907–1917," *Journal of Social History* 35, no. 1 (Autumn 2001): 5–41.

18. "The White Slave System," *The Philanthropist* 4, no. 7 (July 1889): 4.

19. See for example T. W. Snagge, *Report of T.W. Snagge . . . on the Alleged Traffic in English Girls for Immoral Purposes in Foreign Towns* (London: H.M. Stationery Office, 1881); Alfred Stace Dyer, *The European Slave Trade in English Girls* (London: Dyer Bros, 1880).

20. William T. Stead, "The Maiden Tribute of Modern Babylon," *Pall Mall Gazette*, July 6, 1885. Judith Walkowitz, *City of Dreadful Delight: Narratives of Sexual Danger in Late-Victorian London* (Chicago: University of Chicago Press, 1992), 81–120.

21. "The Horrors of the Wisconsin Lumber Camps," *The Philanthropist* 3, no. 11 (November 1888): 8; Kate C. Bushnell, "The Facts in the Case," *Union Signal* 15 (March 7, 1889); "Slavery Up North," *The Daily Inter Ocean* (Chicago), January 6, 1889, 10. On Bushnell see Dana Hardwick, *Oh Thou Woman That Bringest Good Tidings: The Life and Work of Katharine C. Bushnell* (Eugene, OR: Wipf & Stock Publishers, 2002); Kristin Kobes Du Mez, *A New Gospel for Women: Katharine Bushnell and the Challenge of Christian Feminism* (Oxford: Oxford University Press, 2015).

22. Mark Pittenger, *Class Unknown: Undercover Investigations of American Work and Poverty from the Progressive Era to the Present* (New York: New York University Press, 2012); Jennifer Fronc, *New York Undercover: Private Surveillance in the Progressive Era* (Chicago: University of Chicago Press, 2009); Gilfoyle, *City of Eros*, 270–297; On journalism and white slavery see Gretchen Soderlund, *Sex Trafficking, Scandal, and the Transformation of Journalism, 1885–1917* (Chicago: University of Chicago Press, 2013). On the transatlantic dimensions of Progressivism and investigative methods, see Daniel T. Rodgers, *Atlantic Crossings: Social Politics in a Progressive Age* (Cambridge, MA: Harvard University Press, 1998).

23. Ruth Rosen's foundational history of prostitution in the United States estimates that 10 percent of prostitution in the early twentieth century was coerced, Ruth Rosen, *The Lost Sisterhood: Prostitution in America, 1900–1918* (Baltimore, MD: Johns Hopkins University Press, 1982), 133; George Kibbe Turner, "The City of Chicago: A Study of the Great Immoralities," *McClure's Magazine* 28 (April 1907): 581. Edward Bristow has argued that a network of Russian Jews engaged in sex trafficking, Edward J. Bristow, *Prostitution and Prejudice: The Jewish Fight against White Slavery, 1870–1939* (Oxford: Clarendon Press, 1982).

24. In the large literature on anti-vice activism, see especially Mara L. Keire, *For Business and Pleasure: Red-Light Districts and the Regulation of Vice in the United States, 1890–1933* (Baltimore, MD: Johns Hopkins University Press, 2010); Gilfoyle, *City of Eros*; Rosen, *Lost Sisterhood*; Donovan, *White Slave Crusades*; David Pivar, *Purity and Hygiene: Women, Prostitution, and the*

"American Plan," *1900–1930* (Westport, CT: Greenwood Press, 2002); Mark Thomas Connelly, *The Response to Prostitution in the Progressive Era* (Chapel Hill: University of North Carolina Press, 1980); Barbara Meil Hobson, *Uneasy Virtue: The Politics of Prostitution and the American Reform Tradition* (Chicago: University of Chicago Press, 1990); Kristin Luker, "Sex, Social Hygiene, and the State: The Double-Edged Sword of Social Reform," *Theory and Society* 27, no. 5 (October 1998): 601–634; Mary E. Odem, *Delinquent Daughters: Protecting and Policing Adolescent Female Sexuality in the United States, 1885–1920* (Chapel Hill: University of North Carolina Press, 1995); Pliley, *Policing Sexuality*.

25. Pivar, *Purity and Hygiene*, 25–27, 43–45.

26. Ruth Clifford Engs, *The Progressive Era's Health Reform Movement: A Historical Dictionary* (Westport, CT: Greenwood Press, 2003), 20. "Vigilance" committees had been organized in the 1850s to detect slave catchers and protect fugitive slaves.

27. "A National Vigilance Committee," *The Philanthropist* 21, no. 4 (January 1907): 7–8.

28. See Michael Willrich, *City of Courts: Socializing Justice in Progressive Era Chicago* (Cambridge: Cambridge University Press, 2003).

29. James Reynolds to John D. Rockefeller Jr., July 30, 1913, enclosure of a draft letter for Grace Hoadley Dodge to send to Dr. Keyes (n.d.), Folder 30, Box 6, Office of the Messrs. Rockefeller, Rockefeller Boards–Bureau of Social Hygiene, Rockefeller Archives Center, Sleepy Hollow, NY (hereafter RAC); "First Annual Report of the U.S. National Vigilance Association," October 1, 1907, 5, Folder 001742-001-0410, (51777 / 30), Records of the Immigration and Naturalization Service, ProQuest History Vault (hereafter ProQuest INS).

30. "The American Purity Alliance—Objects and Memberships," *The Philanthropist* 10, no. 2 (February 1895): 5.

31. "A National Vigilance Committee," 8.

32. Eva Payne, "Deportation as Rescue: White Slaves, Women Reformers, and the US Bureau of Immigration," *Journal of Women's History* 33, no. 4 (2021): 40–66.

33. Committee on the Judiciary, US House of Representatives, *Grounds for Exclusion of Aliens Under the Immigration and Nationality Act: Historical Background and Analysis*, 100th Congress, 2nd Session, Series No. 7 (September 1988), 7. On the relationship of Chinese exclusion to the control of vice see Ngai, *Impossible Subjects*; Adam M. McKeown, *Melancholy Order: Asian Migration and the Globalization of Borders* (New York: Columbia University Press, 2008).

34. Stuart Creighton Miller, *The Unwelcome Immigrant: The American Image of the Chinese, 1785–1882* (Berkeley: University of California Press, 1969), 163; Luibhéid, *Entry Denied*, 37.

35. Committee on the Judiciary, *Grounds for Exclusion of Aliens*, 10.

36. Committee on the Judiciary, *Grounds for Exclusion of Aliens*, 12–13.

37. Committee on the Judiciary, *Grounds for Exclusion of Aliens*, 14.

38. Act of February 20, 1907 cited in United States Immigration Commission (1907–1910) and William Paul Dillingham, Reports of the Immigration Commission, Vol. 39, 61st Congress, 3rd Session, Senate Document No. 758 (Washington, DC: US Government Printing Office, 1911), 65–66 (hereafter *Dillingham Report*). While federal immigration investigations largely ignored the US–Mexico border, agents there used the 1907 Act to arrest and deport Mexican women as prostitutes. See Katherine Benton-Cohen, "Other Immigrants: Mexicans and the Dillingham Commission of 1907–1911," *Journal of American Ethnic History* 30, no. 2 (2011): 33–57; Peña Delgado, "Border Control and Sexual Policing," 157–178.

39. Peck, "Feminizing White Slavery in the United States," 226–233.

40. Marcus Braun to Sir [Frank H. Larned], September 29, 1908, 2, Folder 001742-003-0400, (52484 / 1-A), ProQuest INS (hereafter Braun, *U.S. White Slavery Report*), 2.

41. Pliley, *Policing Sexuality*, 37.

42. Braun, *U.S. White Slavery Report*, 3–4.

43. Braun, *U.S. White Slavery Report*, 23–24. On Jews and whiteness see Matthew Frye Jacobson, *Whiteness of a Different Color: European Immigrants and the Alchemy of Race* (Cambridge, MA: Harvard University Press, 1999); Eric L. Goldstein, *The Price of Whiteness: Jews, Race, and American Identity* (Princeton, NJ: Princeton University Press, 2008); Yarfitz, *Impure Migration*. On Japanese picture brides see Nancy Cott, *Public Vows: A History of Marriage and the Nation* (Cambridge, MA: Harvard University Press, 2000), 146–151.

44. Braun, *U.S. White Slavery Report*, 8, 2; Report of Special Immigrant Inspector Marcus Braun, August 24, 1903, New York, NY, 95, Folder 001737-007-0001, (52320 / 47), ProQuest INS.

45. Commissioner General of Immigration to White Slave Inspectors, March 10, 1909, Folder: 001742-004-0106, (52484 / 3), ProQuest INS; "Confidential Circular," March 19, 1909, Folder: 001742-004-0106, (52484 / 3), ProQuest INS; *Dillingham Report*, 11.

46. Peck, "Feminizing White Slavery in the United States," 234.

47. For more on the Dillingham Commission, see Katherine Benton-Cohen, *Inventing the Immigration Problem: The Dillingham Commission and Its Legacy* (Cambridge, MA: Harvard University Press, 2018); Robert F. Zeidel, *Immigrants, Progressives and Exclusion Politics: The Dillingham Commission, 1900–1927* (DeKalb: Northern Illinois University Press, 2004).

48. *Dillingham Report*, 10, 34–35, 29.

49. *Dillingham Report*, 23. A number of works have treated the anti-Semitic tone of much of the white slave literature. Scholars have also demonstrated that some Jews participated in organized sex trafficking and tracked the Jewish organizations that arose to combat it. See Bristow, *Prostitution and Prejudice*; Donna J. Guy, *Sex and Danger in Buenos Aires: Prostitution, Family, and Nation in Argentina* (Lincoln: University of Nebraska Press, 1991); Francesco Cordasco, *The White Slave Trade and the Immigrants: A Chapter in American Social History* (Detroit, MI: Blaine Ethridge Books, 1981); Linda Gordon Kuzmack, *Woman's Cause: The Jewish Woman's Movement in England and the United States, 1881–1933* (Columbus: Ohio State University Press, 1990); Pliley, *Policing Sexuality*, 52–53. On anti-Catholicism see Katie Oxx, *The Nativist Movement in America: Religious Conflict in the 19th Century* (New York: Routledge, 2013), 25–52.

50. *Dillingham Report*, 10.

51. On the role played by white maternalist women's organizations in this transformation see Payne, "Deportation as Rescue."

52. Jessica R. Pliley, *Policing Sexuality*, 23–24. The British and European anti-white slavery movements increasingly argued that Jews were responsible for the traffic in women in this period. Rachael Attwood, "Looking Beyond 'White Slavery': Trafficking, the Jewish Association's Representation of 'the Potential Victim', and the Dangerous Politics of Migration Control in England, 1890–1910," *Anti-Trafficking Review* 7 (2016): 115–138.

53. Julia Laite, *Common Prostitutes and Ordinary Citizens: Sex in London, 1885–1960* (New York: Palgrave MacMillan, 2012), 103–106.

54. Rachael Attwood, "Stopping the Traffic: The National Vigilance Association and the International Fight Against the 'White Slave' Trade (1899-c.1909)," *Women's History Review* 24,

no. 3 (2015): 325–350; Laite, *Common Prostitutes and Ordinary Citizens*, 100–115; Walkowitz, *Prostitution and Victorian Society*, 137–148; Stephanie Limoncelli, *The Politics of Trafficking: The First International Movement to Combat the Sexual Exploitation of Women* (Stanford, CA: Stanford University Press, 2011), 42–70.

55. Limoncelli, *Politics of Trafficking*, 8.

56. "Signs of Promise," *The Philanthropist* 14, no. 3 (July 1899): 13. Some women's reform publications were critical of compromise with regulationist governments. See for example "The White Slave Trade," *Woman's Journal* 30 (July 8, 1899): 210.

57. National Vigilance Association (Great Britain), *The White Slave Trade: Transactions of the International Congress*, 16–17.

58. National Vigilance Association (Great Britain), *The White Slave Trade: Transactions of the International Congress on the White Slave Trade*, 8; "International Agreement for the Suppression of the 'White Slave Traffic,'" May 18, 1904, 35 Stat. 1979, 1 L.N.T.S. 83, entered into force 18 July 1905, http://hrlibrary.umn.edu/instree/whiteslavetraffic1904.html; "Historical Summary of the American Government's Attitude Toward Participation in International Agreements on the White Slave Traffic," August 15, 1933, 3, Folder 001742-002-0406, (52483 / 1-B), ProQuest INS.

59. O. E. Janney, "Mr. Wm. Alexander Coote's Visit to America," *Woman's Journal* 38 (February 16, 1907): 28; Theodore Roosevelt and Robert Bacon, "Our Country in Line," *The Philanthropist* 22, no. 3 (October 1908): 9; "La Traite Des Blanches Aux Etats-Unis," *Revue Abolitionniste*, no. 80 (August 1908): 64.

60. Marcus Braun to Commissioner General of Immigration (Daniel Keefe) January 23, 1909, 7, Folder 001742-003-0562, (52484 / 1-C), ProQuest INS.

61. Jill Harsin, *Policing Prostitution in Nineteenth-Century Paris* (Princeton, NJ: Princeton University Press, 1985), 7, xvi. The key text on French regulation is Alexandre-Jean-Baptiste Parent-Duchâtelet, *De la prostitution dans la ville de Paris* (Paris: J-B Baillière, 1836).

62. Marcus Braun to Commissioner General of Immigration (Daniel Keefe), June 23, 1909, 3–4, Folder 001742-003-0586, (52484 / 1-D), ProQuest INS.

63. Elisa Camiscioli, *Selling French Sex: Prostitution, Trafficking, and Global Migrations* (Cambridge: Cambridge University Press, 2024), 199–201.

64. Marcus Braun to Henry White, American Ambassador, Paris, July 27, 1909, Folder 001742-003-0737, (52484 / 1+F), ProQuest INS.

65. Marcus Braun to Commissioner General of Immigration (Daniel Keefe), July 26, 1909, Folder 001742-003-0671, (52484 1-E), ProQuest INS.

66. "Suppression of the White Slave Traffic," January 31, 1910, 61st Congress, 2nd Session, Document No. 214, Part 2, 14.

67. *Keller v. United States*, No. 653, *Ullman v. United States*, No. 654, Decided April 5, 1909, in John Chandler Bancroft Davis et al., United States Reports, Volume 213, *Cases Adjudged in the Supreme Court, October Term, 1908* (New York: Banks & Bros., Law Publishers, 1909), 147; James Thomas Young, *The New American Government and Its Work* (New York: Macmillan, 1915), 188–190.

68. "Reports of the Immigration Commission," 61st Congress, 3rd Session, Senate Document No. 758, 66.

69. "Reports of the Immigration Commission," 66.

70. The letter was one of the only references to homosexuality in the investigations. Marcus Braun to Daniel Keefe August 2, 1909, Folder 001742-003-0671, (52484 1-E), ProQuest INS.

71. For broader histories of the Mann Act, see Pliley, *Policing Sexuality*; Langum, *Crossing Over the Line*.

72. Grittner, *White Slavery*, 86–87; Foster, *Moral Reconstruction*, 186.

73. "To Curb White Slavery," *New York Times*, November 25, 1909; President William Howard Taft, "President's Annual Message," December 7, 1909, 61st Congress, 2nd Session, House of Representatives, *Congressional Record* 45 Part 1: 33.

74. *United States v. Bitty*, 208 U.S. 393 (1908); H.R. 12315, June 25, 1910, 61st Congress, 2nd Session, *Congressional Record* 45 Part 8: 9032, 9120.

75. See Gary Gerstle, *Liberty and Coercion: The Paradox of American Government from the Founding to the Present* (Princeton, NJ: Princeton University Press, 2015), 101, which argues that the Mann Act used a "surrogacy strategy" by invoking the commerce clause.

76. James R. Mann, speaking on H.R. 12315, Wednesday, January 19, 1910, 61st Congress, 2nd Session, House of Representatives, *Congressional Record* 45, Part 1: 805.

77. "An Act to Further Regulate Interstate and Foreign Commerce by Prohibiting the Transportation Therein for Immoral Purposes of Women and Girls, and for Other Purposes," Public Law 61–277, *U.S. Statutes at Large* 36 (1911): 825–827.

78. US Congress, Senate, *White Slave Traffic Act of June 25, 1910*, Presented by Mr. Dillingham, December 13, 1910, 61st Congress, 3rd session, 1910, Senate Document No. 702, 15.

79. *White Slave Traffic Act of June 25, 1910*, 2, 15; On the shifting meanings of consent in the United States see Pamela Haag, *Consent: Sexual Rights and the Transformation of American Liberalism* (Ithaca, NY: Cornell University Press, 1999), 65–67.

80. US Congress, House of Representatives, "White Slave Traffic, Views of the Minority," Presented by Mr. Richardson, January 5, 1910, 61st Congress, 2nd Session, Report No. 47, Part 2: 1.

81. Stephanie McCurry, *Masters of Small Worlds: Yeoman Households, Gender Relations, and the Political Culture of the Antebellum South Carolina Low Country* (New York: Oxford University Press, 1997).

82. "White-Slave Traffic, Speech of John L. Burnett," Jan. 11, 1910, 61st Congress, 2nd Session, *Congressional Record* 45, Part 9: Appendix, 7.

83. 61st Congress, 2nd Session, *Congressional Record* 45, Jan 19, 1910: 821.

84. Pliley, *Policing Sexuality*, 75.

85. James B. Reynolds, "International Agreements in Relation to the Suppression of Vice," *Journal of Social Hygiene* 2, no. 2 (April 1916): 233–244.

86. Pliley, *Policing Sexuality*, 75–76, 80–81.

87. Reynolds, "International Agreements in Relation to the Suppression of Vice," 240–241.

88. Torrie Hester, *Deportation: The Origins of U.S. Policy* (Philadelphia: University of Pennsylvania Press, 2017), 83, 97.

89. Braun, *U.S. White Slavery Report*, 26–27.

90. Kevin J. Mumford, *Interzones: Black/White Sex Districts in Chicago and New York in the Early Twentieth Century* (New York: Columbia University Press, 1997), 158.

91. On Black women's experience in informal labor and commercial sex see, for example, Blair, *I've Got to Make My Livin'*; LaShawn Harris, *Sex Workers, Psychics, and Numbers Runners:*

Black Women in New York City's Underground Economy (Urbana: University of Illinois Press, 2016). On the colored maid trope see, for example, John Couchois Wright, Ella: A Story of the White Slave Traffic (Harbor Springs, MI: John C. Wright, 1911), 85; George J. Kneeland and Katharine Bement Davis, Commercialized Prostitution in New York City (New York: Century, 1913), 6; Clifford G. Roe, Panders and Their White Slaves (New York: Fleming H. Revell Company, 1910), 13–15. Scholars have also noted this trope. Jennifer Fronc, Monitoring the Movies: The Fight over Film Censorship in Early-Twentieth Century Urban America (Austin: University of Texas Press, 2017), 69; Donovan, White Slave Crusades, 81.

92. "Chicago Vice Commission Report," quoted in Clifford G. Roe, Prodigal Daughter: The White Slave Evil and the Remedy (Chicago: L.W. Walker Company, 1911), 388.

93. Blair, I've Got to Make My Livin', 6–12.

94. Saidiya Hartman, Wayward Lives, Beautiful Experiments: Intimate Histories of Riotous Black Girls, Troublesome Women, and Queer Radicals (New York: Norton, 2019), 88–93, 251–256; Anne Grey Fischer, The Streets Belong to Us: Sex, Race, and Police Power from Segregation to Gentrification (Chapel Hill: University of North Carolina Press), 37–41.

95. Blair, I've Got to Make My Livin', 187–222.

96. Dr. D. [David] Newton E. Campbell to Secretary of Commerce and Labor, January 7, 1910, Folder 001742-002-0298, (52483 / 1-A), ProQuest INS.

97. Dr. D. [David] Newton E. Campbell to Secretary of Commerce and Labor, January 7, 1910.

98. "The Laws on the 'White Slave' Traffic Should Protect the Women of All Races," The Broad Ax (Chicago, IL), November 9, 1912; Pliley, Policing Sexuality, 82.

99. Hartman, Wayward Lives, 81–120. On Black women and anti-vice reform see Blair, I've Got to Make My Livin', 187–222.

100. In Interzones, Mumford notes he had not found a single case of a Mann Act prosecution in which a white man was charged with trafficking a Black woman. Mumford, Interzones, 17.

101. "Convicted Under Mann Act. White Man and Negro Woman," The Broad Ax (Chicago, IL), June 2, 1913, 2.

102. Savage vs. United States, Circuit Court of Appeals, Eighth Circuit, March 28, 1914, No. 4038. The Federal Reporter, Vol. 213, Cases Argued and Determined in the Circuit Court of Appeals and District Courts of the United States, June–July 1914, 31–32.

103. "Two Held Under Mann Law," Freeman (Indianapolis, IN), November 30, 1912, 1.

104. "Colored Men Are Held for Violating Mann Act," Anaconda Standard (Anaconda, Montana), March 22, 1914, 10.

105. Pascoe, What Comes Naturally; Mumford, Interzones, 3–18; Pliley, Policing Sexuality, 99–103.

106. On Johnson see Mumford, Interzones, 3–18; Theresa Runstedtler, Jack Johnson, Rebel Sojourner: Boxing in the Shadow of the Global Color Line (Berkeley: University of California Press, 2012); Geoffrey Ward, Unforgivable Blackness: The Rise and Fall of Jack Johnson (New York: Knopf, 2004); Al-Tony Gilmore, Bad Nigger! The National Impact of Jack Johnson (Port Washington, NY: Kennikat Press, 1975).

107. "Year in Cell for Johnson," New York Times, June 5, 1913, 1.

108. Mumford, Interzones, 12; Runstedtler, Jack Johnson, 132–163.

109. For more cases see Mumford, Interzones, 12.

110. For example, "Negro Arrested in Minneapolis for Breaking Mann Act," *Grand Forks Daily Herald* (Grand Forks, ND), March 25, 1913, 1; "White Slavery Charged," *Duluth News Tribune* (Duluth, MN), March 25, 1913, 7; "Arrested With White Girl On Mann Act," *The Broad Ax* (Chicago, IL), March 29, 1913, 4; "Along the Color Line: Courts," *Crisis: A Record of the Darker Races* (New York), June 1, 1913, 68.

111. Pliley, *Policing Sexuality*, 99.

112. Paul Charles Kemeny, *The New England Watch and Ward Society* (Oxford: Oxford University Press, 2018), 189.

113. Sam Erman, "Meanings of Citizenship in the U.S. Empire: Puerto Rico, Isabel Gonzalez, and the Supreme Court, 1898 to 1905," *Journal of American Ethnic History* 27, no. 4 (Summer 2008): 5–33.

114. See for example "Panama a Sodom, Editor Declares," *Chicago Daily Tribune*, June 4, 1907, 10; Neel Ahuja, *Bioinsecurities: Disease Interventions, Empire, and the Government of Species* (Durham, NC: Duke University Press, 2016), 75–77. In 1905 the United States had investigated and dismissed a charge that the US administration had imported Martinican women as prostitutes for Black laborers. See *Investigation of Panama Canal Matters. Hearings before the Committee on Interoceanic Canals of the United States Senate*, 59th Congress, 2nd Session, Doc. no. 401 (Washington, DC: US Government Printing Office, 1907); Greene, *Canal Builders*, 196, 258–260.

115. "Gorgas's Conquest of Disease," *New York Times*, September 22, 1912, Part 8, 7.

116. Noel Maurer and Carlos Yu, *The Big Ditch: How America Took, Built, Ran, and Ultimately Gave Away the Panama Canal* (Princeton, NJ: Princeton University Press, 2011), 71–96.

117. Julie Greene, *Canal Builders: Making America's Empire at the Panama Canal* (New York: Penguin, 2010), 123–158; On Black women's labor see Joan Flores-Villalobos, *The Silver Women: How Black Women's Labor Made the Panama Canal* (Philadelphia: University of Pennsylvania Press, 2023); Alexander Missal, *Seaway to the Future: American Social Visions and the Construction of the Panama Canal* (Madison: University of Wisconsin Press, 2008), 78–79.

118. Ordinance No. 14, An Ordinance Entitled "An Ordinance to Prohibit and Punish Lewd and Lascivious Cohabitation," approved by Governor Charles E. Magoon, November 7, 1905; Harry H. Rousseau, Memorandum for Colonel Goethals, December 3, 1913, Folder 62-B-248, pt. 1, Box 364, RG 185, E30, NACP.

119. "Chapter IV. Adultery," n.d., Folder 62-B-248, pt. 1, Box 364, RG 185, E30, NACP; Case no.730, *Canal Zone vs. Raymond Florimond and Merlina Nortan*, June 8, 1909, RG 21 Records of the District Court of the United States, District of the Canal Zone, 2nd Judicial Circuit, Empire, Gorgonna, Ancon, Criminal Case Files, 1904–1914, Box 4, NADC.

120. On white women's virtue see Wenona Marlin, "Women in Making the Canal," *New York Times*, Sunday, September 22, 1912, X8. On the dangers of Black prostitutes see Walter Stephens to Chester Harding, July 9, 1916, Folder 64-Y-4 part 2, Box 1230, RG 185, E30, NACP.

121. Jeffrey W. Parker, "Empire's Angst: The Politics of Race, Migration, and Sex Work in Panama, 1903–1945" (PhD diss., University of Texas, Austin, 2013), 71.

122. Harry H. Rousseau, "Memorandum," December 4, 1913, Folder 62-B-248, pt. 1, Box 364, RG 185, E30, NACP; Matthew Scalena, "Illicit Nation: State, Empire, and Illegality on the Isthmus of Panama" (PhD diss., Stony Brook University, 2013).

123. Arthur Bullard, *Panama: The Canal, the Country, and the People* (New York: Macmillan & Company, 1911), 61.

124. "In and Out of Town," *Star and Herald* (Panama, Republic of Panama), August 12, 1910, p. 7 c.1; Isthmian Canal Commission, *Annual Report of the Isthmian Canal Commission for the Fiscal Year Ending June 30, 1911*, Appendix N. "Report of Hon. M.H. Thatcher, Member of Isthmian Canal Commission, Head of the Department of Civil Administration," August 1, 1911, 421.

125. Isthmian Canal Commission, "Report of Hon. M.H. Thatcher," 421.

126. Isthmian Canal Commission, *Annual Report of the Isthmian Canal Commission for the Fiscal Year Ending June 30, 1912*, 466.

127. "In and Out of Town," *Star and Herald* (Panama, Republic of Panama), September 2, 1911, p. 6 c.2; "In and Out of Town," *Star and Herald* (Panama, Republic of Panama), August 31, 1911, p. 6 c.2.

128. "In and Out of Town," *Star and Herald* (Panama, Republic of Panama), October 7, 1911, p. 7 c.2.

129. Hartman, *Wayward Lives*, 241–244.

130. J.B. Cooper to Chief of Division of Police and Prisons, September 25, 1911, F 46-D-1, P 1, Box 298, RG 185, E30, NACP.

131. J.P. Fyffe to Jack Phillips, 21 October 21,1911, Folder 46-D-1, part 1, Box 298, RG 185, E30, NACP.

Chapter 4: Policing Women, Protecting Soldiers

1. Maude Miner, "Atlanta, GA," Aug. 30–31, 1917, Box 6, Folder: Atlanta, GA (2 of 3), RG165, E395, NACP.

2. Risa Goluboff, *Vagrant Nation: Police Power, Constitutional Change, and the Making of the 1960s* (Oxford: Oxford University Press, 2016).

3. C. C. Pierce, "The Value of Detention as a Reconstruction Measure," *Public Health Reports* 34, no. 48 (1919): 2711. On arrest statistics see Jessica R. Pliley, *Policing Sexuality: The Mann Act and the Making of the FBI* (Cambridge, MA: Harvard University Press, 2014), 127; Nancy Bristow, *Making Men Moral: Social Engineering During the Great War* (New York: New York University Press, 1996), 129; David Pivar, *Purity and Hygiene: Women, Prostitution, and the "American Plan," 1900–1930* (Westport, CT: Greenwood Press, 2002), 218–219.

4. On the more recent history of philanthropists addressing anti-trafficking see Janie A. Chuang, "Giving as Governance? Philanthrocapitalism and Modern-Day Slavery Abolitionism," *UCLA Law Review* 62, no. 6 (2015): 1516–1556.

5. See, for example, Lisa McGirr, *The War on Alcohol: Prohibition and the Rise of the American State* (New York: Norton, 2015).

6. Michael McGerr, *A Fierce Discontent: The Rise and Fall of the Progressive Movement in America 1870–1920* (Oxford: Oxford University Press, 2005); William A. Link, *The Paradox of Southern Progressivism, 1880–1930* (Chapel Hill: University of North Carolina Press, 1992).

7. Congressional Research Service, "American War and Military Operations Causalities: Lists and Statistics," July 29, 2020, 2, https://crsreports.congress.gov/product/pdf/RL/RL32492.

8. Harrol B. Ayres, "Democracy at Work—San Antonio Being Reborn," *JSH* 4, no. 2 (April 1918): 211.

9. Woodrow Wilson, "President's Message to the National Army," *New York Times*, September 4, 1917, 1.

10. The first published use I could find is in Major Wilbur A. Sawyer's introduction, dated April 3, 1919, to John H. Stokes, *Today's World Problem in Disease Prevention* (US Public Health Service, 1919), reprinted in *JSH* (July 1919), 354. See also Scott W. Stern, *The Trials of Nina McCall: Sex, Surveillance, and the Decades-Long Government Plan to Imprison "Promiscuous" Women* (Boston, MA: Beacon Press, 2018), 121.

11. Brian Donovan, *White Slave Crusades: Race, Gender, and Anti-vice Activism, 1887–1917* (Urbana: University of Illinois Press, 2006), 91.

12. "The Rockefeller Grand Jury Report," *McClure's Magazine*, August 1910, 471.

13. John Farley, *To Cast Out Disease: A History of the International Health Division of Rockefeller Foundation (1913–1951)* (Oxford: Oxford University Press, 2004), 2–5. See also Marcos Cueto, ed., *Missionaries of Science: The Rockefeller Foundation in Latin America* (Bloomington: Indiana University Press, 1994); on the importance of local actors and contexts see Steven Palmer, *Launching Global Health: The Caribbean Odyssey of the Rockefeller Foundation* (Ann Arbor: University of Michigan Press, 2010); Jose Amador, *Medicine and Nation Building in the Americas, 1890–1940* (Nashville, TN: Vanderbilt University Press, 2015). E. Richard Brown, "Public Health in Imperialism: Early Rockefeller Programs at Home and Abroad," *American Journal of Public Health* 66, no. 9 (1976): 897–903; Daniel Immerwahr, *How to Hide an Empire: A History of the Greater United States* (New York: Farrar, Straus, and Giroux, 2019), 138–142.

14. Clifford Roe, "The American Vigilance Association," *Journal of the American Institute of Criminal Law and Criminology* 3, no. 5 (1913): 806–809.

15. Prince Albert Morrow, *Social Diseases and Marriage: Social Prophylaxis* (New York: Lea Brothers and Co., 1904), 25.

16. Pivar, *Purity and Hygiene*, 127–130.

17. J. D. Rockefeller to James B. Reynolds, July 11, 1913, Folder 30, Box 6, Series O, BSH, RAC.

18. Review of James Marchant, *The Master Problem*, *JSH* 3 (October 1917): 581.

19. John Donald Gustav-Wrathall, *Take the Young Stranger by the Hand: Same-Sex Relations and the YMCA* (Chicago: University of Chicago Press, 1998), 9–44; Clifford Putney, *Muscular Christianity: Manhood and Sports in Protestant America, 1880–1920* (Cambridge: Harvard University Press, 2009).

20. Kate Fischer and Jana Funke, "'Let Us Leave the Hospital; Let Us Go on a Journey around the World': British and German Sexual Science and the Global Search for Sexual Variation," in *A Global History of Sexual Science, 1880–1960*, ed. Veronika Fuechtner, Douglas E. Haynes, and Ryan M. Jones (Berkeley: University of California Press, 2018), 51–69.

21. Lina D. Miller, *Directory of Social Agencies of New York* (New York: Charity Organization Society in the City of New York, 1921), 52. On American sexual science see Vern L. Bullough, "The Development of Sexology in the USA in the Early Twentieth Century," in *Sexual Knowledge, Sexual Science*, ed. Roy Porter and Mikulas Teich (Cambridge: Cambridge University Press, 1994), 303–304; on sexuality and social policing see William J. Novak, "Morals, Sex, Crime, and the Legal Origins of Modern American Social Police," in Margot Canaday, Nancy F. Cott, and Robert O. Self, *Intimate States: Gender, Sexuality, and Governance in Modern US History* (Chicago: University of Chicago Press, 2021), 65–84.

22. See John D'Emilio and Estelle B. Freedman, *Intimate Matters: A History of Sexuality in America* (New York: Harper & Row, 1988), 223.

23. Timothy Verhoeven, "'Apostles of Continence': Doctors and the Doctrine of Sexual Necessity in Progressive-Era America," *Medical History* 61, no. 1 (2017): 89–106.

24. Ruth M. Alexander, *The Girl Problem: Female Sexual Delinquency in New York, 1900–1930* (Ithaca, NY: Cornell University Press, 1995), 69.

25. Sarah Stage, "What 'Good Girls' Do: Katharine Bement Davis and the Moral Panic of the First U.S. Sexual Survey," in *The Moral Panics of Sexuality*, ed. Breanne Fahs, Mary Dudy, and Sarah Stage (New York: Palgrave Macmillan, 2013), 154.

26. Katherine Bement Davis, "A Study of Prostitutes Committed from New York City to the State Reformatory for Women at Bedford Hills," in George J. Kneeland, *Commercialized Prostitution in New York City* (New York: The Century Co., 1913), 167, 199, 165, 184–185; Howard B. Woolston, *Prostitution in the United States* (New York: The Century Co., 1921), 16, citing the 1910 census.

27. Davis, "A Study of Prostitutes," 164, 168, 170–171, 175–176, 185.

28. T. N. Bonner, "Searching for Abraham Flexner," *Academic Medicine* 73, no. 2 (February 1998): 160–166.

29. Abraham Flexner, *Prostitution in Europe* (New York: The Century Co., 1914), 16.

30. Abraham Flexner to J. D. Rockefeller, March 26, 1912, Folder 55, Box 7, Series O, BSH, RAC; J. D. Rockefeller to Abraham Flexner, April 10, 1912, Folder 55, Box 7, Series O, BSH, RAC.

31. See, for example, "The Problem of Prostitution," *British Medical Journal* 2, no. 2792 (1914): 30–31. See also letters from French and German abolitionists, Folder 196, Box 9, Series O, BSH, RAC.

32. Flexner, *Prostitution in Europe*, 283, 12.

33. Flexner, *Prostitution in Europe*, 191, 218.

34. Daryl L. Revoldt, "Raymond B. Fosdick: Reform, Internationalism, and The Rockefeller Foundation" (PhD diss., University of Akron, 1982), 74–75. See also Abraham Flexner, *I Remember: The Autobiography of Abraham Flexner* (New York: Simon & Schuster, 1940).

35. Raymond B. Fosdick, *Chronicle of a Generation: An Autobiography* (New York: Harper, 1958).

36. Raymond B. Fosdick, *European Police Systems* (New York: The Century Co., 1916), 375, 384.

37. On red-light abatement laws see Mara L. Keire, *For Business and Pleasure: Red-Light Districts and the Regulation of Vice in the United States, 1890–1933* (Baltimore, MD: Johns Hopkins University Press, 2010); Peter C. Hennigan, "Property War: Prostitution, Red-Light Districts, and the Transformation of Public Nuisance Law in the Progressive Era," *Yale Journal of Law and Humanities* 16, no. 1 (2004): 123–198.

38. Bascom Johnson to G. S. Cole, July 6, 1920, Folder 14, Box 210, ASHA.

39. Matt M. Matthews, *The U.S. Army on the Mexican Border: A Historical Perspective* (Fort Leavenworth, KS: Combat Studies Institute Press, 2007), 67–68.

40. Ronald K. Edgerton, *American Datu: John J. Pershing and Counterinsurgency Warfare in the Muslim Philippines, 1899–1913* (Lexington: University of Kentucky Press, 2020), 15–19.

41. Frederick Palmer, *Newton D. Baker: America at War* (New York: Dodd, Mead & Co., 1931), 296–98; Bristow, *Making Men Moral*, 5.

42. Raymond Fosdick to Newton Baker, August 10, 1916, Folder 6, Box 23, Raymond Blaine Fosdick Papers; Public Policy Papers, Department of Special Collections, Princeton University Library (hereafter RBF).

43. Raymond Fosdick to Newton Baker, August 10, 1916, Folder 6, Box 23, RBF.

44. Max Joseph Exner, "Prostitution in Its Relation to the Army on the Mexican Border," *JSH* 3 (April 1917): 211; James Sandos, "Prostitution and Drugs: The United States Army on the Mexican-American Border, 1916–1917," *Pacific Historical Review* 49, no. 4 (1980): 626. Sandos cites "Pershing's Final Report, enclosure 38." For an account of Pershing's Colonia Dublán camp see Clarence Clendenen, *Blood on the Border: The United States Army and the Mexican Irregulars* (New York: Macmillan, 1969), 334–335. Many of the men at the camp had previously served in the Philippines.

45. Raymond Fosdick to Newton Baker, August 10, 1916, Folder 6, Box 23, RBF.

46. Exner, "Prostitution in Its Relation to the Army," 219, 205–207.

47. Monica Muñoz Martinez, *The Injustice Never Leaves You: Anti-Mexican Violence in Texas* (Cambridge, MA: Harvard University Press, 2018).

48. On Mexican women, sex work, and the border see Peña Delgado, "Border Control and Sexual Policing: White Slavery and Prostitution Along the U.S.-Mexico Borderlands, 1903–1910," *Western Historical Quarterly* 43, no. 2 (Summer 2012): 157–178; Catherine Christensen, "Mujeres Públicas: American Prostitutes in Baja California, 1910–1930," *Pacific Historical Review* 82, no. 2 (2013): 215–247.

49. Raymond Fosdick to Newton Baker, August 10, 1916, Folder 6, Box 23, RBF.

50. Max Exner to John D. Rockefeller, Jr., May 31, 1917, Folder 749, Box 80, Series 100.N, International—War Relief, RG 1.1, Projects, RAC.

51. Exner, "Prostitution in Its Relation to the Army," 219.

52. Raymond Fosdick to Newton Baker.

53. Raymond Fosdick to Newton Baker.

54. Allan M. Brandt, *No Magic Bullet: A Social History of Venereal Disease in the United States Since 1880* (Oxford: Oxford University Press, 1987), 40–41.

55. Brandt, *No Magic Bullet*, 9–10.

56. Raymond Fosdick to Newton Baker, April 12, 1917, microfilm reel 2, Box 3, Folder S, 1917, Newton Baker Papers, Library of Congress, Washington, DC.

57. Fosdick, *Chronicle of a Generation*, 144–45.

58. *Selective Service Act*, Pub. L. 65–12, 40 Stat. 76 (May 18, 1917).

59. Michael Imber, "The First World War, Sex Education, and the American Social Hygiene Association's Campaign Against Venereal Disease," *Journal of Educational Administration and History* 16, no. 1 (1984): 49.

60. Hugh L. Scott to Newton Baker, April 18, 1917, microfilm reel 2, Box 3, Folder S, 1917, Newton Baker Papers, Library of Congress, Washington, D.C.

61. William F. Snow to George E. Vincent (n.d.), Folder 740, Box 79, Series 100.N, International—War Relief, RG 1.1, Projects, RAC.

62. George Chauncey, *Gay New York: Gender, Urban Culture, and the Making of the Gay Male World, 1840–1940* (New York: Basic Books, 1994), 82.

63. Chauncey, *Gay New York*, 82–85.

64. Andrew Byers, *The Sexual Economy of War: Discipline and Desire in the U.S. Army* (Ithaca, NY: Cornell University Press, 2019), 13–14, 91.

65. Brandt, *No Magic Bullet*, 64, 110; On cases of military discipline for masturbation see Byers, *Sexual Economy of War*, 80, 174–175, 180–181.

66. Senate Military Affairs Committee, Hearings, June 18, 1918, 65th Congress, 2nd Session, 1918, cited in E. H. Beardsley, "Allied against Sin: American and British Responses to Venereal Disease in World War I," *Medical History* 20, no. 2 (April 1976): 193.

67. Brandt, *No Magic Bullet*, 14–16.

68. Bristow, *Making Men Moral*, 230–239.

69. American Social Hygiene Association, "Keeping Fit to Fight" (War Department Commission on Training Camp Activities, n.d.) Folder 08, Box 131, ASHA.

70. "Hello, Soldier Sport, Want to Have a Good Time?," n.d., Folder 08, Box 131, ASHA.

71. Army Section, Social Hygiene Division, CTCA, "Syllabus for Use in Lectures on Sex Hygiene and Venereal Disease to Men in Uniform and in Class 1," May 1918, Folder 06, Box 131, ASHA.

72. C. E. Williams, "Make the Army 'Fit to Fight': A Review of the War Department Film by Edward H. Griffith, Exposing the Dangers of Wine, Women and Disease," *Physical Culture* 40, no. 2 (August 1918), 69.

73. Walter Clarke, "Social Hygiene and the War," *JSH* 4 no. 2 (April 1918): 262.

74. Walter Clarke to Surgeon General, Report for weeks ending May 22, 1918 and May 16, 1918, Doc. 32013, Box 73, E 393, RG165, NACP, quoted in Bristow, *Making Men Moral*, 57.

75. Commission on Training Camp Activities, *The War Department, Commission on Training Camp Activities* (Washington, DC, 1917), 13. On the YMCA's sex education and physical programs, see Kristy L. Slominski, *Teaching Moral Sex: A History of Religion and Sex Education in the United States* (Oxford: Oxford University Press, 2021), 80–83.

76. Arthur B. Spingarn, "The War and Venereal Disease Among Negros," *JSH* 4 (July 1918): 338.

77. Glenda Elizabeth Gilmore, *Gender and Jim Crow: Women and the Politics of White Supremacy in North Carolina, 1896–1920* (Chapel Hill: University of North Carolina Press, 1996).

78. Chad L. Williams, *Torchbearers of Democracy: African American Soldiers in the World War I Era* (Chapel Hill: University of North Carolina Press, 2010), 6, 3. For more on Black troops in WWI see Khary Oronde Polk, *Contagions of Empire: Scientific Racism, Sexuality, and Black Military Workers Abroad, 1898–1948* (Chapel Hill: University of North Carolina Press, 2020); Adriane Lentz-Smith, *Freedom Struggles: African Americans and WWI* (Cambridge, MA: Harvard University Press, 2009); Tyler Stovall, *Paris Noir: African Americans in the City of Light* (Boston: Houghton Mifflin, 1996), 1–24; Florette Barbeau and Arthur E. Henri, *The Unknown Soldiers: Black American Troops in World War I* (Philadelphia, PA: Temple University Press, 1974).

79. Spingarn, "The War and Venereal Disease Among Negros," 338. For white officials' refusal to allow Black Atlantans to organize recreation for Black soldiers, see Bristow, *Making Men Moral*, 153–155.

80. "Fit to Fight," Folder 08, Box 131, ASHA.

81. American Social Hygiene Association, "Keeping Fit to Fight," Colored Edition, p. 14, Folder 08, Box 131, ASHA.

82. Polk, *Contagions of Empire*, 130, 140–144.

83. US Surgeon-General's Office, *The Medical Department of the United States Army in the World War*, Vol. VI, Sanitation (Washington, DC: US Government Printing Office, 1921), 938.

84. Brandt, *No Magic Bullet*, 111.

85. L. M. Maus, "A Brief History of Venereal Diseases in the United States Army and Measures Employed for Their Suppression," June 14, 1917, 2, File 3, Box 131, ASHA. On the development of policy in the Philippines see Paul A. Kramer, "The Military-Sexual Complex: Prostitution, Disease and the Boundaries of Empire during the Philippine-American War," *Asia-Pacific Journal* 9, no. 30 (2011): 1–35.

86. See, for example, Edith Houghton Hooker, *The Laws of Sex* (Boston: R. G. Badger, 1921), 356; Edith Houghton Hooker, "A Criticism of Venereal Prophylaxis," *JSH* 4 (April 1918): 179–195.

87. George Walker, *Venereal Disease in the American Expeditionary Forces* (Baltimore, MD: Medical Standard Book Co., 1922), 218–219.

88. Exner, "Prostitution in Its Relation to the Army," 217, 206–207. On the infantilization of soldiers during WWI and concerns over the mixing of draftees from different classes, nationalities, and races see Kimberly A. Reilly, "'A Perilous Venture for Democracy': Soldiers, Sexual Purity, and American Citizenship in the First World War," *Journal of the Gilded Age and Progressive Era* 13, no. 2 (2014): 223–255.

89. Spingarn, "The War and Venereal Disease Among Negros," 336.

90. See Polk, *Contagions of Empire*, 27.

91. Barbeau and Henri, *Unknown Soldiers*, 52–53.

92. Brandt, *No Magic Bullet*, 116.

93. James N. Gregory, *The Southern Diaspora: How the Great Migrations of Black and White Southerners Transformed America* (Chapel Hill: University of North Carolina Press, 2005), 15.

94. See, for example, "Paul Kinsie Report," July 3, 1917, Atlanta, GA (2 of 3), Box 6, RG165 E395, NACP; Maude Miner, "Atlanta, GA," Aug 30–31, 1917, Atlanta, GA (2 of 3), Box 6, RG165 E395, NACP.

95. "Work of the Commission on Training Camp Activities Reviewed and Analyzed in Annual Report of Chairman," *Official U.S. Bulletin*, December 16, 1918: 17.

96. A. J. McLaughlin, "Pioneering in Venereal Disease Control," *American Journal of Obstetrics and Diseases of Women and Children* 80 (December 1918): 639.

97. "I shall send a man to look things over. He will come unannounced, and depart the same way." Raymond Fosdick to Dr. Joseph E. Raycroft, Oct 10, 1917, Folder New Jersey, Box 10, Entry 395, RG 165, NACP.

98. "Reported by P.K.," Hattiesburg, Mississippi, July 27, 1917, Doc. 2702, Box 9, Entry 395, RG 165, NACP.

99. "Preliminary Report by Bascom Johnson," August 29–31, 1917, Doc. 4808, Box 9, Entry 395, RG 165, NACP.

100. Walter Clarke, "Report for Atlanta," Sept. 16, 1917, Folder Atlanta, GA (2 of 3), Box 6, Entry 395, RG 165, NACP.

101. "Preliminary Report by Bascom Johnson," August 29–31, 1917, Doc. 4808, Box 9, Entry 395, RG 165, NACP.

102. "Report by George J. Anderson," September 25, 1917, Doc. 5905, Box 9, Entry 395, RG 165, NACP.

103. Untitled newspaper clipping, Augusta, GA, Sept. 13, [1917], Box 6, Entry 395, RG 165, NACP.

104. Walter Clarke, "Report for Atlanta," Sept. 16, 1917.

105. "Camp Custer Weekly Reports," Folder Michigan, Box 9, Entry 395, RG 165, NACP.

106. *Social Hygiene Legislation Manual, 1921* (New York: American Social Hygiene Association, 1921), 52, 56, 55; George E. Worthington, "Developments in Social Hygiene Legislation from 1917 to September 1, 1920," *JSH* 6 (October 1920): 564. Many states already had laws against fornication on their books, so these new laws may have been restatements of previous laws. See also Kristin Luker, "Sex, Social Hygiene, and the State: The Double-Edged Sword of Social Reform," *Theory and Society* 27, no. 5 (October 1998): 614–615.

107. Bascom Johnson, "Next Steps," *JSH* 4 (1918): 9–23.

108. Worthington, "Developments in Social Hygiene Legislation," chart between 562–563.

109. "Preliminary Report by Bascom Johnson," August 29–31, 1917, Doc. 4808, Box 9, Entry 395, RG 165, NACP.

110. US Immigration Commission, *Report of the Immigration Commission: Immigrants in Industries, Part 23: Summary Report on Immigrants in Manufacturing and Mining* (Washington, DC: Government Printing Office, 1911), 113.

111. For example, in one Atlanta hotel, women paid one-third of their earnings in exchange for a room. Paul Kinsie, Atlanta GA, July 3, 1917, 7 to 12 pm, Folder Atlanta, GA (2 of 3), Box 6, E395, RG165, NACP.

112. "Reported by P.K.," Hattiesburg, Mississippi, July 27, 1917, Doc. 2702, Box 9, Entry 395, RG 165, NACP.

113. Isaac Silberstein, "Report on Vallejo, California," July 5, 1917, Folder California, December 1917, Box 5, E395, RG165, NACP.

114. Pliley, *Policing Sexuality*, 192.

115. "Reported by P.K.," Hattiesburg, Mississippi, July 27, 1917.

116. Elisa Camiscioli, *Selling French Sex: Prostitution, Trafficking, and Global Migrations* (Cambridge: Cambridge University Press, 2024), 8.

117. "Reported by P.K.," Princeton, NJ, Oct. 15, 1917, Doc. 10605, Folder New Jersey, Box 10, E395, RG 165, NACP.

118. Bristow, *Making Men Moral*, 161–62.

119. Baldwin Lucke, "Tabes Dorsalis. A Pathological and Clinical Study of 250 Cases," *Journal of Nervous and Mental Disease* 43, no. 5 (May 1916): 395.

120. Anne Grey Fischer, *The Streets Belong to Us: Sex, Race, and Police Power from Segregation to Gentrification* (Chapel Hill: University of North Carolina Press), 40–41.

121. W. F. Draper, "The Detention and Treatment of Infected Women as a Measure of Control of Venereal Diseases in Extra-Cantonment Zones," *American Journal of Obstetrics* 80 (December 1919): 642–646.

122. Stern, *The Trials of Nina McCall*, 98.

123. Emily Epstein Landau, *Spectacular Wickedness: Sex, Race, and Memory in Storyville, New Orleans* (Baton Rouge: Louisiana State University Press, 2013), 7–9.

124. Walter Clarke, "Report for Macon, GA," Sept. 14, 1917, Folder Macon, GA (2 of 3), Box 6, E395, RG165, NACP.

125. V. H. Kriegshaber to Raymond Fosdick, July 20, 1917, Folder Macon, GA (3 of 3), Box 6, E395, RG165, NACP.

126. "Report by P. K.," Macon, GA, Oct. 11, 1917, Folder Macon, GA (2 of 3), Box 6, E395, RG165, NACP.

127. On the figure of the quadroon prostitute see Landau, *Spectacular Wickedness*, 50–66; Emily Clark, *The Strange History of the American Quadroon: Free Women of Color in the Revolutionary Atlantic World* (Chapel Hill: University of North Carolina Press, 2013).

128. Jaqueline Jones, *Labor of Love, Labor of Sorrow: Black Women, Work, and the Family from Slavery to the Present* (New York: Basic, 1985), 119–120.

129. Tera Hunter, *To 'Joy My Freedom: Southern Black Women's Lives and Labors after the Civil War* (Cambridge, MA: Harvard University Press, 1997), 227.

130. Katie Hemphill, *Bawdy City: Commercial Sex and Regulation in Baltimore, 1790–1915* (Cambridge: Cambridge University Press, 2022), 212–213.

131. "Reported by P.K.," Hattiesburg, Mississippi, July 27, 1917.

132. Frederick Whitin to Raymond Fosdick, August 22, 1917, Folder New Jersey, Box 10, Entry 395, RG 165, NACP.

133. Elizabeth Haiken, "'The Lord Helps Those Who Help Themselves': Black Laundresses in Little Rock, Arkansas, 1917–1921," *Arkansas Historical Quarterly* 49, no. 1 (Spring 1990): 30.

134. "Report by P.M.K.," Atlanta, GA, July 3, 1917, Folder Atlanta, GA, (2 of 3), Box 6, Entry 395, RG165, NACP. As Kinsie noted, "all the hotels in Atlanta that cater to vice have colored porters."

135. Hunter, *To 'Joy My Freedom*, 174.

136. "Report by P. M. K.," Atlanta, GA, July 5, 6, 7, 1919, Folder Atlanta, GA (1 of 3), Box 6, Entry 395, RG165 Box 6, NACP.

137. "Report by P. M. K.," Atlanta, GA.

138. Chauncey, *Gay New York*, 65.

139. Chauncey, *Gay New York*, 65.

140. Maureen D. Lee, *Sissieretta Jones: The Greatest Singer of Her Race, 1868–1933* (Columbia: University of South Carolina Press, 2012).

141. See C. Riley Snorton, *Black on Both Sides: A Racial History of Trans Identity* (Minneapolis: University of Minnesota Press, 2017).

142. Henrietta S. Additon, "Work among Delinquent Women and Girls," *Annals of the American Academy of Political and Social Science* 79 (1918): 152, 153–155.

143. Kathy Peiss, "'Charity Girls' and City Pleasures: Historical Notes on Working Class Sexuality, 1880–1920," in *Powers of Desire: The Politics of Sexuality*, ed. Ann Snitow, Christine Stansell, and Sharon Thompson (New York: Monthly Review Press, 1983), 74–87.

144. H. H. Moore, "Four Million Dollars for the Fight Against Venereal Diseases," *JSH* 5, no. 1 (January 1919): 15–26; Brandt, *No Magic Bullet*, 88–89.

145. Worthington, "Developments in Social Hygiene Legislation," 564.

146. Luker, "Sex, Social Hygiene and the State," 615. For a complete list of states see *Social Hygiene Legislation Manual, 1921*, appendix.

147. Brandt, *No Magic Bullet*, 86. "Detention of Persons with Venereal Disease," *Journal of the American Medical Association* 73, no. 23 (December 1919): 1791.

148. Paul B. Johnson, "Social Hygiene and the War," *JSH* 4 (January 1918): 91–137; Brandt, *No Magic Bullet*, 97; Stern, *The Trials of Nina McCall*.

149. Gertrude Seymour, "A Year's Progress in Venereal Disease Control," *JSH* 5 (January 1919): 53.

150. Philippa Levine, *Prostitution, Race, and Politics: Policing Venereal Disease in the British Empire* (New York: Routledge, 2003), 122–123; see Stern, *Trials of Nina McCall*, 95–96.

151. Mary Macey Dietzler, *Detention Houses and Reformatories as Protective Social Agencies in the Campaign of the United States Government Against Venereal Diseases* (Washington, DC: Government Printing Office, 1922), 31.

152. Elizabeth S. Kite, "Third Report," October 30th, 1917, Folder New Jersey, Box 10, Entry 395, RG165, NACP.

153. Additon, "Work among Delinquent Women and Girls," 156–157. On the overlap between the incarceration of prostitutes and the feeble-minded during the war and the broad influence of eugenic thought on anti-prostitution campaigns, see Wendy Kline, *Building a Better Race: Gender, Sexuality, and Eugenics from the Turn of the Century to the Baby Boom* (Berkeley: University of California Press, 2001).

154. C. C. Pierce, "The Value of Detention as a Reconstruction Measure," *Public Health Reports* 34, no. 48 (1919): 2711. Pliley, *Policing Sexuality*, 127; Bristow, *Making Men Moral*, 129; Pivar, *Purity and Hygiene*, 218–219.

155. Christopher Capozolla, *Uncle Sam Wants You: World War I and the Making of the Modern American Citizen* (Oxford: Oxford University Press, 2008), 19–20.

156. Stern, *The Trials of Nina McCall*, 85.

157. Frank J. Osborne, "The Law Enforcement Program Applied," *JSH* 5 (January 1919): 94; "Quarantine Applied to Men," *Social Hygiene Bulletin* 6 (August 1919): 6.

158. Stern, *The Trials of Nina McCall*, 92.

159. Draper, "The Detention and Treatment of Infected Women," 642.

160. Dietzler, *Detention Houses and Reformatories*, 74.

161. Stern, *The Trials of Nina McCall*, 98–99.

162. Jane Deter Rippin, "Social Hygiene and the War," *JSH* 5 (January 1919), images opposite 130.

163. Dietzler, *Detention Houses and Reformatories*, 170–171.

164. Dietzler, *Detention Houses and Reformatories*, 170–173, 107, 102.

165. Stern, *The Trials of Nina McCall*, 131–160.

166. For more on women CTCA workers see Mary E. Odem, *Delinquent Daughters: Protecting and Policing Adolescent Female Sexuality in the United States, 1885–1920* (Chapel Hill: University of North Carolina Press, 1995), 121–127; Barbara Meil Hobson, *Uneasy Virtue: The Politics of Prostitution and the American Reform Tradition* (Chicago: University of Chicago Press, 1990), 175–182; Bristow, *Making Men Moral*, 114–119.

167. Stern, *The Trials of Nina McCall*, 168–169.

168. See Harrol B. Ayres, "Democracy at Work—San Antonio Being Reborn," *JSH* 4, no. 2 (April 1918): 217.

169. Sarah Mercer Judson, "Solving the Girl Problem: Race, Womanhood, and Leisure in Atlanta during World War I," in *Women Shaping the South: Creating and Confronting Change*, ed. Angela Boswell and Judith N. McArthur (Columbia: University of Missouri Press, 2006), 171. For more on African American women's work during the war see Odem, *Delinquent Daughters*, 118–121. On African American involvement in the social hygiene movement more broadly, see Christina Simmons, *Making Marriage Modern: Women's Sexuality from the Progressive Era to World War II* (Oxford: Oxford University Press, 2009), 49–54.

170. Georgina Hickey, *Hope and Danger in the New South City: Working-Class Women and Urban Development in Atlanta, 1890–1940* (Athens: University of Georgia Press, 2003), 129.

171. Odem, *Delinquent Daughters*, 122–125. For a detailed discussion of elite white women reformers' attempts to stop the arrest and genital inspection of suspected prostitutes, see Stern, *The Trials of Nina McCall*, 164–169.

172. Stern, *The Trials of Nina McCall*, 167.

173. Note by Maurice Gregory, printed as commentary on "Venereal Disease Control: Standards for Discharge of Carriers," July 19, 1918 (Washington, DC: Government Printing Office), reprinted by the World's Purity Federation, January 1922, 3AMS / D / 51 / 01, TWL.

174. Katharine C. Bushnell, "Take warning!," Oakland, CA, 1910. Blackwell Family Papers: Elizabeth Blackwell Papers, 1836–1946, mss1288001328-55, LOC.

175. Capozzola, *Uncle Sam Wants You*.

176. Marjorie Delevan, "American Made," *Michigan Public Health* 8 (February 1920): 61.

177. Laura Lammasniemi, "Regulation 40D: Punishing Promiscuity on the Home Front During the First World War," *Women's History Review* 26, no. 4 (2017): 584–596; Julia Laite, *Common Prostitutes and Ordinary Citizens: Sex in London, 1885–1960* (New York: Palgrave Mac-Millan, 2012), 122–124.

178. Stern, *The Trials of Nina McCall*, 256–259.

179. Andrea Tone, *Devices and Desires: A History of Contraceptives in America* (New York: Hill and Wang, 2001), 102–107; Brandt, *No Magic Bullet*, 112–115.

180. D'Emilio and Freedman, *Intimate Matters*, 233–235.

181. Bristow, *Making Men Moral*, 45–50.

182. Kevin White, *The First Sexual Revolution: The Emergence of Male Heterosexuality in Modern America* (New York: New York University Press, 1993).

183. Stern, *The Trials of Nina McCall*, 202–204; Susan M. Reverby, *Examining Tuskegee: The Infamous Syphilis Study and Its Legacy* (Chapel Hill: University of North Carolina Press, 2009).

184. David Lawrence, "Washington—The Cleanest Capital in the World," *JSH* 3, no. 3 (July 1917): 321.

185. Allison Neilans, "Neo-Regulation in the United States," n.d., 3AMS / D / 51 / 01, TWL.

Chapter 5: The Caribbean Laboratory

1. Inspector T. E. Watson to Director, Department of the South, Guardia Nacional Dominicana, January 5, 1920, L.41-Exp.5, Leg.1700206, Gobierno Militar de Santo Domingo, Digital Collection, Archivo General de la Nación de República Dominicana (hereafter AGN); R. M. Warfield to Military Governor, January 24, 1921, L.41-Exp.5, Leg.1700206, Gobierno Militar de Santo Domingo, Digital Collection, AGN. On the US military government's targeting of Black women see Lorgia García-Peña, *The Borders of Dominicanidad: Race, Nation, and Archives of Contradiction* (Durham, NC: Duke University Press, 2016), 90.

2. Laura Briggs, "Familiar Territory: Prostitution, Empires and the Question of U.S. Imperialism in Puerto Rico, 1849–1916," in *Families of a New World: Gender, Politics, and State Development in a Global Context*, ed. Lynne A. Haney and Lisa Pollard (New York: Routledge, 2003), 41.

3. Warwick Anderson, *Colonial Pathologies: American Tropical Medicine, Race, and Hygiene in the Philippines* (Durham, NC: Duke University Press, 2006).

4. Andrew Byers, *The Sexual Economy of War: Discipline and Desire in the U.S. Army* (Ithaca, NY: Cornell University Press, 2019), 200–203.

5. On Hawai'i see Richard A. Greer, "Collarbone and the Social Evil," *Hawaiian Journal of History* 7 (1973): 3–17; on the Philippines see Andrew Jimenez Abalahin, "Prostitution Policy and the Project of Modernity: A Comparative Study of Colonial Indonesia and the Philippines, 1850–1940" (PhD diss., Cornell University, 2003), 340–349.

6. Kimberly A. Reilly, "'A Perilous Venture for Democracy': Soldiers, Sexual Purity, and American Citizenship in the First World War," *Journal of the Gilded Age and Progressive Era* 13, no. 2 (2014): 223–255.

7. Katrina Quisumbing King, "The Structural Sources of Ambiguity in the Modern State: Race, Empire, and Conflicts over Membership," *American Journal of Sociology* 128, no. 3 (November 2022): 768–819.

8. On patterns of migration and political and intellectual currents see Lara Putnam, *The Company They Kept: Migrants and the Politics of Gender in Caribbean Costa Rica, 1870–1960* (Chapel Hill: University of North Carolina Press, 2002); Anne Eller, *We Dream Together: Dominican Independence, Haiti, and the Fight for Caribbean Freedom* (Durham, NC: Duke University Press, 2016); Nancy Leys Stepan, *The Hour of Eugenics: Race, Gender, and Nation in Latin America* (Ithaca, NY: Cornell University Press, 1996); Franklin W. Knight, *The Caribbean: The Genesis of a Fragmented Nationalism* (Oxford: Oxford University Press, 2011); Stephan Palmié and Francisco A. Scarano, eds., *The Caribbean: A History of the Region and Its Peoples* (Chicago: University of Chicago Press, 2011).

9. On Puerto Rico see Laura Briggs, *Reproducing Empire: Race, Sex, Science, and U.S. Imperialism in Puerto Rico* (Berkeley: University of California Press, 2002); Eileen Suárez Findlay, *Imposing Decency: The Politics of Sexuality and Race in Puerto Rico, 1870–1920* (Durham, NC: Duke University Press, 1999); José Flores Ramos, "Virgins, Whores, and Martyrs: Prostitution in the Colony, 1898–1919," in *Puerto Rican Women's History: New Perspectives*, ed. Linda Delgado and Félix V. Matos Rodríguez (New York: M.E. Sharpe, 1998), 83–105; on Panama see Joan Flores-Villalobos, *The Silver Women: How Black Women's Labor Made the Panama Canal* (Philadelphia: University of Pennsylvania Press, 2023); Julie Greene, *Canal Builders: Making America's Empire at the Panama Canal* (New York: Penguin, 2010); Marixa Lasso, *Erased: The Untold Story of the Panama Canal* (Cambridge, MA: Harvard University Press, 2019); and Jeffrey W. Parker, "Empire's Angst: The Politics of Race, Migration, and Sex Work in Panama, 1903–1945" (PhD diss., University of Texas-Austin, 2013); on the Dominican Republic see García-Peña, *The Borders of Dominicanidad*; Rebecca Ann Lord, "An 'Imperative Obligation': Public Health and the United States Military Occupation of the Dominican Republic, 1916–1924" (PhD diss., University of Maryland-College Park, 2002); Rebecca Ann Lord, "Quarantine in the Fort Ozama Dungeon: The Control of Prostitution and Venereal Disease in the Dominican Republic," *Caribbean Quarterly* 49, no. 4 (2003): 12–29; Melissa Madera, "Zones of Scandal: Gender, Public Health, and Social Hygiene in the Dominican Republic, 1916–1961" (PhD diss., SUNY-Binghamton, 2011); and April J. Mayes, "Tolerating Sex: Prostitution, Gender, and Governance in the Dominican Republic, 1880s–1924," in *Health and Medicine in the circum-Caribbean: 1800–1968*, ed. Juanita De Barros, Steven Palmer, and David Wright (New York: Routledge, 2009), 121–142.

10. On African American soldiers in the Caribbean see Khary Oronde Polk, *Contagions of Empire: Scientific Racism, Sexuality, and Black Military Workers Abroad, 1898–1948* (Chapel Hill: University of North Carolina Press, 2020), 29; Howard L. Kern, *Special Report of the Attorney General of Porto Rico to the Governor of Porto Rico Concerning the Suppression of Vice and*

Prostitution in Connection with the Mobilization of the National Army at Camp Las Casas (San Juan, PR: Bureau of Supplies, Printing, and Transportation, 1919), 51.

11. On the development of scientific racism in relation to sexuality, see Ladelle McWhorter, *Racism and Sexual Oppression in Anglo-America: A Genealogy* (Bloomington: Indiana University Press, 2009).

12. Ellsworth Huntington, *Civilization and Climate* (New Haven, CT: Yale University Press, 1915), 47.

13. Ileana M. Rodríguez-Silva, *Silencing Race: Disentangling Blackness, Colonialism, and National Identities in Puerto Rico* (New York: Palgrave, 2012).

14. Findlay, *Imposing Decency*, 23–24, 78, 88–89.

15. Herman Goodman, "The Anti-Venereal Disease Campaign in Porto Rico, 1918–1920 - Part 1," *Western Medical Times* 42 (October 1922): 119.

16. Goodman, "The Anti-Venereal Disease Campaign in Porto Rico - Part 1," 118.

17. Eileen J. Findlay, "Love in the Tropics: Marriage, Divorce, and the Construction of Benevolent Colonialism in Puerto Rico, 1898–1910," in *Close Encounters of Empire: Writing the Cultural History of U.S.-Latin American Relations*, ed. Gilbert M. Joseph. Catherine C. LeGrand, and Ricardo D. Salvatore (Durham, NC: Duke University Press, 1998), 139–140; Briggs, *Reproducing Empire*.

18. Greene, *Canal Builders*, 337, 123–158.

19. John Lindsay-Poland, *Emperors in the Jungle: The Hidden History of the U.S. in Panama* (Durham, NC: Duke University Press, 2003), 7–8.

20. Harry Alverson Franck, *Zone Policeman 88: A Close Range Study of the Panama Canal and Its Workers* (New York: Century, 1913), 206. While US officials noted that the red-light districts in these cities dated from the early days of the US occupation, it is likely that they had existed prior to when the French attempted to build a canal and possibly to earlier Spanish occupations. See A. T. McCormack to Governor Harding, [first draft] July 22, 1918, F 37-H-10 Part 2, Box 794, E30, RG 185, NACP.

21. Maj. Edgar A. Bocock, "Venereal Disease in Panama," *JSH* 6, no. 4 (October 1920), 620–621; John Hall, *Panama Roughneck Ballads* (Panama and Canal Zone: Albert Lindo, 1912), 10.

22. Mara L. Keire, *For Business and Pleasure: Red-Light Districts and the Regulation of Vice in the United States, 1890–1933* (Baltimore, MD: Johns Hopkins University Press, 2010); Anne Grey Fischer, *The Streets Belong to Us: Sex, Race, and Police Power from Segregation to Gentrification* (Chapel Hill: University of North Carolina Press).

23. On women migrants in the Caribbean see Putnam, *The Company They Kept*; Lara Putnam, *Radical Moves: Caribbean Migrants and the Politics of Race in the Jazz Age* (Chapel Hill: University of North Carolina Press, 2013); Joan Flores-Villalobos, "Gender, Race, and Migrant Labor in the 'Domestic Frontier' of the Panama Canal Zone," *International Labor and Working Class History* 99 (Spring 2021): 96–121.

24. Gasperry Offult to Secretary of State, July 11, 1919, file 819.1151 / 53, RG 59, NACP, quoted in Jeffrey W. Parker, "Sex at a Crossroads: The Gender Politics of Racial Uplift and Afro-Caribbean Activism in Panama, 1918–32," *Women, Gender, and Families of Color* 4, no. 2 (2016), 196; Kern, *Special Report of the Attorney General of Porto Rico*, 32.

25. Lasso, *Erased*.

26. Matthew Scalena, "Illicit Nation: State, Empire, and Illegality on the Isthmus of Panama" (PhD diss., Stony Brook University, 2013), 18–19. As one US official noted, "Ninety percent of

the patrons of the prostitutes of Panama and Colon have been American soldiers, sailors and civilians"; A.T. McCormack to Governor Harding, July 22, 1918, F 37-H-10 Part 2, Box 794, E30, RG 185, NACP.

27. A. T. McCormack to Governor Harding, [first draft], July 22, 1918, F 37-H-10 Part 2, Box 794, E30, RG 185, NACP.

28. As Matthew Scalena has shown, Panamanians increasingly relied on the sale of sex because the US government and American businesses dominated the legal economy. Scalena, "Illicit Nation."

29. Gasberry Offult to the Secretary of State, July 11, 1918, file 819.1151 / 53, RG 59, NACP, in Jeffrey Wayne Parker, "Empire's Angst," 109.

30. On this history see Eller, *We Dream Together*.

31. On the role of ideologies of masculinity and paternalism in the Haitian occupation see Mary A. Renda, *Taking Haiti Military Occupation and the Culture of U.S. Imperialism, 1915–1940* (Chapel Hill: University of North Carolina Press, 2001).

32. Bruce J. Calder, *The Impact of Intervention: The Dominican Republic During the U.S. Occupation of 1916–1924* (Austin: University of Texas Press, 1984), 13, 115.

33. Calder, *The Impact of Intervention*, 16–19.

34. Reynolds Hayden, "Review of the Reorganization of the Sanitary and Public Health Work in the Dominican Republic Under the United States Military Government of Santo Domingo," *American Journal of Tropical Medicine and Hygiene* 2, no. 1 (1922): 41; Military Government of Santo Domingo, *Santo Domingo, Its Past and Its Present Condition* (Santo Domingo City, D.R.: n.p., 1920), 26.

35. Hayden, "Review of the Reorganization," 41–42; on the history of prostitution control in the Dominican Republic see Mayes, "Tolerating Sex."

36. Mayes, "Tolerating Sex," 124–128.

37. J. W. Vann and B. Groesbeck, "The Prevalence of Venereal Disease in the Dominican Republic," *United States Naval Medical Bulletin* 14, no. 4 (October 1920): 683.

38. Hayden, "Review of the Reorganization," 49, 57.

39. Mayes, "Tolerating Sex," 133.

40. Sam Erman, *Almost Citizens: Puerto Rico, the U.S. Constitution, and Empire* (Cambridge: Cambridge University Press, 2018), 148.

41. Briggs, *Reproducing Empire*, 4.

42. Kern, "Special Report," 51.

43. Kern, "Special Report," 5. Between 18,000–20,000 Puerto Rican men served during the war. On Puerto Ricans' military service see Harry Franqui-Rivera, *Soldiers of the Nation: Military Service and Modern Puerto Rico, 1868–1952* (Lincoln: University of Nebraska Press, 2018).

44. Herman Goodman, "The Anti-Venereal Disease Campaign in Porto Rico, 1918–1920—Part 2," *Western Medical Times* 42 (November 1922): 155. At times Goodman separated Puerto Ricans into three racial categories as "white," "mulatto," and "negro." US officials also divided Puerto Ricans into the more familiar categories of "white" or "colored"; Byers, *The Sexual Economy of War*, 134.

45. Kern, "Special Report," 51; Florette Barbeau and Arthur E. Henri, *The Unknown Soldiers: Black American Troops in World War I* (Philadelphia, PA: Temple University Press, 1974), 52–53. Eileen Findlay notes that there was an economic crisis in the 1910s, which led to starvation. It is likely that higher rates of infection reflected poor health caused by poverty. Findlay, *Imposing Decency*, 169–170.

46. Howard Kern to the Judges and District Attorneys of Porto Rico, July 22, 1918, in *Annual Report of the Secretary of War, Vol. 3* (Washington, DC: Government Printing Office, 1918), 618.

47. Kern, "Special Report," 5.

48. Kern, "Special Report," 6–7, 21–22; Herman Goodman, "Genital Defects and Venereal Disease among the Porto Rican Draft Troops," *Journal of the American Medical Association* 72, no. 13 (March 29, 1919): 911. Kern's policy is detailed in Herman Goodman, "A Study on Regulation vs. Abolition of Prostitution—Part 2," *Medico-Legal Journal* 37, no. 5 (September–October 1920): 73–77.

49. Herman Goodman, "The Porto Rican Experiment," *JSH* 5, no. 2 (April 1919): 185–191.

50. Yen Le Espiritu, *Home Bound: Filipino American Lives Across Cultures, Communities, and Countries* (Berkeley: University of California Press, 2003), 47.

51. Kern in *Annual Report of the Secretary of War, Vol. 3*, 618–619; Kern, "Special Report," 25.

52. Gavin L. Payne, "The Vice Problem in Porto Rico," *JSH* 5, no. 2 (April 1919): 238.

53. Kern, "Special Report," 8.

54. Dr. F. Del Valle Atiles, "A Study of 168 Cases of Prostitution," trans. with notes by Herman Goodman, *The Urologic and Cutaneous Review* 24 (August 1920): 438. Goodman cites a study he conducted with 422 whites, 304 mulattoes, and 65 negresses. See also Findlay, *Imposing Decency*, 23–24.

55. Kern, "Special Report," 23.

56. Payne, "The Vice Problem in Puerto Rico," 240. This was a larger number of women in proportion to the population than the number of those arrested in the United States, though the statistics on mainland women's arrests likely undercount the number arrested. Part of Payne's argument was that the US federal government should fund this reform work, suggesting that although the US government adopted reformers' policy of repressing prostitution, it often did not want to fund reformers' broader agenda.

57. Goodman, "The Porto Rican Experiment," 190–191.

58. Kern, "Special Report," 33, 27, 23.

59. Herman Goodman, "Prostitution and Community Syphilis," *American Journal of Public Health* 9, no. 7 (July 1, 1919): 519.

60. Kern, "Special Report," 6–9, 15, 28–30.

61. "Porto Rican Policy Proves Successful," *SHB* 7, no. 3 (March 1920): 7.

62. Goodman, "Prostitution and Community Syphilis," 518–519 [punctuation added].

63. Alyosha Goldstein, *Poverty in Common: The Politics of Community Action during the American Century* (Durham, NC: Duke University Press, 2012), 60; Michael Lapp, "The Rise and Fall of Puerto Rico as a Social Laboratory, 1945–1965," *Social Science History* 19, no. 2 (Summer 1995): 169–199.

64. *Annual Report of the Governor of the Panama Canal* (Washington, DC: Government Printing Office, 1918), 300.

65. A.T. McCormack to Dr. Eusebio Morales, May 13, 1918, F 37-H-10 Part 1A, Box 794, E 30, RG 185, NACP.

66. Hermann Goodman, "The Anti-Venereal Disease Campaign in Panama—Part 2," *Western Medical Times* 43 (March 1924): 268.

67. Hermann Goodman, "The Anti-Venereal Disease Campaign in Panama—Part 1," *Western Medical Times* 43 (February 1924): 231.

68. T. B. Lamoreux to Commanding General, Panama Canal Department, July 20, 1918, F 37-H-10 Part 2, Box 794, E 30, RG 185, NACP; Arthur T. McCormack, *Report of the Health Department of the Panama Canal for the Calendar Year 1918* (Mount Hope, CZ: Panama Canal Press, 1919), 41.

69. Goodman, "The Anti-Venereal Disease Campaign in Panama—Part 1," 231.

70. "The Fight Against Disease on the Isthmus," *JSH* 5, no. 3 (July 1919): 401. On Panamanian resistance to deporting women see Parker, "Empire's Angst," 72–73, 78.

71. Judge S. K. Blackburn to Guy Johannes, August 5, 1918, F 37-H-10 Part 2, Box 794, E 30, RG 185, NACP. Blatchford had previously served in Dakota Territory, Puerto Rico, the Philippines, and France.

72. President of the Ayuntamiento, Arturo J. Pellerano Alfau, and its Secretary, M. A. de Marchena to Señor Regidores, September 25, 1917, Exp. 5, Leg. 2845, Gobierno Militar de Santo Domingo, AGN.

73. Executive Order No. 96, *Republica Dominicana: Colección de Órdenes Ejecutivas* No. 1–116 (November 29, 1916–December 31, 1917) (Santo Domingo: J. R. Vda. García, 1918), 229–230.

74. Hearing, Aug. 16, 22, 23, 1918, L.39-Exp.2, Leg. 1700231, Gobierno Militar de Santo Domingo, Digital Collection, AGN.

75. Hearing, Aug. 16, 22, 23, 1918.

76. Calder, *Impact of Intervention*, 184.

77. Goodman, "The Anti-Venereal Disease Campaign in Panama—Part 2," 269; "Venereal Disease in the Canal Zone," *JSH* 5, no. 2 (April 1919): 263–264.

78. José Amador, *Medicine and Nation Building in the Americas, 1890–1940* (Nashville, TN: Vanderbilt University Press, 2021); "The Fight Against Disease on the Isthmus," *Social Hygiene* 5, no. 3 (July 1919): 399–402. On McCormack see John Ettling, *The Germ of Laziness: Rockefeller Philanthropy and Public Health in the New South* (Cambridge, MA: Harvard University Press, 1981), 139. McCormack would later change his mind and advocate for the May Act during WWII, which made prostitution near a military bases a federal crime. See Marilyn E. Hegarty, *Victory Girls, Khaki-Wackies, and Patriotutes: The Regulation of Female Sexuality During World War II* (New York: New York University Press, 2007), 51–52.

79. Envelope dated 7 / 22 / 18, F 37-H-10—Enclosures, RG 185, E30, Box 794, NARA. For more on the danger of racial mixing see Bocock, "Venereal Disease in Panama," 620; García-Peña, *Borders of Dominicanidad*, 87.

80. A. T. McCormack to Governor [first draft], Panama Canal, July 22, 1918, F 37-H-10 Part 2, Box 794, E30, RG 185, NACP.

81. Goodman, "The Anti-Venereal Disease Campaign in Panama—Part 2," 268–269.

82. F. F. Russell to A. T. MacCormack, August 26, 1918, F 37-H-10 Part 2, RG 185, E30, Box 794, NARA.

83. Goodman, "The Anti-Venereal Disease Campaign in Panama—Part 2," 270–271.

84. H. C. Fischer, *Report of the Health Department of the Panama Canal for the Calendar Year 1919* (Mount Hope, CZ: Panama Canal Press, 1920), 22; "Campaign in Porto Rico and Canal Zone," *SHB* 6 (October 1919): 5.

85. Herman Goodman, "The Anti-Venereal Disease Campaign in Panama—Part 3," *Western Medical Times* 43 (April 1924): 297.

86. Goodman, "The Anti-Venereal Disease Campaign in Panama—Part 2," 271.

87. Goodman, "The Anti-Venereal Disease Campaign in Panama—Part 3," 298.

88. W. C. Rucker to William Snow, December 14, 1921, ICC Papers, File 37-H-10, Part 4, Box 794, E30, RG185, NACP.

89. William Jennings Price to US Secretary of State, November 17, 1921, ICC Papers, File 37-H-10 Part 4, Box 794, RG185, NACP.

90. Hearing and Exhibits, August 23, 1918, L.39-Exp.2, Leg. 1700231, Gobierno Militar de Santo Domingo, Digital Collection, AGN.

91. Hearing, August 16, 1918, L.39-Exp.2, Leg. 1700231, Gobierno Militar de Santo Domingo, Digital Collection, AGN.

92. Hayden, "Review of the Reorganization," 43.

93. Renda, *Taking Haiti*, 158, 212.

94. Major General Commandant to Brigade Commander, Jan. 10, 1919, L.39-Exp.2, Leg. 1700231, Gobierno Militar de Santo Domingo, Digital Collection, AGN.

95. Military Governor of Santo Domingo to Reynolds Hayden, May 14, 1919, L.21-Exp.20, Leg. 1700655, Gobierno Militar de Santo Domingo, Digital Collection, AGN.

96. Lord, "An Imperative Obligation," 137, 116. The *Ley de Sanidad* went into effect in January 1920.

97. Thomas Snowden, "Quarterly Report of the Military Governor of Santo Domingo from October 1, 1919 to December 31, 1919," Military Government of Santo Domingo, RG38, NADC; Lord, "An Imperative Obligation," 207.

98. Executive Order no. 338 (*Ley de Sanidad*), Art. 24, *Republica Dominicana: Colección de Órdenes Ejecutivas*, no. 249–380 (Santo Domingo: J.R. Vda. García, 1919), 374.

99. US Surgeon General's Office, *The Medical Department of the United States Army in the World War, Volume 9: Communicable and Other Diseases* (Washington, DC: Government Printing Office, 1928), 301–305.

100. See, for example, Arthur T. McCormack, *Report of the Health Department of the Panama Canal for the Calendar Year 1918* (Mount Hope, CZ: Panama Canal Press, 1919), 7–9; Mayes, "Tolerating Sex," 133.

101. Kern, "Special Report of the Attorney General of Porto Rico," 13; Dietzler, *Detention Houses and Reformatories*, 171.

102. Payne, "The Vice Problem in Porto Rico," 237–238; The youngest girls held at the Bedford Reformatory were 15 years old. Katherine Bement Davis, "A Study of Prostitutes Committed," 216.

103. Kern, "Special Report," 35, 33.

104. "Dr. Herman Goodman, 76, Dies; An Authority on Dermatology," *New York Times*, Feb. 12, 1971, 40; Payne, "The Vice Problem in Porto Rico," 237.

105. Yordán Pasarrel was from an elite family. His father had been mayor of Ponce. Kern, "Special Report of the Attorney General of Porto Rico," 33, 35.

106. Leo L. Michel and Herman Goodman, "Prophylaxis of Syphilis with Arsphenamin," *JAMA* (December 25, 1920): 1768–1770.

107. Colonial medicine closely linked venereal and "tropical" diseases. See Katherine Paugh, "Yaws, Syphilis, Sexuality, and the Circulation of Medical Knowledge in the British Caribbean and the Atlantic World," *Bulletin of the History of Medicine* 88, no. 2 (2014): 225–252.

108. Kern, "Special Report of the Attorney General of Porto Rico," 32–34, Herman Goodman, "Ulcerating Granuloma of the Pudenda," *Archives of Dermatology and Syphilology* 1 (February 1920): 151, 167.

109. Goodman, "Genital Defects," 907–908.

110. Herman Goodman, "The Anti-Venereal Disease Campaign in Porto Rico, 1918–1920—Part 3," *Western Medical Times* 42 (December 1922): 189. On Puerto Rico and racial classification see Ileana M. Rodríguez-Silva, *Silencing Race.*

111. McCormack, *Report of the Health Department 1918,* 35; Anderson, *Colonial Pathologies,* 90–91.

112. McCormack, *Report of the Health Department 1918,* 35. The practice of removing reproductive organs to treat a range of purported women's diseases, from epilepsy to excessive sexual desire to "insanity," and to prevent women from being ruled by their reproductive organs, harkens to late nineteenth-century medicine. See Lucy Bland, *Banishing the Beast: Feminism, Sex and Morality* (New York: New Press, 1995), 65–67.

113. Briggs, *Reproducing Empire,* 142–161.

114. As Flores-Villalobos argues, "Black women's labor made the Panama Canal," Flores-Villalobos, *The Silver Women.*

115. Parker, "Empire's Angst," 78–79.

116. H. C. Fischer, *Report of the Health Department of the Panama Canal for the Calendar Year 1920* (Mount Hope, CZ: Panama Canal Press, 1921), 22.

117. Fischer, *Report of the Health Department 1919,* 26, 22.

118. Thomas Snowden, "Quarterly Report of the Military Governor of Santo Domingo from April 1, 1920–June 30, 1920," 22, Military Government of Santo Domingo, RG38, NADC.

119. Mayes, "Tolerating Sex," 134; see also Madera, "Zones of Scandal," 75 n207.

120. García-Peña, *Borders of Dominicanidad,* 87.

121. Stephen M. Fuller and Graham A. Cosmas, *Marines in the Dominican Republic, 1916–1924* (Washington, DC: History and Museums Division, US Marine Corps, 1974), 89.

122. Thomas Snowden, "Quarterly Report of the Military Governor of Santo Domingo from April 1, 1920–June 30, 1920," 24, Military Government of Santo Domingo, RG38, NADC.

123. District Commander, Northern District to Commanding General, July 9, 1920, L.1-Exp.31, Leg. 1700192, Digital Collection, AGN; Provost Marshal to District Commander, Southern District, July 17, 1920, L.1-Exp.31, Leg. 1700192, Digital Collection, AGN.

124. Thomas Snowden, "Quarterly Report of the Military Governor of Santo Domingo from April 1, 1920–June 30, 1920," 24, Military Government of Santo Domingo, RG38, NADC; Micah Wright, "Building an Occupation: Puerto Rican Laborers in the Dominican Republic, 1916–1924," *Labor: Studies in Working-Class History of the Americas* 13, nos. 3–4 (December 2016): 83–103.

125. On the role of sexuality in the labor movement in Puerto Rico see Findlay, *Imposing Decency,* 168–171. On Panama see Parker, "Sex at a Crossroads."

126. Kern, "Special Report of the Attorney General of Porto Rico," 11–12, 38.

127. Findlay, *Imposing Decency,* 190.

128. Findlay, *Imposing Decency,* 146, 180; Flores Ramos, "Virgins, Whores, and Martyrs," 97.

129. Robert Langham to Chief Health Officer, September 3, 1918, F 37-H-10 Part 2, Box 794, E30, RG 185, NACP; Parker, "Sex at a Crossroads."

130. West Indian Labour Union to Board of Health August 27, 1918, F 37-H-10 Part 2, Box 794, E 30, RG 185, NACP.

131. Parker, "Sex at a Crossroads," 201–206. As Parker has shown, Pan-Africanist men decried regulated prostitution as a manifestation of US imperialism, though they also placed blame on women themselves. Joan Flores-Villalobos demonstrates that Afro-Caribbean women leveraged discourses about race and sexuality to advance their own goals. See *The Silver Women*, 6–7.

132. Goodman, "The Anti-Venereal Disease Campaign in Panama—Part 2," 266.

133. Record of Proceedings of a Board of Investigation, April 4, 1918, General Corresp. of the Military Govt. of Santo Domingo, 1917–1924, Box 9, RG 38, NADC; Memo, Brigadier General USMC and Acting military governor of Santo Domingo, April 29, 1918, General Corresp. of the Military Govt. of Santo Domingo, 1917–1924, Box 9, RG 38, NADC.

134. Calder, *Impact of Intervention*, 21.

135. Statement by Rubersinda Herrdia, Aug. 11, 1920, L.1-Exp.48, Leg. 1700192, Gobierno Militar de Santo Domingo, Digital Collection, AGN.

136. Madera, "Zones of Scandal," 69–70.

137. Garcia-Peña, *Borders of Dominicanidad*, 87–88.

138. Earl N. Ellis, Memo for Military Governor, Oct. 27, 1920, L.1-Exp.75, Leg. 1700192, Gobierno Militar de Santo Domingo, Digital Collection, AGN.

139. Garcia-Peña, *Borders of Dominicanidad*; Kamala Kempadoo, *Sexing the Caribbean: Gender, Race, and Sexual Labor* (New York: Routledge, 2004).

140. On conflicts between organized labor and elite anti-prostitution efforts in Puerto Rico, see Findlay, *Imposing Decency*, 167–201.

141. See for example Kern, "Special Report," 54–56.

142. Kern, "Special Report," 56–57.

143. Briggs, *Reproducing Empire*, 66–68.

144. Edith Hildreth, "A Campaign for Social Betterment," *Home Mission Monthly* 33, no. 8 (June 1919):180–181.

145. Edith Hildreth, "Impressions of the Hospital at Arecibo," *The Times*, Aug. 24, 1918.

146. Kern, "Special Report," 13.

147. Findlay, *Imposing Decency*, 188–189.

148. Ramos, "Virgin, Whores, and Martyrs," 99.

149. Findlay, *Imposing Decency*, 197; Flores Ramos, "Virgins, Whores, and Martyrs," 99.

150. Briggs, *Reproducing Empire*, 131, 136–137. As Briggs shows, these trials have a complicated legacy because many Puerto Rican women wanted to obtain reliable birth control.

151. Parker, "Empire's Angst," 265, 239–240. On race and national identity across Latin America, see Nancy P. Appelbaum, Anne S. McPherson, and Karin Alejandra Rosemblatt, eds., *Race and Nation in Modern Latin America* (Chapel Hill: University of North Carolina Press, 2003).

152. Hayden, "Review of the Reorganization," 57; see also G. Pope Atkins and Larman C. Wilson, *The Dominican Republic and the United States: From Imperialism to Transnationalism* (Athens: University of Georgia Press, 1998), 56.

153. Lord, "An Imperative Obligation," 169–170.

154. Aquiles Rodríguez, "De la vida moderna: Higiene y Sanidad," *Listín Diario*, March 9, 1920, 6, quoted in Madera, "Zones of Scandal," 72.

155. García-Peña, *Borders of Dominicanidad*, 91.

156. Madera, "Zones of Scandal," 164–228.

157. A. T. McCormack to Governor Harding, July 22, 1918, F 37-H-10 Part 2, Box 794, E30, RG 185, NACP.

158. Hayden, "Review of the Reorganization," 50.

159. Laura Briggs makes a similar argument, *Reproducing Empire*, 9.

160. "Marines Are Told," *The SHB* 6, no. 8 (August 1919): 9.

161. Goodman, "The Anti-Venereal Disease Campaign in Panama—Part 2," 271.

Chapter 6: A "Righteous Crusade"

1. Petition and attached documents, March 27, 1919, Doc. 4712-A-90, Box 85, General Headquarters, AG file, RG 120, NACP.

2. Petition and attached documents, March 27, 1919.

3. Gaetano Liberatore's honorable discharge papers list his character as "excellent" and his physical condition as "good," suggesting the incident with Legros did not result in punishment for him. Fold3, *Gaetano Liberatore* (https://www.fold3.com/memorial/641414743/gaetano -liberatore: accessed October 27, 2023).

4. John D. Rockefeller, Jr., to George E. Vincent, July 14, 1917, Folder 749, Box 80, Series 100.N, International—War Relief, RG 1.1, Projects, RAC.

5. *United States Army in the World War, 1917–1919*, Vol. 1 (Washington, DC: Center of Military History and United States Army, 1988), 3, xxv.

6. On the American Plan on the home front see Alan Brandt, *No Magic Bullet: A Social History of Venereal Disease in the United States Since 1880* (Oxford: Oxford University Press, 1987), 7–95; Nancy K. Bristow, *Making Men Moral: Social Engineering During the Great War* (New York: New York University Press, 1996); Scott W. Stern, *The Trials of Nina McCall: Sex, Surveillance, and the Decades-Long Government Plan to Imprison "Promiscuous" Women* (Boston, MA: Beacon Press, 2018).

7. Oxford English Dictionary, "French," http://www.oed.com/view/Entry /74478#eid55906711; Stephen Shapiro, "The Moment of the Condom: Saint-Méry and Early American Print Sexuality," in *Pioneering North American: Mediators of European Culture and Literature*, ed. Klaus Martens (Würzburg: Königshausen & Neumann, 2000), 129.

8. On *réglementation* see Alain Corbin, *Women for Hire: Prostitution and Sexuality in France After 1850* (Cambridge, MA: Harvard University Press, 1990); Jill Harsin, *Policing Prostitution in Nineteenth-Century Paris* (Princeton, NJ: Princeton University Press, 1985).

9. Goodman, "The Porto Rican Experiment."

10. Charles Brent to Jules Cambon, July 19, 1918, Box 85, General Headquarters, AG file, RG 120, NACP.

11. Mary Louise Roberts argues that the same conceptions of the French as less civilized and sexually immoral shaped the US military's policy in France during World War II. Mary Louise Roberts, *What Soldiers Do: Sex and the American GI in World War II France* (Chicago: University of Chicago Press, 2013), 52.

12. *United States Army in the World War, 1917–1919*, Vol. 1, xii, xiv, 3.

13. Edward M. Coffman, *The War to End All Wars: The American Military Experience in World War I* (Lexington: University Press of Kentucky, 1986), 338–340.

14. On the imperial ambitions that shaped twentieth-century internationalism see Glenda Sluga, *Nation, Psychology, and International Politics, 1870–1919* (New York: Palgrave Macmillan, 2006).

15. Chris Capozolla et al., "Interchange: World War I," *Journal of American History* 102, no. 2 (September 2015): 473.

16. Woodrow Wilson, "President's Message to the National Army," *New York Times*, September 4, 1917, 1.

17. Woodrow Wilson, Address to the Joint Session of Congress, April 2, 1917, 65th Congress, 1st Session, Senate Document No. 5. Available at http://historymatters.gmu.edu/d/4943/.

18. Josephus Daniels, "Men Must Live Straight If They Would Shoot Straight," 16, reprint of an address before the Clinical Congress of Surgeons of North America, Chicago, 1917, Navy Department, Commission on Training Camp Activities, Folder 7, Box 24, RBF.

19. Daniels, "Men Must Live Straight If They Would Shoot Straight," 15–16.

20. Elmore M. McKee, "The Venereal Problem—The Army Viewpoint," *Boston Medical and Surgical Journal* 178 (April 4, 1918): 468.

21. Daniels perpetuated the myth of the Black rapist during his time as a North Carolina newspaper editor. Glenda Elizabeth Gilmore, *Gender and Jim Crow: Women and the Politics of White Supremacy in North Carolina, 1896–1920* (Chapel Hill: University of North Carolina Press, 1996), 83–84. Woodrow Wilson conceptualized the difference between white mainland Americans and African Americans (as well as Latin Americans) through a developmentalist racial framework, in which white Americans had to help their less advanced neighbors of color along the path toward civilization. Mary A. Renda, *Taking Haiti Military Occupation and the Culture of U.S. Imperialism, 1915–1940* (Chapel Hill: University of North Carolina Press, 2001), 108–115.

22. Timothy Verhoeven, "'Apostles of Continence': Doctors and the Doctrine of Sexual Necessity in Progressive-Era America," *Medical History* 61, no. 1 (2017): 89–106, 94.

23. George Walker, *The Traffic in Babies: An Analysis of the Conditions Discovered During an Investigation Conducted in the Year 1914* (Baltimore, MD: The Norman Remington Co., 1918).

24. Brandt, *No Magic Bullet*, 99.

25. Hugh Young, *Hugh Young: A Surgeon's Autobiography* (New York: Harcourt Brace, 1940), 270.

26. Frank W. Weed, "Sanitation in the American Expeditionary Forces," in *The Medical Department of the United States Army in the World War*, Vol. V (Washington, DC: Government Printing Office, 1926), 963.

27. Max Joseph Exner to Raymond Fosdick, June 23, 1917, Folder 749, Box 80, Series 100.N, International—War Relief, RG 1.1, Projects, RAC.

28. Young, *Hugh Young*, 301.

29. Raymond B. Fosdick, "Papers Relating to the Attitude of the A.E.F. in Relation to the Problem of Prostitution" (Washington, DC: n.p., 1918), 12, 20.

30. See H. Gougerot, "Prophylaxie des Maladies Vénériennes—Tracts et Notices de Propagande," *Annales d'Hygiène Publique et de Médecine Légale* 29 (July 1918): 288–304.

31. On French debates over prostitution see Elisa Camiscioli, *Reproducing the French Race: Immigration, Intimacy, and Embodiment in the Early Twentieth Century* (Durham, NC: Duke University Press, 2009); Stephanie Limoncelli, *The Politics of Trafficking: The First International*

Movement to Combat the Sexual Exploitation of Women (Stanford, CA: Stanford University Press, 2011), 112–132; Susan R. Grayzel, "Mothers, Marraines, and Prostitutes: Morale and Morality in First World War France," *International History Review* 19, no. 1 (March 1997): 66–82; Michelle Rhoades, "'No Safe Women': Prostitution, Masculinity, and Disease in France during the Great War" (PhD diss., University of Iowa, 2001). Even during the war French anti-regulationists still communicated with the ASHA. For a French view published in the United States, see Jules Bois, "The New Moral Viewpoint of the French Young Man," *JSH* 3, no. 2 (April 1917): 165–172.

32. On *réglementation* in France see Corbin, *Women for Hire*; Jill Harsin, *Policing Prostitution*; Christian Benoît, *Le Soldat et la Putain: Histoire d'un Couple Inséparable* (Villers-sur-Mer: De Taillac, 2013); Caroline Séquin, *Desiring Whiteness: A Racial History of Prostitution in France and Colonial Senegal, 1848–1950* (Ithaca, NY: Cornell University Press, 2024).

33. Weed, "Sanitation," 899–900.

34. Walker, *Venereal Disease in the American Expeditionary Forces*, 58–61.

35. Walker, *Venereal Disease in the American Expeditionary Forces*, 58–65.

36. Walker, *Venereal Disease in the American Expeditionary Forces*, 31.

37. "Syllabus Accredited for Use in Official Lectures on Sex Hygiene and Venereal Disease," November 1917, reprinted in Walter Clarke, "Social Hygiene and the War," *JSH* 4, no. 2 (April 1918): 291.

38. Max Joseph Exner, "Social Hygiene and the War," *JSH* 5, no. 2 (April 1919): 292–293.

39. "Draft of Bulletin by the Chief Surgeon of the AEF," January 27, 1919, Box 85, General Headquarters, AG file, RG 120, NACP.

40. Hugh Hampton Young, "Preventive Medicine as Applied to Venereal and Skin Diseases," *JAMA* (November 29, 1919): 1670.

41. Young, *Hugh Young*, 308–310.

42. Weed, "Sanitation," 904–905.

43. Georges Clemenceau to Head le Mission Française auprès des Armées Américaines (Ragueneau), February 17, 1918, GR 9 NN 7 1056, Archives de la Grande Guerre, Service Historique de la Défense, Vincennes, France (hereafter SHD).

44. PV of Conference, March 9, 1918, GR 9 NN 7 1056, SHD.

45. PV of Conference, March 9, 1918, GR 9 NN 7 1056, SHD.

46. PV of Conference, March 9, 1918, GR 9 NN 7 1056, SHD.

47. PV of Conference, March 9, 1918, GR 9 NN 7 1056, SHD.

48. PV of Conference, March 9, 1918, GR 9 NN 7 1056, SHD.

49. Fosdick, "Papers Relating to the Attitude of the A.E.F.," 26.

50. Médecin-Major Gastou, Commission d'Études Interalliées pour la Prophylaxie des Maladies Vénériennes, Rapport Présenté à la Sous-Commission, March 25, 1918, GR 9 NN 7 1056, SHD.

51. Fosdick, "Papers Relating to the Attitude of the A.E.F.," 34, 35, 45.

52. PV of Conference, March 9, 1918, GR 9 NN 7 1056, SHD.

53. Fosdick, "Papers Relating to the Attitude of the A.E.F.," 23.

54. Edward H. Beardsley, "Allied Against Sin: American and British Responses to Venereal Disease in World War I," *Medical History* 20, no. 2 (1976): 198–200.

55. *Parliamentary Debates*, House of Lords, April 11, 1918, Vol. 29, no. 17 (London: His Majesty's Stationery Office, 1918), 669–671.

56. "Conference Regarding Venereal Disease and Its Treatment in the Armed Forces," 18, 10 May 1918, WO / 32 / 11404, The National Archives, Kew, Richmond, United Kingdom (hereafter NAUK). On Brent's strong connections to the UK, see Michael Snape, "Anglicanism and Interventionism: Bishop Brent, The United States, and the British Empire in the First World War," *Journal of Ecclesiastical History* 69, no. 2 (2018): 300–325.

57. "Minutes of Proceedings at an Adjourned Conference Regarding Venereal Disease and Its Treatment in the Armed Forces at the War Office," 11, July 11, 1918, WO / 32 / 11404, NAUK.

58. Benoît, *Le Soldat et la Putain*, 300.

59. "Minutes of Proceedings at an Adjourned Conference Regarding Venereal Disease and Its Treatment in the Armed Forces at the War Office," 17–22, July 11, 1918, WO / 32 / 11404, NAUK; Beardsley, "Allied Against Sin," 202.

60. Walker, *Venereal Disease in the American Expeditionary Forces*, 138.

61. On the policing of women on the British home front, see "Regulation 40D: Punishing Promiscuity on the Home Front During the First World War," *Women's History Review* 26, no. 4 (2017): 584–596; Julia Laite, *Common Prostitutes and Ordinary Citizens: Sex in London, 1885–1960* (New York: Palgrave MacMillan, 2012), 119–124; Pamela Cox, "Compulsion, Voluntarism, and Venereal Disease: Governing Sexual Health in England after the Contagious Diseases Acts," *Journal of British Studies* 46, no. 1 (2007): 91–115.

62. Le Préfet de Loir-et-Cher à Le Ministère de l'Intérieur, May 4, 1918, Box 85, General Headquarters, AG file, RG 120, NACP.

63. Fosdick, "Papers Relating to the Attitude of the A.E.F.," 47.

64. Walker, *Venereal Disease in the American Expeditionary Forces*, 48.

65. Fosdick, "Papers Relating to the Attitude of the A.E.F.," 47.

66. Fosdick, "Papers Relating to the Attitude of the A.E.F.," 47–48.

67. Fosdick, "Papers Relating to the Attitude of the A.E.F.," 49.

68. Le Préfet de Loir-et-Cher à Le Ministère de l'Intérieur, May 4, 1918, Box 85, General Headquarters, AG file, RG 120, NACP.

69. Fosdick, "Papers Relating to the Attitude of the A.E.F.," 25.

70. Avery D. Andrews to Commander-in-Chief, G-1 and Chief, French Military Mission, January 22, 1919, Box 85, General Headquarters, AG file, RG 120, NACP.

71. Avery D. Andrews to Commander-in-Chief and C.O. Advance Section S. O. S., January 23, 1919; Division Surgeon's Office, 29th Division to Division Commander, 29th Division, April 17, 1919, both in Box 85, General Headquarters, AG file, RG 120, NACP. Historical Branch, War Plans Division, General Staff, *Brief Histories of Divisions, U.S. Army 1917–1918* (Fort Leavenworth, KS: Army Command & General Staff College, Combined Arms Research Library, 1921), 36.

72. "Report of the Meeting of 19 November 1918 of a Commission Gathered by the Commissariat General of Franco-American Affairs of War on the Subject of Questions of Hygiene Raised by the Presence of American Troops in France," November 19, 1918, GR 17 NN 1, SHD.

73. Benoît, *La Soldat et la Putain*, 300.

74. Le Commissaire Spécial to Gen. Com. of the 10th region, Rennes, June 24, 1918, Box 85, General Headquarters, AG file, RG 120, NACP.

75. Walker, *Venereal Disease in the American Expeditionary Force*, 85, 223–226; Jessica R. Pliley shows that by the 1920–1930s, oral sex had become a more common part of sexual commerce

in the United States, suggesting that Walker made accurate observations about the practice's diffusion. Pliley, *Policing Sexuality*, 191–192.

76. Weed, "Sanitation," 973; Social Hygiene Division, "Will You Go Home with Your Outfit?" (US Army Education Commission, 1918), Box 181, ASHA.

77. Raymond B. Fosdick, *Chronicle of a Generation: An Autobiography* (New York: Harper, 1958), 171–172. See also "Colonel Snow Describes Social Hygiene Abroad," *SHB* 6, no. 7 (July 1919): 1.

78. Weed, "Sanitation," 957. On contact tracing on the home front see Stern, *The Trials of Nina McCall*, 78.

79. The Surgeon, District of Paris to Chief Surgeon, A.E.F., April 30, 1919, Box 5258, Chief Surgeon AEF, RG 120, NACP.

80. George Van Horn Moseley to Commanding General, 29th Division, February 13, 1919, Box 85, General Headquarters, AG file, RG 120, NACP.

81. Chas S. Lincoln, Colonel to Chief of Staff, Memo: "Venereal Conditions in Leave Area," May 3, 1919, Box 85, General Headquarters, AG file, RG 120, NACP.

82. Corbin, *Women for Hire*, 274.

83. Médecin-Major Gastou, Commission d'Études Interalliées pour la Prophylaxie des Maladies Vénériennes, Rapport Présenté à la Sous-Commission, March 25, 1918, GR 9 NN 7 1056, SHD.

84. Young, *Hugh Young*, 283–284, 273–274.

85. Pautrier, "Extrait du Rapport d'Octobre 1918," GR 9 NN 7 1059, SHD.

86. Pautrier, "Extrait du Rapport d'Octobre 1918," GR 9 NN 7 1059, SHD.

87. Michelle Rhoades, "Renegotiating French Masculinity: Medicine and Venereal Disease during the Great War," *French Historical Studies* 29, no. 2 (2006): 323–325.

88. Walker, *Venereal Disease in the American Expeditionary Forces*, 54–55.

89. Byers, *The Sexual Economy of War*, 323.

90. Adriane Lentz-Smith, *Freedom Struggles: African Americans and WWI* (Cambridge, MA: Harvard University Press, 2009), 111.

91. Richard S. Fogarty, *Race and War in France: Colonial Subjects in the French Army, 1914–1918* (Baltimore, MD: Johns Hopkins University Press, 2008), 2.

92. Benoît, *La Soldat et La Putain*, 284.

93. Séquin, *Desiring Whiteness*, 107–108.

94. Weed, "Sanitation," 906.

95. On African Americans' perspectives on military service, see Polk, *Contagions of Empire*; Lentz-Smith, *Freedom Struggles*; Tyler Stovall, *Paris Noir: African Americans in the City of Light* (Boston: Houghton Mifflin, 1996), 1–24; Florette Barbeau and Arthur E. Henri, *The Unknown Soldiers: Black American Troops in World War I* (Philadelphia, PA: Temple University Press, 1974).

96. Lentz-Smith, *Freedom Struggles*, 99. Before the ASHA closed brothels on the US mainland, most maintained segregation based on the race of the customer.

97. On the myth of the Black rapist see Crystal N. Feimster, *Southern Horrors: Women and the Politics of Rape and Lynching* (Cambridge, MA: Harvard University Press, 2009); Estelle Freedman, *Redefining Rape: Sexual Violence in the Era of Suffrage and Segregation* (Cambridge, MA: Harvard University Press, 2013), 89–124; Diane Miller Sommerville, *Rape and Race in the*

Nineteenth-Century South (Chapel Hill: University of North Carolina Press, 2004); Martha Hodes, *White Women, Black Men: Illicit Sex in the Nineteenth-Century South* (New Haven, CT: Yale University Press, 1996), 176–208.

98. Linard, "Au Sujet Des Troupes Noires Américaines," August 7, 1918, Folder 12, GR 16 N 1924, SHD. W.E.B. DuBois collected this confidential memo and reprinted it in the NAACP newspaper *The Crisis* as evidence of the rampant racism against African Americans by US officials. The reprint translates "nos coloniaux expérimentés" as "experienced colonials." "Documents of the War," *The Crisis* 18 (May 1919): 16–18.

99. Young, *Hugh Young*, 320.

100. Young, *Hugh Young*, 362.

101. George Walker to Chief Surgeon, AEF, November 30, 1917, Box 85, General Headquarters, AG file, RG 120, NACP.

102. Polk, *Contagions of Empire*, 140–144.

103. George Walker to Chief Surgeon, AEF, November 30, 1917, Box 85, General Headquarters, AG file, RG 120, NACP.

104. Weed, "Sanitation," 953.

105. Byers, *The Sexual Economy of War*, 151; Lentz-Smith, *Freedom Struggles*, 100.

106. Memo for Commander-in-Chief from Bethel, July 23, 1918, Box 85, General Headquarters, AG file, RG 120, NACP.

107. Walker, *Venereal Disease in the American Expeditionary Forces*, 160–163.

108. Fosdick, "Papers Relating to the Attitude of the A.E.F.," 26.

109. "Alleged Executions Without Trial in France," Hearings Before a Special Committee on Charges of Alleged Executions without Trial in France, 67th Congress (Washington, DC: Government Printing Office, 1923), iv.

110. See "Alleged Executions Without Trial in France," 601–612; Lentz-Smith, *Freedom Struggles*, 134–135.

111. Lentz-Smith, *Freedom Struggles*, 134. On Black-on-white rape scares in France during WWII, see Roberts, *What Soldiers Do*, 195–254.

112. Roberts, *What Soldiers Do*, 254.

113. "Syllabus Accredited for Use in Official Lectures on Sex Hygiene and Venereal Disease," November 1917, Box 5258, Chief Surgeon AEF, RG 120, NACP. This lecture alluded directly to the "rape of Belgium" by German soldiers.

114. Weed, "Sanitation," 906.

115. Séquin, *Desiring Whiteness*, 107–108.

116. Walker, *Venereal Disease in the American Expeditionary Forces*, 122.

117. Walker, *Venereal Disease in the American Expeditionary Forces*, 156.

118. Weed, "Sanitation," 939–941.

119. Walker, *Venereal Disease in the American Expeditionary Forces*, 122. Later experiments on Black men such as the Tuskegee syphilis study would prove Black soldiers correct in their suspicion of doctors. See Susan M. Reverby, *Examining Tuskegee: The Infamous Syphilis Study and Its Legacy* (Chapel Hill: University of North Carolina Press, 2009).

120. Young, *Hugh Young*, 320–321.

121. Thomas Foster, *Rethinking Rufus: Sexual Violations of Enslaved Men* (Athens: University of Georgia Press, 2019), 17–27.

122. Arthur B. Spingarn, "The War and Venereal Disease Among Negros," *JSH* 4 (July 1918): 338–337.

123. Polk calls into question the effectiveness of prophylactic treatments for preventing disease. Polk, *Contagions of Empire*, 138–139, 237n61; Byers argues that prophylaxis was effective. Byers, *The Sexual Economy of War*, 134.

124. Walker, *Venereal Disease in the American Expeditionary Forces*, 156.

125. Brandt, *No Magic Bullet*, 116.

126. Charles E. Marrow to Chief Surgeon, AEF, January 3, 1919, Box 5249, Chief Surgeon AEF, RG 120, NACP.

127. Walker, *Venereal Disease in the American Expeditionary Forces*, 123.

128. Polk, *Contagions of Empire*, 150.

129. Roberts, *What Soldiers Do*, 162, 161.

130. "Colonel Snow Describes Social Hygiene Abroad," 1.

131. George Walker noted that records and questionnaires indicated that 71 percent of all American soldiers in France had sex while there, suggesting that prophylaxis played a crucial role. Walker, *Venereal Disease in the American Expeditionary Forces*, 101.

132. "American Social Hygiene Association Annual Report, 1919–1920," Folder 6, Box 19, ASHA.

133. "Scope of Association Work Is Worldwide," *SHB* 7, no. 4 (April 1920): 6.

Chapter 7: "A World-Wide Influence"

1. Paul Kinsie, "Report on Marseilles, France," January 1–3, 1925, 1–2, Box S174, LNA.

2. Nicholas Hewitt, *Wicked City: The Many Cultures of Marseille* (Oxford: Oxford University Press, 2019).

3. Warren F. Kuehl and Lynne K. Dunn, *Keeping the Covenant: American Internationalists and the League of Nations, 1920–1939* (Kent: Kent State University Press, 1997); Ludovic Tournès, *Philanthropic Foundations at the League of Nations: An Americanized League?* (New York: Routledge, 2022).

4. Rachel Crowdy, "The Humanitarian Activities of the League of Nations," *Journal of the Royal Institute of International Affairs* 6, no. 3 (1927): 156.

5. See Philippa Hetherington and Julia Laite, "Trafficking: A Useless Category of Historical Analysis?," *Journal of Women's History* 33, no. 4 (2021): 7–39.

6. Max J. Exner to John D. Rockefeller, Jr., May 31, 1917, Folder 749, Box 80, Series 100.N, International—War Relief, RG 1.1, Projects, RAC.

7. On the heated debates over the investigators' findings and the formulation of the final report, see Jean-Michel Chaumont, *Le mythe de la traite des blanches: enquête sur la fabrication d'un fléau* (Paris: Decouovert, 2009).

8. Scott W. Stern, *The Trials of Nina McCall: Sex, Surveillance, and the Decades-Long Government Plan to Imprison "Promiscuous" Women* (Boston, MA: Beacon Press, 2018), 99–100.

9. Stern, *The Trials of Nina McCall*, 100, 169. The US Public Health Services took over the functions of the ISHB, but received far less money; Stern, *The Trails of Nina McCall*, 170.

10. Brandt, *No Magic Bullet*, 124.

11. Kuehl and Dunn, *Keeping the Covenant*. Neil Smith argues that US interest in the League was about "fixing the global geography of modernity" as a means of furthering US economic imperialism. Neil Smith, *American Empire: Roosevelt's Geographer and the Prelude to Globalization* (Berkeley: University of California Press, 2004), 141–143.

12. "A History and Forecast," *JSH* 5, no. 4 (October 1919): 554.

13. On international norms and the mandate system see Susan Pedersen, *The Guardians: The League of Nations and the Crisis of Empire* (Oxford: Oxford University Press, 2015), 10.

14. Charles Walter Clarke, *Taboo: The Story of the Pioneers of Social Hygiene* (Washington, DC: Public Affairs Press, 1961), 96. "The Testimonial Dinner Address," *JSH* 23, no. 9 (December 1937): 491. Daniel Gorman states that lobbying by the International Bureau was responsible. Daniel Gorman, "Empire, Internationalism, and the Campaign against the Traffic in Women and Children in the 1920s," *Twentieth Century British History* 19, no. 2 (2008): 198. Limoncelli says that it was the League's bureaucratic desire to oversee the previous 1904 and 1910 conventions that many member nations had signed. Stephanie Limoncelli, *The Politics of Trafficking: The First International Movement to Combat the Sexual Exploitation of Women* (Stanford, CA: Stanford University Press, 2011), 73–74.

15. *The Covenant of the League of Nations*, June 28, 1919, Article 23 (c).

16. Limoncelli, *The Politics of Trafficking*, 73.

17. On disagreements within transnational women's organizations see Leila J. Rupp, *Worlds of Women: The Making of an International Women's Movement* (Princeton, NJ: Princeton University Press, 1997), 150–152. On the ILO see Eileen Boris, *Making the Woman Worker: Precarious Labor and the Fight for Global Standards, 1919–2019* (Oxford: Oxford University Press, 2019).

18. Mir Yarfitz, *Impure Migration: Jews and Sex Work in Golden Age Argentina* (New Brunswick, NJ: Rutgers University Press, 2019); Donna J. Guy, *Sex and Danger in Buenos Aires: Prostitution, Family, and Nation in Argentina* (Lincoln: University of Nebraska Press, 1991); David Petruccelli, "Pimps, Prostitutes and Policewomen: The Polish Women Police and the International Campaign against the Traffic in Women and Children between the World Wars," *Contemporary European History* 24, no. 3 (August 2015): 345.

19. Tiffany Sippial, *Prostitution, Modernity, and the Making of the Cuban Republic, 1840–1920* (Chapel Hill: University of North Carolina Press, 2013), 174–175.

20. Philippa Lesley Hetherington, "Victims of the Social Temperament: Prostitution, Migration, and the Traffic in Women from Imperial Russia and the Soviet Union, 1885–1935" (PhD diss., Harvard University, 2014), 292–348.

21. On Japan, Maki Kimura, *Unfolding the "Comfort Women" Debates: Modernity, Violence, Women's Voices* (London: Springer, 2016), 81–92.

22. Paul Knepper, *International Crime in the 20th Century: The League of Nation's Era, 1919–1930* (London: Palgrave Macmillan, 2011).

23. National representatives came from the United States, Denmark, France, Great Britain, Italy, Japan, Poland, Romania, Spain, and Uruguay. Organizations represented included the International Bureau for the Suppression of Traffic in Women and Children, the International Catholic Association for the Protection of Girls, the Federation of National Unions for the Protection of Girls, the International Women's Organizations, and the Jewish Association for the Protection of Girls and Women. League of Nations, *Report to the Third Assembly of the*

League on the Work of the Council and on the Measures taken to execute the Decisions of the Assembly, Geneva, 1922, 72–73, A.6.1922, LNA.

24. In addition to prostitution, the Trafficking Committee also looked at the employment of women abroad, women police officers, traffic in obscene publications, and age of consent laws. See, for example, Jessica R. Pliley, "Claims to Protection: The Rise and Fall of Feminist Abolitionism in the League of Nations' Committee on the Traffic in Women and Children, 1919–1936," *Journal of Women's History* 22, no. 4 (2010): 90–113. Although the inquiry included children, the investigators did not use the category "child." They attempted to determine if women were 21 years of age, or over the age of consent for each particular country. For more on these debates, see Ashwini Tambe, "Climate, Race Science and the Age of Consent in the League of Nations," *Theory, Culture & Society* 28, no. 2 (March 2011): 109–30. Investigators very rarely, if ever, mentioned boys. The investigators' notes do not include any references to trafficked boys they met. The treaty may have included boys because of the growing concerns over male homosexuality after WWI.

25. League of Nations and Special Body of Experts on Traffic in Women and Children, *Report of the Special Body of Experts on Traffic in Women and Children*, Part 2, Annex III, opposite 196. On the British arguments for excluding India see Ashwini Tambe, "Climate, Race Science and the Age of Consent."

26. Jessica R. Pliley, "Ambivalent Abolitionist Legacies: The League of Nations' Investigations into Sex Trafficking, 1927–1934," in *Fighting Modern Slavery and Human Trafficking: History and Contemporary Policy*, ed. Genevieve LeBaron, Jessica R. Pliley and David W. Blight (Cambridge: Cambridge University Press). For a broader discussion of the battles between abolitionists and regulationists, see Limoncelli, *The Politics of Trafficking*. Limoncelli has shown how diverse coalitions of reformers, sometimes with opposite values and approaches, came together through fighting the traffic in women. Limoncelli's characterization of the two groups, however, does not map onto the ASHA's views of prostitution; it sought both the abolition of state-regulated brothels and strict legal control over sexual morality.

27. On the Dutch anti-trafficking campaign see Petra de Vries, "'White Slaves' in a Colonial Nation: The Dutch Campaign Against the Traffic in Women in the Early Twentieth Century," *Social & Legal Studies* 14, no. 1 (2005): 39–60; Limoncelli, *The Politics of Trafficking*, 95–111. De Vries argues that although Dutch law prohibited brothels, most Dutch abolitionists maintained a more liberal view of sexuality and did not believe the state should interfere with sex between consenting adults, De Vries, "White Slaves," 53.

28. On these ongoing differences see Sonja Dolinsek, "Tensions of abolitionism during the negotiation of the 1949 'Convention for the Suppression of the Traffic in Persons and of the Exploitation of the Prostitution of Others,'" *European Review of History: Revue européenne d'histoire* 29, no. 2 (2022): 223–248.

29. Limoncelli, *The Politics of Trafficking*, 77; Rachel Crowdy to Bascom Johnson, August 10, 1922, LON / 12 / 22452 / 647, Box R636, LNA. Crowdy likely wanted American involvement for financial reasons, since John D. Rockefeller, Jr., funded many League of Nations efforts. See Ludovic Tournès, "La philanthropie américaine, la Société des Nations et la coproduction d'un ordre international (1919–1946)," *Relations internationals* 151, no. 3 (2012): 25–36.

30. Abbott also was involved in the League's Child Welfare Committee and secured Bureau of Social Hygiene funding for child welfare work.

31. Edith Abbott, "A Sister's Memories," *Social Service Review* 13, no. 3 (1939): 356, 374.

32. Grace Abbott to Bascom Johnson, January 20, 1923, S180 / 35 / 2, LNA; Bascom Johnson to Grace Abbott, February 21, 1923, S180 / 35 / 2, LNA.

33. "Traffic in Women and Children, memorandum by Miss Abbott (USA)," March 21, 1923, Geneva, C.T.F.E. 152, R636 / 12 / 27338 / 647, LNA. See also Daniel Gorman, *The Emergence of International Society in the 1920s* (Cambridge: Cambridge University Press, 2012), 74–77.

34. "International Convention for the Suppression of the Traffic in Women and Children," September 30, 1921, Geneva.

35. "Traffic in Women and Children, memorandum by Miss Abbott (USA)," March 21, 1923.

36. Other members of the Trafficking Committee at times saw her as a representative of the US government. See, for example, "1925 Expenditures," R671 / 12 / 35396 / 28269, LNA.

37. "Traffic in Women and Children, memorandum by Miss Abbott (USA)," March 21, 1923.

38. Abbott, "A Sister's Memories," 400.

39. Traffic in Women and Children Committee of Experts, Verbatim report of the third meeting, C.T.F.E. / Experts / P.V.3. (1), 9–10, April 2nd, 1924, Geneva, Box S169 / 24 / 2, LNA. The ASHA also faced harsh criticism from the New York press in the 1920s for entrapping innocent young women through its investigations. See Paul Knepper, "Measuring the Threat of Global Crime: Insights From Research by the League of Nations Into the Traffic in Women," *Criminology* 50, no. 3 (August, 2012): 790–791.

40. The Special Body of Experts was comprised of delegates from Belgium, Italy, France, Britain, Japan, Switzerland, Uruguay, and the United States; Lela B. Costin, *Two Sisters for Social Justice: A Biography of Grace and Edith Abbott* (Urbana: University of Illinois Press, 2003), 93.

41. C.T.F.E. / Experts / P.V.5. (1), 12, October 6, 1924, S169 / 24 / 4, LNA.

42. C.T.F.E. / Experts / P.V.4. (1), 4, April 2, 1924, S169 / 24 / 2, LNA.

43. C.T.F.E. / Experts / P.V.3. (1), 7, April 2, 1924, S169 / 24 / 2, LNA.

44. Knepper, "Measuring the Threat of Global Crime," 779, 784. Mariana Valverde, "The Question of Scale in Urban Criminology," in *International and Comparative Criminal Justice and Urban Governance: Convergence and Divergence in Global, National and Local Settings*, ed. Adam Crawford (Cambridge: Cambridge University Press, 2011), 567–586; Stephen Legg, "Of Scales, Networks and Assemblages: The League of Nations Apparatus and the Scalar Sovereignty of the Government of India," *Transactions of the Institute of British Geographers* 34, no. 2 (2009): 234–253.

45. C.T.F.E. / Experts / P.V.4. (1), 1, April 2, 1924, Box S169 / 24 / 2, LNA.

46. *Report of the Special Body of Experts on Traffic in Women and Children*, Part 2, 6. On the relationship between the national and international spheres see Legg, "Of Scales, Networks and Assemblages," 234.

47. While Galitzi was not yet an American citizen at the time of her investigation (she was originally from Romania), she had filed her "first papers" more than two years prior in 1924 and often championed American social scientific methods. Galtizi's Declaration of Intention for Citizenship (no. 23 42279) is available on ancestry.com.

48. C.T.F.E. / Experts / 3(1), 9, October 4, 1924, Box S169 / 24 / 4, LNA.

49. On interwar eugenics and migration see Alison Bashford, *Global Population: History, Geopolitics and Life on Earth* (New York: Columbia University Press, 2014), 107–132; on identification see Paul Knepper, *International Crime in the 20th Century: The League of Nation's Era, 1919–1930* (London: Palgrave Macmillan, 2011), 58–59.

50. Jeffrey Lesser, *Immigration, Ethnicity, and National Identity in Brazil, 1808 to the Present* (Cambridge: Cambridge University Press, 2013), 4–16.

51. C.T.F.E. / Experts / 3(1), 28, October 9, 1924, Box S169 / 24 / 4, LNA.

52. Lesser, *Immigration, Ethnicity, and National Identity*, 62.

53. Yarfitz, *Impure Migration*, 12.

54. George Worthington, "Open Market—Houses of Prostitution," Mexico City, Mexico, December 5–10, 1924, Box S177 / 32 / 1, LNA. See also Paul Kinsie, "Rio de Janeiro, Brazil, Commercialized Prostitution," May 18–19, 1924, Box S172, LNA.

55. C.T.F.E. / Experts / 3(1), 28, October 9, 1924, Box S169 / 24 / 4, LNA.

56. Elisa Camiscioli, *Selling French Sex: Prostitution, Trafficking, and Global Migrations* (Cambridge: Cambridge University Press, 2024), 17.

57. George Worthington, Havana, Cuba, December 18–20, 1924, Box S173 / 28 / 2, LNA.

58. Charles Winick and Paul M. Kinsie, *The Lively Commerce: Prostitution in the United States* (Chicago: Quadrangle Books, 1971); Paul Kinsie, "Report on Montevideo," May 24, 1924, Box S179 / 34 / 6, LNA; Paul Kinsie, "Report on Le Havre," July 5–6, 1926, Box S174 / 29 / 1, LNA.

59. George Worthington, "Report on Mexicali, Mexico," August 31, 1924, Box S177 / 32 / 1, LNA.

60. Paul Kinsie, "Report on Montevideo," Montevideo, Uruguay, May 24, 1924, Box S179 / 34 / 6, LNA.

61. *Report of the Special Body of Experts*, Part 1, 14.

62. Paul Kinsie, Montevideo, Uruguay, June 15–18, 1924, Box S17934 / 6, LNA.

63. George Worthington, "Open Market—Houses of Prostitution," Tampico, Mexico, December 11–12, 1924, Box S177 / 32 / 1, LNA.

64. Samuel Auerbach, Santander, Spain, January 22–25, 1925, Box S178 / 33 / 8, LNA.

65. Paul Kinsie, "Report on Montevideo," Montevideo, Uruguay, May 24, 1924, Box S179 / 34 / 6, LNA. On the relationship between commercial sex districts and gay and lesbian subcultures see Andrew Israel Ross, *Public City / Public Sex: Homosexuality, Prostitution, and Urban Culture in Nineteenth-Century Paris* (Philadelphia: Temple University Press, 2019).

66. On the problems of recovering voices and "ventriloquizing agency," see Hetherington and Laite, "Trafficking," 21.

67. On Russia in particular see Peter Gatrell, *A Whole Empire Walking: Refugees in Russia during World War I* (Bloomington: Indiana University Press, 2005).

68. Adam M. McKeown, *Melancholy Order: Asian Migration and the Globalization of Borders* (New York: Columbia University Press, 2008), 56.

69. The League of Nations issued 450,000 Nansen passports to stateless people during the 1920s, though the total number of stateless people was far higher. Eric Lohr, *Russian Citizenship: From Empire to Soviet Union* (Cambridge, MA: Harvard University Press, 2012), 149.

70. On France, see Stephen Broadberry and Mark Harrison, *The Economics of World War I* (Cambridge: Cambridge University Press, 2005), 169–201.

71. George Worthington, "Open Market—Houses of Prostitution," Tampico, Mexico, December 11–12, 1924, Box S177 / 32 / 1, LNA.

72. Paul Kinsie, Paris, France, December 13, 1924, Box S174 / 29 / 1, LNA.

73. *Monthly Labor Review* 25, no. 1 (July 1927): 112. Wages are from October 1925 in cities other than Paris.

74. Paul Kinsie, "Traffic in Women and Children," Rio de Janeiro, Brazil, July 9, 10, 1924, Box S172 / 27 / 5, LNA.

75. June Edith Hahner, *Emancipating the Female Sex: The Struggle for Women's Rights in Brazil, 1850–1940* (Durham, NC: Duke University Press, 1990), 100–102.

76. George Worthington, "Report on Mexicali, Mexico," August 31, 1924, Box S177 / 32 / 1, LNA.

77. *History of Wages in the United States from Colonial Times to 1928* (Washington, DC: USGPO, 1934), 373, 224.

78. Paul Kinsie, "Traffic in Women and Children," Panama City, Panama, August 14, 15, 1924. Box S177 / 32 / 6, LNA.

79. *Report of the Special Body of Experts*, Part 1, 23. Paul Kinsie, "Traffic in Women and Children," Vienna, Austria, June 11–12, 1925, Box S172 / 27 / 1, LNA. Her surname and Kinsie's translation of her speech into uneducated dialect suggest she was Jewish. Women's names are generally omitted from the original reports, but Chaumont, Rodríguez Garcia, and Servais, *Trafficking in Women*, includes them.

80. Paul Kinsie, Bucharest, Romania, May 30–31, 1925, Box S178 / 33 / 2, LNA.

81. Ruth Walkinshaw, "Special Report to Miss Grace Abbott Made by Ruth Walkinshaw, Research Worker," January 1925, 10, Box S171 / 26 / 1, LNA.

82. See Theresa R. Veccia, "'My Duty as a Woman': Gender Ideology, Work, and Working-Class Women's Lives in São Paulo, Brazil, 1900–1950," in *The Gendered Worlds of Latin American Women Workers: From Household and Factory to the Union Hall and Ballot Box*, ed. Daniel James and John D. French (Durham, NC: Duke University Press, 1997), 109.

83. Julia Laite, "Between Scylla and Charybdis: Women's Labour Migration and Sex Trafficking in the Early Twentieth Century," *International Review of Social History* 62, no. 1 (2017): 37–65.

84. Committee of Experts, Verbatim Report of the Second Meeting, October 3, 1924, Geneva, C.T.F.E. / Experts / P.V.2(1), 20, Box S169 / 24 / 4, LNA; Paul Kinsie, Panama City, August 22, 1924, Box S177 / 32 / 6, LNA.

85. See also Julia Laite, *The Disappearance of Lydia Harvey* (London: Profile Books, 2022).

86. Paul Kinsie, Genoa, Italy, March 5–6, 1925 Box S176 / 31 / 4, LNA.

87. Bascom Johnson, Argentina Report, Box S171 / 26 / 3, LNA.

88. Paul Kinsie, Genoa, Italy, March 5–6, 1925, Box S176 / 31 / 4, LNA.

89. Paul Kinsie, "Traffic in Women and Children," Panama City and Colón, Republic of Panama, August 23–24, 1924, Box S177 / 32 / 6, LNA.

90. Charles Walter Clarke, Free City of Danzig, n.d., Box S172 / 27 / 3, LNA.

91. *Report of the Special Body of Experts*, Part 1, 43.

92. *Report of the Special Body of Experts*, Part 1, 1, 40, 48. In fact, the Special Body of Experts initially tapped Flexner to lead the investigation, but he was too ill.

93. Bascom Johnson, "The Function of Law and Law Enforcement in Combatting Venereal Disease," *JSH* 8, no. 2 (April 1922): 163.

94. *Report of the Special Body of Experts*, Part 1, 38.

95. *Report of the Special Body of Experts*, Part 1, 47.

96. McKeown, *Melancholy Order*, 320.

97. Aristide R. Zolberg, "The Great Wall against China," in *Migration, Migration History, and History: New Perspectives*, ed. Jan Lucassen and Leo Lucassen (New York: Peter Lang, 1997), 111–121. Erika Lee has shown how this method of border control was a means of Chinese exclusion, Erika Lee, *At America's Gates: Chinese Immigration during the Exclusion Era, 1882–1943* (Chapel Hill: University of North Carolina Press, 2003), 198–199. The Immigration Act of 1924, which also established the quota system, required immigrants to obtain visas from US consular officials. See Martha Gardner, *The Qualities of a Citizen: Women, Immigration, and Citizenship, 1870* (Princeton, NJ: Princeton University Press, 2005), 5n11.

98. *Report of the Special Body of Experts*, Part 1, 18–24.

99. *Report of the Special Body of Experts*, Part 1, 9, 17.

100. Consent and coercion do not have fixed historical meanings. The category of "the traffic in women" foreclosed the possibility of women's consent to sex. See Pamela Haag, *Consent: Sexual Rights and the Transformation of American Liberalism* (Ithaca, NY: Cornell University Press, 1999); Elisa Camiscioli, "Coercion and Choice: The 'Traffic in Women' between France and Argentina in the Early Twentieth Century," *French Historical Studies* 42, no. 3 (2019): 483–507.

101. "Association Notes," *JSH* 14, no. 5 (May 1928): 311.

102. Daniel Gorman, "Empire, Internationalism, and the Campaign Against the Traffic in Women and Children in the 1920s," *20th Century British History* 19, no. 2 (2008): 193.

103. Special Body of Experts, 7th session, 17th meeting, November 24, 1927, Geneva, Box S149 / bis / 4 / 17, LNA.

104. Jean-Michel Chaumont, Magaly Rodríguez García, and Paul Servais, "Introduction," in *Trafficking in Women (1924–1926): The Paul Kinsie Reports for the League of Nations*, Vol. 2 (Geneva: United Nations Publications, 2017), 17–18. Members of the Special Body of Experts were also reticent to contradict the Italian government's statement that there was no regulated prostitution there, even though investigators found clear evidence of systems of licensing and inspections. See PV 7th session, 14th meeting, November 23, 1927, Geneva, Box S149 / 4 / 14, LNA.

105. On controversies over the report see Paul Knepper, "Measuring the Threat of Global Crime: Insights from Research by the League of Nations Into the Traffic in Women," *Criminology* 50, no. 3 (August, 2012): 790–791.

106. Pliley, "Ambivalent Abolitionist Legacies," 104. On Cuba, see *Report of the Special Body of Experts on Traffic in Women and Children*, Part 2, 48, and Sippial, *Prostitution, Modernity*, 148–179. On Hungary, see Circular Decree No. 220.902 / 1924, Issued by the Royal Hungarian Ministry of the Interior, June 27, 1925, Box S176 / 31 / 1, LNA. On Argentina see Donna J. Guy, *Sex and Danger in Buenos Aires: Prostitution, Family, and Nation in Argentina* (Lincoln: University of Nebraska Press, 1991), 117–120. On Uruguay see *Report of the Special Body of Experts on Traffic in Women and Children*, Part 2, 223–224, 182. On Poland see *Report of the Special Body of Experts on Traffic in Women and Children*, Part 2, 143–144; On Japan see "Report on Traffic in Women and Children Translated," *JSH* 14, no. 3 (March 1928): 158; and Maki Kimura, *Unfolding the "Comfort Women" Debates*, 81–92.

107. Advisory Committee on the Traffic in Women and Protection of Children, Minutes of the Fourth Session, May 20–27, 1925, R651 / 12 / 44490 / 13720, 15.

108. Pliley, "Claims to Protection," 100–102. These debates reflected larger disputes in feminist movements around the globe. See Dorothy Sue Cobble, *For the Many: American Feminists and the Global Fight for Democratic Equality* (Princeton, NJ: Princeton University Press, 2021).

109. Paul Popenoe, "Review of *Our Changing Morality*," *JSH* 11, no. 6 (June 1925): 371.

110. Pliley, "Claims to Protection," 100, 103–104.

111. *Report of the Special Body of Experts*, Part 1, 48.

112. See Legg, "Of Scales, Networks, and Assemblages"; Liat Kozma, "The League of Nations and Colonial Prostitution," in *The Routledge Companion to Sexuality and Colonialism*, ed. Chelsea Schields and Dagmar Herzog (Abingdon: Routledge, 2021), 188–198; for broader context see Pedersen, *The Guardians*; Antony Anghie, *Imperialism, Sovereignty, and the Making of International Law* (Cambridge: Cambridge University Press, 1996), 115–195.

113. *Report of the Special Body of Experts*, Part 1, 48.

114. *Commission of Enquiry into Traffic in Women and Children in the Far East: Report to the Council*, 1932, C.849.M.393.1932.IV, 11–12 (hereafter, *Far East Report*).

115. On conceptions of Orient versus Occident see Edward W. Said, *Orientalism* (New York: Random House, 2014).

116. See Erez Manela, *The Wilsonian Moment: Self-Determination and the International Origins of Anticolonial Nationalism* (Oxford: Oxford University Press, 2007); Pedersen, *The Guardians*. On the League and racial segregation see Angela Zimmerman, *Alabama in Africa: Booker T. Washington, the German Empire, and the Globalization of the New South* (Princeton, NJ: Princeton University Press, 2010), 198–202.

117. Julia Martinez, "A Female Slaving Zone? Historical Construction of Traffic in Asian Women," in *Slaving Zones: Cultural Identities, Ideologies, and Institution in the Evolution of Global Slavery*, ed. Jeff Flynn-Paul and Damian Alan Pargas (Leiden: Brill, 2018), 330.

118. On mandates see Pederson, *The Guardians*.

119. Legg, "Of Scales, Networks and Assemblages," 243.

120. Gorman, "Empire, Internationalism," 213.

121. Bascom Johnson to William Snow, September 4, 1930, Folder 07, Box 225, ASHA.

122. Stephen Legg, "Of Scales, Networks, and Assemblages," 244.

123. UK National Archives / Home(Judicial) / 1929 / 775 / 29, in Legg, "Of Scales, Networks, and Assemblages," 244.

124. On their methods for the second investigation see *Far East Report*, 16–17.

125. Bascom Johnson, Traffic in Women and Children Committee, 11th Session, April 4, 1932, Provisional Agenda, LNA, in Julia Martinez, "A Female Slaving Zone? Historical Constructions of the Traffic in Asian Women," in *Slaving Zones: Cultural Identities, Ideologies, and Institution in the Evolution of Global Slavery*, ed. Jeff Flynn-Paul and Damian Alan Pargas (Leiden: Brill, 2018), 327.

126. *Summary Report*, 9.

127. Adam M. McKeown, *Melancholy Order: Asian Migration and the Globalization of Borders* (New York: Columbia University Press, 2008).

128. *Far East Report*, 196; *Summary Report*, 34.

129. *Far East Report*, 39.

130. *Far East Report*, 37, 50, 52. On commercial sex and migration to the Malay peninsula see Sandy Chang, "Intimate Itinerancy: Sex, Work, and Chinese Women in Colonial Malaya's Brothel Economy, 1870s–1930s," *Journal of Women's History* 33, no. 4 (Winter 2021): 92–117.

131. Martyn Housden, *The League of Nations and the Organization of Peace* (Harlow: Longman International, 2012), 63.

132. *Report Summary*, 13. John Pal, *Shanghai Saga* (London: Jarrolds, 1963), 20–21, italics in original.

133. *Far East Report*, 98.

134. On the power of discourses of hygiene to conceptions of modernity in China see Ruth Rogaski, *Hygienic Modernity: Meanings of Health and Disease in Treaty-Port China* (Berkeley: University of California Press, 2004).

135. *Far East Report*, 87–88, 96–97.

136. *Summary Report*, 34; *Far East Report*, 93–96.

137. Elizabeth W. Andrew and Katharine Caroline Bushnell, *The Queen's Daughters in India* (London: Morgan and Scott, 1898); Ian Tyrrell, *Woman's World / Women's Empire: The Woman's Christian Temperance Union in International Perspective, 1880–1930* (Chapel Hill: University of North Carolina Press, 1991), 213.

138. Diana S. Kim, *Empires of Vice: The Rise of Opium Prohibition across Southeast Asia* (Princeton, NJ: Princeton University Press, 2020); Anne L. Foster, "The Philippines, the United States, and the Origins of Global Narcotics Prohibition," 1.

139. Thomas W. Burkman, *Japan and the League of Nations: Empire and World Order, 1914–1938* (Honolulu: University of Hawai'i Press, 2008), 80–86, 106–111.

140. Kimura, *Unfolding the "Comfort Women" Debates*, 81–92. At the same time, groups of Japanese prostitutes and lower-class women worked to reform regulation and improve labor conditions for prostitutes, wary that abolition of regulation would make their lives more difficult. Gorman, "Empire, Internationalism," 212.

141. *Far East Report*, 108.

142. *Sydney Morning Herald*, June 25, 1931.

143. Burkman, *Japan and the League of Nations*. On the League's censure of Japan and Japan's departure see Burkman, 165–193. Similarly, in China a range of actors harnessed conversations about prostitution and trafficking for their own purposes. As Gail Hershatter has shown, Chinese reformers focused on rescuing prostitutes as a means of shoring up national strength and health. Gail Hershatter, *Dangerous Pleasures: Prostitution and Modernity in Twentieth-Century Shanghai* (Berkeley: University of California Press, 1999). Similarly, control of prostitution was crucial to Chinese discourses on "hygienic modernity." See Rogaski, *Hygienic Modernity*.

144. John D'Emilio and Estelle B. Freedman, *Intimate Matters: A History of Sexuality in America* (New York: Harper & Row, 1988), xii; Alys Eve Weinbaum et al., *The Modern Girl Around the World: Consumption, Modernity, and Globalization* (Durham, NC: Duke University Press, 2008); George Chauncey, *Gay New York: Gender, Urban Culture, and the Making of the Gay Male World, 1840–1940* (New York: Basic Books, 1994).

145. See Nicola J. Smith, *Capitalism's Sexual History* (Oxford: Oxford University Press, 2020), 61–102.

146. Limoncelli, *The Politics of Trafficking*, 95–111; Laite, *Common Prostitutes and Ordinary Citizens*, 116–134.

147. On British anti-prostitution and anti-VD measures see Pamela Cox, "Compulsion, Voluntarism, and Venereal Disease: Governing Sexual Health in England after the Contagious Diseases Acts," *Journal of British Studies* 46, no. 1 (2007): 91–115.

148. See Dorothy Ross, "Changing Contours of the Social Science Disciplines" in *The Cambridge History of Science Vol 7: The Modern Social Sciences*, ed. Theodore M. Porter and Dorothy Ross (Cambridge: Cambridge University Press, 2003), 203–237.

149. Katharine Bushnell to Ethel Sturges Dummer, March 10, 1920, Ethel Sturges Dummer Papers, File 484, Schlesinger Library, Radcliffe Institute, Harvard University.

150. Katharine C. Bushnell, *A Brief Sketch of Her Life Work* (Hertford, UK: Rose and Sons, 1932), n.p.

151. *Report of the Special Body of Experts*, Part 1, 14.

152. "1933 International Convention for the Suppression of the Traffic in Women of the Full Age," Geneva, October 11,1933.

153. League of Nations, "Traffic in Women and Children Committee," Eighth Session, April 19–27, 1929, C.294.M.97, LNA.

154. League of Nations, "Traffic in Women and Children Committee," Twelfth Session, April 4, 1933, C.T.F.E. 586, R4666 / 11B / 4116 / 729, LNA.

155. *League of Nations Official Journal*, 950–952. Katherine Lenroot, the director of the Children's Bureau of the US Department of Labor who worked closely with the ASHA, was a member of the Advisory Committee on Social Questions for the League of Nations from 1937 to 1939, so she may have been involved. "Biographical Note," Katharine F. Lenroot Papers 1909–1974, MS#0767, Columbia University Archives and Special Collections.

156. Dolinsek, "Tensions of Abolitionism," 232.

157. Eleanor Roosevelt represented the United States in UN trafficking committee meetings but limited her comments to technical issues. General Assembly, 4th session, 3rd Committee, 237th meeting, September 30, 1949, Lake Success, New York, UN Digital Library.

158. UN General Assembly, Convention for the Suppression of the Traffic in Persons and of the Exploitation of the Prostitution of Others, December 2, 1949.

159. Samuel Auerbach, Rio de Janeiro, Brazil, July 23, 1924, Box S181 / 36 / 4, LNA; Paul Kinsie, Genoa, Italy, March 5–6, Box S176 / 31 / 4, LNA; George Worthington, "Traffic in Women and Children, Open Market—Houses of Prostitution," Mexico City, Mexico, December 5–10, 1924, Box S177 / 32 / 1, LNA; *Far East Report*, 109.

Conclusion

1. Jennifer K. Lobasz, *Constructing Human Trafficking: Evangelicals, Feminists, and an Unexpected Alliance* (London: Palgrave, 2019); Elizabeth Bernstein, *Brokered Subjects: Sex, Trafficking, and the Politics of Freedom* (Chicago: University of Chicago Press, 2018).

2. Michaele L. Ferguson and Lori Jo Marso, eds., *W Stands for Women: How the George W. Bush Presidency Shaped a New Politics of Gender* (Durham, NC: Duke University Press, 2007); Edward Ashbee, *The Bush Administration, Sex and the Moral Agenda* (Manchester: Manchester University Press, 2007).

3. The White House, "National Security Presidential Directive-22 on Combating Trafficking in Persons" (Washington, DC, December 16, 2002), https://ctip.defense.gov/Portals/12/Documents/NSPD-22.pdf.

4. Rep. Christopher H. Smith, "Trafficking Victims Protection Reauthorization Act of 2003," Pub. L. No. 108–193 (2003), https://www.congress.gov/bill/108th-congress/house-bill/2620. (Hereafter TVPRA of 2003).

5. Laura Bush, "Radio Address to the Nation," November 17, 2001; Emily S. Rosenberg, "Rescuing Women and Children," *Journal of American History* 89, no. 2 (September 2002):

456–465; "Afghan Civilians," Watson Institute for International and Public Affairs, Brown University, https://watson.brown.edu/costsofwar/costs/human/civilians/afghan#:~:text=As%20 of%20March%202023%2C%20more,massive%20increase%20in%20civilian%20casualties.

6. "United States Leadership Against HIV / AIDS, Tuberculosis, and Malaria Act of 2003," Pub. L. No. 108–25, 117 Statute 711 (2003), https://www.congress.gov/108/plaws/publ25 /PLAW-108publ25.pdf.; TVPRA of 2003. In 2013, the Supreme Court ruled that imposing the anti-prostitution pledge on American-based organizations violated the First Amendment. But a subsequent ruling in 2020 clarified that the US government can impose the pledge requirement on foreign-based organizations, which do not enjoy First Amendment rights. Since US-based NGOs generally partner with local organizations, they are effectively still required to adhere to the anti-prostitution stance in their foreign HIV / AIDS, malaria, tuberculosis, and anti-trafficking work. *Agency for International Development v. Alliance for Open Society International, Inc.*, 591 U.S. (US Supreme Court 2020); *Agency for International Development v. Alliance for Open Society International, Inc.*, 570 U.S. 205 (US Supreme Court 2020).

7. Esther Kaplan, "Just Say Não," *The Nation*, May 30, 2005.

8. Nicole Franck Masenior and Chris Beyrer, "The US Anti-Prostitution Pledge: First Amendment Challenges and Public Health Priorities," *PLoS Medicine* 4, no. 7 (2007): 207; Michael L. Rekart, "Sex-work Harm Reduction," *Lancet* 366, no. 9503 (2005): 2123–2134.

9. Joanna Busza, "Sex Work and Migration: The Dangers of Oversimplification: A Case Study of Vietnamese Women in Cambodia," *Health and Human Rights* 7, no. 2 (2004): 233.

10. Joanna Busza, "Having the Rug Pulled from Under Your Feet: One Project's Experience of the US Policy Reversal on Sex Work," *Health Policy and Planning* 21, no. 4 (2006): 330–331.

11. "Trafficking in Persons Report" (US Department of State, 2021), 52, https://www.state .gov/wp-content/uploads/2021/09/TIPR-GPA-upload-07222021.pdf. These criteria are also in line with the "End Demand" or "Nordic Model," first implemented in Sweden in 1999. This approach criminalizes the purchase of sex. See Charlotta Holmström and May-Len Skilbrei, "The Swedish Sex Purchase Act: Where Does It Stand?," *Oslo Law Review* 4, no. 2 (2017): 82–104.

12. Caorle J. Petersen, "Sex Work, Migration, and the United States Trafficking in Persons Report: Promoting Rights or Missing Opportunities for Advocacy," *Indiana International & Comparative Law Review* 25, no. 1 (2015): 128–130; John Goodwin, "Sex Work and the Law in Asia and the Pacific: Laws, HIV, and Human Rights in the Context of Sex Work" (Bangkok, Thailand: United Nations Development Program, 2012), https://www.undp.org/sites/g/files /zskgke326/files/publications/HIV-2012-SexWorkAndLaw.pdf; Chi Mgbako and Laura A. Smith, "Sex Work and Human Rights in Africa," *Fordham International Law Journal* 33, no. 4 (2011): 1178–1220.

13. Janie Chuang, "The United States as Global Sheriff: Using Unilateral Sanctions to Combat Human Trafficking," *Michigan Journal of International Law* 27, no. 2 (2006): 439.

14. Stephanie A. Limoncelli, "What in the World Are Anti-Trafficking NGOs Doing? Findings from a Global Study," *Journal of Human Trafficking* 2, no. 4 (2016): 321–322.

15. Laura María Agustín, *Sex at the Margins: Migration, Labour Markets and the Rescue Industry* (London: Zed Books, 2007); Anne Elizabeth Moore, "Special Report: Money and Lies in Anti-Human Trafficking NGOs," Truthout, January 27, 2015, https://truthout.org/articles /special-report-money-and-lies-in-anti-human-trafficking-ngos/.; Anne Elizabeth Moore, "The

American Rescue Industry: Toward an Anti-Trafficking Paramilitary," April 8, 2015, https://truthout.org/articles/the-american-rescue-industry-toward-an-anti-trafficking-paramilitary/.

16. Anne Elizabeth Moore, "Special Report."

17. Elena Shih, "The Trafficking Deportation Pipeline: Asian Body Work and the Auxiliary Policing of Racialized Poverty," *Feminist Formations* 33, no. 1 (Spring 2021): 56–73.

18. Lyndsey P. Beutin, "Black Suffering for / from Anti-trafficking Advocacy," *Anti-Trafficking Review* 9 (2017): 14–30.

19. Kamala Kempadoo and Elena Shih, "Introduction: Rethinking the Field from Anti-Racist and Decolonial Perspectives," in *White Supremacy, Racism and the Coloniality of Anti-Trafficking*, ed. Kempadoo and Shih (New York: Routledge, 2022), 1–13.

20. Katharine Bushnell to Ethel Sturges Dummer, March 10, 1920, Ethel Sturges Dummer Papers, File 484, Schlesinger Library, Radcliffe Institute, Harvard University.

21. See, for example, Juno Mac and Molly Smith, *Revolting Prostitutes: The Fight for Sex Workers Rights* (New York: Verso, 2018); Chi Adanna Mgbako, *To Live Freely in This World: Sex Worker Activism in Africa* (New York: New York University Press, 2016); Melinda Chateauvert, *Sex Workers Unite: A History of the Movement from Stonewall to SlutWalk* (New York: Penguin Random House, 2015).

22. See Mac and Smith, *Revolting Prostitutes*; Mgbako, *To Live Freely in This World*; Chateauvert, *Sex Workers Unite*.

23. "Social Evil Hospital," *Missouri Republican*, December 29, 1872.

24. Samuel Auerbach, "Passengers Mentioned in S.S. Valdivia Report as Having Debarked at Rio de Janeiro," July 25, 1924, Box S181 / 36 / 4, LNA.

25. Blanca Sánchez-Alonso, "The Other Europeans: Immigration into Latin America and the International Labour Market (1870–1930)," *Revista de Historia Economica* 25, no. 3 (2007): 395–426.

26. Mgbako, *To Live Freely in This World*; Crystal A. Jackson, "Framing Sex Worker Rights: How U.S. Sex Worker Rights Activists Perceive and Respond to Mainstream Anti-Sex Trafficking Advocacy," *Sociological Perspectives* 59, no. 1 (2016): 27–45.

27. Asia Catalyst, "Sex Work Is Work, Plenary Speech by Kaythi Win," April 25, 2012, https://asiacatalyst.org/blog/2012/04/25/commentary_sex_work_is_work_plenary_speech_by_kaythi_win/.

28. Meenu Seshu, "Sex, Work and Citizenship: The VAMP Sex Workers' Collective in Maharashtra," in *Organizing Women Workers in the Informal Economy: Beyond the Weapons of the Weak*, ed. Naila Kabeer, Ratna Sudarshan, and Kirsty Milward (London: Zed Books, 2013); Mgbako, *To Live Freely in This World*, 190.

INDEX

Numbers in italics denote images

A NOTE ON THE TYPE

This book has been composed in Arno, an Old-style serif typeface in the classic Venetian tradition, designed by Robert Slimbach at Adobe.